PREVIOUS BOOKS BY TOM CARHART

*Battles and Campaigns in Vietnam*
*The Offering*
*Iron Soldiers*
*West Point Warriors*
*Lost Triumph*
*A Time to Lead*
with General (Retired) Wesley K. Clark

# SACRED TIES

From West Point Brothers to Battlefield Rivals:
A True Story of the Civil War

# TOM CARHART

BERKLEY CALIBER, NEW YORK

THE BERKLEY PUBLISHING GROUP
Published by the Penguin Group
Penguin Group (USA) Inc.
375 Hudson Street, New York, New York 10014, USA
Penguin Group (Canada), 90 Eglinton Avenue East, Suite 700, Toronto, Ontario M4P 2Y3, Canada
(a division of Pearson Penguin Canada Inc.)
Penguin Books Ltd., 80 Strand, London WC2R 0RL, England
Penguin Group Ireland, 25 St. Stephen's Green, Dublin 2, Ireland (a division of Penguin Books Ltd.)
Penguin Group (Australia), 250 Camberwell Road, Camberwell, Victoria 3124, Australia
(a division of Pearson Australia Group Pty. Ltd.)
Penguin Books India Pvt. Ltd., 11 Community Centre, Panchsheel Park, New Delhi—110 017, India
Penguin Group (NZ), 67 Apollo Drive, Rosedale, North Shore 0632, New Zealand
(a division of Pearson New Zealand Ltd.)
Penguin Books (South Africa) (Pty.) Ltd., 24 Sturdee Avenue, Rosebank, Johannesburg 2196,
South Africa

Penguin Books Ltd., Registered Offices: 80 Strand, London WC2R 0RL, England

The publisher does not have any control over and does not assume any responsibility for author or
third-party websites or their content.

PRINTING HISTORY
Berkley Caliber hardcover edition / May 2010
Berkley Caliber trade paperback edition / April 2011

Berkley Caliber trade paperback ISBN: 978-0-425-23910-0

The Library of Congress has catalogued the Berkley Caliber hardcover edition as follows:

Sacred Ties : from West Point brothers to battlefield rivals : a true story of the Civil War /
    Tom Carhart.—1st ed.
      p. cm.
    Includes bibliographical references and index.
    ISBN 978-0-425-23421-1
    1. United States—History—Civil War 1861–1865—Campaigns.   2. United States Military
Academy—History—19th century.   3. United States. Army—Officers—History—19th century.
4. Confederate States of America Army—Officers—History.   5. United States Military Academy—
Alumni and alumnae—Biography.   I. Title.
E470.C23 2010
973.7'3—dc22                                                                    2009050672

PRINTED IN THE UNITED STATES OF AMERICA

10   9   8   7   6   5   4   3   2   1

To my brothers, living and dead,
from West Point's Class of 1966
who endured the sting of battle in an unpopular war,
I here offer them their ultimate accolade:

Well Done.

# Acknowledgments

While writing this book, there have been many moments when I found myself in water over my head. Fortunately, a number of professional librarians, archivists, and just plain smart people have been there to pull me up. My primary resources have been those of the Archives, Library, and Association of Graduates of the United States Military Academy at West Point, New York. I am deeply grateful to the professional staff members there who have guided my every step, including Doctors Steve Grove, Suzanne Christoff, Jay Olejniczak and Alan Aimone, as well as Ms. Elaine McConnell, Ms. Alicia Mauldin-Ware, Ms. Valerie Dutdut, Ms. Susan Lintelmann and Ms. Alicia Muldoon. I am also greatly indebted to Doctor Keith E. Gibson, the Archivist at the Virginia Military Institute in Lexington, Virginia. Doctor Gibson's graciousness extended to allowing my use of the records and other materials found in VMI's Library and Archives, but he also was kind enough to personally give me detailed guides of some key Civil War battlefields in the Shenandoah Valley, as well as to arrange other guided tours by some of his deeply knowledgeable friends who live there. I wish I had written all their names down so that I might formally thank them, but they know who they are and my gratitude is genuine. At the University of Virginia in Charlottesville, let me first thank Doctor Gary Gallagher, who opened some doors for me, as well as Ms. Margaret Hrabe and Ms. Regina Rush, who guided me through the reserve collections of Alderman Library. At the University of North Carolina, I am most grateful to Ms. Rachel Canada and Mr. John Loy, who similarly showed me the way to needed materials in the Special Reserves of Wilson Library. At the Winterthur Museum in Winterthur, Delaware, I extend my deep thanks to Ms. Maggie Lidz, who not only made sure I had access to some key original documents, but also kept my eye on the ball with respect to the DuPont family structure. And finally, my deepest gratitude and undying love go to my splendid wife, Jan, who has endured with the greatest equanimity, kindness, and often-undeserved affection my long periods of submersion while wrestling with this manuscript. Now it is finished, and I hope she and these other key contributors will be as proud of the completed work as I am.

# Contents

# Introduction

In 1989, Kenneth Branagh appeared in a wildly popular film rendition of Shakespeare's *Henry V.* Just before the battle of Agincourt, King Henry gives a speech to his outnumbered soldiers, a speech that, we are led to believe, inspired them to perform heroic feats that brought about their surprising victory. In reality, it was the muddy terrain as well as the use of the longbow and palings (waist-high sharpened stakes driven into the ground at an angle to ward off horses and their riders) that prevented the successful charge of heavily armored French knights through English ranks. Even so, the speech is quite powerful, and the key bonding among soldiers that led to their triumph is attributed by Shakespeare to the king's emotional plea for unity:

> *We few, we happy few, we band of brothers;*
> *For he to-day that sheds his blood with me*
> *Shall be my brother; be he ne'er so vile,*
> *This day shall gentle his condition:*
> *And gentlemen in England now a-bed*
> *Shall think themselves accursed they were not here,*

*And hold their manhoods cheap whiles any speaks*
*That fought with us upon Saint Crispin's day.*

In 1992, a book by Stephen Ambrose entitled *Band of Brothers* was published. The history of the men of E Company, 506th Infantry Regiment, 101st Airborne Division, during World War II, its title connects it to King Henry's men by showing how a close personal bond between soldiers, acquired through training, followed by service together in combat, can result in triumph. Their organizational identity was also extended in some instances by a private familiarity and affection that developed between some individual soldiers, a bond that clearly improved their unit effectiveness. The stories of these bonds and the combat in which these men were immersed are told in the book and the television series of the same name that followed, and both were tremendous popular successes.

This book is about another group of young "brothers" going off to war. Without diluting or discrediting the triumphs of King Henry's warriors or those of the 101st, some distinctions should be made between them and those we will here observe.

In fact, the English troops at Agincourt were no more than ten thousand armed men who had left their farms to fight for their king. Beyond small individual circles of friends from the same region, therefore, only limited personal allegiance among them would have been possible. Their designation as "brothers," then, seems to stretch the term.

The men in E Company of the 506th are different because they started as 140 men training and ultimately fighting together, a number that varied as men who fell in combat were replaced by strangers. Even so, new soldiers in E Company as well as old developed a special trust and identity based on shared harsh experiences and moments of death faced together. Despite the fact that personal familiarity among individuals in a group this size was necessarily quite limited, it was the marked allegiances to each other as group members that allowed Ambrose to use Shakespeare's term "band of brothers" in their description.

But there is another kind of brotherhood among warriors, one closer to the actual meaning of the word.

Brothers who are raised to manhood in the same family necessarily acquire intimate personal knowledge of each other's strengths and weaknesses, flaws and foibles, dreams and aspirations. If, after leaving home, they had fought on both sides in the U.S. Civil War, then you might today read or hear of a case where brother actually fought brother. But despite the enduring popularity of Civil War history, there are precious few memorable stories recording that sort of actual fraternal strife.

If, however, we change our setting from a family to the United States Military Academy, and our characters from blood brothers into West Point classmates closely bound to each other over four or five years as cadets, then many such stories virtually leap from the page.

This, then, is the story of six young men who made the passage through West Point together in the middle of the nineteenth century, when the total number of cadets at the academy at any given time averaged around 250 men. They bonded tightly together there as volitional brothers, then fought for and against each other in the U.S. Civil War.

All West Point cadets were sound-bodied, intellectually gifted young men able to lead as well as to follow. The goal of the academy was to test and harden them through an ongoing series of rigorous trials, and they would be called upon repeatedly to show their own resolute purpose. Cadet life in the nineteenth century was physically challenging, academically demanding, emotionally draining, and relentlessly tedious.

The purpose of this rigid regimen was to prepare them for commissioning upon graduation as officers in the United States

Army. As such, they would serve primarily on America's arduous western frontier, but also remain available for any other military service to country that might be needed.

Thrust together as complete strangers from all sections of the country and living in a sort of "us against them" relationship with the commissioned officers who made up the staff and faculty at West Point, these young men would learn to rely on other cadets for virtually everything. As a direct result, they became intimately familiar with and totally dependent upon the support of each other, not only for success but sometimes even for bare survival.

The Civil War was probably the best demonstration of West Point's central military role in American history, for in virtually all the major battles of that war both sides were commanded by West Point graduates. In the Union army, 328 West Point graduates became general officers, while 164 of the generals in the Confederate army were also West Pointers. By 1865, all the armies on both sides were commanded by West Pointers, as were nearly all of the corps, most of the divisions, and many of the brigades. On both sides, in other words, it was West Pointers who led the soldiers who fought in the Civil War.[1]

In the late nineteenth century, Friedrich Nietzsche famously said "what doesn't kill me strengthens me," and nineteenth-century West Point also adhered to this philosophy. In an effort to strengthen cadets, the academy intentionally subjected them to great duress, so much so that many of them analogized their cadet life—as we will see, not unfairly—to "prison" or "slavery."

While the hardening was no doubt realized, the perhaps more important impact on them, at which we will look, was what occurred after they had been stripped naked psychologically and found that they could only depend on each other for succor and solace. Through the most harrowing of disciplinary experiences, then, they became the closest of friends and quickly learned to lean on their fellow cadets in ways they had never before experienced. So I believe their denomination as "brothers," as will be seen, is a more appropriate and meaningful usage of the term than those of either Shakespeare or Ambrose.

As we take our first look at these six young men, they will be risking dismissal from the academy by breaking the rigid rules in leaving the post without authorization and drinking forbidden alcohol at an "off-limits" tavern. A first question here is simply unavoidable: why were they doing this, why were they taking this great risk? Because together, they were bearding the lion as a group, showing each other and the world that their mutual affection was strong enough for them to accept the greatest challenge then open to them, the risk of getting thrown out of West Point, in order to celebrate, regulations be damned!

But the blunt reality, one perhaps easy for them to ignore at the time, was that they were true warriors-in-waiting. Not too much longer after this joyous celebration, they would take even higher risks, offering their lives for their country in combat. And as we shall see, they would accept those risks with much of the same nonchalance, ignoring any possibility they might draw the card of death.

That will be one of the major distinctions we will see between these men and older officers—the ease with which they will literally lay their lives on the line. That can be described as raw courage, and it is that. But one of its undeniable sources will be their youth, the fact that they have not yet accepted their own mortality. And the more strongly they displayed this risk-taking nature, the less probable was it that they had accepted the inevitability of their own demise, the fact that they, too, would one day die.

This unwillingness to accept one's own mortality is not uncommon among young soldiers. It seems fair to say here that the more idealistic and confident these cadets were in their aspirations toward greatness, the more oblivious they would have been to any real possibility of their own deaths. Given the warrior-king role models to whom they would have been exposed as ideals at West Point, it should not be surprising that they would aspire to a similar demigod status themselves, harboring some personal sense of a great destiny awaiting them. It must have crossed their minds that if Napoleon and Alexander the Great and Achilles could win such battlefield triumphs in their youths, then why couldn't they do the same?

Yes, Achilles was a half-human, half-god mythological figure, while the others had normal human bodies that had physically died. But were they really dead? Yes, their bodies had turned to dust. But despite that inconvenient fact, these men had survived youthful combat and eventually became immortal cultural avatars whose names will live forever.

Why, they must have thought, can't I do that?

All that was needed was a conveniently timed war in which they could show their own flash and brilliance and magnetic leadership, qualities that would shine through, pluck them from the masses and place them at the top. Why not?

And, mirabile dictu, such a war awaited them, one that would embrace them in its not-yet-understood-or-even-recognized bloody maw.

We will take close looks at these six young men, a small group self-selected by their close friendship at West Point who took high risks purely to celebrate the special bond that had grown up between them as cadets. Some were from the North, some from the South, but all had strong regional feelings. And as that political divide cracked our nation open and plunged us into bloody war, some would literally face these, their brothers, in battle.

But their binding friendship would ultimately bridge that political divide. Why? Because they had learned to love each other as cadets, a bond that not even war could destroy. And this is the story of that love and its endurance through the hardest of times.

# ONE

## *Benny Havens*

In the late 1850s, a young man who wanted to attend the United States Military Academy at West Point, New York, had to receive a political appointment from his congressman, each of whom could have only one cadet from his district there at any given time. There were relatively few colleges in this country then, and virtually no other schools of engineering. While students at civilian colleges had to pay their own tuition as well as for their room and board, it was the reverse at West Point: cadets were active-duty members of the United States Army, and even though they were restricted to that army post for training as cadets, they did receive a small stipend each month.

These appointments, then, became popular and were often quite difficult to secure. But rather than just getting a free education in engineering, West Point cadets were primarily being trained for careers as army officers. It was believed at the time that, in order to make the best officer later, cadets had to be put through rigorous paces in order to "toughen them up." This meant that, once enrolled, they underwent a very spartan and difficult regimen of education and training before receiving their diplomas and their commissions as second lieutenants in the United States Army.

The academic curriculum at the academy was rigorous and demanding, the military training was precise and challenging, and the constant discipline cadets endured in their daily lives was severe, strict, and unrelenting. They attended class on six days each week and received a grade on a test they took every day in every subject. They wore only tight, high-collared uniforms, whose coats were studded with three vertical rows of brass buttons shining from their chests. They marched in parades several times each week as well as to and from their classes and meals, and their food was bland, tasteless, and often inedible. Their rooms, persons, rifles, and military equipment were always subject to inspection, and gambling, smoking, and possession of alcohol were strictly forbidden. Cadets could not have a mustache, a wife, or a horse, and they were restricted to the grounds of West Point for their entire time as cadets, save only a ten-week vacation during the summer after their second year. If the inspecting officer found any flaws, or if they violated any of a long list of regulations, they received demerits, and in the event they accumulated more than one hundred demerits in a semester, they would be expelled.

But probably the worst violation of regulations was for cadets to sneak out of their rooms after taps and go off post to a tavern and drink alcohol. In the event they took such a risk and were caught, the punishment for such an offense was immediate dismissal.

Even so, every year some cadets took that risk, perhaps as much to prove they could get away with it as to actually drink forbidden fermented fruit. A cadet dismissed for such an act would sometimes be able to get himself reinstated by the secretary of war, though good political contacts in Washington by the cadet or his family were all-important here. But such reinstatement was not automatic, and any cadet who went "over the wall" after taps was running the very highest risk.

Probably the favorite saloon for cadets taking such a dare was that run by Benny Havens. Benny had started at West Point as a supplier of foodstuffs, and he did quite well, even becoming legendary for his friendly relationships with cadets. But when he was finally caught smuggling alcohol to them, he and his wife were thrown off the post and forbidden to return.

Ever.

This was no doubt a major blow to the Havenses.

But Benny was not one to give up easily, and he set up a saloon a mile or so south of West Point, down near the river and just below the small village of Buttermilk Falls (whose name has more recently been changed to Highland Falls). While popular with both civilians and officers from the staff and faculty at West Point, Benny's most prized customers were cadets sneaking off post after taps. In the common perception of cadets, the staff and faculty charged with their command and education were generally harsh with them, and so were perceived to be the enemy, while Benny and his wife were proven friends.

After his formal banishment, Benny Havens and his bar became quite popular among cadets. Slipping out of their rooms after taps and avoiding the road, they had to make a treacherous approach through the woods on a steep and rocky slope, a foray rendered all the more dangerous on a moonless night. During the winter, however, the trip was made easier simply because they could come and go on the frozen Hudson. There were no icebreakers in those days, and the Hudson would remain frozen for weeks at a time, the ice so solid that you could easily walk across it to the eastern bank. On the rare occasions when officers would be approaching his saloon that late at night, it could only be to catch cadets. But Benny's loyalty to cadets was never even suspect, and when the noise of officers approaching was heard, Benny would hustle them out windows or the back door, released like sparrows to flutter madly through the trees.

Sneaking off post to imbibe at Benny's, of course, was a

high-risk venture. The punishment, as mentioned above, was dismissal, although some superintendents enforced this regulation more strenuously than others. But the threat of dismissal was always there, hanging above the heads of any errant, risk-taking cadets who might be caught at Benny's.

Over the years, sneaking out after taps for a drink at Benny's became almost a rite of passage for the more daring cadets. It was not uncommon, therefore, that cadets were caught, either at Benny's or in the woods as they tried to get away, and some of these were sent packing. But that, of course, often turned on other factors.

One of the most famous cadets to be caught was none other than Jefferson Davis, class of 1828 and a future senator from Mississippi, U.S. secretary of war from 1853 to 1857, and the first and only president of the Confederate States of America. In the summer of 1825, Davis and four other cadets were caught and arrested at Benny Havens's, and all were tried by court-martial in August.

Despite the clever but spurious arguments he made in his own defense, Davis and the others were found guilty and sentenced to dismissal. But Davis and one other cadet were saved because of their good records, while the other three were sent packing. This group included James F. Swift, who might have been considered somewhat special among his classmates in that he was the son of the first man to have graduated from West Point, General Joseph G. Swift, class of 1802. Clearly, then, no favoritism was shown in this area to any cadet with "special connections," which Davis did not have while Swift clearly did.[1]

Even so, this high risk made the experience all the more delicious to those who ran it. And whether they realized it at the time or not, it was also a special preparation for the great pressures they would endure and the risks they might have to run in the Civil War that loomed before them.

In military circles, there has long been interest and debate

over the supposed "principles of war," and there are at least
some common themes upon which there is wide agreement. A
good example of this would be the principles of war as they are
accepted today by the U.S. military and known by the acronym
MOOSEMUSS: mass, objective, offensive, security, economy
of force, maneuver, unity of command, surprise, and simplicity.
But while this list may seem exhaustive, there may be room for
other elements as well, one of which is often crucial to battlefield
success or failure.

That is the spirit of the commander.

Raw personal courage under the life-and-death pressures
of the battlefield is required of that person, but also, given the
predictably slow flow and uncertain accuracy of information or
intelligence reports, a certain levelheaded flexibility is indispens-
able. And that flexibility, to be effective, must include a genuine
willingness to take risks.

In most wars, one can readily detect the presence or absence
of these crucially important elements in the tactics or strategy
implemented by senior leaders, and they are often the keys that
spell victory or defeat. One has only to glance superficially at
major battles from the Civil War to see these aspects of effective combat leadership, or their absence, openly displayed by the
battlefield performance of the commanders.

One well-known example where personal failure of spirit led
to disaster was that of George B. McClellan, the commander
of the Army of the Potomac, at the battle of Antietam. There,
despite his two-to-one superiority in personnel, he failed to
attack (and seems to have quailed at the prospect of attacking)
the Confederate army before him on either 15 or 16 September
1862. When he finally did attack on the 17th, it was with three
uncoordinated assaults at different points and times, a clumsy
strategy that allowed his opponent to maneuver his own troops
from interior lines so as to reject each attack in turn. And at
the crucial moment late in the day, McClellan failed to take

the limited risk of committing his fresh reserves, an action that clearly would have led to a decisive Union victory in an otherwise close contest. In addition, McClellan was careful to personally stay far away from the actual fighting that day, a failure to "lead from the front" that reflected poorly on his battlefield leadership.[2]

His unwillingness to take the risks associated with an attack on all fronts at the same time, and perhaps more importantly, his failure to commit his reserves at the height of the battle, led to his abject failure. His lack of personal courage, of course, had a deep effect not only on his staff and subordinate commanders but even on the common soldiers under his command who never saw him anywhere near the line of battle.

Compare this nadir of command of the Army of the Potomac with the battle of Chancellorsville and the actions there of Robert E. Lee, commander of the Army of Northern Virginia. On 2 May 1863, while facing a Union force more than twice the size of his own, Lee dispatched more than half his army to make a day-long march around the enemy's right flank. Arriving in late afternoon, they delivered a crushing blow against the surprised Union forces and effectively destroyed the fighting spirit of Lee's Union adversary. This luckless and lackluster man, who was taking a cyclical turn in command of the Army of the Potomac, was the already insecure Joseph Hooker. Commonly known in the North by the nickname of "Fightin' Joe," his performance on this battlefield against an opponent of the highest caliber showed him to be something else entirely.[3]

Until that moment, dividing one's force in the face of a superior army had been considered by virtually all "authorities" to be one of the greatest tactical sins a commander could commit. Even today, one would hesitate long before taking such a drastic step. But Lee clearly knew what he was doing, and for a true military genius, all principles and other rules are quickly out the window while other factors, including audacity alone, carry the day. As for individual courage, Lee was often at the very front of battle, risking enemy fire in order to closely observe and sometimes redirect the operations of his troops. At the battle of Spotsylvania on 12 May 1864, for instance, his own men had to pull on the reins of his horse as he moved forward, this to keep him from unnecessarily risking his life by personally leading a counterattack.[4]

And experience in taking risks might well be a key to later military success, such as the risks taken by West Point cadets laughing and singing and drinking illicit liquor with their closest friends at an off-limits bar. To them, the possibility of being dismissed from the academy for that violation of regulations alone was very real. It cannot be denied, therefore, that the act took a certain amount of personal courage and self-confidence, and may well have been just as important a part of their preparations for war as any other.

Indeed, the Benny Havens experience may well have been the highest risk any of them had ever taken. Poised as they were on the precipice of war in 1860, there would be an undeniable relationship between their West Point experiences and their future battlefield performance. Within the next few years they would face higher risks still, risks whose penalties for failure would be colored with blood rather than embarrassment. But for those cadets who took the dare, an illicit run to Benny's provided a fair predictor of the risks they would be willing to run, indeed the courage they would be able to muster, on the battlefields that lay before them.

Once safely arrived at Benny's, cadets could taste special treats that simply were not available inside the academy confines. The specialty of the house was known as "flip": into a large flagon, Benny would pour ale, cider, or rum along with well-beaten eggs, the mixture sweetened and spiced and then heated by plunging a red-hot iron bar, known as a "flip dog," into it. This was a delicate move, for if it was removed at just the right second, it left a delicious caramel-like flavor to the punch, while leaving it in too long could leave a burned taste that ruined it. But Benny was a master at this feat, and when he was serving a group of off-limits cadets, he performed it with relish amid gales of laughter from some homesick and hungry boys. Though sometimes loud and brash seeming, these were really only young lads who had crept through the dark woods, tripping over stones and underbrush, just to find this island of solace in their otherwise harsh and desolate West Point world.

And Benny's wife was a renowned cook as well, serving turkey roasted over the open fire, and sometimes ham, beef, or chicken, too, all accompanied by delicious flapjacks. This combination was attractive, but most normal customers, including officers, went home at a reasonable hour. It was only occasionally and around the midnight hour that cadets would mysteriously creep out of the woods and in the back door. Knowing the risks they were running, and given his own rocky relations with the academy, Benny was benevolent not only in keeping his tavern open but also in providing a watchful eye for officers who might show up unexpectedly.

For those cadets who had shown the spine to sneak out of barracks and through the woods to Benny's, their reward was ample. Not only did they drink brimming glasses of hot flip, they were also served large plates of sizzling hot meat and flapjacks, a veritable feast for these poorly fed boys far from home. But perhaps most of all, it was the mood and the setting that just exuded warmth and welcome, a place where cadets could truly relax until the predawn time came for them to trudge back and get ready for another day of classes. They were all young and strong, of course, and their constitutions could easily handle one night with little sleep but much flip. And the memories no doubt kept them warm through some long and frigid winter nights in their poorly heated barracks.

In the early morning hours of one particular day in April

1860, six West Point cadets were seated comfortably around one of Benny's tables drinking flip as they laughed and celebrated with each other. There may have been three or four other cadets at Benny Havens's that night—or early morning—as well, since the records of the party are somewhat confused. But these six men were there, and they form the centerpiece of our story. They had gathered to celebrate the impending graduation of two of their number: Wesley Merritt and Stephen Dodson Ramseur.

Within only a few years after graduation, both men would find themselves promoted to major general, at which rank they commanded divisions—typically five to ten thousand men—in the Civil War that was still just a looming threat. They were joined in celebration by four other fast friends, who had another year at the academy still left before them: Henry Algernon DuPont, John Pelham, Thomas Lafayette Rosser, and George Armstrong Custer. It was Custer who had organized the party, and he and Rosser would also become generals commanding divisions, one on either side of the Civil War, before four years had passed after their own graduations.[5]

These men were drawn from many states, a genuine cross section of the American population.

Wesley Merritt was born on 16 June 1836 in New York City, the fourth child of John and Julia Merritt. John was a lawyer, but in 1840 the hard economic times of the late 1830s forced him to move his family to southern Illinois. After eight years of farming, they moved to the small town of Belleville, where he became editor of the Belleville *Advocate*. He enjoyed the newspaper business, and after three years, they moved on to the larger town of Salem, where he founded the town's only newspaper, the Salem *Advocate*.

The newspaper was a great success, and John remained the editor through the Civil War. He became a prosperous citizen, and by 1860, he owned property valued at about twelve thousand dollars. He considered himself a political moderate, but he, his wife, and children were all loyal Democrats, as were most of their neighbors. The *Advocate* strongly promoted Stephen A. Douglas, and in 1860 even suggested that southern Illinois join Missouri as a separate western republic in the event of disunion of the states.[6]

From ages fifteen to nineteen, Wesley attended the Christian Brothers School, then studied law under Judge William Haynie in Salem. But his studies ended in April 1855 when he applied for and won the appointment to West Point of his congressman, W. H. Bissell. After receiving the approval of Secretary of War Jefferson Davis, Wesley entered the United States Military Academy on 1 July 1855.[7]

Stephen Dodson Ramseur was born in Lincolnton, North Carolina, on 31 May 1837, the oldest son and second of Jacob and Lucy Ramseur's nine children. Jacob was a farmer, but he also owned a mill and was a partner in a yarn manufacturing company. Young Dod, as he would always be called by family and close friends, grew up hunting and fishing like many country boys. His friends later remarked on the unusual combination they saw in him of gentle behavior and an almost reckless courage in dangerous situations.[8]

Educated at the Pleasant Retreat Academy, Ramseur enrolled in Davidson College in September 1853. He readily adapted to the strong Presbyterian atmosphere at the college, and he found a mentor in his mathematics professor Daniel H. Hill. A West Point graduate himself, Hill promoted Ramseur's interest in the military academy and advised him on the courses he should take in preparation for going there. After Ramseur had spent two years at Davidson, Hill recommended him to Congressman Francis B. Craige. Ramseur won Craige's appointment, and in late June 1855 he made the long trip north and joined Merritt at West Point.

Henry Algernon DuPont was born 30 July 1838 to Henry and Louisa DuPont in Eleutherean Mills, Delaware, the oldest of their nine children. His father, Henry, had graduated from West Point himself in 1833, though he only remained in the army for one year. The DuPont family was already quite wealthy when Henry Algernon was born, having earned their family fortune through the production of gunpowder. Henry Algernon applied to West Point as well as to the Virginia Military Institute, but was admitted to neither. He attended the University of Pennsylvania for one year in 1855–56, and finally won admission to West Point in the summer of 1856.

Thomas Lafayette Rosser was born in rural Virginia on 15 October 1836 to John and Martha Rosser, their second child and oldest son. In 1849, financial reverses caused John to move his family to a 640-acre farm along the Sabine River in Texas, some forty miles west of Shreveport, Louisiana. But he was forced to stay behind, and young Tom, thirteen years old, led the family horses and wagons west, becoming the family man for the trip. Although he owned a few slaves, John's right-hand man in developing the farm was Tom. Wanting him to get an education, however, he sent Tom to a school in a neighboring county for four years.

In 1856 Rosser won an appointment to West Point from Congressman Lemuel D. Evans. He realized that his academic preparation was weak, so he arrived at West Point two months early. He spent that time boning up on his academic skills in the small town just outside the academy's grounds. But his concerns were misplaced, for he would pass all the academic admission tests, and on 1 July 1856 he was admitted to the academy.[9]

John Pelham was born on 7 September 1838 to Atkinson and Martha McGehee Pelham in the plantation home of Martha's father in Benton County, Alabama. Martha was a cousin of the great statesman Henry Clay, and her family was quite wealthy. John was the third of seven children—six boys and one girl—and their father, Atkinson, was a doctor, having graduated from Jefferson Medical School in Philadelphia. He set up his medical practice in nearby Alexandria, but he also owned and ran a thousand-acre plantation adjoining that of his father-in-law. After the secession of Alabama, all six sons would enter Confederate service, though Dr. Atkinson Pelham remained a civilian through the war, and practiced medicine until the day he died in 1880.

John grew up, then, in a wealthy plantation family. He soon became quite an accomplished horseman, and he got the best education available in that area at the time. The Pelham boys gained a local reputation of being a bit wild, and John was certainly at the forefront there. He was very athletic, but also could be quite polished and charming. One of his West Point classmates, Adelbert Ames, later described him as the most popular man in the class, a "gentleman in the highest sense of the term—a discourteous act was wholly foreign to his nature." And so it was that he won an appointment and joined his classmates at West Point on 1 July 1856.[10]

George Armstrong Custer was born on 5 December 1839 in New Rumley, Ohio, to Emmanuel and Maria Custer. Both had been married before and widowed, so they brought their own children to the marriage and added five more who survived infancy, of which George was the first. And clever, mischievous George, an ever-laughing long-haired blond, was the favorite of his parents as well as all his brothers and sisters. They called him "Autie," which was the way he pronounced his own middle name when he was learning to talk.

Emmanuel was a blacksmith, and all these children were many mouths to feed. One of Maria's daughters from her first marriage, Lydia-Ann, married a horse breeder who lived in Monroe, Michigan, thirty-five miles south of Detroit and not too far north of the Ohio line. Ann, as she was called, just adored George, and it was agreed that he would live with her while going to school.

Custer spent many happy years in Monroe, and even when

he moved back to Ohio in 1855 to finish his education, he still thought of it as his adopted home. In 1856, he took a job teaching in Ohio and also applied to Congressman John A. Bingham for an appointment to West Point. Those were political plums, but Custer was persistent, and in January 1857 he won the appointment. That summer he passed the admissions tests at West Point and was admitted to the academy on 20 June 1857.[11]

Looked at objectively, this was a somewhat unusual group. Custer was the great joker of the corps at the time, a man who never took academics seriously, accumulated almost as many demerits as possible without being dismissed, and did just enough to get by. DuPont was more studious and would graduate first in his class, while Custer would graduate dead last. Custer and Rosser had a lot in common, as both were somewhat boisterous types, each as much of a bon vivant as was possible for cadets. Ramseur and Pelham were both quite religious, and Merritt and Ramseur were somewhat stern and serious in their demeanor. So how did they become such good friends, so close as to risk everything for one illicit night out together?

The only fair way to answer that is to try to understand that the pressures on cadets at West Point often forced the most unlikely personalities together and made them dependent on each other, many times in ways they had never thought possible. And this naked exposure of one stripped-down human being under great pressure to another allowed—almost required!—a sort of comfort, familiarity, and camaraderie in which personality types mattered little. All had taken their social masks off and revealed their true selves to each other at some point, and that mutual exposure made them vulnerable to, and comfortable with, each other. They had all been stripped naked by the academy and thrown into the same metaphorical pool, sink or swim together. Now they genuinely relished the deep and trusting friendship that had grown from this. Truly, "brotherhood" only approximates the interpersonal bond they had forged together.

During the Civil War, Custer, Rosser, and Pelham were aggressive extroverts who would fight with wild abandon, openly showing the sort of raw courage in combat that risked their lives but also inspired their men. For their part, Ramseur, Merritt, and DuPont were no less brave themselves, but somewhat more introverted and less given to flash and color. All six would prove to be splendid battlefield commanders, each in his own way. But those actions still lay in their unknown futures, and that night, they had gathered as the closest of friends for one thing only, and that was to celebrate.

As they ate and drank and laughed, they certainly sang as well, for this was a loud and raucous celebration. In that day, long before music could be recorded, singing in such settings was an armywide tradition. One song in particular would have been most appropriate, and they surely sang it, to the tune of "The Wearing of the Green":

> *Come, fill your glasses, fellows, and stand up in a row,*
> *To singing sentimentally we're going for to go;*
> *In the army there's sobriety, promotion's very slow,*
> *So we'll sing our reminiscences of Benny Havens, oh!*

> *Oh! Benny Havens, oh! Oh! Benny Havens, oh!*
> *We'll sing our reminiscences of Benny Havens, oh!*

Yes, it was a song about Benny Havens and his tavern, where they spent some of their happiest high-risk time together as cadets. In 1838, a Lieutenant O'Brien of the 8th Infantry was visiting his friend Ripley A. Arnold, who was about to graduate from West Point, and of course they visited Benny's place. While they were toasting each other there, O'Brien called for pen and paper and wrote the first few stanzas of what has become the most famous and enduring West Point song, entitled simply "Benny Havens."

It is not surprising, given the songwriter's name, that he first sang it to the tune of "The Wearing of the Green," another tradition that has endured. O'Brien wrote a number of verses, including the first, mentioned above. And as the song's popularity took off, many others wrote verses as well, among which the following are probably the best known and most often sung:

*To our kind old Alma Mater, our rock-bound Highland home,*
*We'll cast back many a fond regret as o'er life's sea we roam;*
*Until on our last battlefield the lights of heaven shall glow,*
*We'll never fail to drink to her and Benny Havens, oh!*

*May the Army be augmented, may promotion be less slow,*
*May our country in the hour of need be ready for the foe;*
*May we find a soldier's resting-place beneath a soldier's blow,*
*With room enough beside our graves for Benny Havens, oh!*

*To our comrades who have fallen, one cup before we go,*
*They poured their life-blood freely out pro bono publico.*
*No marble points the stranger to where they rest below;*
*They lie neglected far away from Benny Havens, oh!*

All young men who reported to West Point and began their education and training as cadets in the 1850s were no different from any other frail, flawed human beings, and the same has been true from the days of the academy's founding until the present time. The strongest human instinct among them, of course, the first among Abraham Maslow's renowned hierarchy of human needs, was for simple survival. The prospect, therefore, of these cadets facing death or grievous wounding in combat as a part of their professional commitment after graduation, even though still many years off in the future, could be quite sobering, to say the least.

As young men barely out of their teen years, of course, they were still too young to recognize, let alone accept, their own mortality. Even so, the academy's goal is that, when needed, its graduates will voluntarily step forward and literally offer their lives for our country, no matter the military challenge they may face. And planting that sense of commitment so that it grows and flourishes can be quite a challenge for the academy.

The advantage West Point has here lies in the education and, more particularly, the military training and self-discipline acquired and absorbed by all cadets, a formal program that does provide them a military base on which they will be able to further grow professionally. When they confront hostile fire for the first time, the hope has always been that young West Point graduates will almost instinctively fall back on their training. If they are able to do that, the dread that might otherwise paralyze them is immediately replaced by routine. Concentrating on certain actions as they were repetitively trained to do gives them a different focus, and fear is then generally replaced by dutiful performance. Fear never goes away, of course, but once a young officer learns to control it, he can then perform at his highest level while leading troops into battle.

An important part of this training is the cadets' psychological commitment to their duty, even—and perhaps most importantly— in the very face of death. And so it was, and remains today, that cadets would attempt in many ways to reinforce this dedication, whether through their routine but meticulous appearance in uniform, marching in parades, rehearsing bayonet drill, or even something as seemingly trivial as a group of them singing songs whose words, it was hoped, would dictate their actions.

Before the advent of automatic weapons and devastating artillery rounds in the twentieth century, in all armies there were drummer boys who beat out a loud and steady marching cadence for soldiers in a given infantry unit. And when a soldier was caught up in that unit march, the rhythm of the group took over so that, terrified as he might be personally, it became very difficult psychologically for him to fall out of step and so let his

fears take control of his body. Similarly, the words of songs sung
by West Pointers, and in the case of Benny Havens, words written by West Pointers themselves, had a very powerful effect on
cadets who learned and repeated them.

One other old verse probably best captures their sense of
dedication and resolution in the face of impending battle, a verse
these proud men almost certainly would have sung:

> *And if amid the battle shock, our honor e'er should trail,*
> *And hearts that beat beneath our flag should turn or basely quail;*
> *Then may some son of Benny's, with quick avenging blow,*
> *Lift up the flag we loved so well at Benny Havens, oh!*[12]

These words are far from trivial, of course, for every genera-
tion or so produces a set of West Point classes whose members
will face combat as young officers, some of them, as was the case
with the men we are here observing at Benny Havens, almost
immediately after their graduation. And while most West Pointers thrust into combat show the courage and selfless behavior
desired, it must be recognized that not all are made of the stern
stuff required to lead in battle.

These words that disparage those who cower is a self-statement
by cadets, one that attempts to reinforce the ethic of courage and
self-sacrifice, even to the point of death. Every young officer has
two basic missions in the army: to perform his duty and to take
care of his men. If you fail in the latter, of course, then whatever
the former may be, it becomes all the more difficult to attain.
Taking care of your men means, as a first step, making sure they
are not unnecessarily killed or wounded. And sometimes that
means stepping forward and showing them what to do.

The single ethic of an infantry leader in combat, for instance,
is caught up in his repeating—and given the necessary environment, this is usually done by shouting—to his men the simple
phrase "FOLLOW ME!" after which he steps forward and leads

the way, usually into the face of hostile fire and possibly even death itself. But that leadership is the officer's duty.

The words of the large number of stanzas in the "Benny Havens" song were composed by cadets or recent graduates. Some of them are a clear effort to discourage the "quailing" of West Pointers in the face of battle. For this reason, the words remind any who would hesitate when the gunfire gets heavy that they will later be despised for their reluctance, should it not be overcome, by the majority of other graduates, for the academy calls on all West Pointers to risk everything when answering their call to duty.

Singing this and similar verses served to reinforce the value of selfless courage that is desired of all academy graduates, but as we shall see, there was no need for concern here. When thrust into the furnace of war, each of these six men turned out to be made of gold.

After rousing stanzas and more flip, Custer finally proposed one last toast to Merritt and Ramseur and the rest of their class, which he called the finest class in West Point history. Those words no doubt reflected alcohol-induced inflation, but they do illustrate the way these men felt about each other, the bond they had formed as cadets at West Point. Men in American society have never liked acknowledging that they love other men, but it does seem the only fair way to describe the bond they had formed among themselves.

DuPont, Rosser, Pelham, and Custer stayed behind for one more year as cadets, while Merritt and Ramseur graduated and were commissioned. One of the army's major roles at the time was to protect settlers as they moved west across the Great Plains and Rocky Mountains, and both men were assigned to that duty. They would not stay there long.

# TWO

## *Two Key Institutions*

Two parts of early American history, although not obviously related, would play crucial roles in the fate of these six young men: slavery and the establishment of a professional army in the United States. In order to fully understand our men and the choices they faced, therefore, some cursory look at both is needed.

---

When British subjects began to settle the American colonies, the whole issue of slavery was nothing more than a local property issue, and was so dealt with by early laws. Slavery, however, was the central issue around which the politics of our nation turned for nearly 250 years, ultimately tearing it apart.

In 1619, the first African slaves arrived in Jamestown, Virginia. Almost immediately they were recognized as a low-cost labor force most efficiently applied in agriculture, and slavery gradually expanded into fertile and temperate colonies along the southern Atlantic coast. This meant that, as agriculture developed in some parts of the United States, slavery grew with it.

In the Chesapeake Bay area of Virginia and Maryland, where

tobacco was grown and exported in ever-growing volume, farmers were among the first to adapt to slavery as a most efficient
labor investment. Similarly, the slave population ballooned in
the coastal lowlands and sea islands of the Carolinas and Georgia, where rice and indigo became major agricultural products.

These were areas very receptive to mass labor gangs culti-
vating fields, for the soil was rich in nutrients, the weather was
seldom harsh, and the many navigable rivers allowed agricultural products to be readily shipped to the coast. The large profit
margins realized from the use of slavery resulted in steadily
growing tracts of land under cultivation, always calling for the
use of more slaves. As settlements moved inland, cotton was
planted and quickly flourished, growing in importance during
the 1840s and '50s. But because of the enormous productivity
of their "peculiar institution," the white Southerners who had
originally only tolerated slavery gradually became aware that
theirs had evolved into a slave-dependent society.

In the North, of course, slavery had a different impact. While
the argument has long been made that the heavily forested
rocky hills and difficult winters of New England made slavery
impractical there, other forces also played a major role. Generally forming into small, family-focused and church-centered
communities, the residents of these colonies often brought the
fundamental religious opposition to slavery that had grown up
in England across the Atlantic. The Society of Friends, or Quakers, for instance, had required members to free their slaves, and
Quakers were to provide much of the antislavery leadership in
this country. Over time, other religions joined in, and eventually an abolitionist religious fervor swept through the North.
Though only held by a minority of the population, it resulted in
the gradual abolition of slavery in the North. By the early part
of the nineteenth century, all Northern states had either banned
slavery or were passing through gradual stages of emancipation.

During our first days as a nation, the political tolerance of slavery became a source of great discomfort to many Americans on both sides of the issue. During the summer of 1787, a constitutional convention made up of representatives from the states met in Philadelphia, where they drew up the Constitution. And despite the careful way in which the institution was never called by its proper name, slavery was validated in places where it then existed by the wording of that document. The Constitution was also the first great compromise between Northern and Southern states on the issue of slavery: congressional districts were formed based on the number of white citizens living in a given area, but partial credit was also given for the number of slaves living there.

That same summer of 1787, however, also saw the production of the Northwest Ordinance, which included the first great legal triumph for antislavery forces. In formally organizing land west of the Appalachians, north of the Ohio River, and east of the Mississippi River, Congress expressly stated that slavery would not be allowed in the Northwest Territory, out of which would come the states of Ohio, Indiana, Illinois, Michigan, and Wisconsin.

By the early nineteenth century, slavery was gone from the North, but it was growing like wildfire in the South. The Louisiana Purchase of 1803 brought in territory where slavery had been legal under French rule and whose inhabitants had ranged as far north as St. Louis with their slave property. And as settlements spread to the open West, slave owners and their abolitionist opponents sought to advance their own political causes on the ever-expanding frontier. The representational compromise established by the Constitution helped the South offset the larger and faster-growing citizenry in the North and its population-based power in the House of Representatives, but the South's crucial check was found in the Senate: so long as the number of slave states equaled the number of free states (after the admission of Alabama in 1819 there were eleven of each), the presence of two senators from each state enabled slave owners in the South to use the Senate to block abolitionist legislation coming from the House of Representatives, and they would also use their power in the same body to control the antislavery sentiments of men nominated for appointment to the United States Supreme Court.

The first post-Constitution crisis over slavery occurred in 1819 when Missouri sought admission as a slave state. New York congressman James Tallmadge attached abolitionist language to the bill that passed the House of Representatives but was defeated in the Senate. Serious threats of secession were heard from both North and South, but eventually agreement was reached that Maine, just separated from Massachusetts, would be admitted with Missouri, thus maintaining twelve slave states and twelve free. But most important, agreement was also reached that, other than in Missouri, slavery would not be allowed in territory north of Missouri's southern border, latitude 36 degrees 30 minutes. This was the so-called Missouri Compromise, passed by Congress and signed into law by President Monroe on 6 March 1820. Both sides believed they had gained from it: the South prized the admission of Missouri as a slave state, with the prospect of Florida and Arkansas joining their ranks in the near future; while the North was able to prohibit slavery in the larger part of the territories and also maintain the principle of 1787 that Congress could keep slavery out of the territories if it chose to do so.

As settlers moved west, pro- and antislavery pressures continued to build across the nation. The education of slaves was forbidden by law in most slave-holding states, and abolitionist publications in the North urged slaves to flee their masters, making use of the "Underground Railroad" whenever possible, and promising them safe refuge in the free states of the North or even moving them on to Canada, beyond the reach of American laws. While often condemned in the North on humanitarian, socioeconomic, and religious grounds, slavery was defended in slave-holding regions by plantation owners, political leaders, and clerics who found scriptural, economic, and social justification for the institution. The North was castigated as the home of wage slaves toiling under the yoke of the wealthy upper class, while the South professed itself to be made up of only two classes: the whites, all of whom were considered to be superior to all blacks, and the blacks, whether slave or free, all of whom were described as the lower class.[1]

The crisis of power between North and South took a new turn in 1833 with the reawakening of the battles between state and federal power. The South Carolina state legislature was unhappy with burdensome national tariffs on imports that protected Northern industry at Southern expense. They consequently passed an ordinance in November 1832 that was to take effect in February 1833 stating that the tariffs, which were not specifically authorized by the Constitution, were null and void and would not be enforced by the government of South Carolina. The ordinance then stated that, in the event federal officers tried to collect tariffs in South Carolina or force was used by the federal government, South Carolina would immediately secede from the Union.

Responding to this piece of state legislation, President Andrew Jackson said this nullification ordinance seemed to be based on the unacceptable proposition that South Carolina could remain in the Union while being bound by only those national laws she chose to obey. He then confronted the threat of a state's secession from the Union in a proclamation he issued on 10 December 1832, which includes these words:[2]

*Whether it be formed by compact between the States or any other manner, it is a government in which all the people are represented, which operates directly on the people individually, not upon the States. Each State having parted with so many powers as to constitute, jointly with other States, a single nation, cannot possess any*

*right to secede, because secession does not break a league but destroys
the unity of a nation.*

————

This was precisely the doctrine on which President Lincoln
acted in 1861 when South Carolina, followed by other Southern states, did secede from the Union. In 1833, many South
Carolinians were still hot after hearing Jackson's response, but
they allowed cooler heads to prevail: South Carolina's legislature reconvened and repealed the nullification ordinance. But
as the burgeoning American population moved west, still more
trouble over slavery awaited them.

————

In the late eighteenth century, there were two political parties in this country: the Federalist Party, led by John Adams
and Alexander Hamilton, and the Republican Party (or the
Democratic-Republican Party) led by Thomas Jefferson and
James Madison. Before 1800, their interparty strife sometimes
went to extremes: on too many occasions, American soldiers led
by Federalist officers had cracked heads and wrecked printing
presses and other property, though violent political deaths were
uncommon. Republicans retained a healthy fear of all American
soldiers, for it was clear that troops would be used by their Federalist commanders against American citizens to attain domestic political ends.

In 1798, the possibility of American involvement in a European war grew, and the incumbent Federalists used political
fears to their advantage by, among other things, expanding the
military. Republicans feared this larger army would be used by
the Federalists primarily to silence political opposition. Indeed,
when the Federalists were able to pass the Alien and Sedition
Acts, Republican fears seemed justified. The election of Jefferson in 1800, however, ended the immediate crisis, and he went

right to work to reduce the size and potential threat to freedom of the enlarged army.

In *Mr. Jefferson's Army*, Theodore Crackel holds that Jefferson personally was not at all opposed to the existence of a professional army per se, but only to the American army that existed at the time, and then only because of the political sentiments of its leadership. Nearly all of the officers were loyal to the Federalist Party, and on a number of occasions they had shown themselves willing to oppress Republicans for activities no more serious than the public expression of their political ideas.[3]

Jefferson's initial reduction of the size of the standing army was facilitated by the Military Peace Establishment Act of 1802. Although it was widely portrayed as an economy measure, Crackel shows us that it was little more than a political ruse, and the true purpose of the act was fourfold: to eliminate Federalist control of the army's own power structure; to remove many of the most adamantly anti-Republican Federalist officers from positions of key authority; to provide openings in the army for loyal Republicans; and to establish a steady access to officer commissions for loyal Republicans in the future.

Jefferson was able to change the political coloring of the officer corps of the army dramatically during his tenure in office. Before he was elected, the army numbered over 5,000 men; under the provisions of the Military Peace Establishment Act of 1802, Jefferson reduced the number to 3,289, but by the end of his term in 1809, the numbers had risen again to nearly 9,000 men.

In 1802, he established the United States Military Academy at West Point, New York. He wanted the cadets who would be educated there at public expense to be drawn not from the wealthy big-city political elite of the Federalist Party, but rather to be the sons of men from across the land whose political ideas were more those of the common man.

At the outset of his presidency, more than 90 percent of the officers in the army were Federalists. As a function of his careful reorganization of the officer corps, by 1809 the numbers had reversed; more than 90 percent of the officers were then his political supporters. In Jefferson's eyes, West Point was a key agency through which he could help politically reform the army from within.

In his attempt to establish a military academy that would train politically selected young men from across the nation, Jefferson was taking bold steps, and early success should not have been expected. Indeed, for the first fifteen years of its existence, the structural, political, and organizational problems confronting the new military academy caused it to be of only minimal value.

After Alexander Hamilton's death in 1804, Federalist political power began to fade, but it was their opposition to the War of 1812 that did them mortal damage. The year 1815 brought the formal end of the War of 1812 as well as the end of the Napoleonic Wars in Europe. In the same year, Jefferson's Republican successor, President James Madison, called for adequate military and naval forces in peacetime, direct taxation, and a national bank—things the Republican Party had previously opposed. But by this time, the Republicans no longer feared that the Federalists posed a threat to individual freedoms, and the personal political inclinations of army officers were no longer the central issue to the nation's leadership.

When Jefferson was elected in 1800 and his Republican government came to power, they replaced a Federalist regime whose political ideas of government by wealthy aristocrats were highly antithetical to the beliefs of the great mass of the American people. Jefferson's rise to power and the political reorientation of the government to align itself with the will of the people marks an important sea change in our nascent government and its efforts to preserve our then-frail liberties.

So Jefferson's actions in establishing the military academy can be seen, through the lens provided by Theodore Crackel, to be clearly political in nature. Any historical treatment that ignores the political basis of Jefferson's decision to launch West Point, along with contemporaneous decisions he made to reform the army, risks doing a serious injustice. Though not often recognized as such, this was a very important moment in American history.

Crackel is impressive in his presentation of facts to support his contention that Jefferson slowly and carefully changed the very political nature of the army's leadership. He has collected strong evidence that Jefferson saw a military academy at West Point as a very powerful tool by which he could train and then commission as officers of his army the sons of loyal Republicans. West Point was, in his eyes, a key agency through which he could help politically reform the army from within.

# THREE

## *Cadet Days*

Late in the month of June, throughout the 1850s, when it came time for young men holding political appointments to report in and begin their stage as cadets at West Point, most rode a scheduled ferryboat from New York City that carried them some fifty miles up the Hudson River. Once aboard, they usually found each other out, and soon clouds of anxious anticipation, split by nervous laughter, would be heard wafting out either side of the open boat as it swept slowly northward. But their greatest challenges were still to come; for when they walked up from that dock, they would be molded by the premier professional academy in America.

They intended to take the oath and then hoped to be gradually transformed into true warrior-cum-engineer leaders, men who would serve in the U.S. Army while remaining loyal to the Constitution. And that—the prospect of coming out of the top college in its field and becoming true warrior leaders commissioned in the U.S. Army—was the biggest change for the better that any of them could have imagined.

The United States Military Academy, a sprawling stone for-
tification, looks down several hundred feet to the deep Hudson.
Running from north to south between a small range of wooded
mountains, the river is diverted by a stone mass, erupting as
if from the bowels of the earth, so that it runs directly to the
east for perhaps a quarter of a mile, then resumes its southward
course. Because this rock formation protrudes from the western
bank and changes the course of the mighty Hudson, the plateau
that crowns it has long been called "West Point."

In the 1850s, the academic, parade, and administrative sections of the academy occupied about two hundred acres, at the
center of which remains today a large, level grassy area traditionally known as "the Plain." At the time, the academy buildings occupied the southern side of the Plain, which was roughly
square in shape, while staff and faculty houses were built on
its western edge. Behind these rose a steep, rocky, and thickly
wooded slope, capped by Fort Putnam, a long-unused and
gone-to-seed relic of the Revolutionary War. The northern and
eastern sides of the Plain were edged by trees, from which one
looked down over sharp drop-offs to the river far below. Today,
a few more buildings fill much of the eastern side of the Plain,
but to the north there remains a clear vista of the river. It is a
grassy sward decorated with links of the chain that blocked the
Hudson to the British as well as cannon captured in our nation's
early wars, all crowned by Battle Monument's marble column
intended to honor loyal service. Known as Trophy Point, it is a
splendid parklike area that offers a breathtaking view north up
the river from West Point.

The boat from New York City put in at a wharf far below the
academy, and the aspiring cadets somewhat anxiously climbed
the steep slope and reported in to the adjutant. And this first
arrival at West Point, the steep climb up the hill and arrival
on the Plain, was an experience long remembered by all. The

moment in the late 1850s was perhaps best captured by one who was there, Morris Schaff, class of 1862:

> *The sensations of the new cadet when he reaches the Plain linger a long while. There are two West Points—the actual West Point, and the overarching spiritual one, of which the cadet only becomes conscious about the time when he graduates. The determinate West Point that is to be his master for four years and the shaper of his destiny meets him at the top of the slope with ominous silence. He hears no voice, sees no portentous figure; but there is communicated to him in some way, through some medium, the presence of an invisible authority, cold, inexorable, and relentless. Time never wears away this first feeling; it comes back to every graduate on returning to West Point, let his years and his honors be what they may. And perhaps it is just as well that it is so; that there is one place left in our country where the vanity of asserted ancestry, and the too frequent arrogance of speculative, purse-proud, and fortuitous commercial leadership, find a chill.[1]*

Though written more than a century ago, those words still ring true in the early twenty-first century.

Back in the late 1850s, upon arrival on the Plain, these nervous young men were escorted to the Area of Barracks, where they were first exposed to the closed and cloistered military life of West Point cadets. Their immediate reception was harsh, to say the least. As they were led into the Area of Barracks, they were each suddenly surrounded by two, three, or more seeming fiends, each yelling at the top of his lungs, telling these new arrivals to pull their feet together, stand up straight, and obey orders. These were the upperclassmen—the sophomores (third-class cadets) and seniors (first-class)—who gave the initial instructions, all screaming at the latest wave of eager young men come to join the Corps of Cadets.

West Point has always been quite formal, and rather than calling them "Cadet" So-and-so, all cadets were and are addressed by officers, and introduced to strangers, as "Mister" followed by their surname. New cadets soon learned that they could address only members of their own class by their first names, but all upperclassmen had to be called "Mister." Upperclassmen also called plebes "Mister" in the same way, and only at the end of their plebe year would they be "recognized" by the upperclassmen. That meant that they had gotten past their role as subhuman plebes and would thereafter be on a first-name basis with all other cadets—except for the new, incoming class of plebes, with whom the "Mister" formalities would return.

When new political appointees first arrived at West Point, they were still little more than aspirants, with several hurdles they must take before they would truly become part of the Corps of Cadets. Even so, all were subjected to extreme pressure—go there, do this, get that—all of which tasks would be imperfectly performed, of course, which brought on only more loud fury.

The constant goal of the academy, then and now, is to produce army leaders of competence and character. To attain that mark, the regulations have always been made tighter and the living conditions harsher than those faced by students at all other American colleges. Much tighter and much harsher.

Cadets have always taken classes taught by officers and undergone military training by other officers for four years. The onerous restrictions of old loosened somewhat during the twentieth century, and many classes in recent decades have been taught by civilian academics. But our story takes place during the nineteenth century, when cadets literally stayed at West Point until they graduated, quit, or were dismissed. Their only escape was during the summer after their second year, when they were allowed to go home for ten weeks of vacation—which is why they were not around to greet the newly arrived class of would-be plebes. But for the rest of their tenure as cadets, they were required to remain on post and were seldom if ever allowed to leave, even for such emergencies as a death in their families.

The academy was intent on developing reliability in cadets and toughening them up. The desired end was that, upon graduation, the finished product would be ready to enter the ranks of the active-duty army as commissioned officers prepared to lead.[2]

Cadet appointees came to West Point from literally across the country. In its early days, there was a tradition that the secretary of war would appoint one cadet from each congressional district, but these actions had no legal basis. Finally, in 1843, Congress ordered that the Corps of Cadets would consist of one cadet from each congressional district plus ten who would be appointed "at large" by the president, these latter slots usually reserved for the sons of army officers. So it was that West Point cadets brought with them whatever regional beliefs, prejudices, or traditions they had acquired in their youth, making for a heady political mix.

And it was a strong political brew that bubbled among these young men drawn from across the land, a land that was still not yet truly a nation but rather a conglomeration of states. More important than politics to them, however, would be the personal relationships that would develop among them.

From the mid-1850s through 1861, there was usually a total of about 250 cadets at West Point, sometimes more, sometimes less. But the result of the Corps of Cadets being so small was that they were all intimately familiar with one another. The social interactions of our young men are crucial to our story, but we should never forget that, as part of this "toughening-up" process, cadet life followed a very difficult and sometimes even exhausting regimen.

Cadets had a full day every day, including classes on Saturday mornings—a tradition that endured well into the late twentieth century. They were required to march to chapel on Sunday, and their only free time, really, was Saturday afternoon and evening and Sunday afternoon. But even with this free time, there was very little for them to do. They could not go off post; they could not smoke tobacco, drink alcohol, or gamble; and since there were no sports teams of any sort, their supposed "free time" reeked of boredom. They could not have a wife, a dog, a beard, or a mustache. They were allowed to read in the library on Saturdays, or they could check out books, though these had to be returned on Monday. Reading letters from home and writing responses were among the few escapes from tedium.

But worst of all was probably the food served in the mess hall. Notoriously bad, it ranged from bland to revolting, and there was often little of it, no matter the quality. One cadet described his meals while in summer camp in 1858: for breakfast he had Irish potatoes "with very little meat," coffee, and bread; for midday dinner, he had boiled beef, boiled potatoes, and boiled greens, and for dessert, "bread and molasses, and a kind of pudding made of the food left at the other meals, sweetened, I believe, with molasses and a good deal of spice"; and for supper that evening, he had only bread, butter, and coffee.[3]

Not a terribly attractive diet, particularly when you get, as he did, the same fare every day. But this was no accident, as it was considered part of the "toughening-up" that all cadets had to undergo. There were only a few alternatives for cadets, and these were rare.

The Thompson sisters, two spinsters whose father had been a Revolutionary War soldier, found themselves destitute in 1830. The superintendent at the time, Sylvanus Thayer, had allowed them to live in General Washington's old log quarters at West Point and prepare meals for cadets. This was very satisfactory to them, and although they only had room for twelve, they more than filled their part of the contract. For a cadet, being assigned to take your meals with them was a treasured blessing, for the Thompson sisters ate very well indeed, as did their guests. But it was a cyclical treat, and no sooner did a cadet grow accustomed to eating delicious, filling meals than he found himself back in the mess hall again, condemned to the hated fare on which all cadets had to survive.[4]

Occasionally officers and their wives on the faculty would invite a few cadets to dinner, and this was also a rare and treasured treat. But such escapes were quite irregular, and hunger pangs were particularly unwelcome when added to the other burdens of cadet life.

The only other option cadets had for nourishment was somehow to purloin food of some sort, usually brought in by visitors but sometimes acquired by a cadet's ingenuity alone. Once secured, a group of cadets would gather in the room of the man who had gotten the goods, and together they would cook whatever they had into some kind of stew or other concoction in their fireplaces, with potatoes or other vegetables tucked into the hot ashes below their skillets. This dish, whatever its components, was known as "hash," and the skills of some cadets in preparing it lived far beyond their presence as cadets—like William Tecumseh Sherman, class of 1840 and long renowned as perhaps the greatest hash cooker of all times.[5]

But there were other hash cookers as well. One of the best-remembered moments of illicit food consumption involved a rooster that belonged to a Lieutenant Douglass, whose quarters were near the cadet barracks. So near, in fact, that the rooster's crowing was part of every normal morning. But then one morning, the sun came up with no rooster welcoming it. What had happened to it?

Custer had slipped downstairs the night before, crept into the henhouse and grabbed the rooster by the neck, then quickly scrambled back up to his fourth-floor room in the eighth division. But to understand this, some brief explanation seems in order.

The barracks then at West Point were constructed in an unusual fashion. To enter a door on the first floor, you first had to come up a short flight of stairs to reach its level, half a flight above ground. Then when you went in a door, you were entering what was called a "division," where you would find a short hall, off of which four doors opened, one in every corner and each leading into a two- or three-man room. There was a front and a back door on the first floor of every division, but those were the only ways in or out. There were four floors of cadet rooms in each division, and as you ascended the cast-iron staircase, you found the same arrangement of rooms on each floor, with no horizontal connection to adjoining divisions.

That may have been convenient for some purposes, but if an officer chased a cadet into a division and he went up the stairs, he basically had him trapped in one of the rooms on the second, third, or fourth floors, as there was no way out without wings. But being pursued by an officer means big trouble, so cadets have many times jumped out the second-floor window to make good their escape. This was easy on the southern, or "Area" side, for there was a broad porch on the first floor on that side of the barracks known to cadets by the old Dutch name of the "stoops." Covered by a solid roof with open front and sides, the stoops gave an easy escape to fleeing cadets able to reach the second floor. From there, they had only to climb out a window onto the roof of the stoops and run in either direction to another division, into whose windows they could disappear.

Some cadets have even been known to hang from a third-floor window on that side and drop to the roof of the stoops. But that roof was steeply sloped and therefore dangerous for a cadet who had been consuming illegal alcohol. Even inebriated, however, the fourth floor was just too high for such a stunt, and if an officer ran you up there, you were basically caught.

Once Custer got Chanticleer to his room, he wrung his neck and he and his friends hastily defeathered him. Soon enough, he was boiling in a kettle in Custer's fireplace, the feathers clumped on a newspaper on the floor. Those cadets had a feast that night, but whoever was responsible for getting rid of the feathers did a poor job. At reveille next morning, there was a clear trail of yellow feathers from the door of the eighth division all the way across the Area. Clearly, it was someone who lived in the eighth division who had stolen and eaten Lieutenant Douglass's rooster. No doubt everyone wondered for a long time who that could have been. . . .[6]

For our six cadets, there was the added burden that, in 1854, the duration of the cadet experience had been expanded from four years to five. This change was made with the good intention of giving cadets more instruction so as to better prepare them for the army—teaching them Spanish, more engineering, and more tactical training—and it was directly attributable to two men who had graduated from West Point decades earlier.

The first was a West Point graduate in the class of 1828, Secretary of War Jefferson Davis, later elected a senator from Mississippi and later still president of the Confederate States of America. The second was the superintendent at the time, Robert E. Lee, who had graduated with the class of 1829.

When new cadets arrived at West Point in 1854, they were divided roughly in half, and their age alone dictated the course requirements they would face in order to earn a diploma. Those who were eighteen or older would continue the until-then normal program of four years and graduate in 1858, while those who were younger would be launched on a new and revised academic schedule that would last for five years, so that they would graduate in 1859.

Before that time, cadets were designated by their classes in inverse order, with new cadets in their first year at the academy, or plebes, being members of the fourth class, or fourth classmen. Over four years, they would progress to third, second, and finally, their senior year, first classmen. But under the new five-year program, of course, the new plebes were formally known as members of the fifth class, or simply fifth classmen.

Only two classes, those of 1859 and 1860, went through the full five years, while the class of 1861 was graduated into the Civil War in May, one month short of the scheduled five years. The next class, formerly scheduled to graduate in 1862, actually received their diplomas also in 1861, in June. Thereafter, the course duration was returned to four years and never again expanded to five.

While there were no intercollegiate sports teams at the time, there was a gymnasium, and in addition to marching, cadets did play informal games on the Plain, such as an early form of soccer. On Saturday or Sunday afternoons, they could swim in the river during the summer and skate on it in the winter. After having obtained formal permission, they could also hike or ride horses through the wooded hills that surround the post.

The only two cadet extracurricular organizations were debating societies, the Dialectic and the Amosophic. These met on Saturday evenings to debate issues ranging from the theoretical—"Do the talents of men deteriorate in the Western Hemisphere?"—to the more immediate—"Is the Missouri Compromise Constitutional?"[7]

The only other organization in which cadets could participate was the Napoleon Club. But only a few select cadets were invited to sit in on meetings, as this was primarily an organization whose members were officers on the West Point staff and faculty. At the time, after all, Napoleon was considered the Great Captain of history, alongside of whose triumphant military record no others could stand. One would think that Alexander the Great, Hannibal, Julius Caesar, Gustavus Adolphus, or Frederick the Great might have been competitive. But not so to the members of the Napoleon Club at West Point in the 1850s. For them, the emperor, not yet forty years in his grave, was simply the best there ever was.

When Robert E. Lee was superintendent from 1852 through 1855, he was not only a fervent member, he also gave the club a special room in the academic building in which to meet, on the walls of which were painted large maps of some of Napoleon's campaigns. This club also met on Saturday evenings, and the procedure was that one officer, having had advance notice and a few weeks within which to prepare, would give a presentation on a particular battle or campaign in which Napoleon's army had fought or a logistical or political problem he had faced. The floor would then open for discussion and debate, and it was often loud and even raucous. But for the few cadets occasionally allowed to participate, it was the most fun, and some would even say the *only* fun, they had all week, and they relished it.[8]

Many of the officers who were members of the Napoleon Club, of course, would later command troops during the Civil War. Given that formative experience at West Point, whether as officer or cadet, there seems little doubt that these men would try to emulate Napoleon's actions, though few were able to succeed. George McClellan, one of the brightest officers at West Point, was probably the most fervent and learned member of the club, and his military efforts during the Civil War failed disastrously. In fact, the only high-visibility member whose record shows he used Napoleonic tactics brilliantly was Robert E. Lee.[9]

As soon as these naive young boys passed through the sally port and stepped into the Area of Barracks, upper-class cadets in gray uniforms descended on them, screaming orders at the confused lads still wearing civilian clothes. As of that moment, they were "new cadets." And now that they were on the "inside" and subordinated to enormous pressure from the cadets senior to them, their whole world changed instantaneously. Plebes, they would soon learn, were the lowest form of existence, and they were so treated. Hazing at the time was against cadet regulations and more in the nature of practical jokes, such as cutting a plebe's tent ropes in the middle of the night. But even this generally ended after summer camp, when cadets moved back into the stone barracks built in 1851, barracks that were still in use more than a hundred years later.[10]

One of the first things plebes would do was to take the admissions test. Technically, they were still cadet candidates, as they would not receive their warrants as cadets until after they had passed the general examinations in January that covered their first semester. The first barrier was the admissions test, which they had to pass before they could begin taking academic instruction. Before the Civil War, cadet candidates would take the admissions test soon after arrival, after which a number of them would be dropped from the rolls and they would return home, although some who failed would get a second chance in late August.

But many cadets from the southern and western sections of the country did not have the academic preparation of their peers from the northeast. Congressmen from these sections of the country were tired of their nominees failing the admissions test and so brought pressure to make it somewhat easier. The result was that, for the class that arrived in 1857 and was scheduled to graduate in June 1862, fewer than 10 percent failed the admissions test. But of the original class of seventy-nine, only thirty-four graduated. While it is true that of the forty-five who failed to complete the course, twenty-four left to fight for the Confederacy, another twenty-one quit or, more commonly, failed academically, most of these from the South and the West.

All cadets would spend the summer in tents on the Plain, and new cadets were rushed from place to place: first assigned to their quarters in tents, then sent running around from station to station for medical examinations, measurement for cadet uniforms, and other administrative matters. The uniforms would not be ready for anywhere from days to weeks, during which time they had to wear the civilian clothes in which they had arrived, civilian garb that singled them out for petty harassment by upperclassmen. Those first days were filled with other details that were drowned in a confused blur, with the most remembered experience being their instruction in drill.

They were given too much to do in too short a time, and the result was a confused, exhausted, and often overwhelmed group of young men. But before they knew it, they were learning to march, new rifled muskets on their shoulders, a steady drumbeat drowning out all but the loud directions and reprimands they received from upper-class cadets.

Cadets were paid thirty dollars each month, but the money stayed in their accounts and they could only charge purchases against it. These purchases were limited to uniforms and toiletries, but even so, most cadets were constantly in arrears. To make things worse, they were not allowed to deposit money from the outside to make up their deficits. This was just one more ax metaphorically suspended above their individual heads, but it was only one of many.

These boys-quickly-turning-into-men soon learned that West Point is a closed society. No matter how wealthy or well-born a new cadet might be, all members of this new class were here treated the same: like dogs. But they also learned that plebe year would be the great rite of passage that loomed before them, that they were being tested for admission into a very elite group at a select institution.

This first year at West Point would prove to be the most rigorous experience virtually all of them had ever faced. And perhaps the crucial aspect of plebe year, something new for all, was the extent to which they were required—forced, really—to rely on each other.

This was done intentionally, of course. If one plebe in a squad or platoon was late for formation, for instance, or wore the wrong uniform, then none of them would be recognized as having arrived on time. All plebes in that squad or platoon had to be standing in ranks correctly attired. This meant the slow were necessarily helped along by the quick, the sloppy by the neat, and a concept of teamwork among classmates sprang up and became heavily embedded in all.

"Cooperate and graduate" the saying goes, and it cut across all aspects of West Point. If one classmate was slow in mathematics or French or drawing fortifications or shining brass, a classmate who was strong in that area would devote extra time and effort to coach or assist the weaker member. The result was a bonding among these young men, a bond the authorities intended to result in extra effort being extended by one man for another, both at the academy and later in the army.

The pressure on plebes was intense, of course, and this special bonding built up very fast. And it worked. No matter how smart or dumb, swift or slow, strong or weak, organized or confused a given plebe might be, he could always expect to be called upon to help a classmate. And, in turn, should he need it, he could count on receiving help from another classmate, instantly and without any question.

During the summer months, the Corps of Cadets was housed in a small city of tents with wooden floors on the Plain. But this was a formal military camp, and presiding over all were the somewhat larger tents in which the tactical officers who technically commanded them, all the way up to the commandant of cadets, also lived for the summer. There would be no academic courses until September, and this was the time when great focus was placed on soldiering.

Reveille was at 5:00 a.m., followed by roll call and "police of the area," which means meticulously picking up and disposing of trash, litter, or anything else that didn't belong there. From 5:30 to 6:30, cadets had their first drill session. For the next half hour, they had to raise their tent walls, arrange their bedding, and get equipment and uniform ready for morning parade. At 7:00, there was another roll call, after which they marched to breakfast in the mess hall. At 8:00 was morning parade, followed by guard mounting. From 9:00 to 10:00 was artillery drill, with no other formal duties (other than cleaning and polishing musket and equipment in preparation for evening inspection) until roll call and march to dinner at 1:00. All gentlemen at the time were skilled in dancing, and dancing class was from 3:00 to 4:00, after which there was another police call, followed by the companies being turned out to take their muskets from the stack. From 5:30 to 6:45 was afternoon infantry drill, followed by evening parade and inspection until about 8:00. Then came another roll call and march to supper. Tattoo roll call was at 9:30 and taps (lights-out) at 9:45.[11]

If they did not quit or get dismissed during plebe year—and a high percentage fell to one of the two—these men would learn more about themselves and what they could do or endure than they had ever thought or even suspected possible. And they would also have earned membership in a special fraternity on which they might rely for the rest of their lives. For truly, after plebe year, these men were closer than brothers.

At the time, anywhere from a quarter to a third of their number would fall by the wayside during the first year. But for those who made it, their lives and their world were changed forever. Here they would grow into manhood, making lifelong friendships and forming their true characters based on personal honor and devotion to duty. And those who stayed did so because they had all fallen under the spell of West Point.

After plebe year, of course, that fraternal affection extended to all other cadets as well. Seen from the outside, then, all cadets seemed to have a sort of siege mentality as regarded the officers who made up the staff and faculty, a sort of "us against them" outlook that permeated all. And there is no question that this bonded all contemporaneous cadets in later years, whether in the army or as civilians.

Even so, cadet life was rigorous. Perhaps some better sense of this can be found in the words of one of our six men, Henry DuPont. In a letter to his mother dated 1 November 1856—the fall of his plebe year—he refers to her recent visit:

> *You seem to infer that because I was not in very good spirits then, that I am regretting that I came to West Point. It seems to me that it is*

*analogous to this, no person would ever regret having taken medicine to do him good and cure him, if sick, no matter how bitter or disagreeable it might be. Now you seem to me, from your letter, to think that every one should like his medicine, and take it with the greatest joy and delight. I, however, disagree with you and think that, if he is sensible, he should take it willingly, but that he has a right to make faces and complain of its tasting bad, so that he drinks it all.[12]*

---

Another key aspect of West Point was competition. Cadets were required to pass not only the academic admissions test, but also to be healthy and sound medically. And once classes began, all cadet grades were posted every week outside the adjutant's office for all to see. Periodically, the "sections," as the dozen or so cadets taking instruction in a given classroom were called, would be reorganized according to grades.

This was done so that the smarter students would be grouped together, as would be those who needed to work harder. But more important to cadets, it was also a listing of each cadet's rank, or "standing," in each class. This academic ranking, along with disciplinary records and other military records of achievements or failures, determined a cadet's overall class standing.

Class standing would count at graduation for such things as branch and assignment selection, and it would follow a man all his life. In one's later career, if two men had been promoted through the ranks together, then calculating who outranked whom, and thus who would take command, might well depend on class rank at West Point. And while competition may have been most prominent in academics, it permeated all aspects of cadet life.[13]

While academic grades counted heavily in determining class rank, there were other factors as well. Discipline, as measured primarily by the number of demerits a cadet acquired, was important. A cadet could receive no more than one hundred demerits in a given six-month period, and exceeding that number meant automatic expulsion. Custer brushed that number twice, including having received ninety-nine demerits more than a month before the end of a semester. That situation caused Custer to be extraordinarily careful for the next thirty days, being a better cadet than he had ever been before or, indeed, than most of his fellow cadets had even thought possible.

Another major element of class rank turned on every cadet's aptitude for the service as a commissioned officer in the army. Each of the four companies of cadets had an officer assigned to it who was personally responsible for the military training and demeanor of every man in his company. These officers, denominated as "tactical officers" (or "tacs" in cadet slang), were technically in command of each of these companies. But as a practical matter, it was cadet company commanders who ran things, though under the supervision and command of their tacs.

Most tacs were not long or favorably remembered by cadets, as they were often harsh and exacting—which, after all, was their job. But occasionally, one would come through who would encapsulate all those attributes of an officer to which cadets aspired, including the ability to be supportive and inspiring while still maintaining cadet performance and adherence to regulations at a high level.

Usually lieutenants or captains, these tacs worked for the commandant of cadets in the military chain of command, and they managed cadet discipline by doing such things as inspecting their rooms or their persons and issuing demerits for flaws they found and, when they could, detecting and punishing cadet violations of regulations, violations for which they also issued demerits. After a cadet had acquired a certain number of demerits during a month, every additional one received had to be worked off by marching extra guard tours.

The usual ratio was one hour of marching an extra tour for each demerit, and they were marched on Saturday afternoons during what otherwise was cadet "free time." But before marching, each cadet being punished would be inspected by the officer of the day, and this inspection could turn into a venomous downward spiral: if any flaws were found, such as "improperly shined brass" or "dirty weapon," then the cadet would receive more demerits, which would mean more punishment tours.

As a practical matter, these tacs also filled an important paternal role, particularly for the younger cadets in their company who were far away from home for the first time. But their job also included the subjective rating of each cadet relative to his peers, and thereby providing an assessment of his potential aptitude for service. And this measurement, which was used to determine cadet rank, for instance, was also an important component in class standing.

Any officer at West Point could, at any time, write a report on a given cadet, either good or bad, and submit it to that cadet's tactical officer. Each company tac, in turn, might use these reports to modify his perception of a given cadet's aptitude.

As we look back to a time of wooden ships and horse power, an era long before airplanes, internal combustion engines, penicillin, or even electricity, such cadet competition may today seem to us somewhat superficial, even silly. But it was far from either, and a good example of this comes to us from Henry DuPont. In 1855 he had applied from his home in Delaware both to West Point and to the Virginia Military Institute. He was not admitted to either, so he went to the University of Pennsylvania, of Ivy League renown, for one year. But his prominent family was politically powerful, so in 1856, he was admitted to West Point and began his plebe year that summer. In a letter home, he says:

*There is something very exciting in the competition for "standing" in our studies. I have been working incessantly since January, and must*

*go on until June. To stop my exertions for a time is to be beaten.
I think that a high rank in the class in this institution is well worth
studying for, though it was not at college. There is something radically
wrong in the system of our universities and colleges and they never will
flourish as they would do, were they to adopt the plan of arranging the
students by their merits, and instead of expelling the lazy and stupid,
who in some places, as at the University in Philadelphia [University
of Pennsylvania], form the majority and give the tone to the whole
institution. I think now that my obtaining an appointment was one
of the most important events in my whole life, and I am very glad
that I left college where, in comparison to what I am learning here, I
learned nothing at all.*[14]

---

And the competition was not just in classrooms, either, as much of
the instruction in military areas took place outdoors. For instance,
in addition to taking instruction in mathematics, engineering,
geography, drawing, chemistry, physics (then called "natural philosophy"), English, French, and ethics, cadets also took infantry
tactics, artillery tactics, cavalry tactics, ordnance, and gunnery.
Some of this was classroom instruction, but there was abundant hands-on instruction outdoors as well, where cadets could
become familiar with the weaponry, tactics, and common day-to-
day experiences of the active-duty members of the army in which
they would soon serve as officers. And while the competition in
some areas was sometimes fiercer than in others, it was always
there, a sort of leitmotif of the West Point cadet experience.

Riding, of course, was essential for cadets, and while some
arrived at the academy as accomplished equestrians, others had
never ridden at all. Even so, all went through a regimen of rigorous training.

Part of this was many long, jarring hours astride a horse trotting around the riding hall, either bareback or with their stirrups
crossed over the saddle in front of them so that cadets could not

insert their feet into them for support and balance. Some good riders took this easily in stride, while others squeezed their legs around the torso of the horse, squeezing for all they were worth and trying desperately not to fall off. And falling off, of course, was a normal experience for the uninitiated. But when a cadet fell, he was invariably required to remount and continue to ride around the hall with his classmates until the instructor stopped the group.

As their skill increased, they began other exercises, such as "cutting heads." Leather balls filled with straw were placed atop posts of different heights, always including a few on the ground. Cadets would then ride past them at a gallop and thrust at or cut these "heads" with their sabers, including those on the ground, which required a deep and often precarious lean.

The ability to jump fences on horseback was another skill thought necessary for future officers. But when bars were put up for this, some of the horses cadets had been assigned to ride became balky and refused the jump. That meant that, from a gallop, they suddenly stopped short just before the jump, often causing their rider to slide forward over the horse's head and crash into the bars or onto the sawdust-covered floor.

Any of these exercises could send horses into bursts of bucking and kicking, a nearly uncontrollable behavior that made cadet lives even more miserable. But cadets tried to be patient because they knew that when they became seniors, or first classmen, they would be able to select their horses, and there were many good ones.[15]

Even horseback riding was not without its dangers, of course. Cadet John Pelham had a bit of a scrape, which he mentioned in a letter to his mother:

*I was kicked by a horse on the 23rd. The cavalry plain is covered with snow and ice, and we have to ride in the riding hall. We have heads, rings, lances, and bars arranged around the hall, which we have to cut, thrust, parry, and jump, each one taking his turn. Sometimes miss-cuts are made and the horses' ears or legs are struck; this makes them foolish and hard to get out of ranks. While attempting to force a vicious one—I don't mean my horse—he let fly both feet, which took me on the leg. This compelled me to dismount and go to the hospital. My leg is quite sore, but the bone is not injured, the kick was on the muscle.*

John, in fact, was an excellent horseman. He, Rosser, and Custer were considered the best riders in the Corps of Cadets, and if a horse couldn't be ridden by one of them, other cadets believed, it just couldn't be ridden.[16] In 1860, the Prince of Wales, the future king Edward VII of England, visited West Point. While there, he watched a performance that included a mounted Pelham, whose grace and form, he commented, impressed him.[17]

Another amusement with which to fill their free afternoons Saturday and Sunday was dancing, and again, John Pelham was quite the dancer. During the cold winter months, few visitors came to West Point, so the cadets danced with each other, even as they had taken dancing instructions with classmates as partners. But during the summer, there were more "hops," to which women were invited. And while the warm sun shined, girls came to West Point in droves. They cruised the academy grounds, their brightly colored crinoline skirts rustling, their parasols shading them as they, not so secretly, hoped to find the man of their dreams wearing cadet gray.

But John tended to avoid these female temptations, as he was a strong member of the "confirmed bachelor" club. It wasn't that he disliked women or was not attracted to them, for he eagerly studied them through a telescope as they walked around the Plain. But he also thought that, as a young officer, he needed to maintain his independence and focus on his military duties. He wanted a family in due course, but had resigned himself to waiting it out. As he wrote to his mother,

*I think a young officer ought to play his hand alone for four or five*
*years at least, after graduating. He ought to rough it on the frontier for*
*several years and learn whether Fate is propitious, and in what direc-*
*tion Fortune showers her favors. That is the road I'll take.*[18]

———————

Dod Ramseur wrote to a friend describing the rigors he faced. He
said that, before accepting the appointment, he had thought long
and hard about his ability to succeed at West Point. He believed
he had considered all the difficulties and hardships he might face
there. But no one, he said, could ever "*imagine* the severity of the
West Point course." All the stories he had heard about the hardships that must be endured by a plebe, stories he had thought
inflated, turned out to be true. This helped him better understand
why so many Americans were reluctant to join the army, as few
were willing, in peacetime, to subject themselves to the "severe
and almost tyrannical laws which are necessary for the preservation of order and discipline in a standing army."[19]

It is now difficult to determine who roomed with whom in
the 1850s, as roommates were often changed and all pertinent
official records have long disappeared. We can only know such
details through memoirs and letters, but it looks pretty certain
that John Pelham, a blue-eyed blond from Alabama, roomed
with big Tom Rosser from Texas, at least for part of their time
as cadets.[20] One of his classmates, Adelbert Ames—later a major
general in the U.S. Army—described Pelham as follows:

*He was a gentleman in the highest sense of the term. A discourteous*
*act was wholly foreign to his nature. He was a favorite in the Corps of*
*Cadets, and I think I am safe in saying, the most popular man in our*
*class. . . . I recall one instance when, as a young cadet, he was trying*
*to get on the "color guard." Success depended on military bearing,*
*cleanliness of gun, and condition of dress and accoutrements, including*

*every possible detail. Half a dozen classmates surrounded him, eager
to prepare him for the adjutant's critical inspection. One brought him
a bayonet scabbard better varnished than his own—another a waist-
belt thought to be better than the one he had on—a third was wiping
his gun with a handkerchief to remove any possibly neglected particle
of dust—time, effort and interest they would hardly give themselves
for themselves. He, all the while, was protesting they were too kind,
and acknowledging his appreciation of their attention with merry
laugh and twinkling eyes. He made the color guard.[21]*

———

Once summer encampment on the Plain ended, cadets moved back
into barracks in preparation for class and arranged their meager
possessions according to regulations. These were an iron bedstead,
a table, a straight-backed chair, a lamp, a mirror, a washstand, and
a mattress and blanket (these last two were folded up when not in
use). In addition to their uniforms, cadets were authorized only a
few other private possessions outside of what they had been issued,
such as toiletries and letter paper. But for the most part, that was
what each cadet had in his room, and nothing more. Running
water was available in sinks found in the basement, as were toilet
facilities. Room ventilation was bad, which meant they were hot
in the summer and cold in the winter. The only heat came from
an open fireplace, which was both inefficient and ineffective during cold New York winters, especially at night.[22]

Though most of the prankish hazing ended with camp, some
endured into barracks. For instance, it was not uncommon for
upperclassmen—usually new sophomores, or "yearlings"—to
sneak into a barracks room shared by two plebes in the dead
of night, grab them by the ankles and jerk them out of bed and
onto the floor, then run away laughing.

Such physical harassment was against regulations, of course.
But it was almost impossible for the perpetrators to get caught
and punished, so it continued on an unpredictable basis—usually

when sophomores stayed up late studying (also against regulations, but they hid their lights with blankets tacked over their windows) and felt like some deviltry before finally going to bed themselves.

Once they had been through its rigors themselves, of course, many upperclassmen, in particular new sophomores who had just finished their own year of turmoil, simply delighted in tormenting the next batch of plebes. Sometimes it was done mirthfully, other times with a sense of payback or even vengeance. And one of the biggest jokesters was Custer.

One night another cadet, Morris Schaff, was startled awake by a sudden crash inside a plebe room down the hall, a noise that seemed to shake the whole building. It seemed that the plebe occupants had been jerked out of their beds the previous night, and they didn't like it. So in order to give them early warning of any repeat effort, they had leaned an elaborate and precarious structure made up of their two washstands and their two chairs against their closed door. And when the pranksters had sought silent entry that night, they instead brought the whole contraption crashing to the floor. A silence was broken by a loud voice demanding:

*"Who lives in here?"*

The responses were meek: "Sir, Mister Robbins." "Sir, Mister Higgason."

*"Good God! Mister Robbins, come out of this!"*

The next noise was of the two screaming plebes being dragged down the hallway by their ankles, after which the two invaders slipped down the stairs, leaving the pair of angry, cursing plebes behind.[23] The invaders were Custer, of course, and his roommate at the time, George Watts of Kentucky,[24] and they later admitted that the booby-trapped door had scared the daylights out of them both, and they laughed hard about it for a long time.

And there were other times as well. When Jasper Myers

arrived from Indiana with the class of 1862, he wore a full beard, which was strictly forbidden for cadets. But before he was ordered to shave, Custer walked up to him and confronted him not as a new plebe, but rather matter-of-factly as an adult. He told him there must have been some mistake, so he was to return home, as it was his boy who should have taken the appointment, not the old man.[25]

# FOUR

## *Impending Disunion*

In 1857, the Dred Scott decision was handed down by the Supreme Court, holding that neither slaves nor their descendants could ever become citizens of the United States, and that the U.S. Congress had no authority to prohibit slavery in federal territories. In addition, this decision held that slaves had no right of action to sue in court, and that slaves, as private property, could not be taken from their owners without due process of law.[1]

This, of course, was a major body blow to those opposed to or even just uncomfortable with slavery. There were not many cadets who were open abolitionists, and those who were usually concealed it. As Custer later recorded, this was not a popular stand for a cadet to take:

> *As the pronounced abolitionist was rarely seen in Congress in those days, so was his appearance among the cadets of still rarer occurrence; besides it required more than ordinary moral and physical courage to boldly avow oneself an abolitionist. The name was considered one of opprobrium, and the cadet who had the courage to avow himself an*

*abolitionist must be prepared to face the social frowns of most of his comrades and at times to defend his opinions by his physical strength and mettle.*[2]

———————

Despite the extreme positions of some of the Southern zealots among them, most cadets during the mid to late 1850s held somewhat moderate views on national policy issues and usually found themselves in the political middle. Even though political tension was growing, cadets tried always to act like gentlemen and so avoided, in their discussions or even casual conversations, touching on such sensitive subjects as slavery. Besides, as potential servants of the people, cadets knew they would be bound to serve their country despite which political party or philosophy might win dominance at the ballot box. Such political controversy, most believed, was strictly out of bounds at West Point.[3]

But as the political storm over slavery slowly grew into a hurricane that was to rip our nation apart, the political passions of the American people were mirrored among cadets. Regional origins of cadets, which had been little more than an interesting curiosity, now became the base on which increasingly rigid social lines began to grow. And among this group of hormone-engorged young men training to become warriors, innocent acts that formerly would have passed without comment now became slights or even insults, and the resulting anger sometimes turned into rage and even fistfights.

Wesley Merritt came from Salem, a small town in southern Illinois whose residents were generally more closely associated with the cotton/pork/tobacco/molasses/rum culture of the South than the wheat/beef/coffee/dairy/whiskey customs of the North. And although there was no slavery in southern Illinois, there was in Missouri off to the west, Kentucky to the east, and the vast depths of Dixie to the south, so there were pressures pulling him both ways.

Wesley's personal political views reflected those of his father back home in Salem, in that he was a middle-of-the-road moderate who despised abolitionists but also hated the "fire eaters" who would break up the Union over slavery. He was somewhat reserved, but his reluctance to argue was partly an effort to mask his furious temper, which he worked hard to control. But after hearing another cadet braying his strong abolitionist beliefs, it became too much for him, and the two ended up in a fistfight.[4]

Dod Ramseur's father had been a prosperous merchant, but in the falloff of 1857, he was cheated out of nearly everything he owned by a partner who happened to be from the North. The very idea that his family had been, as he described it, "robbed of all earthly goods by the damning treachery of a miserable Yankee, a villain, a liar, a fiend of Hell" was enough to enrage Dod, and he harbored a bitterness over this event for the rest of his life. Added to that was his anger over the failure of the pro-slavery Constitution in Kansas, which caused him to breathe fire on the North: "I am a *Secessionist* out and out," he said, "in favor of drawing the dividing line from the Atlantic to the Pacific." If Kansas were to enter the Union as a free state, he believed the South would have no alternative but to establish an independent nation founded on "*Liberté et Egalité.*" He predicted that tar and feathers would be the fate of any Yankee foolish enough to trespass there a first time, and a hangman's noose, he believed, should await a second transgression.[5]

The most important political event before the Civil War that occurred while our men were cadets was probably John Brown's attempt to take the arsenal at Harpers Ferry and start a race war in which he intended to arm freed slaves and turn them against their masters. And the response among cadets largely reflected that of the American people. Until the late 1850s, the extremes of abolitionism or slaveholding as national models had attracted little support among most cadets and were largely ignored. The situation was probably not unlike that one finds in college students of modern times over sensitive political issues like abortion or gun control: yes, there are champions of both extremes to be found in the student body, while most others just ignore their political recruiting efforts. But in the wake of the Harpers Ferry raid, support for or opposition to slavery became a loud debate, and cadets slowly began to draw lines between themselves on that basis.

Henry DuPont came from a prominent family in Delaware, which was technically a slave state, though by 1860 the number of slaves there had shrunk to 1,798 while free blacks numbered 19,829.[6] DuPont gives us a view of the situation in 1859 that was probably typical among West Point cadets at the time. In a letter to his father (also a West Point graduate, in the class of 1833) dated 29 October 1859, he says:

> *What an outrageous affair was that at Harpers Ferry. I suppose that the Mr. George Turner, a graduate of West Point whom the abolitionists shot, was your old friend.[7] The most disgusting part of the business though, I think, are the meetings of the republicans of Chicago and of various towns of Massachusetts to express their sympathy with Brown and regret at the failure of his plans. A great deal of political capital will I suppose be made out of the affair.[8]*

It is important here for us to remember, as Bell Wiley so graphically shows in his most insightful book *The Life of Billy Yank*, that there was a great deal of racism among white Union army soldiers during the Civil War. Most of them accepted with little thought that all African Americans were automatically inferior to them, many holding them to be of a lesser race. Seeing the same sort of attitudes among cadets at West Point who came from Northern states, then, should come as no surprise, for cadets truly reflected the societies they had left behind when they had come to West Point.

Merritt and Ramseur graduated with their class on 1 July 1860, and for them, that climactic event made mere political differences fade into the background. Of the 121 cadets who had entered with them in 1855, only 41 would graduate. During the Civil War, 32 of these men would remain loyal to the Union, while the other 9 would resign their commissions in the U.S. Army and fight for the Confederacy. One-quarter of the class would not survive the war.[9]

On the Sunday before graduation, the traditional pregraduation service was held in the chapel. And the lower classes of the Corps of Cadets sang a special song for them, a song which was only sung each year at this time. It was sung to the cadets about to leave by those who were to stay behind. It has a lovely melody, but the central words are haunting, particularly at this time:

> *When shall we meet again?*
> *Meet ne'er to sever . . .* [10]

Merritt's first assignment was to the 2nd Dragoons, then stationed at Camp Floyd in Utah. This illustrious unit was then commanded by Colonel Philip St. George Cooke, who had written "System of Cavalry Tactics," which, with some amendments, was to become the standard guidebook for cavalry until the turn of the century. Cooke was himself from Virginia, and while he remained loyal to the Union during the Civil War, his daughter's husband, then-captain J. E. B. Stuart, resigned his commission and joined the Confederate army.

In June 1862, Cooke would find himself in command of a Union cavalry force in pursuit of a Confederate cavalry force on a reconnaissance mission that boldly rode around McClellan's entire Union command. And that Confederate column was commanded by none other than his son-in-law, now a general. McClellan had ordered Cooke to pursue Stuart no faster than a Union infantry force that accompanied him could march, which meant that the riders in gray got clean away. While this outcome may have caused a minor embarrassment to Cooke within Union ranks, it was no doubt good news for his daughter.

Merritt's company commander was Captain John Buford, and another officer in the 2nd Dragoons was Captain Alfred Pleasonton. Within a short time, Buford would be Merritt's commander in the 1st Cavalry Division and Pleasonton would command the entire cavalry force of the Union Army of the Potomac. Both considered Merritt an almost ideal young lieutenant, and that appreciation would count for a lot in the menacing war that was already at their doorstep.[11]

Ramseur was commissioned in the 3rd Regiment of Artillery, but his first duty was to return to West Point later in July and testify before a congressional commission organized and run by Senator Jefferson Davis. Ramseur proposed that the infantry training for cadets be curtailed and replaced by instruction in artillery tactics and that more experience with astronomical and surveying instruments would be beneficial. He was thanked for his input and dismissed, after which he reported to the new artillery school at Fort Monroe, Virginia. After many months of instruction, he was reassigned to a light artillery battery in Washington, D.C.[12]

Rumors and currents of war waiting for them coursed through the Corps of Cadets in the late 1850s. In the run-up to the presidential election in the spring and summer of 1860, presidential politics dominated cadet discussions, and Lincoln had few supporters. An unofficial straw ballot was held in the barracks in September, and 214 cadets voted by secret ballot. The results were 99 votes for the Southern Democratic candidate, John C. Breckinridge (who would become a Confederate general); 47 for the Northern Democratic candidate, Stephen A. Douglas; 44 for the Constitutional Union candidate, John Bell; and only 24 for the Republican candidate, Abraham Lincoln.[13]

On 5 November, the day before the presidential election,

Rosser wrote to Sam Houston, the governor of his home state of Texas, offering his services in the event Texas should secede. Houston, despite his Virginia roots, was a strong supporter of the Union, and in his answer (which he wrote and Rosser received after Lincoln's election), he was distressed by the possibility of civil war and encouraged the aspiring soldier to "give your whole time and attention to your studies in order that you may be prepared to assume the position to which your graduation would entitle you."[14]

On 6 November 1860, Lincoln was elected. Very quickly, the political outrage from the South turned into an uproar. The quickly ensuing political machinations in the "lower South" states of South Carolina, Georgia, Florida, Alabama, Mississippi, Louisiana, and Texas were most threatening, and it soon became clear that the white citizens of those states were willing to go to great lengths, even to fight a bloody war, in order to attain their independence from the Union.

In December, South Carolina seceded, to be followed in early 1861 by the six other states mentioned above. This was sobering, to say the least. From those very moments of secession, and although the Civil War had not yet started, U.S. Army officers from the seceded states began to resign their commissions, as did some cadets. Anxiety hung thick in the air, particularly at West Point, and cadets began to realize that they might even one day become personal adversaries.

Now some important decisions had to be made, and very quickly, by many cadets. One of these was Pelham, who had been elected president of the Dialectic Society. He was quite torn, and in a letter to his father of 11 December 1860, he poured his heart out, saying that he had hoped to graduate from West Point, that it would have been "exceedingly gratifying," for himself as well as for his family, to "receive a diploma from this institution, but Fate seems to have willed it otherwise." He said that he saw no other honorable course for him to take but to resign from West Point when Alabama left the Union and offer his sword to her. He mentioned that he had written to the chief justice of the Alabama Supreme Court, who had responded with advice that he should do precisely that. He also said, "In this I have not acted precipitately, but in a manner worthy of myself, of my family, and of my section of the country."[15]

On 17 December, Rosser wrote to Jefferson Davis, then a senator from Mississippi but with a much larger destiny still before him. In his letter, Rosser said that he could never accept a commission from Abraham Lincoln, though he thought his military career would be significantly enhanced if he stayed a few more months and received his diploma. But he would still feel obligated to resign if Texas seceded, as he wanted to offer his services in defense of the "Honor and Liberty of the South which would be sacrificed by submission to Republican Rule."[16]

On 9 January 1861, Mississippi seceded from the Union, and Davis soon resigned from the U.S. Senate and returned to his plantation in that, his home state. But he was a towering political figure in the South, and on 18 February 1861 he was appointed "Provisional President of the Confederate States of America." That formal title was to endure until he was formally elected president on 6 November 1861.

Meanwhile back at West Point, as each day passed after the November 1860 election, something new was occurring, or rumored to be occurring, on the national political scene. Efforts to mediate between the two sides were constant, but neither side wanted to give much ground. As rumors flew back and forth, occasionally punctuated with revelations of events far worse than those suspected, the noose began to tighten around the necks of cadets from the slave states, whether seceded or not. Clearly Pelham, Rosser, and many others were in a terrible predicament.

Still, many other cadets were deeply sympathetic. DuPont, in confronting the whole situation, told his mother that he sympathized with army and navy officers from South Carolina who were resigning their commissions. "I know if Delaware were in a similar position to South Carolina I should consider it my duty to resign at once and go home."[17]

But as other Southern states began to follow South Carolina in seceding, the pressure on Southern cadets at West Point only grew. DuPont told his mother as much in another letter, in which he said that he did not know when he had been in such a state of mind over politics. He thought the Civil War the most horrible thing imaginable, and had little patience with the loud celebrations of some cadets from the North. He thought every man of proper feelings, though he may think it the right thing to do at the time, would later regret plunging us into "the untold horrors of civil war and the dipping of our hands in the blood of our countrymen," and he found the "sanguinary and blood-thirsty speeches" being constantly made "perfectly revolting."

He also tried to explain the difficult situations in which Pelham and Rosser found themselves. DuPont told his mother that both had been offered positions in the rebel armies of their home states, but both had so far refused them, despite the fact that these had been published in local papers in their home states. But both realized that, if called upon by their state governors, they would feel bound to resign from West Point and return home. The thought of giving up their diplomas when they were so close to them after five years of hard work was jarring. But if offered commissions to serve in the armies of their home states by their governors, both had told DuPont that they would be bound by both duty and honor to accept them.[18]

Cadets from the South had begun to leave West Point as early as November 1860, but there were clearly mixed emotions among them.

Cadets at West Point in the winter of 1860–61 found themselves in an extraordinary place at an extraordinary time. Looking into the eyes of their best friends, many of them saw their future adversaries. And while the competition bred into cadets over their whole time at the academy endured, this time the competition would be waged on bloody fields with truly lethal weapons.

The split was sudden, and it was shocking. In the new year, many more Southern cadets began to turn in their uniforms and equipment and leave the academy as civilians, though everyone knew where they were going. But that act did not end their brotherhood with other cadets, even those from the North, and they were sometimes even carried down to the docks on the shoulders of their Yankee classmates.

Custer tells us of one such moment, though he acknowledges that the departure of friends from the South was wrenching:

> It cost many a bitter pang to disrupt the intimate relations exist-
> ing between the hot-blooded Southron [sic] and his more phlegmatic
> schoolmate from the North. No schoolgirls could have been more
> demonstrative in their affectionate regard for each other than were
> some of the cadets about to separate for the last time. And under
> circumstances which made it painful to contemplate a future coming
> together.[19]

On 23 January 1861, Captain Pierre Gustave Toutant Beauregard, who had graduated second in the West Point class of 1838 and was from Louisiana, arrived to replace Richard Delafield as the new superintendent. By then, Louisiana had seceded, and cadets from that and other seceded states were leaving West Point in large numbers. Soon after Beauregard arrived, a cadet from Louisiana called on him and asked whether or not he should also resign. Beauregard's answer was "Watch me, and when I jump you jump. What's the use of jumping too soon?" But Beauregard's political sympathies were already suspect in Washington. To preclude public embarrassment of the army, then, he was relieved of that command on 28 January, after only five days as superintendent, and replaced, once again, by Delafield.[20] But this man's second tour as superintendent was brief and he, in turn, was replaced within a few weeks by Colonel Alexander H. Bowman.

On 21 February 1861, an order from Colonel Bowman directed that

> the Officers and Professors on duty at this Post will assemble at 11:30 a.m. on the 22nd instant in the Chapel, to commemorate the birth of Washington, and to listen to the friendly counsels and almost prophetic warnings contained in his Farewell Address to his Countrymen.
>
> All Academic duty will be suspended at 11 a.m., and at 11:30 the Companies of Cadets with side-arms only, accompanied by the Band, will be marched to the Chapel for the purposes before mentioned.[21]

Once all were assembled in the chapel, George Washington's entire Farewell Address was read. While it is quite long—more than six thousand words—a pertinent passage reads as follows:

> The Unity of Government, which constitutes you one people, is also now dear to you. It is justly so; for it is a main Pillar in the Edifice of your real independence; the support of your tranquility at home; your peace abroad; of your safety; of your prosperity in every shape; of that very Liberty, which you so highly prize. But as it is easy to foresee, that, from different causes, and from different quarters, much pains will be taken, many artifices employed, to weaken in your minds the conviction of this truth; as this is the point in your political fortress against which the batteries of internal and external enemies will be most constantly and actively (though often covertly and insidiously) directed it is of infinite moment, that you should properly estimate the immense value of your national Union to your collective and individual happiness; that you should cherish a cordial, habitual,

*and immovable attachment to it; accustoming yourselves to think and*
*speak of it as of the Palladium of your political safety and prosperity;*
*watching for its preservation with jealous anxiety; discountenancing*
*whatever may suggest even a suspicion, that it can in any event be*
*abandoned, and indignantly frowning upon the first dawning of every*
*attempt to alienate any portion of our Country from the rest, or to*
*enfeeble the sacred ties which now link together the various parts.*

――――――――

Those were profound words, of course. But by this time, with a
half dozen slave states having already seceded, it was too late for
them to have had any meaningful effect, not only for the cadets
and faculty then listening to them, but especially for the leaders
of the already-seceded or soon-to-secede states. And so, despite
prescient warnings from the father of our country, the provin-
cially patriotic peoples of the Southern states started slowly to
slip away.

And the regional distinctions had become too open to ignore.
There were no cadet duties for the rest of that day, and as was
the custom on Washington's birthday, the entire West Point
band took the place of the drum corps for tattoo. As it marched
toward the barracks, cadets hung out every window.

While marching through the sally port, the band struck up
"The Star-Spangled Banner." The barracks were formed in an L
shape, so that the two wings formed two sides of a square, and
as the band came into this area, the music swelled and boomed.
While loud yelling by cadets was forbidden, Custer leaned out
his window and spontaneously started a thunderous cheer that
rolled down the two rows of barracks, amplified by a host of
other Union-supporting cadets who also were hanging out their
windows.

Then the band struck up "Dixie," and the Southern cadets, led
by rabble-rousing Tom Rosser, tried their best to outdo the Yankee
cadets they loved but whose politics they despised. Then the band

stopped playing and marched away, but cadets kept the music and cheering up by shouting the words of both songs at the top of their lungs. And back and forth the cheering went, the Northerners led by Custer, the Southerners by Rosser—two best friends who would, soon enough, face each other on the field of battle. But that was still unknown to all, and so the raucous laughter and celebration went on well into the night.[22]

On 27 February, not having received a response to his earlier letter, Rosser again wrote to Jefferson Davis, by then the president of the Confederate States of America. In this letter, he offered his services to the growing Confederate army. But he added a caveat, saying that, since he intended to devote his life to service as an officer in that army, he thought his abilities might be enhanced if he stayed at West Point to receive his diploma in June.[23]

John Pelham also wrote to Jefferson Davis on 27 February, and his letter reads as follows:

*Dear Sir,*

*Being still a member of the Mily Acad'y, I don't think it would be exactly proper for me to offer my services to the new government, but I am anxious to serve to the best of my ability. If you think it would be better for me to resign now rather than to wait and graduate which will be in June a single word from you will cause me to resign and as soon as my resignation is accepted I will consider myself under your orders and repair to Montgomery without delay.*

*I am a member of the 1st class which graduates in June next—you know the importance of that portion of the course still to be completed, and also whether my services are needed at present. May I expect a recall if needed?*

*Most Respect'y*
*Your Obdt Serv't*
*Jno. Pelham[24]*

Their proposals were acted upon, as their commissions as first lieutenants in the Confederate army date from 16 March 1861. While they soon learned of this, both men were still in a quandary as to what they should do.

Pelham happened to have an aunt, Martha Wright, and her daughters, Marianna Pelham Mott and Ellen Wright, were his cousins. Although these ladies were abolitionists, they were also family, and such was clearly more important to John than their personal politics. Martha and Ellen were both expected to be in Philadelphia within a few weeks to celebrate the golden anniversary of other relatives, and on 26 March 1861, Pelham wrote to Marianna. In the text, one notes not only his enduring confusion, but also the affection, no doubt mutual, that he shared with Rosser:

*West Point N.Y.*
*March 26th / '61*

*Dear Cousin*

*I am just in receipt of your kind letter of the 23rd Inst.*

*I would like above all things to meet your Mother and Sister in Phila.—it may be the only opportunity I will ever have of seeing them. I am most anxious to see them, but can not say when I will leave. If I remain to get my diploma I will have to wait till 15th June. But whether I will stay till then is the question. I am not master of my own acts at present. I have been appointed a 1st Lieutenant in the Army of the "Confederate States of America." My appointment has been confirmed by the Congress. The appointment was made without my consent or knowledge. I cannot accept an appointment from them as long as I am a member of this Institution, but if I am recalled by the Authorities, I will obey it. I have thus far resisted every overture, on the part of my friends, to resign, disregarded their advice and braved their anger. My father and* brothers alone wished me to graduate. I had no idea I was so well supplied with friends. All seemed to vie with each other in attempting to force me to resign. I have worked almost five years for my diploma, and it pains me to give up the undertaking now—besides all this, it chagrins me to be forced to leave an undertaking unfinished. I believe there are only two Cadets here at present from the Seceded States—myself and a classmate from Texas [his roommate, Tom Rosser]. We will leave together—in June—or before, as the fates will it. We have been living together for three or four years, and I feel like we are inseparable—like his presence is necessary to my happiness. If we leave before June, it will be in about two weeks. You must allow me to introduce him.

I suppose you have heard of Bro' Charles' Marriage, through Aunt Ann or some of our Kentucky kin. I believe Aunt Martha knew Bro' Chas—if so, tell her, he married one of the nicest ladies in Ky. So they all write—I have never seen her.

I had a letter from Henry Pelham [a Kentucky cousin] a few days since, he says all are well in Ky. Sister is almost crazy about her Sister—it is the first she has ever had [John had five brothers but only one sister]. I think it would be doing her a kind and brotherly act to present her with another, but none of the girls will have me. It's the most unaccountable thing I ever heard of—don't you think so?

I can let you know definitely in a week or two whether I will have the pleasure of visiting you before you leave Phila.

If anything could compensate me for giving up my dearest object—graduating—it is the pleasure I would have in visiting your family, your Mother & Sister.

Tell Cousins Belle & Emily [Marianna's daughters Isabel, fifteen at the time, and Emily, thirteen, whom John had met on an earlier visit to Philadelphia] we may get another ride together—and then I will teach them to ride like Cavalry officers. Give them my best love. Remember me kindly to Mr. Mott.

*Affectionately*
*Jno. Pelham*[25]

But from the tenor of a letter Pelham wrote the very next day to a judge who had promoted his cause to Jefferson Davis, it's apparent that he really wanted to stay and get his degree if at all possible:

*27 March, 1861*

*Hon. A. J. Walker*

*Dear Sir,*

*I received your favor on the 25th yesterday. Until it came I was quite uncertain whether I could graduate—now I think I shall, President Davis advised some of my friends here to graduate, by all means and gave sufficient reasons. . . . Mr. Lincoln does not seem to be very anxious for war, and I guess everything will remain quiet till June—in the mean time I will better qualify myself for a position in life especially for the military profession. As soon as I graduate I shall resign, and apply for an appointment in the Southern Army. . . .*

*I thank you sincerely for visiting the President and the Sec'ry of War in my behalf, and for all the kindness and friendliness you have ever evinced for me.*

*Your most obliged friend,*
*Jno. Pelham*[26]

———

Custer tells us of the departure of two of his friends from Alabama, Charles P. Ball and John H. Kelly. Both were very popular men at West Point, and both would become prominent Confederate officers, though Kelly would be killed in battle. After Alabama had seceded, they both resigned on a Saturday, changed into civilian clothes, and were about to walk down to the boat in civilian clothes. Suddenly a host of cheering classmates descended on them and lifted them onto their shoulders for the short walk down the hill.

Custer at the time was "walking an extra," which means he was spending what otherwise would have been his Saturday afternoon free time marching punishment tours, rifle on shoulder, uniform and accouterments all neat and polished. This was because he had accumulated too many demerits, and walking "extras" had become a rather usual experience for him. He had been inspected by the officer of the guard before beginning his tour, and as noted earlier, if his shoes or brass had been found not to have been polished to a high enough sheen or his rifle had been dusty or any of a long list of military minutiae for whose perfection he was responsible, that would have meant more demerits. And more punishment tours.

He, as well as Rosser and even Pelham, was the sort of "good bad West Point cadet" so accurately described by Pulitzer Prize–winner Rick Atkinson in *The Long Gray Line*: well liked by classmates, but men who did just enough work to get by and also flaunted regulations whenever they thought they could get away with it. They often did not, hence the numerous punishment tours.[27]

As Custer watched, Ball and Kelly were a hundred yards away or more. But they both saw Custer and waved their hats at him. Custer, of course, was in a precarious position, for if he waved back and got caught, that would only mean more punishment tours. So he compromised. "First casting my eyes about to see that no watchful superior was in view, I responded by bringing my musket to 'present'." That means he stopped, stood at attention, and brought his musket up and held it in front of him vertically, which is the way a soldier carrying a long-barreled weapon traditionally salutes. A man walking punishment tours, of course, is not allowed to do that, to "present arms" as a salute to departing friends. But this time, he got away with it.[28]

Then the inevitable happened on 12 April 1861. Cannon under the command of Confederate general Pierre G. T. Beauregard, who had been West Point superintendent for five days in January 1861, opened fire on Fort Sumter in the harbor of Charleston, South Carolina. Since a Union fleet intended to resupply them had steered away, it took less than two days, with no bloodshed on either side as a result of hostile fire, before it fell to the forces in gray.

But despite the lack of bloodshed before Major Robert Anderson's agreement to surrender Fort Sumter, an unforeseen tragedy still occurred. While the men in blue were firing a salute to their flag before abandoning the fort, one of their guns exploded and killed a crew member, Private Daniel Hough, thus making him the first true casualty of the Civil War.

Now that the Stars and Stripes had been fired upon by rebellious Southerners and a Union fort surrendered to them, it was time for uproar in the North. On 15 April Lincoln called for 75,000 volunteers to serve for three months in the militia, and furious public meetings and cries of alarm in Northern newspapers resulted in a massive response. But this mobilization in the North also tipped several other slave states from the "upper South" into rebellion, particularly Virginia, although the exchange of gunfire in Charleston Harbor would seem to have led to no other possible outcome. And now the Southern leaders suddenly realized that the Yankees would fight to maintain the Union, and they began to arm as well. Now it seemed there was no way back, and the long-threatened war had become inevitable.

When the news from Fort Sumter reached West Point, a group of cadets from the North gathered in and around one cadet's first-floor room, where they sang "The Star Spangled Banner" so loud, one participant said, that it could have been heard on the other side of the river. He also said that it was the first time he had seen the Southern contingent, or what was left of it, given their steady resignations, cowed. All of their Northern allies had deserted them, and they were stunned.[29]

Now all cadets from all areas in the country knew that they were at war, and they all grimly assessed their own futures. For Yankees it was easy, but for Southerners, it was a bit harder. If they were to leave before graduation, that meant they would literally walk away from their investment of up to five years at West Point with no hope of serving in the U.S. Army, which had been their goal all along. Even so, many were to take that step.

After the fall of Fort Sumter, the numbers of cadets resigning and heading South began to swell. But Rosser and Pelham, roommates that year, kept hanging on, hoping desperately that all this would somehow blow over and they would be allowed finally to receive their diplomas. Then on 17 April, the Virginia Convention met in Richmond and voted to secede, and that was the final blow for many.[30]

Rosser and Pelham left the academy on 22 April, and although the army authorities allowed Southern officers and cadets to resign with no interference from them, the same was not true elsewhere. Civilians in the North who expressed opinions about secessionists used the word "traitor" a lot, and newspaper stories of violence against people from the South traveling through Northern cities caused them to take a roundabout route to Alabama.

Bypassing New York City, they went to Philadelphia, where they spent a few days with Pelham's aunt, Martha Wright, her daughter Ellen, and a few of Pelham's other relatives. From there they headed west through Harrisburg, Pennsylvania, but they had no problems until they arrived in New Harmony, Indiana, where they were stopped and questioned on their destination by the police. Having resigned from West Point, it was clear to Pelham that he was no longer bound by the cadet honor code.

Although there was no written honor code at the time, cadets were trusted on their word, and any cadet who lied or stole was usually subject to immediate expulsion. In 1970, one scholar writing about West Point before the Civil War said:

> *The highly legalistic, minutely regulated, cadet-administered honor code of today was unknown in antebellum West Point. The cadet of that era, like his officer counterpart, was expected not to lie or steal, and if apprehended in either of these offenses, he risked dismissal, although in a few cases, mitigating circumstances reduced the penalty.*[31]

The same was not true of cheating, however, as cadet attitudes were heavily weighted toward a sense of "us against them," with the other side including not only tactical officers who enforced the rules but also academics, who always had the power to fail a cadet—and failing only one course was grounds for dismissal—and thus force him to leave West Point. For cadets in academic trouble, then, cheating was either ignored or condoned by other cadets, and sometimes even assisted.

Now finding himself at high risk if the truth of their situation were learned, Pelham made up a ridiculous story about how they were special couriers with secret messages from General Winfield Scott, the commanding general of the U.S. Army. Impressed and satisfied, the local police let them go, showing once again that the bigger the lie, the more likely you are to get away with it.[32]

But now there was only one last barrier, and that was the Ohio River—how were they to get across? There are several stories about this, most no doubt apocryphal. Given his acknowledged good looks, the one that sounds the most credible has Pelham stop a pretty girl in the street. As he rambled over nothing, she blushed at this smiling, handsome young man and his courtly manners—at the time, not at all an unlikely event. And this was just what he wanted. Soon enough, he talked her into renting a skiff for a "pleasure ride" with himself and his companion, Rosser.

But once they were out on the river, he revealed their identities and intentions to her as they rowed toward the Kentucky shore. She first urged him to stay with the Union army, but seeing that his mind was made up, she relented and enjoyed the ride as much as she could. When Pelham and Rosser jumped off into Kentucky, they at last felt free. Despite powerful internal political pressures, Kentucky had not yet seceded, and in fact was one of the four slave states that would not secede. But it was still a slave state, and so Rosser and Pelham could finally stop lying, drop their guard, and proceed to Montgomery without fearing for their lives.[33]

On 6 May 1861 forty-five members of the class of May 1861 received their diplomas. The man who ranked first in that class, Henry Algernon DuPont, was commissioned in the Corps of Engineers. Even that long ago, choosing that technical branch was already somewhat of a tradition for those men who graduated from West Point at the top of their class. But unlike some of his peers and somewhat surprisingly, as we shall see, his choice of that branch of the army would end up costing him in terms of early promotion.

Arthur Harper Grimshaw, M.D., was born in Philadelphia in 1824 and graduated from the University of Pennsylvania in 1845. In 1849, he moved his medical practice to Delaware and thereafter became closely connected with the DuPont family. Like many other prominent figures across the country, he was to be commissioned a colonel and tasked with mustering the 4th Regiment of Delaware Volunteer Infantry, still loyal to the Union. In early May 1861, he met with young Lieutenant DuPont in Washington and urged him to accept a commission as a major in his regiment. He said that he could arrange the matter, and that the regiment was much needed back home to control the rebellious forces he said were brewing and frightening those who did not want Delaware to secede.

In May 1861 considerable political wrangling was going on in the four so-called border slave states of Missouri, Kentucky, Maryland, and Delaware over possible secession, but the controversy was least of all in Delaware.[34] In 1860 there were nearly 20,000 free blacks in Delaware and fewer than 2,000 slaves. Henry had a rough idea of these proportions and so doubted Dr. Grimshaw's dire predictions.

He wrote to his father and asked his advice on 10 May, saying that while he would have enjoyed the prospect of serving near home, he somehow thought his service would be more needed with the regular army. On 14 May he stepped forward and took his place as a lieutenant with the 5th U.S. Artillery. But despite his willingness to lead his men into battle, he soon became regimental adjutant, and as such, spent the next few years in a purely administrative role in the rear. He would not actually see combat for several more years, but when he did, in the Shenandoah Valley, his personal leadership and courage would be so extraordinary as to win him a Medal of Honor.

Only six men in the class of May 1861 had left West Point before graduation in order to fight for the South, including John Pelham and Thomas Lafayette Rosser. But because of the impending war, the academy quickly reverted to the four-year schedule, and on 24 June 1861, thirty-four men graduated with the class of June 1861. This number included George Armstrong Custer, who graduated thirty-fourth, or dead last, in the class.

However, since December 1860, twenty-four other members of the class had left the academy to serve in the armies being raised by the Southern states that were their homes. Had they stayed and graduated, it is clear that a number of them, having even less lustrous academic records than Custer, would have prevented his graduating as the class "goat." Even so, his final class rank marked him permanently. In view of his later battlefield triumphs, however, this fact alone provided compelling evidence that measuring West Point cadets by their academic prowess was not a reliable way of predicting their future personal success under arms in time of war.

The ominous drumbeats of armies assembling and glaring at each other resonated through the land. There would soon be a battle in northern Virginia, no doubt of that, and the troops of the Union and Confederate armies, though still willow green, would begin shooting at each other, daubing fields and trees along Bull Run a hot scarlet.

On 30 June, having graduated from West Point a week earlier, the members of the class of June 1861 were commissioned and released to their assignments. Giddy with anticipation, a thick stream of these new lieutenants gorged the railroad cars to Washington. Union forces were assembling there, and still quite naive, most of these men were eager to be tested in the battlefield skills they had spent the last four years developing. But not all of them were part of this almost joyful throng heading off to war.

Though he strained at the bit to go off to war with them, one of the most colorful members of the class found himself held back at the academy while his classmates flooded south. On 29 June, his very last day as a cadet, he had stepped over the line one last time. But unhappily for him, he was caught in the act, and so was forced to stay behind to face trial by court-martial. And that man, almost predictably, was George Armstrong Custer.

On 29 June, the last day before he would have received his commission and in what would clearly be his last official duty at West Point, Custer served as cadet officer of the guard for the annual cadet encampment on the Plain. As the sun was setting, two of the newly arrived cadet candidates began to argue

over their place in a line for water. Yelling led to pushing and
then they were trading blows. Surrounded by their new classmates, the two tussled until Custer arrived on the scene.

His official duty as C.O.G. required him to stop the fight and
reprimand or even arrest the two miscreants. Instead, his boyish self reappeared, and he pushed his way to the front, loudly
instructing the other new cadets, "Stand back, fellows, let's
have a fair fight!" But the officer of the day, Lieutenant William
B. Hazen, had also been attracted by the commotion and was
approaching behind him as he shouted those commands. When
all the cadet candidates abruptly ran in all directions, Custer
turned to face an angry man in blue. Unusually for him, he was
suddenly at a loss for words.

This instance of the cadet officer of the guard wildly flaunt-
ing regulations was all the more serious because it was done in
the presence of new cadets. The news spread fast and the academy authorities felt they had no choice but to enforce the regulations rigidly. So Custer was arrested, and as his classmates left
on the very next day, he stayed behind.

On 15 July he was charged at court-martial with "neglect
of duty" for failing to suppress a quarrel. The judge advocate
general was Lieutenant Stephen Vincent Benet (grandfather of
the poet of the same name), and having been caught red-handed,
there was really no defense Custer could make. The two cadet
candidates who had been fighting both testified that it was no
more than a scuffle that made little noise and resulted in no inju-
ries to either man, and Lieutenant Hazen reported favorably on
Custer's previous conduct.[35]

It is unknown whether a telegram from Washington ordering him to proceed there immediately forced the issue or, given
the pressing nature of the looming war, the court-martial had
decided on no more than a slap on the hand. But whatever the
motivation, Custer was sentenced only to be reprimanded in

orders. This was a modest administrative check mark against him in his records that, in light of his future performance in the Civil War, would do him no harm whatever. He headed south on the next train, stopping in New York City only long enough to buy a saber, a pistol, and spurs. He arrived in Washington at dawn on 20 July.

# FIVE

## *The Fighting Begins*

We will follow our six men after they have donned their officer's uniforms and moved into leadership roles at the front. But it is important to remember that there were hundreds of thousands of soldiers on either side in the Eastern Theater of the Civil War. The likelihood, therefore, that any of their paths might cross, or even that they might hear of one another, was remotely small. However, as they rose in rank later in the war to command brigades and even divisions, there were moments of professional contact between some of them serving in the same army that included moments of joyful personal reunion.

Similarly, with three of them commanding units on each side, there were battles in which some of them faced each other. Though they occasionally knew ahead of time the units and commanders they would fight, they almost always later learned the identity of the men they had defeated or to whom they had lost.

The central theme of personal competition they had learned at West Point was deeply rooted, and it clearly came to the fore in those moments—without question, there was no more worthy opponent they might face than a classmate and friend. This does not mean they sought to kill or injure each other individually, as they clearly did not—in particular, for a close group of friends like our six men, the personal affection that had grown between them at West Point was too strong to be so easily reversed. On the few times any of them faced another, they did call up all their courage and ingenuity and did everything possible they could to defeat the other. And for the winners, as we shall see, such a victory turned out to be a moment of singular and enduring triumph.

After Fort Sumter fell, the ranks of the U.S. Army as well as those of the Confederate army trying to come to life were flooded with volunteers. Most of these men, however, had virtually no military experience whatever, and so trainers had to be found who could whip them into shape. But particularly in the South, the search was for more than new recruits, which were plentiful. Rather, there was a desperate need in Dixie for veterans or other experienced people who knew how an army was supposed to function and who could help launch the new Confederate force.

The first capital of the Confederacy was Montgomery, Alabama, and that's where Rosser and Pelham went after they left West Point in May 1861. That month, Virginia offered to make Richmond, the largest city in the Confederacy, the nation's capital. The offer was accepted and the change took place that summer. But Rosser and Pelham were commissioned as Confederate lieutenants in Montgomery while it was still the capital, then were sent off to help get this new army up and running.

The most important knowledge armies needed as they formed was technical, particularly in the artillery branch. That was because infantry or cavalry tactics were pretty uniform and could be readily learned by conscripts; standing up to enemy fire, of course, was another matter altogether, a life-preserving courage necessarily learned by troops when they went into battle.

But just to be fired, the breech-loading cannon used by both sides in the Civil War required a well-trained crew with detailed knowledge of each of their individual roles. But since enemy return fire could be expected to wound or kill crew members of a given gun, each man also had to be able to assume the role of any other crew member immediately, else the wounding of only one or a few could end the fire of that piece.

This, of course, took knowledge and training. Lots of training.

Most cannon used by both sides during the Civil War typically required a crew of nine to eleven men to service each of them, and each crew member had specific duties to perform in concert with the others. To be effective, then, gun crews had to practice their routine repeatedly. But when hostile fire began knocking out crew members in battle, some took on multiple roles, and in a pinch, one gun could be loaded, fired, and reloaded by as few as three or four well-practiced men, though with a dramatically lessened rate of fire.

Once such a crew became well rehearsed in the roles required to fire a particular field piece, of course, the next key issue was accuracy of fire, another technical issue relating to ordnance, range, and direction. This also required intensive training. All West Point cadets, of course, were well schooled in artillery drill, making them invaluable for training green recruits on both sides at the outbreak of the war.

Initially, the new Confederate army had little structure or efficient organization, as Pelham and Rosser would soon learn. Upon receiving their commissions, Rosser was sent to perform recruiting service in North Carolina, while Pelham was assigned to take charge of Confederate ordnance in Lynchburg, Virginia. Both men were very unhappy with such assignments as war clearly loomed; both wanted to serve at the front, to test their manhood in the ways they had learned at West Point. But for the short term, there was little they could do but wait for things to develop.

For his part, their old friend Ramseur had already been serving in the artillery branch of the U.S. Army since before the fall of Fort Sumter. His absorption into the new Confederate army, therefore, was very smooth: he simply resigned his Union commission and went to Montgomery, where, on 22 April 1861, he received his commission as a lieutenant in the Confederate army. But only days later, he received a telegram from North Carolina's governor, John W. Ellis, informing him that he had been elected captain of the Ellis Light Artillery of the North Carolina State Troops in Raleigh. With this news, he immediately went back to his home state and assumed command. And within three weeks there, he was promoted once again, this time to major, though he stayed in command of the same unit.

From the state arsenal, the governor issued him six pieces of artillery of varying caliber and quality, a few wagons and forges, and little else. But Ramseur went right to work, drilling his men for up to twelve hours each day. While this was taxing to the newly enlisted civilians at first, they soon began to function well. By July 1861, the more than 100 men in the Ellis Light Artillery began to take on the look of a well-trained regular army unit.[1] In the words of a major North Carolina newspaper, "A better drilled and equipped corps cannot be found in the Army."[2] At the end of that month, Ramseur and his unit were sent to serve with John C. Pemberton's brigade of Benjamin Huger's division on the southern bank of the James River. They would remain there, protecting access to Richmond from the river, through the rest of 1861 and into the spring of 1862.

After a few frustrating weeks in Lynchburg, Pelham was able to express his displeasure at having merely a support role to General Joseph E. Johnston, who was organizing the Army of the Shenandoah in Harpers Ferry. This was basically just a plea from one West Pointer to another, but Johnston was unable to do anything until 8 June, when Virginia's soldiers were formally made part of the Confederate army. Within days, he sent for Pelham, who arrived in Harpers Ferry on 15 June 1861.

His assignment was as lieutenant and drillmaster of the Alburtis battery of Martinsburg, and he was told to take charge and train them in their duties as fast as possible. Organized soon after the John Brown Raid in 1859, the battery was little more than symbolic. Armed with four smoothbore six-pounder bronze guns, they were without horses and had received no training at all in field artillery use. Its commander was a Captain Ephraim G. Alburtis, a leading citizen of Martinsburg, but like his men, he was without any military operational knowledge.

When Pelham arrived, he could have caused considerable social discomfort by abruptly taking over from a man old enough to be his father. Instead he used the tactful approach of reporting to Captain Alburtis and telling him that he had been assigned to help him, but as a junior officer asked for his permission to do so. Alburtis graciously turned over control of the battery. That very day Pelham asserted himself, spoke to the men, and established a training schedule.

During the Civil War, Pelham would show himself to be not only an extremely competent artillerist, but also a man of great daring who many times outdueled his opponents, usually with fewer guns than his adversaries were firing. He became renowned on both sides for his use of surprise as well as for venturing far in front of Confederate lines to take out a particular target, a very high-risk venture. His guns were Napoleons— smoothbore muzzle-loading brass pieces; various cast-iron rifled cannon known as "rifles"; and howitzers.

The Napoleons and the rifles fired solid shot, canister (a spray of lead rifle bullets with the effect of a giant shotgun, mostly used against troops), or shells that exploded when they hit, like modern artillery. The howitzers fired only explosive shells and, with a smaller charge, were of shorter range but just as deadly. The rifles were the most accurate but, made of cast iron, were sometimes prone to have their barrels burst, their elevation screws break, or simply to malfunction in some other way.

One of the most difficult tasks in the Civil War was firing an artillery piece so that its projectile would hit its target. This required aligning the tube of the piece in the right direction and, more important, accurately estimating the range to target. Relative elevation of gun and target could play a role, as could wind, and most artillerists learned simply by trial and error. John Pelham was one of the best shots on either side, a man who seemed to have some sort of almost instinctual feel that made every shot he aimed and fired deadly.

For the next month, Pelham's unit trained every day between Winchester and Martinsburg. Sixty-three soldiers were assigned to man the four guns, and Pelham was able to acquire forty-three horses, four jury-rigged caissons, and one homemade forge wagon. Soon he was also able to acquire gunpowder, solid shot, and canister, with which they further refined their training. And before long, the formerly clean businessmen of Martinsburg had been transformed into sweating, grime-encrusted apprentice artillerymen. They trained for seven hours every day, the routine rigid and the discipline strict. One blunder, even one minor mistake by a gun crew member, could result in no fire from that gun or, worse still, the death or dismemberment of crew members. This was a harsh reality, and so they readily absorbed the lessons in which this young lad of twenty-two instructed them.

As they trained, they were almost always watched by women—their wives, sweethearts, or just curious girls attracted to all that manly heaving and grunting and gun firing. Among them were the Dandridge girls, Serena and Sallie, and their cousin Lily. The three young women then lived in a splendid house on an immense plantation owned by their father and known as the Bower. The three of them were much taken by the handsome blond lieutenant just arrived from West Point, and they went out of their way to find excuses to flirt with him.

While Pelham drove his men hard, he also got in there with them and showed them with his own hands precisely what to do and how to do it, an active participation in the rough, dirty, and dangerous work that appealed not only to his artillerymen-in-training, but also to their female observers. After the day's work was done, he was regularly invited back to the Bower to dine with the family. But his presence as favored guest of the lord of the manor was a social experience already quite familiar to him from growing up on his father's Alabama plantation, so much so that he was always quite correct, but also relaxed and even humorous. His gracious manners charmed them all, men as well as women.

As July approached, tension continued to mount on both sides. A Union army under General Robert Patterson was growing to some 15,000 men in nearby Harpers Ferry. But although they clearly outnumbered the 10,000 or so under Johnston at Winchester, these troops in blue were just as green as those in gray. Consequently, commanders on both sides carefully kept their men away from those on the other side while they trained.

Meanwhile, stories of potential or actual combat elsewhere raced through the towns as well as through the ranks. In northwestern Virginia, it was said that a few thousand troops under McClellan and William S. Rosecrans were facing similarly sized Confederate forces under Richard B. Garnett and John Pegram, and though combat had not yet been joined, both sides were maneuvering for advantage. Then came shouts of "On to Richmond!" in the Northern papers. Patterson's army of 15,000 was facing a smaller force under Johnston near the mouth of the Shenandoah Valley, while Irvin McDowell in Washington had 35,000 men or more, blocked only by Beauregard and his 20,000 at Manassas. "What are we waiting for?" asked the newspapers. Crush the rebellion! Hang Jeff Davis! On to Richmond!

As the pressure in the North continued to build, commanders

on both sides remained cautious. Patterson moved forward to Martinsburg, and on 4 July Johnston moved out of Winchester to face him. Patterson was not that bold, however, and he kept his army locked in its town redoubts. But Pelham's training was relentless, and by the middle of July, the Alburtis battery was performing very well.

It remained to be seen how they would behave under actual fire. But Pelham knew that the more they trained to perform their duties as arms and legs of the fire-belching beast, the more they would feel part of it and so not have time for personal fears. On 18 July the orders came from Richmond: McDowell was on the move south, and Johnston was to hurry his army down to Manassas and support Beauregard.

Custer arrived in Washington on 20 July. Getting off the train in a strange city, he first went to the Ebbitt House Hotel, where he knew a few others who had been cadets with him at West Point were staying. Delayed by his own boyish antics and their reverberations, he had received his commission a few weeks after the rest of the class. But this made no difference to any of them, and they laughed and rejoiced as he told them the tale of his trial by court-martial for not having arrested those two squabbling new cadets.

After this brief but pleasant interlude, he was directed to the army's administrative headquarters. Before leaving West Point, he had been ordered to report for duty to the army's adjutant general, which he tried to do in the early afternoon. But when he entered the headquarters area, Custer found himself in the midst of a crowd of staff officers scurrying up and down halls, in and out of various offices, their arms heavily laden with various packets, documents, and maps. He was finally able to arrange an appointment with the adjutant general and reported to him for orders. As the A.G. was about to pass him on to a subordinate officer for specific assignment orders, he turned to Custer. Since Custer had just arrived from West Point, the A.G. asked if he would like to be presented to General Scott, the commanding general, before he left for duty.[3]

To Custer, of course, General Winfield Scott was an almost godlike figure. Though not a West Point graduate himself, Scott had become a great national hero because of his success as a commanding general in the Mexican-American War some fifteen years earlier. At the time there was no army requirement for an officer to retire at a certain age, and indeed there were no provisions for a paid retirement. It had thus become quite common, in time of peace, for army officers to stay in uniform as long as they could minimally continue to perform their duties. Health issues among senior officers were either ignored or leniently treated by the army, and this often meant that men stayed in command well into their dotage, often practically until the day they died. By the time Custer arrived in Washington, it was felt by many critics that, with a war between the states breaking out, General Scott had already outstayed his practical ability to function effectively as commanding general.

Scott did suffer severely from gout and rheumatism. His body having swollen to more than three hundred corpulent pounds, he was simply unable to ride or even mount a horse, a physical limitation that would have greatly limited his abilities as a field commander. But his mind was still quite sharp.

He had shown this a few months earlier when he had proposed to Lincoln an efficient, effective, and—in terms of blood and treasure—quite inexpensive way to defeat the rebels. All it would take, he said, would be to blockade Southern ports and so cut the Confederate states off from the European markets where they sold their cotton, tobacco, and other agricultural products. At the same time, he proposed sending some 60,000 Union troops down the Mississippi River and stationing them at forts located at strategic points south of Cairo, Illinois, reaching all the way down to the Gulf of Mexico. This, he argued, would effectively isolate the South. And since he did not believe that most people living in the seceded states supported the rebellion, he proposed that the federal army would then just wait for the Southern people to turn on their political leaders and, eventually, replace them with men who would willingly rejoin the Union.

Lincoln listened carefully. But upon reflection, he decided that trying to enact such a bold set of plans in what was perhaps still an avoidable war against the seceded states was simply impractical. But Scott had also sent the idea, in confidence, to General George McClellan, his young protégé who had graduated second in West Point's class of 1846 and had recently left civilian life to take command of the Ohio Volunteers. Trusting him as he did, Scott even proposed that McClellan play a crucial role in command of the 60,000 troops who, under his plan, would control the Mississippi.

A brilliant, popular, and charismatic man who was already widely known as "Young Napoleon," McClellan had enormous ambition. While pretending to be Scott's loyal subordinate, in fact he was already conspiring to replace him at the top of the Union army. When he received Scott's plan in early May 1861, he scorned it to his friends, calling it a passive "boa constrictor" plan that could never work. He was eventually able to get his political allies on Capitol Hill to pressure Scott into resigning, in November 1861, and then ascended to that post himself. But in May 1861, Scott was still unaware that McClellan was secretly his political rival, and his plan was soon leaked to the press, where it was strongly criticized as an "Anaconda Plan." Although denials were quickly made, its publication seemed to have McClellan's fingerprints all over it.

Thereafter, Scott was ridiculed by public figures writing in newspapers North and South, often much younger men who thought his plan verged on the cowardly and mocked him for it. While it would later turn out that domestic opposition to the rebellion in the South was not nearly as strong as Scott had suspected, by 1864 the Union seizure of the Mississippi and blockade of Southern ports he had first recommended became precisely the method used to isolate and eventually defeat the Confederate states.

Such high-level political machinations were entirely foreign to Custer, of course, and he remained in awe of Scott. When he went into his office, he was cordially received and given his choice of training new troops or joining a regular unit on the edge of battle. When he chose the latter, Scott complimented him, then asked him to return in a few hours and carry messages from him to General McDowell, the Union army commander at Manassas. But his first problem would be to find a horse, a task Scott predicted might be quite difficult.

Beaming with pleasure, Custer soared out of Scott's office on wings of joy. But once he had checked with various stables, he found Scott's prediction was accurate. At a loss for a mount to carry him as the commanding general's emissary, he happened to see a familiar face on the street. It was one of the sergeants from an artillery battery that had trained cadets at West Point, a unit that had left the academy to join the regular army only a few months before Custer did.

When he asked the sergeant what he was doing, he learned that he had been sent back to Washington on one horse to pick up another and intended to lead him back to Manassas with him. That was right where Custer wanted to go, and the sergeant quickly suggested he ride the second horse. He asked the sergeant to wait for a few hours that he might pick up Scott's messages and then ride forward to the army with him. And when all was ready, Custer was thrilled to learn that the horse the sergeant had been sent to retrieve was none other than Wellington, a former West Point mount often ridden and much favored by Custer and his classmates.

That night, the two men set out on a long ride, arriving at Manassas just before dawn on Sunday, 21 July. Custer delivered the messages to a staff officer, then was directed to his company in the 2nd U.S. Cavalry Regiment, where he was warmly welcomed.[4]

At the beginning of the Civil War, U.S. Dragoon Regiments were renamed as U.S. Cavalry Regiments, including the 2nd U.S. Cavalry Regiment to which Custer here reported. As the Army of the Potomac grew after Bull Run, its cavalry corps became the 1st, 2nd, and 3rd cavalry divisions, under each of which were two or three brigades. These brigades, in turn, were made up of four to six cavalry regiments, and the 1st, 2nd, 5th, and 6th U.S. Cavalry Regiments became part of the Reserve Brigade in the 1st Cavalry Division. The other two dozen cavalry regiments in the Army of the Potomac were named after the states where they had been raised (e.g., 5th Michigan), but in battlefield performance U.S. and state regiments became indistinguishable. Their nomenclature endured, however, and can be confusing.

During that same night, Confederate forces had begun to consolidate south of a stream called Bull Run and close to the town of Manassas. Johnston's army had begun their movement on 18 July, and most of his infantry had been sent to the Manassas area over several days by train. The cavalry and horse-drawn artillery, however, made the trip on roads that threaded through the Blue Ridge mountain range.

During the second day's march, most of the artillery, including Pelham's Alburtis battery, was gathered into a separate column. Their horse-drawn guns, caissons, and forges used back roads devoid of troops, which allowed them to make very good time. Shortly after midnight, in the early morning hours of Sunday the 21st, they reached Beauregard's army and went into camp.

A few hours later, Union troops began to move forward, threatening to cross Bull Run at a bridge, but actually sending most of the army on a long march west along the northern bank of that stream. With most of these soldiers brand-new and having acquired little in the way of order and march discipline, the movement of the blue force was easily tracked by their gray adversaries as much loud blundering occurred.

When they finally crossed the stream and began moving toward the Confederate positions, their arrival was no surprise. Still, with their superior numbers, they drove the forwardmost rebel units back.

Some Confederate artillery that had been firing for several hours seemed threatened by this sudden wave of oncoming blue-coats and was ordered to pull back, including the Alburtis battery commanded by Pelham. One of the other artillery officers, Lieutenant William T. Poague, later commented on this:

> *I was riding at the rear of the battery in column and behind me came Alburtis' guns in charge of a young officer. Just as we reached the top of the ridge next to Bull Run, he exclaimed 'I'll be dogged if I'm going any further back!' and wheeled his guns into battery. From reading the reports of the battle I find that these guns performed most valuable service in stopping the advance of a Federal Brigade up the hollow from the direction of Bull Run; for if unchecked it would have gotten right in rear of our line of battle as it was struggling to hold onto Henry House plateau. I have also learned beyond a doubt that this young officer was Lieutenant John Pelham.*[5]

In early afternoon, General Barnard Bee tried to stop his flee-ing men by pointing out that one Confederate unit was standing fast: "Look, there stands Jackson like a stone wall." Those words had barely been shouted before Bee was himself killed by Union fire. But his description of Thomas J. Jackson was to stick and even attain a sort of immortality that shone brightly for centu-ries still to come.

Jackson's brigade, known ever after as the "Stonewall Bri-gade," stood its ground and returned fire into the advancing blue ranks. Pelham's battery was stationed with others on the flank of that brigade, and they poured volley after volley into the advancing enemy ranks. Eventually this combination of cannon and rifle fire slowed the Union advance, then stopped it.

Jackson's men, with cannon on their flanks, formed a sort of human barrier that blocked the Union advance. This courageous stand in the face of hostile fire at first slowed the flight of Confederate soldiers. Then, as they passed and realized that they were seeing a force in gray that would not yield, they began to re-form their ranks on either side of this salient unit. The Union advance was surprised by this, and they soon stopped as the men in gray they had just been pursuing turned on them and poured fire into their ranks.

Now the Union momentum disappeared, and two rough lines of soldiers faced each other, hurling fire and brimstone at each other and painting the fields with their blood. Suddenly the outcome was no longer as clear as it had been only moments before.

It was at that critical time that Beauregard's infantry flooded onto the field from the west, having only moments earlier dismounted from their trains. As they swept forward with the first version of the keening yell that was to strike terror into the hearts of Union soldiers throughout the war, they stunned the Union soldiers who thought they had already won the day. While some Union units maintained their cohesion in the face of this sudden reversal, most soldiers in blue simply panicked and fled to the rear, their formations dissolving like smoke hit by a gust of wind. The panic was contagious, and soon there were only masses of men in blue running in terror, throwing their weapons and knapsacks to the side to speed their flight. They ran blindly to the north, back across Bull Run and then as far as they could get in as short a time as possible.

Custer saw little that day other than Union cavalry and infantry forces maneuvering in different directions. His unit was held in reserve, and though he saw no combat, he did play a minor role in helping his retreating army cross Bull Run, but this time moving north. His company was one of the last organized units to move in that direction, covering the rear of the units that had already streamed past him. Fortunately for the fleeing Yankees, in the wake of battle the victorious rebels were almost as disorganized as they were. There was no real risk of a crushing pursuit that a more experienced and better-trained army would have made, and the Union army got back to the pastures of northern Virginia across the Potomac from Washington with no real enemy hindrance.

Upon its return to the Washington area, Lieutenant Custer and G Company of the 2nd U.S. Cavalry were united with four regiments of New Jersey Volunteers. Their commander was General Phil Kearny, a one-armed legend who had fought in the Mexican-American War as well as with the French army in Algeria. A wealthy soldier of fortune who had earned the reputation of being both a rigid disciplinarian and a tough battlefield warrior, Kearney established a strict regimen to whip his troops into shape, and Custer thought him superb.

After a few weeks of training, three hundred of Kearny's men were ordered to make a night attack against a Confederate picket post that was less than ten miles away. This was an unauthorized raid, of course, and when an officer from headquarters was sought to accompany the lieutenant colonel in command, Custer was thrilled to be selected as Kearny's representative.

The column of men moved as silently as possible, and they actually reached their destination. But when they deployed and moved into position for the attack, they were detected by the rebels, and a sharp volley rang out. The men in the Union force, finding themselves suddenly under fire, showed no hesitation at all as they turned and ran for their lives.

But these men were all green, and the only combat any of them had seen to date was the utter rout of Union troops at Bull Run. This mass rush for safety when fired upon, therefore, was not the slightest bit surprising. Clearly, more training and rigid discipline would be required before these men could be expected to stand their ground and return enemy fire. That would happen in due course, but the early fighting in the east was largely disastrous for Yankee forces.

In August 1861 Custer was reassigned to the 5th Cavalry, but he remained in the Washington area, and, like all troops in the Army of the Potomac, his unit was involved in no combat whatever with the Confederates. Then in October he fell ill and requested permission to return to his home on sick leave. With no military action impending during the winter, his request was granted, and he was soon on a train to Monroe, Michigan.

Custer was to stay in Monroe with his sister Lydia-Ann until February, and he was an impressive presence socially. The woman he would marry a year or so later was Elizabeth Bacon, the only daughter of a widowed local judge. They had not yet been formally introduced, but she and her father were both witnesses to an embarrassing bout of public drunkenness one evening by our blond lieutenant, after which he disappeared into his half-sister's house. This was a time of widespread temperance fervor, and when Custer reappeared the next day, he had sworn to Lydia-Ann that he would never touch alcohol again. More than a trivial act, he never broke that pledge, even many years later when his wife served liquor to invited guests inside his own home.

After the Union army was routed at Bull Run, it was clear to all that the top military leadership had to change. Having recently won some minor clashes in western Virginia, an area across the Blue Ridge Mountains in what would become the State of West Virginia, General George McClellan was being loudly celebrated by his many fans in Northern newspapers as well as enthralled members of Congress. Still only thirty-four years old, he was widely seen as a military phenomenon, a "Young Napoleon," though, because of his diminutive size, some also called him "Little Mac" behind his back. Right after

Bull Run he was called to Washington and given command of all Union troops in the area, what would become known as the Army of the Potomac.

In July and August 1861, he met with President Lincoln as well as with various cabinet members and military leaders, including General Winfield Scott. This must have been quite a meeting, for McClellan, through his political supporters on Capitol Hill and in the newspapers, was secretly trying to bring Scott down and replace him. While still unaware of these political efforts, it was Scott who promoted McClellan as his special protégé. For his part, while smiling to his face, McClellan despised Scott, disparaging and belittling him behind his back. His self-love was beginning to grow out of control, ever dangerous for a military commander, and that is easily shown by his own words in a letter he sent to his wife on 27 July 1861:

> *I find myself in a new & strange position here—Presdt, Cabinet, Genl Winfield Scott & all deferring to me—by some strange operation of magic I seem to have become the power of the land . . . I almost think that were I to win some small success now I could become Dictator or anything else that might please me—but nothing of that kind would please me—I won't be Dictator. Admirable self denial![6]*

So early in the war, Lincoln knew very little about military affairs, let alone effective battlefield leadership. He was to set himself the task of learning everything he could, and he devoured books on military strategy, tactics, weapons, maneuvers—no military topic was out of bounds. And within a very short time, he began to surprise his generals with how much he knew. But that was still in the future. For now, in the wake of the defeat at Bull Run, the tumult of praise for McClellan emanating from Capitol Hill and many newspapers simply swept him along.

After Bull Run, the Union army in and around Washington numbered fewer than 40,000 men, and they were almost all brand-new soldiers who barely knew how to march or fire a weapon. Demoralized by defeat, these men needed organization, training, and a morale boost. And McClellan was just the man for that. But leading them into battle was something entirely different, a task for which "Little Mac" would prove himself to be far less suited.

After Bull Run, Johnston and his Confederate army settled into and around Centerville, a small town some thirty miles west of Washington, a presence that was somewhat unsettling to civilians in the nation's capital. While he insisted that his own Union soldiers were not yet ready for battle, McClellan at least sought to gather intelligence about the Confederate army's deployment. And the means he chose was in keeping with the image of himself he promoted, this time as the young, energetic, and creative leader who had arrived from success on the battlefield of western Virginia to save the nation.

In June 1861, before the battle of Bull Run, a young entrepreneur named Thaddeus Lowe had been able to rise above Washington in a gondola slung below a balloon. Tethered to the ground, Lowe sent a telegraph message to Lincoln, thus impressing him with the potential of using manned balloons for aerial observation and surveillance.

After Bull Run, the Union army retreated to the immediate environs of Washington, while the victorious Confederate army remained only a few miles away. McClellan replaced McDowell, and as part of his intensive training of Union troops, he decided to try Lowe and his balloon for intelligence gathering.

Several flights were quite successful, leading to more detailed maps of the Confederate army's deployment. With balloons secured to the ground by ropes, men went aloft in their gondolas and used telescopes to look far behind the front lines. This was a rousing success until the Union balloons were subjected to the first antiaircraft artillery fire, apparently the idea of Lieutenant Tom Rosser.

During the battle of Bull Run, Rosser's howitzer battery was the only one from his battalion that was absent. Detailed to accompany Richard S. Ewell's brigade toward Fairfax Courthouse, the noise of the battle brought them hurrying back, but the fight was over before they got there. Rosser was sorely distressed, but a few weeks later he got another chance to fire his weapons at the enemy.

At the time, Rosser was the newly commissioned commander of the Lafayette Artillery from New Orleans. He watched while riflemen shot at the balloons, but the balloons were generally beyond rifle range. Even if they had been closer, however, bullets would have done little damage, and certainly not deterred those spies in the sky. But then he had a bright idea.

The artillery support on both sides was primarily "direct fire," meaning that they fired their projectiles in relatively flat trajectories at targets they could see with the naked eye. Consequently, the muzzle of each cannon could not be raised high enough, perhaps forty-five degrees or more, to shoot at a balloon, and bringing down a balloon with cannon fire seemed impossible.

But as Rosser thought about how he could elevate the muzzle, he came up with an ingenious idea. First, he ordered the crew of one gun to get some shovels and dig a hole in the ground several feet deep behind it. Once that was done, they pulled the gun back and lowered its trails into the hole, thus raising the muzzle of the gun high into the sky.

Now that he could fire a cannonball high enough to reach the balloons, Rosser had no idea what charge to use or how to gauge the fall of the round as it sped on its way. So he just decided to "eyeball" it and fired the first round directly at a balloon several hundred feet above the ground and about a half mile away. The first round fell short, so he dug the trails a few inches deeper and fired again. And again. And again.

After a number of cannonballs missed, one finally ripped

through the net of ropes that attached the balloon to the gondola below it, severing some and scaring the life out of the screaming crew members. Their cries of distress could be clearly heard as their ground crew pulled the balloon down to safety, and the crew's loud and desperate prayers were answered when they finally reached terra firma.

After that, such balloons were only launched from well behind Union lines, which meant they were far less effective. And the ground crews paid closer attention, ready to pull them down if they were brought under fire by Confederate artillery. That reduced the effectiveness of spies aloft in balloons, of course.

Rosser was to be promoted to captain in September 1861. He had been a very competent and valuable officer commanding an artillery battery in combat, but the promotion also recognized his role in the first successful use of antiaircraft artillery fire. Though he only forced the balloon to be pulled down, he did hit it with his cannonball, and the effect was the same as if he had shot it down.[7]

On 26 July, Lincoln named McClellan commander of what would become the Army of the Potomac. At the time, that included virtually all Union armies, some of them beyond McClellan's personal control when he sailed to the Virginia Peninsula. But the formal elevation only inflated his amour propre. His new title and authority at the top seemed only to fan the fires of his arrogance, and, coupled with the open disdain and mistrust McClellan felt for his superiors, this made for a poisonous stew.

Indeed, the attitudes he shared with many in letters and conversations should have sounded an alarm. But even if that happened for some, it went ignored and the handsome young military-genius-in-waiting rode forward unimpeded.

The efforts of Union army officers in Washington then were not all focused on training. On 5 August, Henry Algernon DuPont wrote a letter to his mother describing how he was sent to recapture an escaped prisoner of war. The man had managed to change into civilian clothes and get away to the town of Alexandria, where his parents as well as his wife and her family lived. Resting unarmed and surrounded by blood relatives as well as in-laws, he thought himself safe and protected when DuPont and his party arrived. Surprise on their part was followed by horror, and for a moment DuPont thought he was going to have to shoot someone before recapturing the prisoner and bringing him back. He thoroughly disliked that duty and hoped he would never have to repeat it.[8]

A few weeks later, Henry wrote to his aunt, and this letter reflects the depression that must have inhabited the entire Union army. He said that he did not foresee a very bright future, and he was especially downhearted when he saw the list of new brigadier generals published in newspapers in the North. He was distressed by the number of newspaper editors and minor politicians whose names he recognized on the list of generals, and thought this further evidence that all politicians then were innately and hopelessly corrupt. He also believed the government "incapable of controlling the destinies of an immense people like our own" and that while he hoped for the best, he didn't anticipate any great successes in the Union's immediate future.[9]

On 16 August 1861, a newly promoted McClellan wrote to his wife:

> *I am here in a terrible place—the enemy have from 3 to 4 times my force—the Presdt is an idiot, the old General in his dotage—they cannot or will not see the true state of affairs. Most of my troops are demoralized by the defeat at Bull Run, some even mutinous—I have probably stopped that—but you see my position is not pleasant.[10]*

But despite his repeatedly expressed self-confidence, McClellan continued to find excuses for not crossing the river and attacking the rebels.

Alburtis's battery, commanded by Pelham, had been among the artillery batteries specifically complimented by Stonewall Jackson in his after-action reports, and his reputation was spreading. As the armies of Johnston and Beauregard melded after Manassas, William N. Pendleton planned a complete reorganization of the artillery. One of his recommendations was for the creation of the 1st Regiment of Virginia Artillery, with Pelham as a company commander, inspector, and mustering officer. Because of political opposition in Richmond, however, this was never more than a paper organization. But Pelham continued to train Alburtis's battery every day, and he drove them hard. By the end of August, he had brought them along so far that they were widely respected as the best trained artillery battery in Johnston's army.

In that same August, General Johnston had recommended organizing a brigade of cavalry under the command of J. E. B. Stuart. Promoted to general on 24 September, Stuart had wanted a battery of horse artillery as part of his command, although his early efforts to have an unschooled friend named to command it were blocked. But he had heard about Pelham's mastery of his guns at Bull Run, of his daring courage at the very front, aligned next to Jackson's brigade and pouring death into the advancing Yankee ranks.[11] The reputation this young man had built so quickly attracted him.

On 29 November 1861, Special Orders No. 557 signed by General Johnston directed that "Captain Pelham will report with his Battery to Brig. Gen. J. E. B. Stuart for service as horse artillery."[12] There is little doubt that Stuart had arranged this, and it was a military marriage that would prove to be one of the most successful ever in the Army of Northern Virginia. Stuart had already shown himself to be a furious and ferocious cavalry commander whose pace few artillery commanders could match. Fortunately for him, Pelham would show that he had all of Stuart's fire and aggression, perhaps even more.

While it was never mentioned by either of them, here or in any other operational connection between officers, there was an unspoken bond between these two men. In the midst of the huge armies on both sides in the Civil War, West Point graduates generally found themselves surrounded by men who knew nothing whatever about the military art. In that setting, if they were able to find and work with another West Pointer, the application of their shared experiences gave them an important base on which they could build and in very short order hope to attain extraordinary success. It didn't always work that way, of course, but it did so regularly enough that it gave any team, group, or even pair of West Pointers who were able to combine their efforts a very decided advantage in the Civil War.

Stuart had graduated from West Point seven years before Pelham, and his immediate service as a young officer had been on the western frontier. As a cavalry leader, he and other soldiers played a sort of constabulary role, trying to control and protect the ever-building wave of white migrants surging across the Mississippi. These were men and families who wanted either to settle and farm on the high plains or, especially after the gold strike of 1849, to move on through the Rockies to California.

But the plains were already inhabited by tribes of a fierce indigenous people called Indians by white settlers. The largest tribes lived a nomadic life, following the enormous buffalo herds that seasonally drifted north and south and on whose meat and skins they were totally dependent. So they were startled at first by the waves of white settlers who arrived uninvited. These invaders either passed through on their way west or simply stopped and began to farm these Indian hunting grounds, planting crops and building fences to enclose their livestock.

This was just too much, and bands of fierce marauding warriors who were willing to kill and even die tried to stop them. The well-armed white settlers, of course, exhibited the fierce independence of the day and were not easily controlled. This meant a lot of Indians killed settlers, and a lot of settlers killed Indians.

Whether or not this white migration is accepted as seen today as an attack on the native peoples already living there, the settlers wanted protection and the government back east sent army soldiers for that purpose. And the tribes of Indians they fought proved to be worthy adversaries for the U.S. Army. When the Civil War broke out in 1861, most combat-experienced soldiers on either side were those fresh from fighting on the frontier.

When the armies of North and South formed in 1861, Stuart had already shed his own blood as well as that of his adversaries. Although fresh out of West Point, Pelham was not only well trained and strongly self-disciplined, he was also a fast learner. And as they worked together, Stuart's role as commander was enhanced by the role he also took on as Pelham's almost-older-brother. Their close interaction in the early days after Manassas led to a personal bond based on trust as well as affection, their rehearsal performance over the fall, winter, and spring of 1861–62 that of a well-oiled machine. When the fighting began again, their battlefield performance in tandem would become the envy of commanders on both sides, the very stuff of legend.

North of the Potomac that same fall, McClellan's poisonous comments about the civilian leadership of the government continued in another letter to his wife written on 10 October 1861:

> *When I returned yesterday after a long ride I was obliged to attend a meeting of the Cabinet at 8 pm. & was bored & annoyed. There are some of the greatest geese in the Cabinet I have ever seen—enough to tax the patience of Job.*[13]

———

When General Winfield Scott finally resigned on 1 November 1861, McClellan, of course, was named to replace him. And after reaching the top of the military command structure, his hubris knew no bounds. But he still had no plans to attack the Confederate forces deployed menacingly nearby. And whenever he was asked, even by the president, why he wasn't using his army to attack the Confederates, he had endless excuses.

He spoke vaguely of making a frontal attack on Centerville, though as the moment to move the army grew near he made a change of strategy. His next proposal was to take his army up the Rappahannock and get between Johnston and Richmond, then move overland to take the Confederate capital. Lincoln favored a direct overland attack, and discussions went on over the winter with no resolution.

As the army's soldiers became more competent in their craft, the highly political newspapers were far from idle. And while all in the North were initially supportive, they soon began to tire of McClellan's excuses, and public discomfort with his lack of action began to build. Then in early December, Young Napoleon fell seriously ill with typhoid fever, and while he convalesced, all military activity, even the training, basically stopped. In the new year, the early weeks of 1862, the heated support of McClellan that had been heard from his allies and supporters in Congress, even from members of the president's cabinet, began to cool.

When he had recovered enough to resume his military duties, McClellan finally realized that his position was at risk. There was a new political climate in the air, and gentle nudging from Lincoln told him he had to deliver, that no more indefinite delays would be accepted. For the first time, he feared his job might be in jeopardy, and he felt that he had to take offensive action against the Confederates or he would be replaced.

Then on 9 March General Joe Johnston, fearing a Union move by water up the Rappahannock that would cut him off, withdrew his army south of that river. Then the debate was between a frontal attack by land or a new movement by water that McClellan proposed.

McClellan's plan was to send his army of over 155,000 by ship to Union-held Fort Monroe on the tip of the Virginia Peninsula between the James and York Rivers. Once landed, he planned to march them up the peninsula some fifty miles and attack Richmond from the southeast. Lincoln did not approve of the plan, but he reluctantly acquiesced.

On 9 March, as part of the larger movement of the Army of the Potomac, a long Union infantry column began to march southwest toward Centerville, only a few miles from Manassas. Joe Johnston's men had just abandoned the area, and the Union column was led by Custer's 5th Cavalry. So far down the chain of command, Custer did not know that this column was only a feint, a ruse intended by McClellan to mask loading his army aboard water transport bound to Fort Monroe. Most of the officers in the 5th Cavalry were off on other duties, and the movement would only last a few days. During this time the regiment would be commanded by Major Charles Whiting, while Custer was the only officer in his company. That meant he was the acting company commander, a fact of which he was very conscious and a set of responsibilities to which he was strongly committed.

At that point in the war, a company, or "troop," as such units were designated in the cavalry, consisted of about one hundred horses and their riders, further subdivided into four platoons of twenty-odd horsemen. As the column moved south, newspaper reporters, eager for some good news after Bull Run, hovered expectantly nearby. This may have been only a feint in the minds of the Union generals, but as far as Custer was concerned, they were, in the parlance of the time, moving "on to Richmond," and spirits were high.

Their first day of movement was little more than a ride in the country, and no contact with enemy soldiers had been made, nor had any even been seen, so they stopped short of Bull Run and camped. Next morning, they saw many Confederate cannon set in positions on hillcrests that dominated the road on which they were advancing. But the cannon remained silent as they grew closer, which was somewhat unsettling. They were further confused when they detected no human activity at all within what were presumably Confederate lines.

Thinking this artillery had been abandoned, Custer and a few other officers rode right up to the mouths of the guns, only to discover that they were not cannon but blackened logs, the "Quaker guns" about which McClellan was to be derided in the press. Confederate forces had only recently left, and the air was still heavy with the stench of bacon and other supplies they had simply burned to keep from falling into Yankee hands.

Word of this went back to General George Stoneman, who commanded the column. Like his men, he was unhappy with the licking they had taken at Bull Run and he wanted to strike a telling blow. With so much sign of their recent departure, Stoneman felt he might catch the rebels still, and he ordered the cavalry to pursue them with all haste.

A few hours later, scouts came racing back with news that they had seen Confederate pickets stationed on the next rise, and Major Whiting immediately sent this information and a request for orders back to General Stoneman. Custer had left his troop under the command of his first sergeant and ridden back to Major Whiting's location to stay abreast of developments. When the courier rode back from General Stoneman, Major Whiting read his response aloud: "Drive in the pickets." Custer immediately asked Whiting if his troop could have the honor of carrying out Stoneman's order, a request that was quickly granted.

Custer led his troop to the front of the formation, then led them down the road in a column of fours. It wasn't long before Custer spotted what he instantly knew was the Confederate picket line, though they wore no uniforms. Rather, the silhouettes of mounted men wearing civilian farmer clothing lined the top of the next ridge. And they all carried guns.

Custer had segments of the fences on either side of the road removed, then spread his troop out side by side in the fields. He started them forward at a walk, an array of a hundred horsemen spread out over several hundred yards.

For Custer, this had to be an anxious moment since this would be his first time under fire. The men in front of him up on that hilltop weren't just farmers, they were enemy soldiers. They were just as green as his own men, perhaps even less well-trained, but the weapons they brandished sent a clear message. As his line moved forward, Custer felt confident that the enemy horsemen would turn and ride away, but not before shooting at him and his men. And he was ever aware that this was his first proving ground, that to be an effective leader he must now show courage in combat.

As he had been taught at West Point and believed, courage on the battlefield is not the absence of fear. Far from it, for all soldiers under hostile fire fear death. No matter how Custer may have felt that day, his ability to control his fear and lead his men in an attack would evidence not only his own personal courage but also his capacity to inspire bravery in others.

The looming death from bullets fired by those anonymous gray figures atop that ridge—that was exactly what Custer wanted to face. His testing moment as a warrior, a moment for which he had trained so long and hard at West Point, had suddenly arrived. This day he would prove his worth, for others but also, and perhaps mostly, for himself. This day he would live out the line that he and other young officers had become fond of shouting, almost joyously: "Glory and promotion or a coffin!"

As the troop reached the foot of the hill, those gray ghost horsemen rebels had disappeared from sight, but enemy bullets ripped the air over their heads. The horses were still moving at a walk and started up the hill, and the bullets whizzing by were quite unsettling. But Custer had more on his mind, for his commands now were crucial.

Cavalrymen on both sides in the Civil War usually carried a

rifle, a pistol and a saber. In a headlong charge, Custer did not want his men to stop or even slow their horses to take better aim with pistols. He noted that many of his men held their pistols, ready to shoot. But he didn't want that, so he ordered them to fire their pistols, then holster them and draw sabers. Some fifty yards from the crest, he raised his saber, yelled "Charge!" and dug in his spurs.

When they reached the top, those shadowy riders were gone, but that didn't even slow Custer's men down. Racing down the far side of the ridge and across the field at its bottom, they saw no enemy anywhere. Slowing to a trot in midpasture, their confusion was cleared by a sudden volley of flame from the bushes along Cedar Run to their front. Custer had "driven in the pickets," so he stopped his men, turned them around, and led them out of rifle range.

Their damage was slight: a bullet had split one man's scalp, and one horse had been wounded. They trotted back to the head of the column, and Custer was little short of jubilant when he reported "mission accomplished" to Major Whiting. But this report no sooner made its way up the ranks when General Stoneman's courier brought orders to the cavalry column. The exercise was over, so they rode back to Alexandria and prepared for embarkation.[14]

On 11 March, even as the ships were loading, Lincoln decided he needed to help McClellan focus on the coming operation. To that end, he relieved him of command of the entire Union army, save only the Army of the Potomac with which he would sail to Fort Monroe. He explained this to McClellan, and, given that man's ego, there can be little doubt he did not like the action. However, in the middle of March, the ships began to load, and on 4 April, McClellan himself set foot in Fort Monroe.

# SIX

## *Fighting on the Peninsula*

Movement by ship from Washington to Fort Monroe was a slow process, and it took many weeks for all of McClellan's troops to complete the transit. Finally, by the first week in April, the enormous blue host moved out of Fort Monroe on dry land. But on 5 April, McClellan also got news from Lincoln that he was not sending McDowell's corps of 40,000 men to join him on the peninsula.

Lincoln had discovered that McClellan had not left as many troops as he promised to guard Washington. In addition, Lincoln was becoming increasingly uneasy because General Stonewall Jackson was loose in the Shenandoah Valley. Harpers Ferry, situated at the northern end of the valley, was only forty miles northwest of Washington, and Lee had directed Jackson to attack Union forces there in the hope this would frighten Lincoln's government so much that he would order troops drawn back from McClellan to protect Washington.

Lee's plan worked perfectly. Using forced marches, Jackson maneuvered his 18,000-man "foot cavalry" to shock, confuse, defeat, or escape from the three different Union armies—some

60,000 men—trying to catch him. They failed utterly, and Jackson's operations in the Shenandoah Valley have become the stuff of military legend. So this threat by Jackson was probably the major reason Lincoln refused to release McDowell's corps of some 40,000 men to McClellan.

This decision was crucial, for that added increment might well have changed the whole outcome of Union operations against Richmond and even the state of our nation. If McClellan had been operating with another 40,000 men, there is the distinct probability that he would have not just defeated but overwhelmed Johnston's army at the battle of Fair Oaks. He would then have taken the Confederate capital at Richmond, captured Davis and the administrative government of the Confederacy with all its elements, including its treasury, and so crushed the rebellion in its infancy.

Such an event in June 1862, of course, would have been several months before Lincoln announced the Preliminary Emancipation Proclamation in September 1862, which promised freedom to all slaves in states still in rebellion on 1 January 1863. Had Richmond so fallen, it seems that the reasonable outcome would have been for the Confederate states to return to the Union peacefully, with slavery intact in the states where it was then legal.

Some political compromise probably would have been brokered over such hotly contested prewar issues as the Fugitive Slave Act and the legalization of slavery in some new territories, with a simply unknowable outcome for the American people of all races. Probably, however, that would have included the legal existence of slavery in some parts of the United States until perhaps as late as the early twentieth century.

So it seems that Lincoln's refusal to release those 40,000 men, or perhaps Lee's order to Jackson to cause the havoc in the Shenandoah Valley that frightened Lincoln into retaining those troops, may have been the single most important set of decisions that kept the Civil War going long enough for Lincoln to free the slaves.

McClellan would whine about this cut in his troop strength for a long time. But before he had received that message from Lincoln, McClellan had already started his ponderous move toward Richmond. And once under way, he really couldn't stop it, mostly because of the major political damage that would have done to him. So it was that, though slowed by enormous trains of troops, cannon, and supplies, the Army of the Potomac began slowly to creak up the Virgina Peninsula toward Richmond.

In that spring of 1862, General Robert E. Lee, West Point class of 1829, was military adviser to Confederate president Jefferson Davis, who had graduated from West Point in 1828. At a time when there were around two hundred cadets of all classes at West Point, this meant that the two had necessarily known each other since early manhood. In addition, the two men had known most of the senior leaders in both armies from shared service in the pre–Civil War army, particularly when both men fought in the Mexican-American War of 1846–48.

This familiarity was shared on both sides in the Civil War armies, of course. But in addition, Davis had been secretary of war from 1853 to 1857, while Lee had been superintendent at West Point from 1852 to 1855. It was during that time that the two had, among other things, extended the duration of the West Point education from four to five years. But they had also grown even more personally familiar with the young officers who would rise to general's rank on both sides during the Civil War.

McClellan had been a special protégé of Davis when he was secretary of war, and he knew "Little Mac" to be a brilliant man. For the use of the army, McClellan had translated from French a booklet on bayonet drill, and for the same purpose had written his own book on cavalry tactics. He had even developed the military saddle (McClellan saddle) that won the 1859 competition for a standard U.S. Army saddle. As he led his Army of the

Potomac northwest toward Richmond, then, he was seen by both sides as a brilliant military leader.

With McClellan as yet untested, his reputation was based on a minor victory in what was to become West Virginia and the public image of himself that he had worked hard to create. But not for long.

The Confederate forces tasked with stopping McClellan were under the command of General John B. Magruder. They were deployed in an array of defensive lines that stretched across the peninsula, with one end pinned to the fortified port city of Yorktown. As the blue army approached in early April, McClellan launched a number of probes against Confederate lines.

On 4 April 1862, Custer's regiment marched north along the James River out of the fortress while another cavalry column marched parallel to them along the York. After less than fifteen miles, they came to the Warwick River, a stream on the far side of which the Confederates had built a series of strongpoints. This Confederate line ran all the way across the peninsula, which was only about ten miles wide here.

On the York River side of the peninsula, the rebels had fortified Yorktown, and McClellan decided that town was the key to success. In his detailed initial planning, he had proposed to transport a large force by boat to land in its rear and overwhelm the weak side of its defenses. But the force that had been scheduled for this was McDowell's corps of 40,000 men, a force whose departure from the Washington area Lincoln had refused. So he sent for his heavy siege guns while launching probes over the various defended waterways to its south and west. The Union cavalry columns waited ten days for the infantry and artillery to march up to their positions, and the heavy siege operations took McClellan a month to complete.

While the Union cavalry was held in place, Custer was sent to General William F. "Baldy" Smith's staff. He first supervised the digging of rifle pits along the Warwick River at night, then was sent up in a balloon to make assessments of the Confederate defenses that lay before them. He did this a number of times and finally, on the night of 4 May, he noted a number of huge fires inside the Confederate defenses at Yorktown. He came down immediately and reported what he had seen to General Smith, surmising that the rebels were destroying supplies as they evacuated. Custer and another officer volunteered to cross the wide stream between Union and Confederate lines and investigate and found, as he had predicted, that the rebel lines were empty.

Custer's insight was noted, and when Smith's Union column crossed the stream and headed north toward Williamsburg the next day, the weather was cold and wet and the dirt roads soon became mud. While the main column struggled, Custer was allowed to ride out in front in search of solid detours that would get them to Williamsburg, the next prepared Confederate stronghold in their path.

There were still many bridges over the streams that obstructed their movement, bridges the rebels had not yet removed. As he approached the one that crossed over Skiff Creek, Custer saw someone had just set a fire in the middle of it. He dug in his spurs, then pulled up short and leaped onto the boards, kicking at the burning sticks and logs, throwing some over the side into the water. He ignored the bullets whizzing by overhead, and in very short order he had saved the bridge. For this, Baldy Smith cited him for gallantry, the first in a long series of plaudits he was to receive for courage in combat.[1]

Joe Johnston was in full retreat, and he had detailed Stuart's cavalry as well as a large force of infantry to slow the Yankee pursuit. His infantry lodged itself in a large earthwork on the Yorktown–Williamsburg road that had been built earlier by General Magruder and so was called "Fort Magruder." Joseph Hooker's division was leading the Union pursuit, and when they attacked the line of rifle pits and other fortifications at Fort Magruder, they were bloodily thrown back. Counterattacks by

James Longstreet's men threatened to overwhelm Hooker, who withdrew. Then Winfield S. Hancock's brigade of Baldy Smith's division, with Custer along as lead scout, arrived on Longstreet's left flank and occupied two abandoned Confederate redoubts. But they drew heavy fire from a bigger redoubt, which seemed to be the main Fort Magruder. Reluctant to plunge into this unknown force, Hancock stopped and tried to connect with Smith and with Hooker on his left. If he could take this strongpoint, he believed he could turn the enemy line, but his brigade would probably need a lot more help to do that.

After several hours and still with no movement from Hooker or Smith, Confederate soldiers came pouring out of the trees behind the fort. These were two regiments of General Jubal Early's Virginia infantry, 1,200 men with no artillery support. But no Confederate reconnaissance had been done, and Early didn't even realize what size force he was attacking. Hancock had 3,400 men and eight artillery pieces, and they stood their ground. But the rebel yell and the gray wave approaching them were terrifying to Hancock's soldiers. Then, seeing the size of the attacking rebel force, Hancock ordered his own men to fix bayonets and charge into them. In response they slowly began to form ranks, but the howling gray wave rushing toward them seemed too much, and, paralyzed by fear, they stayed frozen in place. Shocked stock-still they stood, and shouted orders to charge went unheard.

Then their tension was broken by a flashing, yelling apparition. It was Custer on horseback, now out in front of them and waving his hat, shouting encouragement as he urged them forward. It was unexpected and unheard of—no, ridiculous—a young boy with long yellow hair laughing in the face of death, dancing before them on a horse, a much bigger target to enemy fire than were they at ground level. He pranced down their line, mocking the oncoming rebels while calling on the men in blue to join him in the fight.

As stunned as they were by the rebel yell, Custer's startling appearance was also jolting and allowed them to find their fighting spirit. A deep roar burst from their lungs in answer to the rebels, newfound strength churning through their chests as they surged forward.

The Confederates saw at once that they were far outnumbered, and as the first clash subsided, most of their unwounded turned and fled. This was that last bastion protecting the end of their line, and now Hancock could move into their rear. In the defensive works of that stronghold was found an abandoned Confederate battle flag, the first to be captured in combat by the Army of the Potomac.

The collapse of their line meant the rebels were flanked at Williamsburg, so that night they pulled out of their carefully constructed defenses and withdrew up the peninsula. Hancock was praised for his brigade's actions, and he also applauded Custer's bravery in battle, his second citation of the day.[2]

But men were also praised on the Confederate side. In Stuart's official report, he told of one artillery battery,

*composed mostly of raw militia from Floyd County, Virginia, who had received but a few weeks drill yet, under the indefatigable exertions of Captain Pelham, ably seconded by his lieutenants and noncommissioned officers, they that day won the name of veterans.*[3]

———

The Army of the Potomac continued its cautious movement forward, and Custer rode out in front as a scout. Toward the end of May, the Union army controlled ten miles of the banks of the Chickahominy River. They were now close enough that, on Sundays, the men could hear the bells at St. Paul's in Richmond, the Episcopalian church where Robert E. Lee and other senior officers in the Army of Northern Virginia habitually attended services.

Yes, they were close now, very close. One morning Custer accompanied Brigadier General John G. Barnard, the chief engineer in McClellan's army, to the banks of the Chickahominy River. They were at a bend in the river, between the picket lines of the two forces now but out of sight to both. Having heard from his men that the river was shallow and perhaps fordable here, and having heard of Custer's daring exploits, Barnard asked him to try to get across.

Wading in with his pistol held over his head, Custer found the water reached as high as his shoulders, but no deeper, and he was able to keep walking on the bottom. Once on the other side and armed only with that still-dry pistol, he cautiously crept some distance through the thick forest. Not only did he find pickets walking their assigned posts, but he also discovered their main guard post, where they apparently rested between tours of duty, just as Custer and his friends had done back at West Point. And because this guard post was forward enough that it was caught within the bend of the river, it seemed a federal raiding party might sneak across the river and surprise them. They could, Custer believed, capture whatever rebel soldiers they caught on picket duty, and then get them back across the river before any higher Confederate command might even suspect their presence.

With Custer still soaking wet and muddy from his foray behind enemy lines, Barnard took him back to Army of the Potomac headquarters, where he was asked to explain what he had found to General McClellan. Custer, like most other soldiers in his army, simply adored McClellan, and he must have felt just the slightest trepidation because of his appearance. But Little Mac listened patiently to the tale of this young lieutenant crawling around within Confederate defenses.

Little Mac was most impressed. After he had heard a detailed report from Custer of what he had seen and asked him a few other questions, McClellan decided to strike. He ordered a crossing by the 4th Michigan Infantry Regiment, to be guided by Custer. They captured thirty-seven Confederates and brought them back across the river while killing and wounding many more who had to be left behind. The total Union cost for this venture was two Union soldiers killed and a half dozen wounded.[4]

McClellan called Custer back to his headquarters after the raid and told him he was just the sort of officer he was looking for. He invited him to join his staff, which would mean an immediate brevet promotion to captain. Having been asked to work on the staff of the general he then admired above all others, Custer was simply delighted to accept.[5]

But for McClellan, this was not the sort of major success in the war he was still hoping to find, and at best it was only a minor accomplishment, for bigger things still bedeviled him. If we presume, as I think we must, that there was no conscious collusion to inflate Confederate numbers between him and his civilian chief of intelligence, Allen Pinkerton, then the intelligence reports on enemy strength that flowed into his headquarters every day must have weighed heavy on his mind.

McClellan was ever conscious of the possibility that he might stumble into an enormous Confederate army that would trap and overwhelm his Army of the Potomac down here in southern Virginia. After deliberate consideration of his intelligence reports, whether he knew them to be exaggerated or not, he thought that a frontal attack on the defenses of Richmond would mean an all-out battle to the end with the Confederate hordes he believed to be protecting Richmond. Too far from home, deep in the enemy's rear, and massively outnumbered, that was just too big a risk for him to take.

In reality, by this time there were about 105,000 Union soldiers under McClellan's command outside of Richmond. His adversary, Joe Johnston, had only about 60,000 men to defend that city. And this massive delusion was to add hesitation to McClellan's steps, a hesitation he could ill afford.

Taking all his information into consideration, McClellan believed that the most prudent path for him to follow would be to slowly but steadily bring on more forces and besiege Richmond, then pound it into submission with his heavy artillery and mortars. But that would take time, and he knew he would hear about it again from above. So he tried to prepare Henry Halleck and President Lincoln and the others back in Washington for what he believed was going to be a slow but steady seizure of the Confederate capital.

Then on 31 May, in what would be known as the battle of Fair Oaks, General Joe Johnston attacked a large body of Union troops he thought separated from the rest of McClellan's force on the south side of the Chickahominy River. The Confederate assault was not well coordinated, but it was able to push the blue force back while inflicting many casualties. But then things started to drag as both sides threw in reinforcements. The Union lines recovered some ground and eventually were stabilized, but Johnston had been seriously wounded and was evacuated to Richmond. The next day the Confederates renewed their attack, but now the Union forces were ready for them and they made little headway. Both sides claimed victory.

Indeed, it was a bloody fight, with the Confederates suffering perhaps 6,000 casualties and the Army of the Potomac some 5,000. And the blood and horror of war were beginning to have their effect on McClellan. In a letter he wrote to his wife after the battle was over, he said:

> I am tired of the sickening sight of the battlefield, with its mangled corpses & poor suffering wounded! Victory has no charms for me when purchased at such cost.[6]

———

There is no denying that McClellan was a spectacular trainer. Most beloved by the troops, he probably did more to elevate their spirits than any previous American general had. But clearly he was not the man who should have been leading the Army of the Potomac when it went to war. As Napoleon famously said:

> *The man who cannot look upon a battlefield dry-eyed will allow many men to be killed uselessly.*[7]

On 5 April 1862, Stephen Dodson Ramseur received orders transferring him and his unit to the peninsula. Upon arrival, General Magruder was impressed not only by his demeanor but also by the competence of the Ellis Light Battery he had so carefully trained. Thinking Ramseur too valuable to be in charge of only a single battery, the general made him commander of a full battalion of artillery. On 16 April, he was able to repel a Union attack without suffering any casualties, though he knew more serious combat lay ahead.

Ramseur then heard that a new regiment was being formed back home in Raleigh, and he contacted political friends, asking for help while assuring them that he was right for that command. On 21 April he received word that he had been elected colonel of the new 49th North Carolina Infantry Regiment. He immediately returned to Raleigh and took command. But he found that the soldiers of this unit were all raw recruits, and not only did they show no fire in their bellies, most seemed reluctant to go into battle at all. Ramseur was disappointed, but he swore that he would, once again, turn these raw recruits into disciplined and reliable troops.[8]

Unfortunately he had little time for this daunting task, for McClellan was on the move. But it took nearly a full month for McClellan to bring up the heavy siege guns with which he intended to batter Yorktown into submission. When they were finally in place and ready to fire, however, Magruder slipped his men out of their positions, on the night of 3 May, and retreated north to another defensive line. McClellan continued to grind slowly north behind them, but now Davis and Lee had seen how McClellan reacted when faced with the need for offensive action: instead of risking a fight, he had called on siege equipment.

This may have been the first indication Davis and Lee had that Little Mac preferred maneuver and siege over bloody battle. These were established military methods that saved on manpower and were widely practiced before the French Revolution. It was only an indication, but Lee would soon follow it up and use McClellan's hesitation to close with enemy forces, and the insecurity that betrayed, on the battlefield against him.

Before 1789, many armies in Europe were made up of well-armed, trained, and disciplined professional soldiers, often hired mercenary units from other lands. With some exceptions, such as those inspired by religious zealotry, wars were between kings and were generally fought over control of territory. Their armies, of course, preferred to engage in maneuver and siege rather than bloody battle. In such cases, generals would try to maneuver their armies so as to control key pieces of terrain—river crossings, road intersections, mountain passes—from which they would then simply threaten their adversaries.

In such a contest, the soldiers on either side usually did not really want to actually fight and kill, let alone die, for they had no personal stake in the contest and were merely there representing their employer king. And even if such maneuvering did not end in a suspension of hostilities, the result was usually that the outmaneuvered army would withdraw into a fortified city. That would be followed by a siege of weeks or months, which would eventually cause one side to run out of food. If that were the besieging army, it would simply withdraw; if it were the besieged army that had exhausted its sustenance, it would surrender the town, with the understanding that captured soldiers would later be released unharmed. So "wars" between royal states often involved minimal bloodshed.

Then came the French Revolution and the overthrow of the king followed by the attempted rule by representatives of the people. Other royal families in Europe were unhappy with this, and they proposed to send armies of professional soldiers to overthrow these upstarts and return rule of France to the Bourbon throne. But the French response was the *levée en masse*, the mobilization of the common people willing to fight and even die to defend their overthrow of the monarchy and the political freedoms that implied.

A new sense of patriotism for the newly won freedom of the people seemed to be the driving force that, with structural assistance from military veterans, converted armed mobs into soldiers. In 1792, at the battle of Valmy, a sprinkling of old soldiers supported by a mass of raw volunteers was able to stop and defeat an army of highly respected Prussian professional soldiers. That was the "new" military tactic of mass killing and driving enemy forces from the field rather than just maneuvering and besieging.

And now it looked to Lee and Davis as though McClellan was trying to fall back on the "old" military methods of maneuver and siege. If that were true, it seemed that he could be undone by bloody battle that would overwhelm his ideas of a clean and bloodless war.

On 5 May, Hooker's division caught up with Magruder's rear guard in earthen defense works near Williamsburg. Attacking immediately, the soldiers in blue were stopped. But Hooker had left his left flank open and it was there that Longstreet counterattacked, driving that wing back. Pelham and his horse artillery were ordered to come up by Stuart, and he raced to the front around two o'clock. He had only brought three guns with him, but they were enough and he delivered devastating fire for the rest of the afternoon, firing 360 rounds and driving the Yankees steadily back. He reported casualties of two men wounded and four horses killed, three wounded, and thirteen escaped from their holders, all but two of which were later recovered.[9] But before the Confederates could break through, reinforcements under Kearny arrived and stemmed the tide.

The major Confederate port of Norfolk fell to Union forces on 9 May, and Ramseur's 49th North Carolina received orders to Petersburg, just south of Richmond. Arriving in the first week of June, they learned that in the battle of Fair Oaks on 1 June, General Joseph Johnston had been wounded. Despite his wounding, the battle ended as a draw, and Johnston was replaced by Robert E. Lee in command of what he would designate as the Army of Northern Virginia.

Lee focused at first on strengthening Richmond's defenses, but he also needed to know the disposition of McClellan's forces, particularly his right wing. Accordingly, he sent J. E. B. Stuart, with a force of 1,200 horsemen, on a deep reconnaissance raid around McClellan's right flank. From 12 to 15 June Stuart and his men rode around McClellan's right and made a complete circuit around his army, destroying supplies and startling the men in the Union rear as he smashed through them.

In 1861 McClellan's commander of cavalry, General Philip St. George Cooke, had refused to follow his native Virginia into the Confederacy. Loyal to the Union, he became a brigadier general of volunteers, while his son-in-law, J. E. B. Stuart, and Flora, his daughter and Stuart's wife, went south. Now, ordered to pursue and destroy his son-in-law, he was caught up in family anguish.

Though he came close, he never caught Stuart, and although it is not clear whether that was because he was ordered not to go any faster than the infantry that accompanied him or out of concern for his daughter will never be known. At any rate, it meant the end of his career, and when McClellan's force returned to Washington, Cooke asked to be relieved of command. But one of the brightest stars on his staff was Wesley Merritt, who also left McClellan's command and spent the next year shuffling papers in Washington.

On 23 June, General Beverly H. Robertson, commander of the 4th Virginia Cavalry Regiment, was sent forward with two infantry regiments, two cavalry regiments, and two artillery pieces to engage the enemy near Mechanicsville. This artillery, commanded by Captain Thomas Lafayette Rosser, had only one piece that was rifled, the other being a smoothbore howitzer. Rosser struck the first blows, and part of Robertson's official report captures his action well:

> The rifled gun, being speedily placed in position, opened fire upon the enemy's cavalry, drawn up on the opposite hill, doing considerable execution, as was plainly visible. The enemy soon opened a battery of six pieces and rapid firing was kept up for a considerable period of time. As our gun was completely sheltered, the enemy did not obtain its range, and hence few or no casualties occurred on our side.[10]

The next day saw more skirmishing, until Robertson received an order to retire behind the Chickahominy River. He had the two artillery pieces open up and withdrew his men across the river under the cover of their fire. Robertson again tells of Rosser's performance:

> Captain Rosser received a severe flesh wound in the arm, which, though, did not prevent his commanding the pieces while the engagement continued. . . . Captain Rosser displayed much judgment in placing his pieces, which, under his personal supervision, were served in the most handsome style.[11]

Lee was finally ready to take the offensive, and on 25 June he launched his opening attack on McClellan's troops, which was the beginning of a series of fights that were to be remembered as the Seven Days Battles.

That day, Union and Confederate forces clashed at the minor Battle of Oak Grove. McClellan held his ground at first, but quickly lost the initiative as Lee began a series of attacks. On 26 June he hit Union forces at Beaver Dam Creek (Mechan-icsville), where Captain Thomas L. Rosser, commanding the Washington Artillery, was wounded in the arm. It was not a grievous wound, but it was serious enough for him to be evacuated to Richmond, where he spent several weeks recuperating.

The Yankees slipped away that night, but Lee caught them at Gaines Mill the next day, 27 June, and attacked them in the early afternoon. Pelham's horse artillery, trying to reach the fighting while accompanying the cavalry division, was hin-dered by thick brush as well as poor roads and trails. When they finally found their place on Jackson's left, they were held in reserve and did not participate in any fighting, primarily because of the dense forest and undergrowth that covered much of the terrain. But they were harassed by a painful thorn in their side: eight Union artillery pieces were firing on them from beyond rifle range.

Stuart called Pelham forward, and although he had only two guns with him, a Blakely and a Napoleon, he immediately unlimbered them and opened fire. Stuart summarized Pelham's action here in his official report:

> *The Blakeley was disabled at the first fire, the enemy opening simul-taneously eight pieces, proving afterwards to be Weed's and Tidball's batteries. Then ensued one of the most gallant and heroic feats of the war. The Napoleon gun, solitary and alone, received the fire of those batteries, concealed in the pines on a ridge commanding its ground, yet not a man quailed, and the noble captain [Pelham] directing the fire himself with a coolness and intrepidity only equaled by his previous brilliant military career. The enemy's fire sensibly slackened under the determined fire of this Napoleon, which clung to its ground with unflinching tenacity.[12]*

After nearly an hour of this unequal fight, three Confederate batteries came forward to join Pelham's fire, which soon drove the Union guns down the road at a gallop.[13]

On the 28th, Stuart's advance squadron located a gunboat tied up to the wharf at a landing on the Pamunkey River known as White House. Stuart decided the way to drive it away was with sharpshooters, so he brought forward some seventy-five of his own dismounted men and they opened fire on the gunboat and its crew.

The Union response, however, was to return fire with its own sharpshooters. Stuart thought this a waste of time, so he brought Pelham forward with a howitzer. His first round burst directly over the gunboat, which caused a hurried reboarding by the Union sharpshooters. The gunboat soon untied from the wharf and headed downriver, pursued by Pelham's fire and never to be seen by Stuart again.[14]

Lee pursued and caught McClellan on 29 June at Savage's Station. Once again, he smashed into them, though the fighting remained inconclusive. Next morning, the men in blue were gone, but Lee's pursuit was unrelenting.

On 30 June at Glendale, Longstreet's corps led the attack. Uncharacteristically, however, Jackson failed to come up on his flank in time to deal the decisive blow that would have crushed their blue opponents. After dark, the Union soldiers withdrew to Malvern Hill, atop which they built strong defenses with interlocking fields of rifle and artillery fire over cleared ground. Clearly, if Lee's men attacked them there they would be slaughtered.

It is not surprising, then, that for the Confederates, the 1 July fight on Malvern Hill proved to be the worst of the Seven Days. Thinking the Union soldiers psychologically whipped and ready to fold, Lee launched almost suicidal frontal assaults against well-defended infantry and artillery positions covering a flat plateau with deadly fire. But Lee had presumed too much, for the Yankees held their ground, slamming into Confederate ranks with sheets of fire and lead.

Ramseur had about 500 riflemen in the 49th North Carolina at Malvern Hill, and they were held back through the earlier fighting. In late afternoon, they were moved forward to a position no more than two hundred yards from the Union line but were protected by a bluff and so out of sight of their enemy. Then about twilight, they were ordered to attack.

They rushed forward, still unseen by the Yankees in the shadows. When they got to within about one hundred yards of the Yankee line, a rebel yell echoed down their line, and all hell broke loose. Union guns were swung around to meet them, rifle and cannon fire shredding their serried ranks. Ramseur led from the front and was one of the first men hit, taking a rifle ball in his right arm just above the elbow. The 49th got to within about twenty yards of the Union line before it ground to a bloody halt, then the men pulled back over the edge of the bluff, dragging their wounded with them as best they could.[15]

During the Seven Days, Lee's army had remained constantly on the offensive and suffered more than 20,000 dead or wounded, including about 100 from the 49th North Carolina who went down on Malvern Hill. Having fought primarily from strong defensive positions, McClellan's army was not as badly bled, but still paid the price of 16,000 casualties. But after every one of those battles, despite his often significant successes, as on Malvern Hill, a clearly intimidated McClellan had continued to withdraw until 2 July. Only then did he finally reach a safe refuge at Harrison's Landing, a strongly defended river landing covered by Union gunboats on the James River. Although Lee paid a heavier price in blood, then, it was without question McClellan who had lost the contest of wills.

On 10 June, when he returned to duty, Rosser was pleased to learn that he had been promoted to lieutenant colonel of artillery. Then on 24 June he was promoted to colonel and given command of the 5th Virginia Cavalry Regiment under General J. E. B. Stuart. Back at West Point, Rosser, along with his two close friends Pelham and Custer, had been considered among the best riders at the academy, and this transfer to the cavalry was something he had long sought. Another personal delight, of course, was that he would now serve closely with Pelham, his former roommate and one of his closest friends at the academy.[16]

Ramseur was only one of thousands of wounded Confederate soldiers evacuated to Richmond, but because of his senior officer status, he was treated in the quiet of a private residence, thus avoiding the putrid conditions found in the overcrowded hospitals. As he recovered, he was pleased to see his name prominently mentioned in his brigade commander's official report as follows: "I should do injustice if I failed to mention the conspicuous conduct of Colonels Rutledge, Ransom, and Ramseur, the two latter being severely wounded." After a few weeks of rest in Richmond, Ramseur went home to North Carolina for an extended convalescence leave.[17]

On 2 July Stuart harassed or captured any retreating Union soldiers he found, mostly stragglers, and he sent Pelham farther forward in reconnaissance. Stuart got word from him that night that McClellan had reached Harrison's Landing. But Pelham also said he had discovered a plateau, Evelington Heights, from which he felt he could fire artillery into the heart of the Union camp. Stuart forwarded this news to Lee through Jackson, then set out himself to join Pelham.

Arriving the next morning, his men easily drove off the Union cavalry squadron they found on Evelington Heights. Then Stuart had Pelham open fire on the sprawling Union camp below. Pelham only had one gun with him, but he started lobbing shells into the rows of tents, and Stuart was delighted as he watched the surprised Yankees scramble.

The Yankees sent infantry and artillery to drive that gun off the plateau, but Stuart's dismounted sharpshooters were able to delay their advance. Finally, at around two o'clock in the afternoon, Stuart learned that Jackson and Longstreet were still far off, and it was not clear they were even coming to his support. He remounted his sharpshooters, then had Pelham limber up, and they abandoned the plateau to McClellan's soldiers.[18]

On several occasions over the next few days, Pelham engaged in duels with enemy detachments of two or three guns on the far side of the river, and in every case he drove them back. Then on the 6th, 7th, and 8th of July, McClellan sent out large parties in an attempt to drive Stuart's cavalry away from their strong posts along the river road. But the 5th Virginia Cavalry was there, and the commander of that regiment, Tom Rosser, was able not only to inspire his men, but also to dismount and arrange them in defensive positions that allowed them to resist and reject the Union attacks effectively, for which he won praise from Stuart in his official report. Thereafter, Stuart's men set up pickets to monitor McClellan, and the rest of his force screened Lee's withdrawal to Richmond.[19]

In his final report of 15 July on the period from June 26 through July 10, Stuart was most complimentary to Pelham:

> *Capt. John Pelham, of the Horse Artillery, displayed such signal ability as an artillerist, such heroic example and devotion in danger and indomitable energy under difficulties in the movement of his battery that, reluctant as I am at the chance of losing such a valuable limb from the brigade, I feel bound to ask for his promotion, with the remark that in either cavalry or artillery no field grade is too high for his merit and capacity. The officers and men of that battery emulated the example of their captain, and did justice to the reputation already won.*[20]

# SEVEN

## *Second Battle of Bull Run*

Barring minor clashes between men from Stuart's force and the Union troops at Harrison's Landing, a month of inactivity on both sides followed the Seven Days Battles. As the Union army lingered in its strong position along the James, Lee knew that he had crushed whatever fighting spirit McClellan may have had. McClellan was locked tight in his defenses while Lee's army returned to the Richmond environs.

Lincoln, of course, was very unhappy with McClellan's failures. But he was also quite displeased by the actions or inactions of some of his other commanders as well. As mentioned in chapter 6, from the last days of May through the first ten days of June, Stonewall Jackson and some 15,000 men had demonstrated classic military maneuver and shock action in the Shenandoah Valley. During that time, with remarkable speed and deception, Jackson's force had defeated, pinned down, or befuddled three separate Union armies whose total strength was more than three times its own. Not only was this bad for Union morale, but it also kept McDowell's corps of 40,000 from joining McClellan on the peninsula, a force that might have made the difference.

Lincoln wanted no threat from the Shenandoah, and on 26 June, he created the Army of Virginia and appointed General John Pope to command it. Made up of the armies of Nathaniel P. Banks, John C. Frémont, and McDowell, and a few other small units, it was hoped that Pope would be able to accomplish three tasks. The first was to protect Washington against attack by Lee's army or any portion of it; the second was to control the Shenandoah Valley; and the third, to draw Confederate troops away from Richmond—the reverse of Jackson's mission in the valley—thus making McClellan's attack there easier.

On 11 July 1862, Lincoln appointed General Henry W. Halleck commanding general of all Union armies. On the 14th, a large Union cavalry force under Colonel Edward Hatch was taken from Banks's army and sent to Gordonsville in the hope of being able to destroy a key Confederate rail line junction there. But McClellan's "slows" seemed to afflict many Northern generals, and Hatch didn't get near that town until the 19th, by which time Jackson had arrived and was there to defend it.

Halleck visited McClellan at Harrison's Landing on 27 July, and after discussions, ordered him to return his army to Falmouth, on the north side of the Rappahannock River across from Fredericksburg and less than forty miles south of Washington. McClellan was very unhappy with this, and he was to obey these orders only very slowly. Meanwhile, Lee had reinforced Jackson's army to nearly 25,000 and released him on Pope, a part of whose army was by then near Cedar Mountain, thirty miles west of Fredericksburg. On 9 August, Jackson attacked, but it was a confused clash with no clear victor. On 12 August, Jackson withdrew to Gordonsville, which confirmed to Lee that he would have to lead his entire army north in order to defeat Pope.

On 24 August, the two armies glared at each other across the Rappahannock, Pope's 75,000 confronting Lee's 55,000. The next morning, Jackson led half of Lee's army on a forced march to Orleans, twenty-five miles to the northwest. Stuart went with him, and they crossed the Rappahannock on the Waterloo Bridge and moved north. Among other things, Stuart's cavalry was tasked with maintaining connections with Longstreet's half of the Army of Northern Virginia. In late afternoon of the 25th, Stuart left outposts to cover the bridge, which, as he was to report, was crucial:

> My command had hardly recrossed the Rappahannock when that portion of it left on outpost duty on the river became engaged with the enemy, who advanced on the opposite bank. It was soon apparent that the enemy meditated the destruction of the Waterloo Bridge, the only bridge over the stream then standing. Appreciating its importance to us, I directed the sharpshooters of the two brigades to be sent to its defense, and the command of this party, numbering about 100 men, devolved by selection upon Col. T. L. Rosser, Fifth Virginia Cavalry, whose judgment in posting his command enabled him to prevent the destruction of the bridge in spite of desperate attempts to reach it, and held possession all day and night against infantry and artillery until the next day, when he turned over his position and the bridge intact to a regiment of infantry sent to relieve him.[1]

On the 26th, Jackson moved twenty-odd miles east, deep into Pope's rear. Stuart led his advance and, with Isaac R. Trimble's infantry following them in support, reached the Manassas Junction area after dark. Met by canister fire as they approached, Stuart called the infantry up to maneuver against the enemy artillery. They easily took the position, scattering most of its few defenders while capturing many others, along with numerous artillery pieces. And most important, they had captured an enormous Union depot containing, in Stuart's words, "millions of stores of every kind."[2]

Jackson arrived early the morning of 27 August. After sending some of Stuart's cavalry regiments off to the north and east to sever Union supply lines and reconnoiter, he spent all day organizing captured supplies while his men and horses gorged themselves on the Union plenty. That night, after returning cavalry had reported having seen only the backs of fleeing Yankees, the rebels secured four days' rations and every supply they could carry or load on captured wagons, then burned the rest. Still wanting to confuse Pope on his location, Jackson had his brigades leave on several roads leading to the north and west.

Next morning, as Union troops began to return in strength, they found their warehouses at Manassas reduced to ashes and destruction. The Confederate force that had done this, Jackson and his men, had simply disappeared, leaving tracks in many directions. Pope was confused, and his men had no idea where the rebels had gone.

By the evening of the 27th, Lee was already north of Orleans with Longstreet's corps, the other half of his Army of Northern Virginia, and McClellan had arrived back in northern Virginia from the peninsula with the bulk of his Army of the Potomac. But McClellan felt personally offended by his partial loss of military power to Halleck, and he seems to have actually wanted Pope to experience defeat at Lee's hands. There was really no chance, therefore, despite repeated urging, that he would send any of his troops, recently landed at Falmouth, forward to support Pope.

That didn't really trouble Pope, however, for he was a smart man and a competent military strategist. On the morning of the 27th, learning that Jackson was at Manassas Junction, he realized Lee, improbably, had divided his army in half. That, he believed, gave him a splendid opportunity: if he moved with alacrity, he could interpose his own army between Longstreet and Jackson, then turn on them and defeat them in detail.

He decided to move first against Jackson, whose force he presumed to be still at Manassas Junction. But by that night, Jackson had simply disappeared and no one on the Union side seemed to have any idea where he had gone. Stuart's cavalry was still with him, and Rosser's regiment, after having established connections with Longstreet, joined Jackson's force the afternoon of 28 August in their strong defensive positions.

They were on the gentle slopes of Stony Ridge, hidden in the wood line that ran parallel to the Warrenton Turnpike a mile or so to their southeast. Between them and the turnpike was Brawner's Farm, and just behind them up the ridge was an unfinished railroad cut.

Having hit and dispersed Union infantry and supply wagons on a private road some miles to the south earlier that day, Rosser took Jackson back to show him the precise spot. But Jackson saw no opportunity there, so they returned to the ridgeline. Then just at sunset word arrived that another blue column of troops was moving in the open on the Warrenton Turnpike. Jackson's men were alerted, and when the column got precisely in front of Jackson's position, his men came out of the woods, bayonets gleaming in the sun, and opened fire.

With his regiment covering Jackson's right flank during this fight, Rosser was to report capturing many Yankee prisoners. But the brutality of this fight on Brawner's Farm was something neither side had expected, and the slaughter on both sides that occurred that evening was only the opening act of what would become one of Lee's greatest triumphs.[3]

When Jackson's men opened fire, the Union troops they struck did not simply turn and run away, as might have been expected of green troops this early in the war. The unit marching down the turnpike in front of Jackson's men was the 1st Brigade of General Rufus King's division of Ambrose Burnside's corps. But these were no ordinary paper-collar city boys; rather, they were hardened western men wearing their trademark black hats, three regiments from Wisconsin and one from Indiana. Instead of taking cover or retreating when fired upon, they turned and fired back, then maneuvered toward Jackson's men. Now there were 2,000 Yankees charging fearlessly uphill to counterattack a line of just over 3,000 rebels.

These Yankees earned their name that day as the "Iron Brigade." Before nearly being destroyed as a unit at Gettysburg, the men recruited to this brigade from Wisconsin, Indiana, and later Michigan were to win fame as the toughest unit in the Union army. And that day, they faced and fought against the brigade that bore the same reputation in the Confederate army, the Stonewall Brigade. Given their aggressive fighting styles and the massive casualties both units suffered throughout the Civil War, those designations would prove to be most appropriate.

Even as Jackson's infantry attacked, he sent for Pelham's twenty artillery pieces. Having been promoted to major on 16 August, Pelham was eager to show that he was worthy of the rank and went racing forward with the three guns he had with him, sending orders to the others to move forward. But those orders seem to have lost their way, and with shadows falling as they raced down a twisting path in the forest, one of the three guns he had with him missed a turn and was lost. But the other two stopped when they heard a volley no more than fifty or sixty yards to their front.

Pelham approached the edge of the wood line on foot and could see that he was well in advance of Confederate infantry on his left. He knew that the lines of blue coming up the slope before him were the enemy, so he drew his two guns to the edge of the trees, unlimbered them, and opened fire.

The men before him were from the 19th Indiana and the 6th Wisconsin, roughly 800 men and half of John Gibbon's brigade. The rebels they engaged on Pelham's left were the 700-man Stonewall Brigade commanded by William S. H. Baylor as well as some soldiers from William B. Taliaferro's brigade. For more than an hour, Pelham's guns held the Yankees at bay. They did not retreat before the Confederate artillery and rifle fire crashing into their ranks, but rather stood their ground and returned blow for blow.[4]

Two more regiments from another brigade in King's division soon arrived, building Union strength on Brawner's Farm up to some 2,600. Jackson fielded only two understrength brigades—Baylor's and Trimble's—and a few regiments from two other brigades, for a total of just over 3,000. The combined strength of the four partial Confederate brigades barely outnumbered the six Union regiments opposing them, though there were many rebel regiments nearby who might have pitched into the fight if they had been so ordered. Communication difficulties being understood, they either were not or simply didn't get there in time to join the fight.

Because Jackson's two division commanders, Ewell and Taliaferro, were wounded, he struggled to have his orders carried out. He even led two regiments into the attack personally, something no major general should ever do. But the battle went on for several hours with neither side giving any quarter. It was a stand-up, slug-it-out fight with no cover for either side at a range between combatants of less than one hundred yards.

The casualties were appalling. Still, the fighting went on until full nightfall, when the darkness allowed Union forces to pull back. And they did. This bloody battle between the best infantry troops on either side ended as essentially a draw, and both sides needed to lick their wounds.[5]

Later that night, realizing he was outnumbered by Jackson's corps and fearing that Longstreet might be nearby, King conferred with his four brigade commanders. With two brigades badly hurt by the day's fighting, all agreed that the most prudent thing to do was to march the division to Manassas Junction, where they hoped to find Pope's army concentrated. They did spend some time attempting to recover dead and missing, then moved away from the battlefield in the early morning hours.

Their casualties were appalling: out of the 2,900 men engaged that day from six Union regiments, some 900 had been killed, wounded, or were missing.[6] Confederate losses were almost a mirror of that: of the 3,500 rebels who fought on Brawner's Farm, 1,100 were casualties, nearly one-third of their number and closely reflecting the bloody price paid there by the Yankees.[7]

After several days of marching his troops back and forth fruitlessly, now Pope had finally found Jackson. But it took him most of the day to assemble his divisions and launch an attack on Jackson. He believed that Longstreet's force was too far off to arrive in support that day, and he threw four divisions against Jackson's line. But these attacks were all made directly into his frontal defenses, were made piecemeal, and were poorly coordinated.

The result was that, though badly bled and pressed by a force many times its own size, Jackson's men held their ground and repelled the attacks. Longstreet came up on Jackson's right by noon that same day, but remained concealed and did not engage the Union army.

As the fighting opened, Pelham was moved to Jackson's right flank, where he found three other Confederate batteries firing at enemy positions. He went two hundred yards past them on their left, deployed his guns on a ridge, and joined the barrage. After about two hours, he had exhausted his ammunition for all but one gun. Sending the others to the rear, he noticed that the other three batteries with which he had been firing in concert had retired, leaving him alone with his single gun.

He sent a sergeant to the rear to ask for reinforcements and more ammunition, but that man returned empty-handed. Pelham would not give up, however, and he kept that single gun firing until one of its trails was shattered by enemy counter battery fire and so knocked it out of commission. Reluctantly, he had it hitched up and pulled to the rear along with its wounded crewmen.[8]

Lee did not expect Pope to attack again on the 30th and was

formulating plans to get around to his rear. Then, at around 1:30 in the afternoon, to Lee's surprise, Pope attacked Jackson's 25,000 frontally with most of his full force of 60,000, punishing the rebels badly, with General Fitz John Porter's corps making ground against Jackson's right.

Lee's initial response was to have Longstreet open a massive artillery bombardment on Porter's men, which surprised them and drove them back. Seeing his opening, Lee then had Longstreet's five divisions launch an all-out attack on Pope's exposed left, which swept ahead with little opposition. Stuart was covering Longstreet's right flank, and saw his opening:

> I directed Robertson's brigade and Rosser's regiment to push forward on the extreme right, and at the same time all the batteries I could get hold of were advanced at a gallop to take position to enfilade the enemy in front of our lines. This was done with splendid effect, Colonel Rosser, a fine artillerist as well as a bold cavalier, having the immediate direction of the batteries.[9]

In desperation, Pope pulled troops from his right to stop Longstreet, but Jackson saw this and launched his own counterattack on a now-open Union right. Many units of the Union's Army of Virginia basically collapsed, and Pope tried to reassemble them as his soldiers were forced back. Some units were orderly in their withdrawal, however, and, given their great numbers, they were able to stop and hold on Henry House Hill, the center ground of the first battle of Bull Run.

Fighting ended at dusk, but Pope had seen enough. He quickly formulated plans for a withdrawal to Centerville, which started as soon as it was dark, and within a few days his men were back within the Washington defenses. His losses, from 16 August to 2 September, were about 1,750 killed, 8,500 wounded, and 4,300 missing or captured, while Lee's were about 1,600 killed, 7,800 wounded, and 110 missing.[10]

The mood on the Union side was glum, not only among the troops but among the people and all the way up the government to the White House. Once again the Confederates had whipped a larger Union army and sent it streaming north for protection. And Pope, the man Lincoln had hoped would turn things around, had failed miserably.

McClellan, of course, had managed to keep his Army of the Potomac safe and secure in Falmouth. Despite urging from Halleck and Lincoln, none of his divisions had gone to the support of Pope, which was probably a key element in his shameful defeat. And Little Mac was still posturing and complaining, warning against impending peril for the republic unless he were returned to command all Union armies.

The entire military situation was most distressing to Lincoln. Hoping to have found a general who could fight and defeat these numerically smaller Confederate forces, he had been vastly deceived. And now at summer's end, the soldiers of the Confederate Army of Northern Virginia lay menacingly just across the river, with no one willing or able to attack them, let alone defeat or even drive them away.

Pope was reassigned to command the Department of the Northwest from St. Paul, Minnesota, and his Army of Virginia was dissolved into the Army of the Potomac. The men and officers who had served under him still clamored for McClellan, and Lincoln, realizing he was probably the best commander available, decided to give him another chance.

# EIGHT

## *Battle of Antietam*

In the Army of Northern Virginia, spirits were high. Lee's triumphant success against Pope was an enormous boost to Confederate morale, and he became even more of a hero across the South. Having thrown the Union back on its heels militarily, he wanted very much to take the fight into Maryland. Most of all, he wanted to retain the hard-won initiative in the fighting, and a victory north of Washington might win recognition of the Confederacy in Europe.

His overall plan called for him to head for Harrisburg, Pennsylvania, and cut the major east–west railroad lines. From there, he would threaten Philadelphia, Baltimore, and Washington. It was also hoped that his presence in the unseceded slave state of Maryland might spark a revolt there. And perhaps as important to Lee as any other reason was that the movement he planned into Maryland and Pennsylvania would take the devastation away from Virginia, his most beloved land, already so ravaged by war.

He began crossing the Potomac on 4 September and almost immediately began sending his forces off on various missions over a distance of some thirty miles. General J. E. B. Stuart and his staff crossed the Potomac into Maryland on 5 September and were cheered on by Southern sympathizers while ignored by Yankees. When they reached the town of Urbana, they were well received, and Stuart and his staff were invited to set up their headquarters tents in the garden of a private home. As part of their town tour, they were shown a large, empty building that had formerly housed a private school and was referred to as "the academy."

Stuart was so delighted by the town and the supportive people he met there that he told his aide, Major Heros von Borcke, to organize a ball at the academy. And this he did, right down to coming up with invitations and decorations. Even a band was found, that of the 18th Mississippi Infantry.

So it was, on the evening of 8 September, that a ball was held celebrating the arrival of Stuart's cavalry in Maryland. Stuart had kept only Wade Hampton's brigade in Urbana, sending the others to towns some ten miles or so apart. This was done so that the men would be able to live off the land without depriving the residents of all their foodstuffs. And they didn't just seize food and fodder, but rather paid them with IOUs that were rather risky. These would have been honored by the Confederate government had they won the war, and they might or might not later be honored by the federal government.

The dance was in full whirl when a messenger came bursting in and shouted the news to Stuart that their pickets had been driven in and the town was being attacked by Union cavalry. The dance was instantly forgotten as the men from Mississippi put their instruments aside and picked up their rifles. Women screamed and clutched at their children as officers bolted out the door to their horses. Stuart and von Borcke and a few other staff officers raced to the front, only to find that things weren't as bad as reported, that they had been attacked by a small force, perhaps only a regiment of Union cavalry that was moving through the night and had lost its way.

As officers scrambled to get their regiments in line to block the Yankee attack, Pelham's guns were already pouring round after round into their ranks, which lost some of their formation then began to visibly falter. Stuart ordered several regiments to make a general advance, and the soldiers in blue soon turned their horses and ran. The 1st North Carolina chased them for several miles, until they got away in the dark around midnight. With a great sense of relief, the Confederate cavalrymen returned to Urbana, only to find that the now-armed musicians were waiting in the academy, and many of the invited civilians were still in the area. By then it was around 1:00 a.m., but Stuart told the band to recover their instruments and strike up a tune. Within half an hour, most guests had returned, and the dancing went on until predawn pink streaked the sky.[1]

A few days later, orders arrived that moved Stuart's entire force to the north, and soon they were stretched out to form a screen barrier between Lee's main force and McClellan's pursuit. On the 13th, Stuart and his command set up in the small town of Middletown, only to be attacked by an enormous Union force. Driven through town, they burned the only bridge over the Kittochtan Creek, which slowed the blue pursuit somewhat.

Stuart and his staff rode on and joined Fitzhugh Lee's brigade in Boonesborough at nightfall. From them they learned that Pelham, who had been moving with Lee's brigade, had stayed behind too long in a skirmish earlier that day and some reported having seen him after he had been cut off and was about to be captured by the Yankees. Always one who tried to get in the last shot of a fight before withdrawing, it looked like Pelham's luck had finally run out, and his loss was greatly mourned.

Next morning, the 14th, Pelham rode into Boonesborough alone, having cut his way through the Yankee lines and saved himself, in von Borcke's words, "by his never-failing coolness and intrepidity."[2]

On 13 September McClellan reached Frederick, where a Union soldier had just found a document in an abandoned Confederate camp. Wrapped around three cigars, it was a copy of Lee's entire plan of operations, a document that must have been dropped or mislaid by a staff officer. Only hours old, its contents laid out all of Lee's plans in great detail, and its discovery was an enormous boost to McClellan. He now expressed confidence in his impending victory over Lee's army, a confidence that he had seldom expressed in the past. But this crucial piece of paper in his possession had him almost crowing to his staff that now he would finally destroy Lee's army. Even so, he delayed sixteen hours before he got his huge army moving.

Lee soon learned that McClellan had found a copy of the orders and was now moving in his pursuit. He called his divisions in from their various tasks, including Jackson, who had been assigned to take the U.S. garrison and armory at Harpers Ferry. On 14 September, Union forces were slowed by much-outnumbered Confederate units at the battles of South Mountain and Crampton's Gap. Then on 16 September, McClellan's Army of the Potomac confronted Lee's force lined up defensively behind Antietam Creek and perhaps a half mile in front of the town of Sharpsburg. He did nothing that day but skirmish, send out scouting parties, and plan his offensive, which allowed the rest of Jackson's troops to join Lee that night. But despite that strengthening of the Confederate position, by the next day McClellan had at least formulated a plan:

> The design was to make the main attack on the enemy's left—at least to create a diversion in favor of the main attack, with the hope of something more, by assailing the enemy's right—and as soon as one or both of the flank movements were fully successful, to attack their center with any reserve I might then have on hand.[3]

Though vague, it was at least a plan. No written order for the attack was ever issued to his corps or division commanders, and it wasn't carried off in precisely the order specified of attacking the Confederate left, then their right, and finally their center. Still, with nearly 80,000 men under his command to Lee's less than 45,000, the plan, though vague, might have been carried out and won a stunning victory. But because his attacks on Lee's left, center, and right were made consecutively rather than at the same time, McClellan failed to overwhelm and possibly capture all or most of Lee's army, which could have ended the war.

Early on the morning of 17 September, Union forces opened an artillery barrage on Lee's center. At the same time, a massive infantry attack was launched against the Confederate left, meeting little resistance as it surged forward. But as Union soldiers entered a cornfield and two patches of trees that flanked it, remembered today as the "East Woods" and the "West Woods," a mass of John Bell Hood's screaming rebels suddenly rose and slammed into them, forcing them back. Union artillery then pounded the cornfield, after which the Union attack that had been earlier rejected by Confederates was repeated.

Stuart was tasked with covering the Confederate left flank, and Pelham's guns were crucial here. On his own initiative and with his telling eye for key artillery terrain, Pelham positioned more than a dozen artillery pieces on Hauser's Ridge, a half mile west of the cornfield. Because it was protected from the view of Union artillery, his position could not be engaged by their counter battery fire, yet Pelham was able to sweep the open ground north of the Dunker church. That meant that every time the Yankees attacked, Pelham's shell, canister, and solid shot ripped great holes in their right flank.

The men in blue were never able to successfully attack Pelham's position or even to slow his fire. Consequently, as long as they continued to attack at the left end of the Confederate line, this terrible artillery barrage against the Union forces continued unabated.

Historian Jennings C. Wise has called Pelham's actions

> *one of those masterstrokes by a subordinate of highly developed initiative . . . no one movement on either side bore a greater influence upon the final issue of the battle than did the advancement of Pelham's group. . . . This was a move on the chessboard, though perhaps by a pawn, which baffled the most powerful pieces of the enemy.*[4]

Stonewall Jackson had arrived on the battlefield the night before from Harpers Ferry, and he commanded on this left wing, though some of his men were still strung out on the road. The butchery from the cornfield back to the walls of the Dunker church a half mile south of it continued, with control of this area changing many times over until late morning. Only then did the firing there fade and the much-bled troops were content to simply stand their respective ground.

It was around this time that Union general William French led his division against the center of the Confederate defenses. Confederate infantry under the command of General D.H. Hill, Ramseur's former math professor at Davidson College, was in a strong position there, his men well protected while firing from a sunken road. Between 10:00 a.m. and 1:00 p.m., Northern soldiers attacked this position four times and were bloodily thrown back in every case.

This sunken road had already won the name of "Bloody Lane" from soldiers on both sides, but at around 1:00 p.m., some Southern soldiers there apparently misunderstood an order and pulled back. Because of this partial withdrawal, or perhaps because of Yankee ferocity alone, two blue regiments pressed forward and attained enfilading fire on Bloody Lane. After a few minutes of crushing fire from one flank, the Confederate soldiers still stuck in that scarlet-streaked sunken road who were able to do so pulled back, and a lull fell over the center of both lines.

The final Union blow was against Lee's right flank, where there was a bridge over Antietam Creek. Though the water was only knee-deep, neither side realized that, and furious fighting followed. Because the Yankees thought themselves constricted to the narrow passage over the bridge, fewer than 500 rebel riflemen delivering a murderous fire held them at bay. Finally, Union troops under General Ambrose Burnside crawled and crab-walked over not-yet-cold corpses in blue to get across that cursed bridge. But once on the other side, Burnside's force paused to re-form and recover, which was a great blunder.

Before Burnside's men could drive the few gray soldiers before them back into Antietam, A. P. Hill's division finally arrived from Harpers Ferry. This was Lee's last absent unit to make it back, and they burst squarely on Burnside's left flank. This stopped the Union advance on Sharpsburg and sent the blue soldiers scrambling back to safety.

Next morning, neither army made a move. They made the conventional temporary truce to recover dead and wounded, but no offensive action came from either side as they stayed in place and glowered at each other. But because he had "interior lines" and McClellan's attacks had all been made sequentially rather than all at the same time, Lee had been able to shift his meager forces from one section of his lines to another and thus to hold off one Union attack after the other.

That night, the 18th, Lee began moving his army back to a nearby ford over the Potomac River, which was less than a mile behind the village of Sharpsburg. During the hours of darkness, the Army of Northern Virginia pulled back into Virginia, leaving the Army of the Potomac in control of the battlefield. Having discovered at first light that Lee was gone, McClellan crowed of his victory to Washington. But he fatally failed to pursue Lee, a shortcoming that, a month later, would finally cost him his job.

On 17 September 1862, somewhere between 6,300 and 6,500 men were killed or mortally wounded at the battle of Antietam, and more American soldiers died that day than on any other day in the nation's military history. That day produced a larger number of American battle deaths than were suffered by our country's military in all other wars of the nineteenth century—the War of 1812, the Mexican-American War, the Spanish-American War, and all the Indian wars—*combined*. In addition to those deaths, another 15,000 men were wounded and recovered, at least partially. But many of these wounded men were so grievously injured that their productive lives were over.[5]

The battle of Antietam has been described by many Civil War aficionados as a fight to a draw, but that is misleading. Although he technically wasn't driven from the field, by his withdrawal Lee did concede the ground to McClellan. And the most important measure of victory in the nineteenth century was probably just that: after the fighting ended, the army in control of the battlefield had almost always won the battle. The battle of Antietam, then, was a Union victory.

Lincoln had wanted to announce the Preliminary Emancipation Proclamation for some time, but he had been awaiting a Union victory so that outsiders would not think it no more than a last desperate outcry. He decided that Antietam was enough, and on 22 September, he announced:

> *on the first day of January . . . all persons held as slaves within any State, or designated part of a State, the people whereof shall then be in rebellion against the United States shall be then, thenceforward, and forever free.*

This was to be a telling political blow against the Confederacy, and it was a two-edged sword. Before the Civil War, according to the 1860 census, there were four million slaves in the United States, out of a total population of thirty-one million.

After this Preliminary Emancipation Proclamation, and particularly after the actual Emancipation Proclamation that followed it on 1 January 1863, hundreds of thousands of slaves ran away from slavery to Union lines or the protection of invading Union armies. Not only did this dramatically reduce the work that got done on the home front of the Confederacy, but many of these escapees also took up arms to fight for the North. By the time of Lee's surrender at Appomattox, there were 190,000 black male soldiers in the Union army, most of them escaped slaves.

Lincoln was also concerned about talk by officers within Union army ranks that the war was not really being fought seriously, that McClellan's slow movement showed that he was not even trying to destroy Lee's army because of some supposed larger political plan. Some specification of this came to him a few days after the battle of Antietam when he was told that one staff officer in the War Department, a Major John Key, had been telling friends that there was no effort to catch Lee after the battle because "that was not the game." Key supposedly then said that the overall plan called for both armies to fight without defeating each other, but rather just to exhaust their solders without either victory or defeat, after which peace would be made and slavery saved.

Lincoln was particularly concerned about this because he learned that Key's brother was a colonel on McClellan's staff. He called Major Key in and asked if he had made the remark. When Key confirmed that he had, Lincoln revoked his army commission on the spot. He had heard there was talk of such a "game" among McClellan's staff officers, and he said he intended to "break up the game."[6]

Clearly McClellan got the message, and on 7 October 1862, he issued a general order that included the following words:

*The Constitution confides to the civil authorities—legislative, executive, and judicial—the power and duty of making, expounding, and executing the Federal laws. Armed forces are raised and supported simply to sustain the civil authorities, and are to be held in strict subordination thereto in all respects. This fundamental rule of our political system is essential to the security of our republican institutions and should be thoroughly understood and observed by every soldier. The principle upon which, and the object for which armies shall be employed in suppressing rebellion, must be determined and declared by the civilian authorities, and the Chief Executive, who is charged with the administration of the national affairs, is the proper and only source through which the needs and orders of the government can be made known to the armies of the nation.*[7]

While perhaps overly verbose, that is a precise statement of the relationship between the soldiers of our country and our elected president, who is the only individual with the constitutional authority to make (or delegate) all policy decisions relating to any use of the military. It is an open-and-shut case, and while Lincoln was no doubt pleased to see such a formal acknowledgment from McClellan, there had doubtless been times over the past year when he might have wished to remind him of their relative authorities. Despite McClellan's post as commanding general of the Union army, he was still subordinate to the president, who is, after all, the military commander in chief. McClellan sometimes seemed to have forgotten that.

Lee's Army of Northern Virginia had not won the impressive victory in Maryland he had hoped for, but when his army crossed the Potomac River, it was not pursued by the Union army under McClellan. Now back in Virginia, Lee told Stuart to take two of his brigades of cavalry, two regiments of infantry, and his horse artillery commanded by Pelham and move upriver fifteen miles to the town of Williamsport. From there, he was to recross back into Maryland, then put on a demonstration that would convince McClellan the Confederates were there in force.

This was accomplished, and the first contact was with two

squadrons of Union cavalry that Stuart surprised and charged soon after his force was back inside Maryland. An hour or so later, Union reinforcements began to arrive. But Stuart was ready, and a lively skirmish ensued, complete with cannonades from Pelham. The Union forces withdrew toward Hagerstown, and Stuart's force followed them, but slowly.

The next day, Pelham made a long reconnaissance ride and learned that a large Union cavalry force was gathering nearby. He reported that to Stuart, then he rode up to Stuart's Prussian aide-de-camp and companion, Major Johann August Heinrich Heros von Borcke, and invited him to ride down to a peach orchard he had found a quarter mile away. Down there, Pelham said, they could climb a tree, eat peaches, and watch as Yankee horsemen approached.

Von Borcke accepted, and soon enough, the two men were perched in the branches of a peach tree, hidden from sight by the leaves while enjoying the lusciously sweet ripe peaches of late September. The Yankees were not more than a half mile away, and there seemed to be four regiments, while a cloud of dust in the distance told them that more were on their way, probably infantry.

Clearly Stuart had accomplished Lee's mission of fooling McClellan into believing Confederate soldiers were there in force. Now the two of them decided to get back behind their own lines. Unless they could discover another source in the country they rode through, their diet was restricted to often unpalatable army food. But now, refreshed by the succulent peaches whose sweet juice beaded von Borcke's beard and ran in sticky rivulets down Pelham's smooth cheeks and jowls, they dropped out of the tree, mounted their horses, and dug in their spurs.[8]

After an afternoon and evening of skirmishing, J. E. B. Stuart slipped back across the river into Virginia, his mission accomplished. The Yankees were left scratching their heads as they fruitlessly scoured the farms and woodlands of northern

Maryland for their elusive foe. Having paralyzed McClellan's entire army once again, Stuart was the toast of the South, and even in the North his daring exploits were fast becoming legend. And McClellan himself was far from eager to cross the river and once again face generals who were clearly his battlefield masters.

So long as no large Union force followed them into Virginia, it was time for the Army of Northern Virginia to rest and recuperate. J. E. B. Stuart then placed his men in a long arc some thirty miles long that extended from Harpers Ferry to Williamsport. In late September, Stuart established his headquarters on the Bower, that plantation along the Opequon Creek near Martinsburg owned by Colonel Adam Dandridge that was so well known to Pelham. And sure enough, the original three beautiful Dandridge girls were still there, but now they were joined every day and evening by many other young beauties drawn from near and far. They had heard of handsome and gallant young Confederate officers at the Bower and, not surprisingly, had managed to wangle invitations.

A sea of white tents occupied by Stuart's staff was set up on one side of the big white mansion, in which perhaps a hundred young men slept. These were mostly staff officers, though there were also many orderlies who would carry messages to and from Stuart's subordinate commanders as well as to and from his own commander, General Robert E. Lee. As many as two hundred of their horses grazed freely on the lush grass that filled the adjoining fields. The Dandridge family was an old and wealthy one, well connected to powerful people on both sides of the war. Indeed, Martha Washington had been born a Dandridge and had spent part of her youth on this very plantation.

Colonel Dandridge's two daughters, Sallie and Serena, lived on the plantation with him, as did a niece named Lily. Training filled every day, and Pelham made sure his men, particularly the replacements who had just arrived, were fully schooled on the duties of every member of the crew that serviced each of his guns. And if practice makes perfect, then by the end of a week his men were approaching just that.

Stuart's men had their own mess tents and facilities, and their fare was enriched from the neighboring hills bursting with tasty game, from pheasant and partridge to wild turkey and deer. Even so, the main house was like a magnet to these young officers each evening. There were even formal dances joined by young ladies from other plantations or the town of Martinsburg. Some even came from Winchester, for the word was out that many handsome young officers were staying at the Bower, where music and dance and perhaps inappropriately carefree laughter burst forth every evening.

Pelham had been writing to Sallie since he first met her while training in the Shenandoah more than a year earlier. Now that he was staying in a tent right outside her bedroom window, it was a story-land romantic dream come to life. Every night, music rang out from Stuart's banjo player right after supper, and other instruments almost magically appeared and added to the chorus. Dance was the centerpiece of that world, and joy, laughter, and lightly tapping sandals offset by clumping boots rang through the house. Even so, John and Sallie seldom danced with anyone else. No, in the midst of violent war, this was their time for each other, and no one else would be allowed to intrude.

Truly they lived in their own world, largely oblivious to all that went on around them. They rode horses into the countryside together, rowed on the river in the moonlight, sat with each other at evening picnics or around an open fire, and often just walked through the fields hand in hand. They even borrowed a yellow wagon, which Stuart's men had captured from the Yankees, to go for long rides. Smiling and foolish after training had ended each day, both practically bubbled over as their young love burst into bloom against the backdrop of this beautiful Southern plantation.

They could not hide it, of course, and J. E. B. Stuart finally asked John if all this romance wasn't going to spoil his love of fighting. John knew he was still a fierce warrior, and no one could deny that. Still, now that he was in Sallie's company, something was oddly wrong with that, though he knew not what. He told Stuart that, yes, he still loved fighting, but he would be happy when the fighting was finally over and he could settle down and raise a family.

As love swept them away, he gave Sallie his greatest treasure—the Bible his mother had given him when he first left for West Point. Yes, the war was still there, but they tried to ignore it, tumbling through a romantic trance together as September slid into October.

Then it was time to fight. From 10 October through the 12th, Stuart led 1,800 handpicked men, including Pelham and four of his artillery pieces, on a long raid deep into enemy country. Leaving at night, they rode hard up to Chambersburg, Pennsylvania. Once there, they captured and burned mountains of Union military supplies. Both on the way north as well as on the way back, they scoured the countryside for horses and took every one they found. They very courteously gave the Confederates receipts explained earlier to their owners, though they usually met scowls, for these did not always result in repayment out of Pennsylvania state or U.S. coffers.

On the way back, they rode around McClellan's entire Army of the Potomac, thumbing their noses at his impotence. When they rode back across the river into Virginia, they took with them some twelve hundred fresh horses they had collected in Pennsylvania. And, given the form of their operations and the high turnover in mounts they experienced, most of these horses never again left Stuart's cavalry.

Their raid was painted in banner letters across the front pages of the nation's newspapers, North and South, as a laughing adventure. And given the near impunity with which they conducted it—suffering losses of one man wounded while two fell asleep and were captured—such a designation was not far off. Their adrenaline was still gushing when they returned to the Bower, and it took a few days to release all the heated passion their ride had sent coursing through their bodies. They were to have more than two weeks of calm in which they could rest and recover. But just as they began to truly relax, the war called.

On 29 October they finally broke camp. McClellan's 110,000 men had finally crossed the Potomac and were looking for Lee's 70,000. Now it was time for Stuart's men to perform some of the impenetrable screening and aggressive reconnaissance that had made them famous.

A series of moving fights ensued, clashes with blue cavalrymen who usually outnumbered them and were increasingly supported by infantry. The contact on 3 November was typical, with advancing blue columns forcing Stuart and his men to abandon the small town of Upperville: Union soldiers rode into one side of town as the last of Stuart's cavaliers rode out the other.

But Pelham had taken his guns around town on a back road and set them up in a strong position about a mile away. After a brief flurry of gunfire exchanged with pursuing Yankees, Stuart's riders became a bit disorganized, some of them bleeding and some on foot as they passed their own guns. Soon enough, a column of blue cavalry appeared in their wake, so many hounds in eager pursuit of a wounded deer. But Pelham broke up their column, killing or scattering the hostile horsemen with canister fire.

A half mile or so behind him, groups of Stuart's troops were trying to re-form so as to meet the steady, grinding Union advance. But now Pelham found himself in a risky position, as some 200 Union cavalrymen had dismounted and taken cover behind a thick stone wall to their front. Although they were still some two hundred yards away, their carbine fire was having a telling effect, wounding his crew members and killing his horses. But even this bloody reduction of his gun crews had little effect on their rate of fire, for Pelham was in there with them.

Hard at work in his shirtsleeves, he helped load, aim, and fire the guns himself. But the canister, which he had chosen to take out a maximum number of Yankee soldiers, was having no effect on the thick rocks behind which they took cover. So he changed his fire to solid shot, and his guns were soon tearing great chunks out of the wall, hurling stone fragments that themselves killed or wounded many previously concealed Yankee sharpshooters.

Now the tables had turned. The Union soldiers behind the stone wall soon realized that they would be killed if they didn't move. So they stood up and ran. But they didn't get far, for some of Stuart's horsemen had seen Pelham's predicament and had come back to rescue his battery. As they arrived, they saw only the backs of running blue soldiers, whom they pursued, cut down, or captured.

The Union command decided to pursue Stuart no farther that day or night, and he pulled his force back to the countryside near Ashby's Gap. From there the lower country beyond Upperville could be easily seen, and the great dark lines of Union infantry, cavalry, and artillery headed their way gave strong evidence that their earlier withdrawal had been most prudent.[9]

Over the next several weeks, this kind of moving engagement continued, and Pelham's matchless use of his guns to delay Union pursuit was the telling difference. His crews were badly bled, but from Stuart's cavalry a bountiful supply of eager volunteers was always ready to join this elite "flying battery." New crew members were quickly trained, and Pelham's gun crews continued their superb performance without skipping a beat.

It was Pelham's extremely accurate fire that routinely destroyed or disabled Union batteries, smashed into lines of federal cavalry or infantry, and effectively staved off much larger Union forces as they continued to screen Lee's forces. Finally, Stuart joined Longstreet's corps in Culpeper. In the first week of December the entire Army of Northern Virginia set up a strong defensive position behind the Rappahannock River near the old colonial town of Fredericksburg.

In early November, after reinforcements had arrived and stragglers and others absent from Antietam had been rounded up, Lee's Army of Northern Virginia had swollen to some 85,000. The Union Army of the Potomac, meanwhile, had also grown to nearly 120,000. But McClellan had been so slow in his pursuit that, on 7 November, Lincoln relieved him of command and replaced him with Ambrose Burnside. All this took place within a year after McClellan had so roughly elbowed Winfield Scott aside and taken his place at the top army command post.

McClellan went home to New Jersey and would use his political skills to win the Democratic nomination for president in 1864. Though he would be badly beaten by Lincoln, he proved to be a better politician than he had been a general, and he would serve as governor of New Jersey from 1878 to 1881. But by then his time on the national stage was past, and his military star and place in history had faded dramatically.

Ramseur was still recuperating back in South Carolina, but he was far from forgotten. By this time, he had missed the battles of both Second Manassas and Antietam. And to his great dismay George Burgwin Anderson, one of his greatest personal heroes, had been seriously wounded at Antietam. After graduating from West Point in 1852, Anderson had taken his commission in the dragoons and had served most of the period between 1853 and 1860 on the western frontier, protecting settlers from Indian attacks.

Resigning in 1861 to join the Confederate army, Anderson was soon promoted to general and given command of a brigade of four North Carolina infantry regiments. And from the earliest days of the war, he had become an important role model, even a hero, for Ramseur and many others. Like Ramseur, he had been wounded at Malvern Hill, but not so grievously. That meant he was back on duty before Lee moved into Maryland in early September.[10]

He was there hit by gunfire again, though this time his wounds were frightful. He was evacuated to North Carolina, and Ramseur had even visited him on several occasions. But his condition suddenly worsened, and he died on 16 October 1862 at the age of thirty-one.

Now Lee needed a leader to command that brigade. He knew that Ramseur had shown splendid abilities in training green troops and then leading them into battle. But perhaps most impressive was the raw guts that man had shown at Malvern Hill, where he had risked his life in an openly courageous way by leading his men from the front.

This was just the sort of leadership Lee was looking for, and on 26 October he recommended Ramseur for promotion to brigadier general and the command of the brigade formerly commanded by Anderson. The administration slowed things somewhat, but on 6 November 1862, the Army of Northern Virginia was informed that President Davis had approved certain promotions, including that of Ramseur. Thus, at the age of twenty-five, Dod became a brigadier general, the first of our group of six to attain that august rank.

It is noteworthy, as an indication of the steady loss of leadership on both sides, that in that same report of 26 October, Lee reported three of his general officers had been killed and eight others had been wounded and were convalescing. Even so, for Ramseur and all officers in the armies of both sides, elevation to general officer's rank was an undeniable mark of dramatic success in the military profession.[11]

When McClellan left the army, his staff was somewhat adrift. Custer went home to Ohio to await orders, which would take some time. As usual, he returned to Monroe, Michigan, and on Thanksgiving Day was at a party where he was formally introduced to Miss Elizabeth Bacon. Only a few years younger than Custer, Libbie was the beautiful only daughter of a local widower judge, a man who disliked the idea of his daughter socializing with soldiers. But Libbie had other ideas.[12]

In the small town of Monroe, she and Custer had long observed each other at a distance. That Thanksgiving meeting was fascinating to both, and Custer even later told her that was when he first fell for her. It was the start of the romance that would fill his life and, through her person as his widow, prolong his fame long after his death.

But he was also using his time at home to seek the command of the 7th Michigan Cavalry, which was then being formed from volunteers in the state. As a West Point graduate with considerable combat experience, he thought himself perfectly suited to be named colonel of that regiment, for which he earnestly applied.

But this was a political patronage position, most commonly given to the man who had raised the regiment. This was usually an older man who had become an important political personage regionally, which would give him the local prominence necessary to attract young men to the colors. Custer, of course, was only a young man, and even though he was fresh from the front, that gave him no political clout in Michigan.

In addition, the governor was a Republican, and Custer himself was well known to be a Democrat from a Democratic family in Ohio. Although he was able to get a prominent Republican judge to advance his cause to the governor, and a number of general officers to sign letters of support, Custer was still only a young staff officer of no particular personal significance. Consequently, the political line remained impermeable and Custer's informal request for the command was politely refused.

# NINE

## *The Battle of Fredericksburg*

The Union war strategy was in some disarray, but as the new commander of the Army of the Potomac, Burnside decided to move directly south and attack Lee's forces wherever he found them. They were not hiding, and early in December Burnside found them just west of the old colonial town of Fredericksburg on the banks of the Rappahannock River.

The Army of Northern Virginia was arrayed in a strong defensive position on a ridge running parallel to the river and about a mile to its west. The Confederate positions covered a front of perhaps four miles. Jackson and 35,000 men were on the right of the line, with his center on Prospect Hill, and Longstreet with another 35,000 were on the left, atop Marye's Heights. Longstreet's left was pinned to the river while Jackson's right was covered by Stuart's cavalry, which included Pelham's artillery.

On 13 December, after having taken several days to cross, Burnside finally moved his forces forward in two elements. General William Franklin arrayed his 60,000 men a few miles south of town and parallel to the river, facing Prospect Hill. Burnside's original plan called for the main attack to be made by Franklin, while the other 60,000 Union troops under General Edwin Sumner and General Joseph Hooker lay to the north of his and would play a supportive role. Unhappily for the Union, there was to be virtually no coordination between these two attacks.

Franklin's was the first move, and after the heavy fog had lifted between 9:00 and 10:00 a.m., he ordered General George Meade's division forward. Launched against Prospect Hill and supported by the divisions of Abner Doubleday and John Gibbon, this was to be the primary Union attack. Before they stepped out, however, von Borcke had been sent to warn Jackson of this impending attack, to which he responded, "Major, my men have sometimes failed to take a position, but to defend one, never! I am glad the Yankees are coming."[1]

Jackson then gave the order for Stuart's horse artillery to open fire on the enemy's flank immediately.

The Union troops would have to cover perhaps a half mile of open ground, then to attack Confederate defenses concealed in the forest that covered the hillside. When he got the order, Pelham could see Meade's men forming up and preparing for their attack. He begged Stuart to be allowed to advance his two light pieces to the intersection of two roads out in the open, a position on the left front of Meade's formation. From there, he said he would be able to pour a murderous fire into the blue ranks, and Stuart gave him free rein. Pelham immediately went racing out into the open, unlimbered his two guns—a smoothbore Napoleon and a rifled Blakely—and poured a deadly fire into the dense blue columns. Their response was initially paralysis, and then flight, with panic driving the feet of Yankee riflemen. But as the Union commanders struggled to bring order to their units, Pelham kept up his fire. Soon enough, he had stampeded the extreme left of Franklin's army, and terror gripped the men in blue.

Several Union batteries opened up on Pelham, but he was as elusive as he was destructive. He would fire a few shots, then limber up and race fifty or a hundred yards to a new site, unlimber, and open up again. This use of horse-drawn artillery clearly confused and even paralyzed Franklin's entire command, and more Union batteries were brought to bear, with as many as thirty-two guns trying to hit him with a sweeping fire.

But Pelham never even slowed down until the Blakely was hit and disabled by Union artillery fire. He had it drawn off the field, then continued his dance of death, now reduced to one gun and crew. As he continued his fire, members of his crew were increasingly wounded and rode to the rear, so that eventually, each time the gun was unlimbered, he had to dismount and assist in the loading, aiming, and firing of the piece.

Commanders on both sides were stunned in rapt attention as they watched this daring young man and his crew race across the battlefield, fire, then move and fire again, almost taunting the Yankee cannon crews. Stuart sent von Borcke to tell Pelham to retire, but his response was that he could hold his ground and he would only leave the scene when he was out of ammunition. With that brief cry to von Borcke, he was on the move again, racing from place to place, raking the Union lines and preventing their intended attack.

His mobile fire continued to smash through Union formations, bringing bloody havoc to blue ranks, for their artillery just couldn't stop him. Three times the call to retire was repeated, and three times it was ignored. Lee, watching from Marye's Heights, said, "It is glorious to see such courage in one so young." Pelham finally did take his single piece off the field, but only after he had fired his last round at the enemy.[2]

The other guns in Stuart's horse artillery, meanwhile, were adding to Pelham's fire, though from protected positions. Jackson was watching, and, remembering Pelham's splendid behavior at Second Manassas, he sent fourteen more guns forward to help keep up the fire. Pelham had retired from the immediate front of the Union troops and was back within Confederate lines, but he set these guns as well as his own so that fire would be at right angles with that of another fourteen Confederate guns on the ridge. In this way, they made a death trap of the area across which Union troops would have to move if they wanted to attack the Confederate line.

That day, Pelham's battlefield performance was most impressive. His fire had delayed Franklin's attack for a key period of time, and Robert E. Lee spoke of this in his preliminary report:

> General Stuart, with two brigades of cavalry, was posted in the extensive plain on our right. As soon as the advance of the enemy was discovered through the fog, General Stuart, with his accustomed promptness, moved up a section of his horse artillery, which opened with effect upon his flank and drew upon the gallant Pelham a heavy fire, which he sustained unflinchingly for about two hours.[3]

It was an exceptional event when Lee praised anyone below the rank of general in his formal battle reports, so this was high praise indeed. And far from transitory, this story of Pelham's individual bravery was repeated in his formal report, written in April 1863:

> Dense masses appeared before A. P. Hill, stretching far up the river in the direction of Fredericksburg. As they advanced, Major Pelham, of Stuart's Horse Artillery, who was stationed near the Port Royal road with one section, opened a rapid and well-directed enfilade fire, which arrested their progress. Four batteries immediately turned upon him, but he sustained their heavy fire with the unflinching courage that ever distinguished him. Upon his withdrawal, the enemy extended his left down the Port Royal road and his numerous batteries opened with vigor upon Jackson's line.[4]

While Pelham was freezing the Union left, the other half of Burnside's army was still in Fredericksburg. Finally, around 11:00 a.m., with Franklin's force still tied in Pelham's knot, men from French's division under Sumner spilled out of the western side of town. Forming up in the open, they began moving forward to assault Marye's Heights, bristling with Confederate cannon. Between the ridge and town was an open field, and Longstreet's artillery fire covered every inch of it. Marshy terrain prohibited movement by a large force on the northern side of this field, so in order to take the Confederate position, the soldiers in blue had to cross that field.

On the far side of the field from Fredericksburg and at the base of the ridge ran a sunken road, in which was stationed a Georgia brigade. Heavy traffic had lowered the road's level, and a stone retaining wall provided a ready-made trench for these rebel defenders. It ran for about four hundred yards, covering that end of the field. The result, when the Union force attacked, would be a sheet of fire pouring into their ranks.

The first attack was an utter failure, the men in French's division struggling to get even halfway across the open field before being driven back. More divisions, those of Hancock, Oliver O. Howard, and Samuel D. Sturgis, took their turns in the killing field. All were utter failures, leaving behind, as they raced for the rear, serried rows of bleeding blue bodies.

At the southern end of the battle, Franklin's men were long stymied by the thunderous Confederate artillery fire that pounded their ranks. Gradually, counter battery fire began to tell, and Meade got his men across the open area and into the forest. Gibbon's division, on Meade's right, also got across, but the two divisions soon lost contact in the dense woods.

Then a furious counterattack by Jackson's men drove them back down the hill and across the open ground. Some hours later, Jackson even tried to get several of his infantry divisions across that field to attack Franklin's force, which now was pinned against the river, but heavy Union artillery fire held him back. Franklin, however, had been cowed, and his force would take no more significant action that day. Seeing that, Jackson

moved George E. Pickett's division from Prospect Hill to Marye's Heights.

Sumner's corps having tried and failed to take the Confederate stronghold at the base of Marye's Heights, Burnside passed
the duty to Hooker. At around 3:30, Charles Griffin's division
tried the assault, followed by that of Andrew A. Humphreys at
4:00. Neither of these divisions even reached the sunken road,
leaving piled corpses and moaning wounded men in their wake.
The last assault was made by George W. Getty's division at dark,
but with the same bloody result.

On the next day, 14 December, both armies stayed in place
and strengthened their positions. A truce was called for burying
the dead and evacuating the wounded from those blood-soaked
fields, but nothing else happened. Lee no doubt hoped Burnside
would renew his assault on the 15th, but his army had slipped
back across the river during the night of 14–15 December.

After Fredericksburg, there would be no more major battles
in the east for some time, and the Army of Northern Virginia
settled into its winter quarters. That gave Pelham a chance to
get to know William W. Blackford, and though he was not a
West Pointer, they became close. They slept in adjoining tents,
they often ate in each other's company, and their horses were
stabled together. On many evenings they read aloud to each
other from *History of the War in the Peninsula and in the South of
France*, General Sir William Francis Patrick Napier's book on the
Napoleonic Wars from the British perspective. Blackford would
later write a compelling history of his Civil War experiences,
entitled *War Years with Jeb Stuart*, in which he described Pelham:

> There was Pelham, who commanded the horse artillery but who
> always lived at headquarters as a staff officer, as the General [Stuart]
> would not agree for him to do otherwise, for he loved him dearly. Only
> twenty-one or two years old and so innocent looking, so "child-like
> and bland" in the expression of his sparkling blue eyes. . . . He was

*tall, slender, beautifully proportioned and very graceful, a superb rider,*
*and as brave as Julius Caesar.*[5]

Pelham spent most of February 1863 in Fredericksburg,
though he did go to Culpeper with Stuart, where he spent several weeks. On 23 February Lee's chief of artillery, General
William N. Pendleton, asked if Pelham could be promoted to
lieutenant colonel and sent to command a battalion under him.
On 2 March Lee wrote to Jefferson Davis recommending Pelham for promotion to that rank but with him staying in command of Stuart's "flying artillery."[6]

In the middle of March, Stuart went back to Culpeper for a
court-martial and Pelham went with him. Then on 17 March
they were awakened with the news that a Yankee cavalry unit
had crashed across the Rappahannock at Kelley's Ford. Fitzhugh
Lee's troops, though far outnumbered, were fighting valiantly as
they fell back, and by late morning, both sides had artillery firing in their support.

To Pelham, this was a call to play a game he loved, the game
of combat. Dressing hurriedly, he mounted a borrowed horse
and then he and Stuart and a Major Gilmore headed for the
sound of battle, all eager for the fight. Some 2,000 Union cavalry under General William W. Averell had crashed across the
Rappahannock, and pickets from Fitzhugh Lee's brigade raced
to him with the news.

Having a normal strength of about 1,900, the winter had
been hard on the brigade's horses, and more than half the men
were on leave to find new mounts (Confederate cavalrymen
owned their horses). That meant that Lee had available only
about 800 men from the five regiments in his brigade at the
time, the 1st, 2nd, 3rd, 4th, and 5th Virginia cavalry regiments.
Rosser immediately led his 5th in a screaming attack that jolted
the Yankees while Fitzhugh Lee was scrambling for more troops.

When Pelham arrived on the scene of battle, his artillery had not yet come up, though he had sent for it. The most commonly told story of what followed has the 3rd Virginia forming up for attack, and Pelham staying by them or riding with them, standing up in his stirrups, waving his hat or his sword and cheering them on: "Forward! Forward!" But soon after those words left his lips, a Yankee shell exploded above and behind him, and a piece of shrapnel, later said to be the size of the end of one's finger, pierced the back of his head at the hairline. The charge by the 3rd went on as Pelham fell from his horse.[7]

Soldiers ran to his side, and although they could see no wound, he was unconscious. Then Captain Harry Gilmor arrived, and after telling two soldiers to get Pelham back on his horse and take him to the nearest ambulance, he rode off to find Stuart. When he found him, he told him Pelham had been hit, though he knew not where, but he hoped that by this time he would be in an ambulance headed for Culpeper. They still didn't know if he was dead or alive, though both presumed the latter. Even so, they didn't know where in his body or how badly he had been wounded. But the news of Pelham's loss and, God forbid, possible death was stunning to Stuart, who is said to have leaned over his horse's neck and wept.[8]

The fight was fierce as blue and gray riders smashed into each other and recoiled. Death flashed from their pistols, scarlet streaked their sabers. Rosser was seriously wounded, hot blood pulsing through the new hole in his boot, a minié ball lodged in his foot. But he stayed at the front of his regiment, re-forming them, cheering them on, and leading them again and again in charge after charge.[9]

Having found Stuart, Gilmor went back to look for an ambulance and check on Pelham's condition. Unbeknownst to him, the two soldiers had presumed Pelham dead and loaded him across the saddle of his horse like a sack of grain, then started walking toward Culpeper. When Gilmor caught up with them, he had them lay Pelham in the grass and, pressing his ear against Pelham's chest, could still detect a faint heartbeat. Then an ambulance arrived and Gilmor accompanied Pelham into Culpeper.

He was taken to a private home, still breathing but unconscious. Stuart sent three physicians to attend to him, and they discovered that a piece of lead had pierced the back of his head and broken a great deal of bone, but apparently had not injured the brain. Even so, given the medical situation during the Civil War, there was little hope that he would recover. Indeed, he died that night without ever having regained consciousness.

Stuart was devastated, as was his entire command. Though deadly in combat, in the safe rear area Pelham had always seemed to exude a sort of youthful glee despite his surroundings. And now he was gone. With him was also gone his own special spark, a rejuvenating good humor that could always bring cheer to a camp, no matter how solemn the occasion might have been.

Von Borcke was detailed to escort the body to Richmond and make arrangements for it to be further transferred to Pelham's home in Alabama. He was able to find a solid iron coffin, and he had a glass window placed over Pelham's face, that his sweet face might continue to charm and beguile the many Southerners who adored him.

He lay in state for several days in the Confederate Capitol Building in Richmond, and Sallie Dandridge was able to make it through the lines from Martinsburg just to kneel at his coffin and feel herself by his side one last time. In his personal effects was a folded note from a Yankee officer, clearly Custer, that had somehow made it through the lines:

> *After long silence, I write. God bless you, dear Pelham; I am proud of your success. G.A.C.*[10]

On 20 March, Stuart published General Orders No. 9, formally announcing Pelham's death to the men of his cavalry division:

*The memory of "the Gallant Pelham," his many manly virtues, his noble nature and purity of character, are enshrined as a sacred legacy in the hearts of all who knew him. His record has been bright and spotless, his career brilliant and successful. He fell the noblest of sacrifices on the altar of his country, to whose glorious service he had dedicated his life from the beginning of the war. In token of respect for his cherished memory, the Horse Artillery and division staff will wear the military badge of mourning for thirty days, and the senior officer of staff, Major Von Borcke will place his remains in the hands of his bereaved family, to whom is tendered in behalf of the division the assurance of heartfelt sympathy in this deep tribulation.[11]*

Written in camp soon after Pelham's death by John Esten Cooke, one of his friends and a staff officer for Stuart, is another plaint, this one more personal:

*To him who writes these lines, the death of this noble youth has been inexpressibly saddening. It has cast a shadow on the very sunlight, and the world seems, somehow, colder and more dreary since he went away. It was but yesterday almost that he was in his tent, and I looked into his frank, brave eyes, and heard his kind, honest voice. . . . All who knew him loved him for his gay, sweet temper, as they admired him for his unshrinking courage. . . . "Pelham is dead!" It is only another way of saying "honour is dead! Courage is dead! Modesty, kindness, courtesy, the inborn spirit of the true and perfect gentleman, the nerve of the soldier, the gaiety of the good companion, the kindly heart, and the resolute soul—all dead and never more to visit us in his person!"[12]*

A train carried him home in solemn state. After crossing the state border, it stopped at every station so that the many Alabama women of all ages who were still in Pelham's thrall could come aboard and place flowers on his coffin. Then came his last stop, where his mother held him in her arms and wept. Then the family buried him in the small cemetery of Jacksonville, Alabama. The Gallant Pelham had finally come home.[13]

Rosser's wounding was to have a happier outcome for him. Back at Kelley's Ford that day in March, after an afternoon of fighting and killing, General Averell's force of Union cavalry withdrew across the ford in early evening. The bullet was removed from Rosser's foot and he somehow was able to avoid infection. However, he needed to rest and recover, and that meant he would not rejoin his unit until 12 May. But he had other things in mind for May.

Earlier in the war, Rosser and several other young officers had ridden past a big house in front of which two young boys stared at them in awe. It was a hot day, so Rosser called out to one of them, who told him his name was Will Winston. Rosser then said that if Will would bring him a drink of water, he would come back someday "and marry your sister!" Will ran and got the water, and then the men rode on. A year or so later, Rosser was again in the area, and, hoping to borrow a pen and ink, he knocked on the front door of a large house that he did not consciously remember. Yet it was the same house, and the door was opened by a wide-eyed Will, who went running back into the house, yelling for his sister: "Sis Betty! Sis Betty! Here's that man come to marry you!"

Sis Betty turned out to be a charming nineteen-year-old beauty, and Rosser was smitten. He began to court her whenever he could get away from the war, with letters filling the long stretches when he couldn't.

His wound healed, he rejoined the 5th Virginia on 12 May, and on 28 May 1863, he and Betty were married. The wedding was attended by Generals J. E. B. Stuart and Fitzhugh Lee, and many staff officers as well, including Major Heros von Borcke. And fittingly, their maid of honor was Sallie Dandridge.[14]

# TEN

## *Battle of Chancellorsville*

At the end of October 1862, Ramseur had gone to Richmond in hopes of finding the best medical treatment for his mangled arm, treatment that he hoped would end the pain and partial paralysis. This meant he was in town on 1 November 1862, when Confederate secretary of war George W. Randolph signed the orders promoting him to general officer.

He was enormously gratified by this formal recognition of his martial competence, and very pleased indeed to have reached the high rank of general at the tender age of twenty-five. Still, Dod knew and understood the gravity of this promotion and the increased responsibilities it meant.

Old friends, particularly from his regiment, the 49th North Carolina, were quick to congratulate him, many of them hoping they might be able to serve under his command. But still in need of further rest for his wound, he went back home to North Carolina in mid-November. Further improvement in the condition of his arm was his primary goal, and that was most important. But now there was someone else who added spice to his life.

From the day he was evacuated from the battle, his wound,

though painful, could be bandaged and so concealed. Consequently, he had long been able to travel and maintain some sort of social life. Early in his convalescence, therefore, he had traveled to the small town of Milton, North Carolina, where his cousin Ellen Richmond lived with her father on his estate, known as Woodside. Though he had not seen her in many years, she had, as he expected, grown into a beautiful young woman.

He was nearly three years older than she, but any differences melted away when they met again, though in many ways it was for the first time. It may be hard for some to accept the concept of "love at first sight," particularly since the two had known each other many years earlier. But however it is described, the relationship that sprang up between them was that sudden and dramatic. Dod extended his stay at Woodside and, not surprisingly, very soon realized that he had fallen in love with her. To his great joy, she told him that she had also fallen in love with him.

In largely rural America of the time, travel and communication were seriously constrained, and important decisions often had to be made within a short span of time or even on the spot. These limitations of time and space also meant that letters were often the sole contact between people over extended periods. They carried, therefore, much more meaning and value than they have since high technology has largely obliterated their importance for spanning vast distances with written words.

But love letters have always been love letters, the carefully crafted specification of inner passions. Still, during the Civil War, time was short for extended romances before marriage, and there was generally no room for either party to play coy, as there was simply too much at risk. Some letters Dod sent to Nellie that Christmas unveiled his true feelings when he called her "the source of all my joys, how infinitely much I owe to you, how inexpressibly much I love you for all this newfound happiness" or wrote "Every day I love you more fondly and more devotedly, the sentiment fills every corner of my heart until it has become as essential to my happiness as the heart is to existence."[1]

Any wound suffered by a soldier during the Civil War was automatically a major threat to his life. This was before the discovery of antibiotics, of course, and the capabilities of medical treatment in general were quite limited. That meant that if a bullet, a bayonet, or a piece of artillery shrapnel pierced the trunk of a man's body or his skull, those were basically untreatable wounds and almost certainly meant death, often slow and agonizing.

A similar wound to a soldier's arm or leg, given the general lack of cleanliness in a soldier's life, almost always required amputation. But after the amputation had been performed, the stump had to be seared with a hot iron, which sterilized it and so stopped the spread of infection. Infection, however, was only part of the risk, for amputation was a major shock to the body that was often lethal all by itself.

Indeed, roughly half the amputations during the Civil War resulted in death, including that of Stonewall Jackson. It is widely known that he was accidentally hit in the arm by rifle fire from his own men during the battle of Chancellorsville. But he did not die from his wounds. Rather, his death was brought on by what was described at the time as pneumonia, but has more recently been assessed as a pulmonary embolism, a blood clot that traveled from his amputation site to his lungs and killed him.[2]

Ramseur's wound had been cleaned, dressed, and bandaged, and he was fortunate to avoid infection. By January 1863, he had recovered enough that he was able to join the brigade he had been named to command in their winter camp at Fredericksburg, Virginia. Consisting of the 2nd, 4th, 14th, and 30th North

Carolina Infantry Regiments, they had been commanded since the battle of Antietam by Colonel Bryan Grimes of the 4th. Since the fatal wounding at that battle of their previous commander, General George Anderson, Ramseur thought they had lost much of the organization, dedication, and esprit their former commander had instilled in them. But Ramseur was confident that, with a little hard work, they would soon be in "fine fighting trim" before they were attacked by General "Fightin' Joe" Hooker, the new commander of the Army of the Potomac.[3]

Ramseur drilled his men hard through winter and early spring, but while they spent long, boring hours on picket duty, he had most evenings free. The result was almost a deluge of letters to his one true love. He spoke of their time together at Woodside, and he shared his dreams with her of their future together when he might be stationed as a Confederate officer in an eastern caserne or perhaps even somewhere in the West. He was desperately in love, and he pleaded with her to marry him the next summer rather than waiting until the end of the war.[4]

His letters were filled with political commentary on everything from condemnations of Lincoln to his distress with the thoughtless or evil ways in which the countryside of Virginia was being devastated by the wicked Yankees. But the leitmotif to which he always returned was his undying love for her and his desperate longing to be with her.

Then on 27 April, a large portion of Hooker's army simply disappeared and was later reported by Confederate agents to be moving north along the Rappahannock. Earlier that month, Wesley Merritt had been picked up on the staff of General George Stoneman, commander of Hooker's cavalry corps. On 29 April Stoneman had been sent on a deep cavalry raid to destroy Confederate communications, leaving only one brigade with the Army of the Potomac to perform reconnaissance duties. Hooker had intended to draw Lee's entire army west to defend against this cavalry move, and then cross the river and hit him from behind. But as Stoneman delayed and dithered, Hooker realized that his plan was not going to work.

The cavalry raid did go deep into Confederate territory, but it was to be largely a failure. Merritt distinguished himself by leading a party of some fifty men to burn bridges on the South Anna River, which he did with dash and courage. However, the raid deprived Hooker of most of his cavalry for the looming battle, although, given the terrain, their absence was to make little difference in its outcome.

Hooker was a smart man, and seeing that his original plan would not have its desired effect, he soon devised a better one. He decided to move far upstream to the northwest with 70,000 men, cross the river, and then move southeast to hit Lee from the rear. Meanwhile, his other 40,000 men, under General John Sedgwick, were to cross the river at or near Fredericksburg and attack Lee's defenses frontally. Trapped between these two massive armies, Lee would surely be crushed. But as Army of the Potomac commanders before him had repeatedly done, Hooker badly underestimated Lee.

When he heard earlier that the Union had loaded its XI Corps on steamers at Hampton Roads, Lee had detached Longstreet with two divisions to protect the Virginia-Carolina coast. Now, when Fightin' Joe and most of his immense army had disappeared, Lee carefully studied his map and soon determined what Hooker's plan must be. If he made a long, roundabout march and then reappeared from the north or west, say, Lee would find himself trapped between two armies and at a major numerical disadvantage. But Lee had neither the time nor the inclination to wait on Hooker.

Little more than one large brick house at a road intersection, Chancellorsville was in the middle of an area known as "the Wilderness." This was a genuine tangle of second-growth oak and pine, with thick undergrowth that made passage off the roads very difficult for individuals and virtually impossible for vehicles or any formation of troops. Adding to its impenetrability, it was crisscrossed by swampy brooks, and the only high ground in the area was known as Hazel Grove, less than a mile southwest of Chancellorsville. In case of battle, the terrain would give a decided advantage to defenders, for neither cavalry nor artillery could be used with any effect.

On 29 April Lee heard from Stuart that a large Union force had crossed the Rappahannock at Kelley's Ford, some eighteen miles upriver to the northwest from Fredericksburg. Though Lee did not know it at the time, this was Hooker with 54,000 men, and they immediately began to move southeast. Suspecting he had guessed right, Lee sent Anderson's division west as a stopgap measure while he tried to further determine Yankee plans through intensive cavalry reconnaissance.[5]

On 30 April another 20,000 Union soldiers crossed at U.S. Ford, only six miles upstream from town, and joined Hooker. Now he had more than 70,000 men approaching Chancellorsville from the northwest while another 40,000 were crossing the river a few miles south of Fredericksburg and threatening the Confederate positions there. Hooker's vise was starting to close.

That day, Lee heard from Anderson's division near Chancellorsville that a large Union army was advancing on them and pushing them back. Still entrenched in strong positions on high ground, Lee immediately saw that the force closing on Chancellorsville was the more serious threat, and he gave orders for 43,000 of his men—including Ramseur's brigade in Robert E. Rodes's division—to move west and defeat this blue army in the Wilderness. To hold off Sedgwick, he left Early behind with 10,000 men spread out on the high ground west of the river, much of it the same high ground that Lee's army had occupied during the battle of Fredericksburg only months earlier.

As Hooker moved forward, intending to attack Lee's rear, his one brigade of cavalry was simply unable to penetrate Stuart's mounted screen. That meant he was moving forward blind, with no idea of what Confederate forces lay before him. But his numbers were so great that he was not deterred by this in the slightest, and he moved forward confidently in three strong columns.

Two of these columns pushed past Chancellorsville, with the XI and XII Corps under Howard and Henry W. Slocum moving southeast on the Plank Road and the II and V Corps under Hancock and George Sykes heading in a more easterly direction on the turnpike. The third column under Meade, meanwhile, moved along the south side of the river and, meeting no resistance, had soon flanked Lee's army without realizing it. But in late morning Jackson's men, moving west on the Plank Road to join Anderson, ran into Slocum's XII Corps while still two or three miles short of Chancellorsville.

Two brigades from Anderson's Confederate division were driven back by the men in blue, and Jackson told Rodes to send another brigade forward. He sent that of Ramseur, and his brigade slammed into the Union advance party. These Union soldiers were then hurled back in some confusion, and Ramseur's men drove them hard, capturing arms and baggage for as much as two miles. He drove his men forward until about 6:00 p.m., when they confronted a larger force deployed before them. But Ramseur simply deployed his artillery to pour grapeshot through the trees as his men continued their advance. Finally, as dark set in, they stopped, put out a strong picket line, and slept on their arms.[6]

That night Hooker's courage seems to have failed him. Anxious about these aggressive Confederate columns attacking from the east, he called all his troops back into a defensive position around Chancellorsville. There, they built strong defenses based on log breastworks and other obstacles.

Lee's forces had followed Hooker's men as they withdrew, ever suspicious they might fall into some sort of trap. But on 1 May, Lee realized that Hooker had simply quailed. Ever aggressive, he deployed his forces into positions facing Hooker's line but soon realized that he could never overcome this much larger Union army. Time was of the essence here, and he sent out reconnaissance parties, hoping to find a weakness in Hooker's line. Then Stuart arrived with the news that Hooker's right was wide open, suspended "in air," and could easily be attacked and turned. This was good news to Lee, and he used it to make his plan.

That night he ordered Jackson to take 26,000 men and make a wide circular march of some fourteen miles around the Union right. Once in position, he would array his troops in a long north–south line and then smash it into the exposed and unsuspecting Union right flank.

While Jackson was doing that, Lee would use the remaining 17,000 under his command to keep Hooker engaged in their present positions. And to carry this off, Lee could only hope that Early's 10,000 outside of Fredericksburg would not be attacked by Sedgwick's 40,000, for that would be a crushing blow from which they would not have much hope of recovery.

On 2 May, Jackson's men moved out at dawn, marching southwest at first before looping out to the west and then north to get behind Hooker's line. This was a risky move, for it divided Lee's army into three parts, each out of supporting distance of the other two. But Lee was willing to gamble, for he knew that the Confederacy's only hope of survival against a vastly superior Union army lay in such high-risk moves.

Several Union pickets detected Jackson's move and relayed the word up their chain of command. Sickles got permission from Hooker to send parties out on reconnaissance, which he converted into attacks. These did some damage but could not stop Jackson's column. Hooker interpreted this as a retreat to the south and west, and he gave orders to prepare a pursuit, though nothing came of that during the afternoon.

Jackson had his troops in place on the Union right flank by

midafternoon, but the heavy brush delayed his reorganization into an attack line. That portion of the Union line was occupied by Howard's XI Corps, and many of his officers reported a large Confederate force on their right flank. But Howard apparently didn't believe them, for he simply ignored these warnings.

Then, at around 6:00 p.m.—this was before daylight savings time and about two hours before dark—rabbits and foxes and even deer suddenly came streaming from the west and bounded through the XI Corps camps, startling the Union soldiers. Most of them had just stacked their rifles for supper, and before they could understand what was happening, Jackson's men exploded out of the woods on a front more than a mile wide and several divisions deep. With the blood-curdling rebel yell echoing before them, the gray line smashed into the open blue flank, shooting and bayoneting the stunned Yankees who didn't run.

The surprise was total, and pandemonium quickly set in. Those who didn't run faced certain death, and their panic was contagious as they ran headlong through the thick underbrush. One brigade in rifle pits facing west was able to stop Jackson's center, but as soon as they were flanked at both ends, they climbed out of their defensive positions and joined the panicked retreat.[7]

Ramseur's brigade was part of Rodes's division, on the southern end of the front echelon and covering the right flank of Alfred H. Colquitt's brigade. They moved forward steadily, capturing hundreds of prisoners as they overwhelmed Union breastworks. Two quickly planned counterattack efforts were made, but after brief pauses Ramseur's men repelled them and drove on. They kept moving until dark, then again slept on their arms.[8]

As the sky darkened, Stonewall Jackson had moved forward with a few staff officers, looking for a way they could deny use of U.S. Ford to their enemy. Upon his return, he was fired upon by nervous Confederate pickets, grievously wounding him in the arm. He was evacuated from the field in an ambulance and his arm was amputated just below the shoulder. But the shock was too great, and, given the rudimentary nature of medical treatment, he died on 10 May.

Within Southern ranks, however, Jackson's wounding was considered little more than a rumor that night and next day, and it did not even slow the headlong advance of his men. But Jackson was gone from the field, and on 3 May Stuart took command of Jackson's corps. At first light, the divisions of Rodes, Raleigh E. Colston, and Henry Heth continued their attack from the west while the divisions of Lafayette McLaws and Richard H. Anderson, who had stayed in position with Lee, attacked from south and east.

Once his men had taken Hazel Grove, Stuart recognized its importance and placed forty artillery pieces on it. From there, they were able to pour a deadly cannon fire into the Union positions that were formed in a giant teardrop shape below them while Confederate infantry assailed them on the ground. But the Union defenses had solidified and the first such attacks were rejected. When Rodes's division came forward, it deployed on both sides of the turnpike, and the thick underbrush and the noise of battle made control of these men very difficult.

Ramseur's brigade in that division moved forward together on the road. But then his men were blocked by Confederate troops whose attack had been repelled earlier, many of their officers dead or wounded or mysteriously absent. They cowered in captured Union entrenchments, and they refused to advance or even move aside.

Ramseur tried first to reason with them, then to plead with them, and finally to order them, but all to no avail. Frustrated, he found Stuart and asked if he could move through them or over them. Stuart encouraged him to do so, and he went back to his men, where he shouted, "Forward march!" At that word, his North Carolinians pushed through the milling throng and eagerly went over the top. They stepped into a true hail of gunfire, but as men were hit and went down, the rest simply closed ranks and pressed forward resolutely.

At the same time, two other brigades from Rodes's division also advanced, but all of them into a barrage of deadly bullets. Eventually, the Confederate advance was stopped, but not rejected. Then, at about 9:30 a.m., Hooker sent word to his men to pull back to prepared positions a mile north of Chancellorsville. Because of that, the Union forces in front of Rodes's division and the rest of Stuart's command suddenly withdrew. So in an abrupt move, and after a fierce morning of fighting, the rebel army had won control of Chancellorsville as their blue adversaries disappeared into the Wilderness to their north.[9]

By nightfall Hooker had established a semicircular perimeter more than three miles long and descending to within a mile or so north of Chancellorsville, with both ends tied to the Rappahannock River behind them. But there was now great danger to Lee looming in the east. Having acted a bit late, Sedgwick had burst through Early's defense and was heading west to join the fight.

By now Hooker had been thoroughly cowed, and his men huddled in their strong defenses with no thought of offensive action. On 4 May, therefore, Lee left Stuart with four divisions of 25,000 men to cover Hooker's 75,000. He then headed back east with his other two divisions, totaling perhaps 12,000 men. He reunited with Early, and their combined force of 21,000 trapped Sedgwick on three sides against the Rappahannock. But confusion and fog delayed the attack that would have captured or destroyed Sedgwick, and, during the night, his blue army slipped across the river on a pontoon bridge brought up that day.

Lee turned back toward Chancellorsville on 5 May, intending to overwhelm Hooker, despite the fact that he was far outnumbered. But on the night of 5–6 May, Hooker also pulled his troops back across the river, leaving Lee in possession of the battleground after what many have called his greatest victory.

During the battle, Ramseur's brigade suffered heavy casualties, with 151 men killed, 529 wounded, and 151 missing or captured.[10] Ramseur was himself one of those wounded, but he remained with his command throughout the fight.[11] As A. P. Hill said in his report, "Ramseur's brigade, under his gallant leadership, was conspicuous throughout the three days' fighting."[12] Later he was taken to Richmond, where his wound was treated. He then went back to North Carolina for his convalescence and was able to spend much of that time in the company of his one true love, Nellie. But those precious days flew by, and on 20 May he rejoined his unit.[13]

On 6 May Lee had been bitterly disappointed when he learned that Hooker had been able to cross the Rappahannock with the remaining 75,000 men in the Army of the Potomac and thus get away. He had very much wanted to crush Hooker's army and so, with his victorious army poised within reach of a defenseless Washington, win the war for the Confederacy. And delivering such a crushing defeat on the main Union army in the east remained his goal.

On 22 May Hooker relieved Stoneman of command and replaced him with General Alfred Pleasonton. Merritt stayed on the new commander's staff, and he was soon delighted to find that another staff member serving with him was Custer. Though spirits were down generally in the Army of the Potomac after Chancellorsville, this reunion was a source of great pleasure for the two old friends.

In the wake of Chancellorsville, Lee had been able to convince Jefferson Davis and members of his cabinet that the best next move would be for him to lead the Army of Northern Virginia north into Pennsylvania. In a report he wrote on 31 July, he explained his justifications for this:

It would force the Army of the Potomac to withdraw from their positions across the Rappahannock River from Fredericksburg.

It would force the Union army to withdraw from the Shenandoah Valley.

It would take the initiative away from Hooker and disrupt any plans he might be making for operations in Virginia that summer.

It would transfer the major fighting in the east out of Virginia and north of the Potomac River.

It was hoped it would require Union troops to be removed from other parts of the country and brought east to defend against Lee.

And finally, it might offer an opportunity for Lee to "strike a blow at the army then commanded by General Hooker."[14]

This last reason was really at the heart of Lee's operations throughout the war. In his mind it was not enough for him to defeat a Union army and drive it away, for with their superior numbers and resources, that army could be refurbished and strengthened with reinforcements, then return to the field to give battle once again. But if he could corner and destroy the Army of the Potomac, then there would be no Union armed force of any significance left between the Army of Northern Virginia and the capital city of Washington. This, a crushing victory over the Army of the Potomac, was the most expeditious way he saw in which the Confederacy might win its war for independence outright.

On 27 June, with most of the Army of Northern Virginia in

Pennsylvania and in the belief that Hooker and the Army of the Potomac were still south of the Potomac, Lee said the following to Confederate general Isaac Trimble:

> *When they hear where we are, they will make forced marches. . . . They will come up, probably through Frederick, broken down with hunger and hard marching, strung out on a long line and much demoralized, when they come into Pennsylvania, I shall throw an overwhelming force on their advance, crush it, follow up the success, drive one corps back on another, and by successive repulses and surprises, before they can concentrate, create a panic and virtually destroy the army . . . we shall fight a great battle, and if God gives us the victory, the war will be over and we shall achieve the recognition of our independence.*[15]

With Jackson gone, Lee decided to reorganize his army into three corps. The I Corps remained under the command of General Longstreet, while the new II Corps and III Corps were led by General Richard Ewell and General A. P. Hill respectively. The three new corps would consist of three infantry divisions each, and artillery forces were distributed to their commanders individually while Lee retained personal control over his eight cavalry brigades under General J. E. B. Stuart. On paper, Lee had about 80,000 men under his command, but on 30 June, just before the battle of Gettysburg, he had only some 70,000 men present for duty.

The movement north started in early June, and on the 8th of that month, the I Corps under Longstreet and II Corps under Ewell had both gotten to Culpeper Courthouse while the III Corps under A. P. Hill had stayed outside of Fredericksburg. Lee wanted the Yankees to think that the entire Army of Northern Virginia was still there, when in fact two-thirds of it was already thirty miles away and headed across the Blue Ridge Mountains into the Shenandoah Valley.

Stuart and his cavalry were also east of Culpeper, and reports to Hooker indicated that Lee might be moving his forces north. To investigate this, at dawn on 9 June some 10,000 Union horsemen were sent across the Rappahannock at Beverly and Kelley's fords.[16]

Captains Custer and Merritt and another staff officer named Elon Farnsworth, it is important to understand, were often the bearers of orders to subordinate units. This meant that when they spoke, it was with the authority of their commanding officer, General Pleasonton. For instance, if Custer had been sent by Pleasonton to tell a given division commander to advance, retire, or stay in place, his directions were heard as those of the commanding general and were obeyed as such.

Such staff officer duties were not always as simple as they may sound, particularly in the midst of combat. But both Custer and Merritt truly relished fighting, so for them, carrying a message forward in combat was a delight. And there was sometimes much more direct engagement in operations expected of them as the eyes and ears of the commanding general.

In the lull after Chancellorsville, while the Army of the Potomac hesitated in fear of Lee, the Army of Northern Virginia was resting, recovering, rearming, and undergoing significant reorganization. In addition to restructuring his force into three corps and filling their ranks with soldiers drawn from other regions of the Confederacy, Lee was also careful to augment Stuart's cavalry as much as he could before moving into Pennsylvania. Brigades were brought in from the Shenandoah Valley and North Carolina, and suddenly Stuart had more than 9,500 horsemen under his command.

Through the month of May, Stuart drilled his new force relentlessly, and on 22 May held a grand review for three of his brigades at Brandy Station, a small railroad depot between Culpeper and the Rappahannock River. He was very pleased by that, but it wasn't enough, so on 5 June he held another review, to which he invited Lee. Although trainloads of civilians did come from Richmond and elsewhere to watch the show, Lee was unable to attend. Nevertheless, on the morning of the 5th, Stuart had his guests assembled on the slopes of Fleetwood Hill near Brandy Station. From there, they beheld his nearly 10,000 horsemen arrayed in a great field below them.

When all was ready, Stuart personally galloped along their line with his staff. Then he came back up on Fleetwood Hill, and, as bands played, the brigades passed in review several times below the spectators. They started at a walk, then a trot, and finally a gallop. As they spurred their horses forward this last time, the men in gray all raised their sabers and emitted a rebel yell that might have raised the dead. Then they wheeled off in formation, and each brigade charged in mock combat against prepositioned artillery pieces that fired blank rounds. Color, glamour, pageantry—they had it all, and as word spread, Stuart's fame and luster in Southern cities mushroomed.

That evening, Stuart hosted a grand ball attended by his officers and many of the ladies who had come as spectators. While they danced, however, many of his enlisted men tending their horses grumbled about Stuart's wearing out men and horseflesh for meaningless pomp. But they were able to sleep undisturbed by the war that night, and any such rest they got was gratefully received.

The ceremonial display was such a great success, in fact, that on 7 June, Lee sent word to Stuart that he would be pleased to attend a repeat performance the next day. The proper arrangements were made and on the morning of 8 June, the show was repeated. But this time, instead of a hill covered with male and female spectators, their place was occupied by the 10,000 Confederate infantrymen that Hood had brought with him. There was nothing else in the way of entertainment available to them, and all loved the show.

The men who performed in it, however, were worn out, as

were their horses. To their relief, they were allowed to sleep on their arms that night in the fields around Brandy Station. But this time many of them felt as exhausted as if they had fought in a major battle.[17]

Rosser rode in both reviews, but after the 8 June performance, he was sent off on picket duty in the Warrenton area. If he had known when he left that night that he would miss a full day of pitched battle between the largest cavalry forces on either side, he would surely have protested. But as it was, he simply wasn't there.

In early June, Hooker did not know Lee's intentions. He did know, however, that Stuart's cavalry was assembled near Brandy Station, a mass of horsemen that might even be as large as his own. He didn't know why they were there, and he suspected something else was afoot. He therefore quietly assembled his own cavalry under Pleasonton nearby, though north of the Rappahannock, and ordered Pleasonton to cross the river with his large cavalry and infantry force at two fords on the morning of 9 June. Once on the southern side of the water, his orders were to attack Stuart's men in their camps.[18]

And so it was that, at dawn on 9 June 1863, the 8th New York Cavalry crashed through the Confederate pickets at Beverly Ford. In his customarily fearless fashion, Custer, as Pleasonton's personal representative, led the way. This was the lead regiment of a brigade commanded by Colonel Benjamin Davis.

Once having driven in or killed the pickets, they charged through open fields, shooting at Stuart's men as they galloped over them. Totally surprised, many men in gray were caught still asleep on the ground. But they were all brusquely awakened to what must have seemed to be their worst nightmare ever.[19]

This was the beginning of what would be the largest cavalry fight of the war, with the Union sending about 11,000 horsemen supported by 3,000 infantry across the Rappahannock to engage some 9,500 Confederates. The Union infantry would be little engaged, and the fight would take place over miles of open terrain, ideal cavalry country that consisted mostly of open fields with stone walls dividing them. And with control of ground almost constantly changing, the engagement would last the whole day long.

With the initial noise of battle at two fords, word quickly spread through rebel ranks of the Yankees' arrival in force. But there were just too many blue riders racing into their ranks at the outset, and Stuart's horsemen, trying desperately to saddle their horses and form up, were pushed back quite some distance, lucky at that point just to stay alive.

Soon enough, however, Confederate companies and squadrons had recovered and were counterattacking these brazen intruders. Now two mounted forces of roughly the same size were heavily engaged, and the fighting went back and forth. This was very serious business, of course, and soon enough Colonel Davis was killed.

But Custer quickly assumed command of the entire brigade, made up of the 8th New York as well as the 8th Illinois and the 3rd Indiana, and he led them in a ferocious charge that scattered gray horsemen before them. At the end of such a successful charge, cavalrymen slow their momentum and often tend to become disorganized, whether by obstacles or unfamiliar terrain. If that happens, they suddenly become vulnerable to a counterattack.

In this case, there was not yet enough organization in Confederate ranks for such a feat. Rather, the men in blue found themselves increasingly surrounded by a mass of gray horsemen arriving on the scene, their number growing all the time. But Custer was not one to hesitate. He immediately turned the brigade around and led them in another violent saber charge that broke through the Confederate horsemen and reached safety with their blue brethren. Now clearly in his element, Custer was to lead a number of other charges throughout the day.[20]

Back in Washington, Merritt had been able to maneuver himself so that he returned to a fighting unit, and he was also there. Though only a captain, he found himself in command of the 2nd U.S. Cavalry Regiment, with which he had served before the war when it had been called the 2nd Dragoon Regiment. After crossing at Beverly Ford, he and his men spent an hour or more chasing and banging sabers with recently awakened Confederate horsemen who were milling around with little organization. Confusion reigned in most Confederate units as more and more men in blue kept pouring across the river and smashing their way forward.

Then, about two miles from the ford, the Confederates drew up a line of artillery and brought the Yankees under fire. Union guns were brought up, and Merritt and his regiment were detailed to guard them for the better part of an hour. By that time two other Union cavalry regiments, having charged and been rebuffed, were retreating across the front of the Confederate guns, which opened on them. Seeing this, Merritt led his men in their direction. But the Confederate artillerymen saw them coming with enough time to limber up and get away before the blue horsemen could reach them.

Pleasonton had ordered half his force to cross the Rappahannock at Beverly Ford and the other half at Kelley's Ford, two miles to the south. Because of fog, misdirection, and poor leadership, the half crossing at Kelley's Ford did not join the battle for several hours. Stuart's headquarters was atop Fleetwood Hill, and in late morning he watched his men off to his east counterattacking the Union troops who had come across at Beverly. Then columns of Union cavalry that had been delayed before crossing at Kelley's Ford came bursting out of the woods to his south and caught him unawares.

He had only a few men and one artillery piece on top of Fleetwood, and a few rounds from that gun stopped the Union horsemen while he called for reinforcements. But after a pause,

the Yankees charged, drove Stuart off the hill, and took control of it.

In response to Stuart's call for help, Confederate cavalry regiments to his east came racing to the rescue, and they soon took
back the hill crowned by their commander's headquarters tents.
Control of this key bit of terrain was to change hands several
times during that day's fight. But as the gray lines before him
had thinned, General Buford, commander of the Union forces
that had crossed at Beverly, called on his men for one last effort
to burst through.

He sent four infantry regiments in first, and they drove a
wedge through the only line of foot soldiers, these dismounted
rebel cavalry. The 6th Pennsylvania Cavalry flooded through
this opening, but the 9th Virginia had been held back for just
such an event. Now released, they slammed into the Pennsylvania men, driving them back into Union lines.[21]

This was to be Merritt's moment as he led his 2nd U.S. Cavalry in the charge of his life. They crashed into the flank of
the 9th Virginia, and the combat dissolved into swirling individual pistol and saber fights that were often little more than
personal duels. After emptying his pistol, Merritt drew his saber
and slashed wildly. Then, suddenly, he and one of his lieutenants found themselves alone facing several senior Confederate
officers.

He and the lieutenant had somehow been separated from
their men, and though he heard a voice crying "Kill the damned
Yankee!" Merritt never lost his brazen panache. Pointing his
saber at the senior officer, he spurred his horse forward while
yelling, "Colonel, you are my prisoner!"

Probably a Confederate brigade commander and a general
rather than a colonel, the man answered, "The hell I am!" and
swung his own saber at Merritt's head. While he was able to
raise his own blade enough to partially parry the blow, it still cut
through his hat and sliced his scalp. Other rebels then opened

fire on him and his lieutenant, but they missed, and the two Yankees were able to burst through their adversaries and make it back to the 2nd U.S., then in the process of withdrawing to Union lines. Though Merritt's head wound bled heavily, his skull was not damaged and it was soon bandaged, only briefly causing him to leave the field.[22]

The fighting flowed back and forth across the fields all day with neither side able to wrest full control of the fields from the other. Finally, in late afternoon, Rodes sent part of his division forward to help Stuart, including Ramseur and his brigade. But Union soldiers saw them coming, and as they sent word to Pleasonton that a large Confederate infantry force was approaching, he decided to pull his men back across the river.[23]

Pleasonton heard from his subordinates of the great courage both Merritt and Custer had shown on the field of battle, and he had even watched parts of their action himself. Both men had not only fought like demons, but they had also been great inspirations to the men they led, and Pleasonton was very proud of them. Several of his older brigade commanders had shown their hesitance and weak leadership that day, and he needed some young, courageous generals to command his men if they were to win battles. The performance of Merritt and Custer that day would be a major factor in his decision, within only a few weeks, to recommend each man for promotion to brigadier general and command of a cavalry brigade in the Army of the Potomac.

The Union force withdrew from the fields of Brandy Station in good order, and although they didn't defeat Stuart, neither were they themselves defeated. They never learned that Lee was massing his forces in Culpeper in preparation for his move north, but this was the first time Union cavalry had been able to hold its own against Stuart and his "Invincibles." It was a strong indication that the cavalry tables had begun to turn, and their performance in this battle was to be a great source of pride among Union horsemen for the rest of the war.

Stuart was then assigned to keep the curious Yankees away from the passes through the Blue Ridge and so deny them knowledge of Lee's Army of Northern Virginia moving north along the Shenandoah Valley. There were thus sequential cavalry clashes over the next few weeks at Aldie, Middleburg, and Upperville, Virginia, and Custer and Merritt were both heavily involved. Custer was only an aide to Pleasonton, but Merritt still commanded the 2nd U.S. Cavalry Regiment, and both men's fighting skills and raw courage were widely noted. Although Stuart's horsemen were able to hold off their Yankee counterparts in these fights, Union infantry was eventually brought up and this combination of mounted and foot soldiers steadily pushed Stuart's men back.[24]

On 21 June Pleasonton's men drove Confederate cavalry out of Upperville at the base of the Blue Ridge Mountains, but they were unable to get through Ashby's Gap, now defended by rebel infantry as well as cavalry. However, a company of the 8th New York claimed to have used back roads and cross-country movement to reach the crest of the mountains north of Ashby's Gap.

What they did or didn't see has always been open to question, but Pleasonton reported to Hooker that Lee was moving north down the Shenandoah and was prepared to move north across the Potomac River. Pleasonton then withdrew his force and rejoined the Army of the Potomac.[25]

# ELEVEN

## *The Battle of Gettysburg*

After the cavalry clash at Brandy Station, Lee continued to move his troops north into the Shenandoah Valley. Ewell's II Corps was in the lead, and Albert G. Jenkins's cavalry rode with him. On 14 June Rodes's division moved nineteen miles in a very fatiguing march, finally stopping near Martinsburg, Virginia, in late afternoon. They were within ten miles of the Potomac, and a Union brigade was drawn up in battle formation outside of town with cavalry, infantry, and artillery forces prepared for mutual support. Rodes then asked the Union commander to surrender, a request he refused.

Rodes then arrayed his own cavalry and artillery units on both sides of town. When the infantry finally came up in the center, he put them in position for attack. He then ordered Ramseur to "advance with speed upon the enemy's position" and drive the Yankees from Martinsburg. But once Ramseur's men got moving, the Union brigade collapsed before them. At nearly a run, they chased the Yankees for two miles beyond the edge of town, capturing five artillery pieces with plentiful ammunition and six thousand bushels of "fine grain."

On 15 June Rodes's division crossed the Potomac at Williamsport and rested there for three days while Jenkins's cavalry scoured the countryside for livestock, food, gunpowder, and other necessities. The private owners of these goods were either paid (in Confederate money) for what was taken or given promissory notes.

Before crossing the Potomac, Stuart had asked Lee if he could take three of his seven cavalry brigades—those of Hampton, Fitz Lee (which included the 5th Virginia commanded by Rosser), and W. H. F. "Rooney" Lee (the latter commanded by Colonel John R. Chambliss on this operation)—and ride around the entire Army of the Potomac for a third time. Lee gave his assent, just so long as Stuart came up on the right of Lee's army as they moved into Pennsylvania.

Stuart left on 25 June, but he was first delayed by the passage of Union divisions in front of him. He managed to avoid detection, but that cost him two days. Once across the Potomac and inside Maryland, he captured 125 wagons laden with Union army supplies that would clearly be invaluable to Lee in Pennsylvania. Consequently, Stuart's advance had to stay on roads and could only move at the speed of the wagons. But this restriction meant that he soon lost all contact with Lee and searched for him all the way north to Carlisle, Pennsylvania, without finding him. He would be out of contact with Lee from his departure on 25 June until he finally rejoined the Army of Northern Virginia at Gettysburg on 2 July.

When Lee crossed the Potomac, the other four brigades of cavalry were still with him. Those of William E. "Grumble" Jones and Robertson were left at Harpers Ferry to guard the crossing, while the commands of Jenkins and John D. Imboden stayed with Lee's army. They met virtually no resistance as they moved into Pennsylvania and Lee sent his corps off in different directions to terrify the people and gather supplies. But his discipline was very strict, and theft from civilians or the plunder of their possessions was strictly forbidden. They were to be seen as a powerful army invading the north and destroying or taking only military goods or installations, and were not to injure noncombatants in any way.

As Hooker's army began to follow Lee's, it went through some major changes. First, Lincoln's patience with Hooker ran out, and on 28 June, he was replaced by General George Gordon Meade. Although this man didn't really want the job, he was bound by duty to accept it. And no sooner had Meade taken command than Pleasonton recommended promotion of three captains on his staff to brigadier general: Merritt, Custer, and Elon J. Farnsworth, the latter having been educated at the University of Michigan rather than West Point.

Such a promotion from captain to brigadier general was almost unheard of, skipping as it did over the ranks of major, lieutenant colonel, and colonel. Pleasonton presented a very persuasive case of his need for fighting generals, however, and Meade immediately approved the promotions and forwarded their names to Halleck. Within hours, the formal order promoting those men came back to Meade and they pinned on their stars. And so it was that at the age of twenty-three, Custer became the youngest man ever to reach the rank of general in the U.S. Army.

Generals Buford, David M. Gregg, and Judson H. Kilpatrick commanded the three cavalry divisions within the Army of the Potomac. Custer and Farnsworth were made commanders of brigades under Kilpatrick while Merritt was given a brigade under Buford.[1]

The armies of North and South fought over three days at Gettysburg, with the battle lasting from 1 July through 3 July 1863. On 1 July Merritt was sent south of Gettysburg to join Buford's division, and he saw no fighting until the last day of the battle. But late in the afternoon of 3 July, his brigade was southwest of Big Round Top, probing north up the Emmitsburg Road. A messenger to Kilpatrick alerted him to his presence, and he told Merritt to overlap the road and extend his right to connect with Farnsworth's brigade.

An hour or more of long-range gunfire followed, after which Merritt advanced, led by a screen of dismounted skirmishers. Soon they began running into firm resistance, and Merritt dismounted more of his men to fight as infantrymen. He had them try to advance on foot, but facing Evander M. Law's Alabama brigade some 2,000 strong and not armed or trained to fight on foot, they were unable to gain any ground.

On his right, closer to the southwestern slope of Big Round Top, was General Kilpatrick, commander of the 3rd Cavalry Division, with Farnsworth's the only brigade from his unit present on the field at the time. Kilpatrick loved to be known as a fighter, but his aggression was usually little thought out and often foolhardy. Known behind his back as "Kill Cavalry" because of the frivolous ways in which he often wasted his men's lives, the fighting here bore witness to that.

On 3 July Kilpatrick ordered Farnsworth to lead his brigade in a mounted attack against an unknown number of Confederate infantrymen in thick woods on hilly ground littered with large boulders. Farnsworth first tried to tell him this was terrible cavalry country and no such attack had any hope of success, but Kilpatrick would have none of it. So Farnsworth led a ridiculously suicidal cavalry attack into the heavy brush, and he was killed, along with many of his men. No ground was taken, no enemy artillery silenced, and no Confederate soldiers killed or captured to justify these deaths. Unhappily, this was just the sort of operation for which Kilpatrick got the nickname that made his men cringe.[2]

The brigade of which Custer was the new commander was known as the Michigan Brigade, for it consisted of the 1st, 5th, 6th, and 7th Michigan cavalry regiments. The 7th, of course, was the very regiment of which he had asked the command from the Michigan governor. But now, on demonstrated merit alone, he had won command of the entire brigade. At first its officers were surprised and a bit offended that this blond, boyish-looking captain had been jumped over them to general's rank. But within a very few days, he would prove his mettle to them.

In those days, general officers were allowed great freedom in choosing their uniforms. Somehow, and on a day's notice, Custer was able to acquire a black velvet jacket with double rows of gold buttons down the front and large gold braid loops sewn on its cuffs. As a new general, he took command wearing this jacket and a wide-brimmed black hat with a silver star pinned to it, with the final touch of a small red kerchief around his neck. It was certainly a flamboyant outfit, and one of his officers described him as "a circus rider gone mad."[3]

This was the same extravagant, flamboyant Custer he had always been, though now he could actually wear a some-what unusual uniform with impunity. But his model for this was Napoleon's famous cavalry commander, Marshal Joachim Murat, who wore gaudy uniforms of bright colors with gold braid, feathers, or anything else he thought bright and attractive. His purpose was to be readily identifiable by his men in battle, and Custer's goal was the same. Both men led from the front, and their uniforms made them stand out and this often raised the morale of their men beyond measure.

One of his key subordinates, Captain James H. Kidd, described Custer as follows:

*A keen eye would have been slow to detect in that rider with the flowing locks and gaudy tie, in his dress of velvet and gold, the mas-ter spirit that he proved to be. That garb, fantastic as at first sight it appeared to be, was to be the distinguishing mark which, during all the remaining years of that war, like the white plume of Henry of Navarre, was to show us where, in the thickest of the fight, we were to seek our leader—for, where danger was, where swords were to*

*cross, where Greek met Greek, there was he, always. . . . Showy like*
*Murat, fiery like Farnsworth, yet calm and self-reliant like Sheridan,*
*he was the most brilliant and successful cavalry officer of his time.*
*Such a man had appeared on the scene, and soon we learned to utter*
*with pride the name of—Custer.*[4]

Meade finally caught up with Lee on 1 July—or rather, Lee
descended on the advance elements of the I Corps of the Army
of the Potomac a few miles northwest of Gettysburg. A. P. Hill's
corps slammed into them there, coming out of the northwest.
The Yankees recoiled, and then Rodes's division of Ewell's corps
came down Oak Hill from the north and hit their right flank.
But his initial attacks were stymied by Union soldiers behind a
stone wall, and Rodes tells us of the key role Ramseur's brigade
played:

> *Ramseur's brigade. . . . was ordered forward, and was hurled by its*
> *commander with the skill and gallantry for which he is always con-*
> *spicuous, and with irresistible force, upon the enemy just where he had*
> *repulsed O'Neal and checked Iverson's advance.*[5]

After he had sent two of his regiments to support another
brigade that was crumbling, Ramseur was ordered to take his
last two regiments and rescue still another brigade whose men
had been badly bloodied and were being driven back. We get
more detail of this incident from Ramseur's official report:

> *I found three regiments of Iverson's command almost annihilated, and*
> *the Third Alabama Regiment coming out of the fight from Iverson's*
> *right. I requested Colonel Battle, Third Alabama, to join me, which*
> *he cheerfully did. With these regiments (Third Alabama, Fourteenth*
> *and Thirtieth North Carolina), I turned the enemy's strong position*
> *in a body of woods, surrounded by a stone fence, by attacking en*
> *masse on his right flank, driving him back and getting in his rear.*

*At the time of my advance on the enemy's right, I sent to the commander of the Twelfth North Carolina, of Iverson's Brigade, to push the enemy in front. This was done. The enemy, seeing his right flank turned, made but feeble resistance to the front attack, but ran off the field in confusion, leaving his killed and wounded and between 800 and 900 prisoners in our hands.[6]*

Around noon, the Union XI Corps under Howard arrived in Gettysburg, and after leaving one division in reserve on Cemetery Hill just south of town, he sent the other two forward to hit Rodes in his left flank. But those fresh Yankee divisions were themselves hit in their right flank by Early's division, which came booming out of the northeast, its cannon fire shredding Howard's ranks and the soldiers' keening rebel yell terrifying all. Soon after this, both the Union I Corps and XI Corps retreated in some disorder, then basically collapsed and were driven through town.

The division Howard had left atop Cemetery Hill became the rock around which most of the fleeing Union soldiers were able to coalesce. Some of them were also sent to Culp's Hill, a mile to the east, and soon a solid defense was set up on these hills and the high ground between them. Other Union corps arrived during the night, and as they came up Meade assigned some to Culp's Hill, others along the crest of a ridge running south from Cemetery Hill and known today as Cemetery Ridge. When the black of night faded to the predawn gray on 2 July, lines of robust Union defensive positions bristling with cannon covered each other with interlocking artillery and rifle fire.

But there was one notable exception.

Unlike most of his peers at the time, the Union's III Corps commander, General Dan Sickles, was a political general with no military background. When he saw the low-lying section of Cemetery Ridge to which his corps had been assigned, he thought his force would be too vulnerable if he placed it there.

He decided on his own, therefore, without orders, clearance from above, or even notification to his commanding general, that he would move forward about a mile and set his corps up on high ground marked by a peach orchard and a wheat field. Once there, he placed his men along a V-shaped line. But it was too long a line to be covered by the 10,000 men in III Corps, and it projected west for nearly a mile, which would allow Confederate artillery to assail it from two directions.[7]

Lee had ordered Longstreet's I Corps to assault the southern end of the Union line on 2 July, but this was delayed by various factors. Finally, at around 4:00 p.m., the attack was launched. Pickett's division had not yet arrived, so Longstreet sent those of Hood and McLaws as well as Anderson's division from A. P. Hill's corps, forward in waves. Meade kept sending reinforcements to Sickles as they came up and even took units from other parts of his line and threw them into the fight. But the Confederate force was too strong, overwhelming the Yankees and driving them back to Cemetery Ridge.

Both sides were badly bloodied, and Longstreet's men had basically destroyed Sickles's III Corps. But when the fighting stopped at around 6:00 p.m., they had not been able to take Little Round Top. By dark, the Union line ran from that key hill two miles north to Cemetery Hill, then looped east another mile to Culp's Hill, thus taking on the traditional "fishhook" shape by which it is remembered.

———————

On 2 July 1863, Custer's brigade of Michigan cavalry caught up to the rear of Hampton's brigade just outside of Hunterstown. This was at around 4:00 p.m., just about the time of Longstreet's attack on the main Gettysburg battlefield some four miles away. And in his first cavalry charge led as a general officer—he had led charges by regiments and even a brigade earlier as a captain—Custer performed a master stroke that is generally misunderstood and dismissed as an arrogant and foolish act on his part.

Custer and his brigade came over a rise in the woods to see a wide plain spread before them, mostly corn on the left, wheat on the right. A road went straight ahead, splitting the area into two sections of fields, both crisscrossed by fences. The road itself was lined with a sturdy wooden fence on either side, so that only four to six horses could move down it side by side at a gallop. A half mile or so down that road, Custer could see a dozen or two Confederate soldiers stretched across the road, some mounted, some on foot. Beyond them, he could see a number of gray soldiers moving around at the edge of another wood. The group on the road was obviously a rear guard, but what were they protecting?

There was only one way to find out. Custer thought it was a large group of Confederate cavalry, perhaps a brigade or more. But given the lay of the land, how could he maximize the blow he would deliver? Clearly, the narrow road and the fences crossing the fields precluded his moving the entire brigade into an all-out sweeping attack. If he sent a handful of men down the road to act as bait and then had them race back to a prepared killing ground, the rebs might shoot at them, but would probably dismiss them as scouts or couriers, and no large force would pursue them. But if he sent a company down to smash into them, draw serious blood, then turn and flee back to the ground Custer would prepare, why, that might just do the trick.

With the bulk of his force still concealed by the woods, Custer moved the dismounted 7th Cavalry forward into the corn on his left, keeping them close to the road but out of sight. Similarly, he dismounted the 6th Cavalry and aligned them on the other side of the road, concealing them in bushes or the wheat field, with many of them hidden in the large Felty Farm barn on one side of the road. He left the 1st and 5th Michigan mounted but out of sight at the edge of the woods, and deployed Alex C.M. Pennington's guns in the same area, pointing down the road. Any

Confederate force that chased his bait and got this far would ride around the corner of the barn and find themselves looking into the business end of Pennington's guns.

Once his brigade was so deployed—and only Custer would have had the authority to order this—he had A Company of the 6th Cavalry, some sixty men, line up in the road in front of the Felty barn. They then drew sabers and, yelling maniacally, Custer led them galloping down the road.

The Confederates on the road were stunned and quickly pulled out of the way. A Company charged through the surprised and dismounted gray troopers, only to meet the fury of the Cobb Legion, a regiment-sized unit that attacked in formation.

A Company was hit hard, and Custer's horse went down, though he was pulled up onto the back of a private's horse and got away. The much-depleted A Company raced back, pressed hard by howling Confederate horsemen. But as these gray pursuers passed the Felty barn, a prearranged storm of gunfire met them. Those who could struggled back to their own lines, and after a ragged artillery exchange at dusk, both units moved away from each other.

Custer suffered thirty-two casualties that day, which was probably more than he expected. Still, his plan worked, for Hampton paid a still higher blood price. While it is difficult to determine from the official records just exactly how many casualties he suffered, one of Hampton's biographers says he lost sixty-five men, and one of Custer's says that twenty-two dead Confederates were left in the road as they retreated.

The 3rd of July, of course, was the key day on which the battle was decided. For a long time, most historical treatments have reinforced the idea that the so-called Pickett's Charge was Lee investing everything on one throw of the dice in his central effort to win by frontal assault. After a two-hour artillery bombardment, he sent nine brigades, some 13,000 men, across an open field more than a mile wide against the heart of the Union defenses. That meant he was sending only about 20 percent of his available soldiers in the single most important attack of his life while the rest of his army quietly waited.

We are supposed to accept, then, that Lee believed those 13,000 men could break through Union lines at the "copse of trees" below Cemetery Hill and then somehow defeat Meade's force of more than 80,000 men who awaited that attack in their strong defensive positions with powerful artillery support.

In light of all the evidence available, does that seem credible today?

Apparently not. Recent explications of various pieces of evidence indicate that Lee ordered a bold and high-risk three-pronged attack that day, an attack that, if successfully carried out, might have given Lee a great victory at Gettysburg, destroyed the Army of the Potomac, and perhaps even won the Civil War for the South. This belief has been echoed by many in recent years, including at least two Pulitzer Prize–winning military historians.

Counted among the greatest living authorities on the Civil War, James M. McPherson won the Pulitzer Prize in 1989 for *Battle Cry of Freedom*, generally considered one of the very best twentieth-century Civil War histories. In *This Mighty Scourge* McPherson writes:

> *As late as the morning of July 3—perhaps even as late as 3:30 that afternoon—Lee still hoped and planned for a Cannae victory. His orders for July 3 included not only the attack we now call Pickett's Charge—or the Pickett-Pettigrew assault—but also an attack on Culp's Hill and a coup-de-grace strike by Stuart's six thousand cavalry swooping down on the Union rear while Pickett and Ewell punched through the center and rolled up the right.*
>
> *By 4:00 P.M. on July 3 these hopes had been shattered.[8]*

Another well-respected historian with a similar pedigree is Walter A. McDougall, who won the Pulitzer Prize in 1986 for *The Heavens and the Earth*. In his more recent book *Throes of Democracy: The American Civil War Era, 1829–1877*, he says:

> *Is there anything new and important to say about Gettysburg? Perhaps so. Perhaps Lee's imagination and patience did not falter after the abortive attacks on the second day. Perhaps his plan for the third day was the most brilliant of all: he just kept the fact of its failure secret out of concern for his army's morale. That plausible plan concerns something everyone knows—J. E. B. Stuart's belated return on July 2—and something many people may not know: the action Stuart's men fought on July 3 well behind Culp's Hill. It is always assumed that Stuart just meant to disrupt the federal troops' supplies and reinforcements or harry their expected retreat. But strong circumstantial evidence suggests that Lee sent Stuart around the northeastern tip of the Union lines with orders to circle back west and charge Cemetery Ridge from the rear in support of Pickett's charge from the front. Why didn't Stuart deliver that mortal blow? Because 2,700 cavalrymen from Michigan, in fighting trim thanks to Hooker's attention, defeated Stuart's 6,000 gray ghosts about four miles short of their goal.[9]*

An understanding of the three elements of Lee's plan that failed, then, sheds a new light on that famous battle.

The first of his planned three attacks was "Pickett's Charge" by nine brigades, about 13,000 men, as mentioned earlier.

The second attack was to have been launched by Ewell's corps against Culp's Hill and the right end of the Union line. During the night of 2–3 July, Lee increased the strength of Ewell's force at the bottom of Culp's Hill from three to seven brigades, about 10,000 men. When the Union XII Corps began to return to the area at first light on 3 July, they opened fire on Stuart's infantry brigade, which was then occupying some of the abandoned Union trenches low on the hill. Over the next few hours, two attacks were made on Culp's Hill by three Southern brigades and one by two brigades. Culp's Hill was then defended by three Union brigades, about 3,000 men. At around 10:00 a.m., Ewell got a message from Lee to stop fighting and wait for Longstreet's attack, at which time he would launch his own. This would have been the second of Lee's planned attacks. But after Ewell pulled his men out of combat at around 10:30, no later concerted attack was ever launched by these seven brigades. Why not?[10]

Because the triggering event for that attack would have been Lee's third planned attack, the arrival in the rear of Culp's Hill of about 6,000 screaming rebel horsemen. This was Stuart's cavalry force that Lee had sent three miles northeast of town that morning on the York Pike: the brigades of Fitzhugh Lee, Wade Hampton, and Colonel Chambliss, all of whom had been with Stuart in his ride around the Union army, and Jenkins's brigade, the only other cavalry brigade Lee had immediately available in Gettysburg on 3 July. This brigade was made up of about 1,200 mounted infantrymen, who used horses as transportation, then, at the point of contact with enemy forces, dismounted and, armed with the 1859 Enfield rifle and sword bayonets, fought on foot.[11]

From their position on the York Pike, Stuart's men came south to the woods atop Cress Ridge, then fired cannon shots signaling their arrival to Lee. According to Major Henry McClellan, Stuart's adjutant, the scene upon their arrival was "as peaceful as if no war existed," and "not a living creature was visible on the plain below." That "plain," of course, was East Cavalry Field.[12]

At around 1:00 p.m., back on the main battlefield, Lee opened his artillery bombardment of the Union lines focused on Cemetery Hill and the Copse of Trees. This fire was answered by Union artillery pieces, and the bombardment went on for about two hours, until roughly 3:00 p.m. Some time before the artillery barrage opened on the main battlefield, Stuart discovered a body of Union cavalry at the southern end of East Cavalry Field.

This was Custer's brigade of the 1st, 5th, 6th, and 7th Michigan Cavalry, perhaps 1,800 men in all. They were supported by
another 600 men from Gregg's cavalry division, the 1st New
Jersey and 3rd Pennsylvania cavalry regiments, and Purnell's
Legion.

Technically, the ranking officer on the field, and Custer's
commanding officer, was Brigadier General David McMurtie
Gregg, who commanded the 2nd Cavalry Division, while
Custer's brigade was part of the 3rd Cavalry Division under Kilpatrick. Earlier that morning, when Stuart had moved his force
out onto the Baltimore Pike, he was observed by Howard's XI
Corps on Cemetery Hill.

The news was sent to the commander of the Union cavalry
corps, Major General Alfred Pleasonton, who in turn sent Gregg
to cover the southern end of East Cavalry Field with his division
of some 2,500 men as a blocking force. But Gregg pleaded with
him to give him another brigade as reinforcement, since they
might have to face a much larger force under Stuart. Pleasonton
eventually agreed to do so and had Custer's brigade diverted for
that purpose.

When Gregg got to the southern end of East Cavalry Field,
Custer was already in place. Gregg then began dispersing his
own men off the potential battlefield to positions of relative
safety. Colonel J. Irvin Gregg's brigade, for instance, was posted
as a long picket line that stretched from the lower end of East
Cavalry Field some two miles southwest to Wolf Hill. General
Gregg was able to post other regiments to flank and rear security
posts so that finally he had only 600 of his own men on the field
as well as Custer's 1,800.

That was a questionable act on his part, for any good commander would have sent Custer's men off to fill the support
duties and kept his own men on the field. The reason is that
he would have known something about his own men and their
commanders. Even if some of them were new or otherwise less

reliable than others, at least he would have known that and so been able to distribute his forces appropriately when the crunch came. With Custer's men making up the great majority of his troops, however, they were complete strangers to him, and he would have had no idea whatever which were the stronger or weaker troops.

It seems clear that, by conveniently transferring nearly 80 percent of his troops off the field, Gregg was trying to avoid facing Stuart and his Invincibles, a cavalry force that had yet to be defeated by Union horsemen. His actions also show that he was willing to let Custer bear the ignominy that might come from his troops being trampled by Stuart. But after Custer was able to stop and defeat Stuart, General Gregg tried to elbow him off the table and take credit for the victory himself, as evidenced by his after-action official report:

> *Brigadier General Custer, commanding Second Brigade, Third Division, very ably assisted me in the duties of my command. Colonel J. B. McIntosh, commanding First Brigade of my division, handled his brigade with great skill, and deserves particular mention for his gallantry and untiring energy throughout the day. The Third Brigade, Second Division, Col. J. Irvin Gregg [General Gregg's nephew] commanding, was held in reserve upon the field.*

That sounds like Gregg's men did all the fighting, while Custer only "ably assisted" him. In fact, the butcher's bill tells a different story: of the 254 Union casualties suffered on East Cavalry Field, Custer's men accounted for 219, including 32 fatalities. Gregg's 35 casualties included no fatalities. That tells a story far different from the one in Gregg's official report, and since he played no significant role in the actual fighting, we will turn the page on him.

After a brief exchange of artillery fire with Custer, Stuart dismounted Jenkins's brigade and ordered their advance, firing their new long-range rifles at the blue cavalrymen, some of whom were also dismounted. In that day, when a cavalry unit, whether mounted or dismounted, was fired upon by infantry, they normally just remounted if necessary and rode away. They had neither the weapons—usually carbines, less accurate and shorter range than the foot soldiers' rifles—nor the training to effectively counter a line of infantrymen. But in this case, Custer simply dismounted his 5th Michigan Cavalry, whose soldiers were armed with Spencer repeating rifles, not carbines, and moved them forward to return the fire of the gray infantry sweeping their way.

A certain amount of back-and-forth fighting between dismounted cavalrymen ensued, and eventually, Confederate horsemen joined the fray, pushing the 5th Michigan Cavalry to the southern end of the field. Custer responded by leading the 7th Michigan Cavalry in the first Union charge of the day. And he rode well out in front of them, a single rider defying death in a way that seemed almost magical.

At least five horses would be shot under Custer during the Civil War, probably quite a few more. But he was never touched, and he was to continue leading from the front all through the war. Given the amount of hostile gunfire exchanged all around him, his repeated return from battle unscathed baffled all. He seemed to some to be charmed, to have some almost magical ability to avoid bullets, a gift referred to behind his back as "Custer's luck."

Unfortunately, near the northern end of the field, they ran into a sturdy wooden fence that stopped them but simply would not go down, and they were soon under fire from three sides. They were driven back to the southern end of the field, where dismounted riflemen from parts of the 5th and 6th Michigan cavalries finally repelled their gray pursuers. The two sides then separated and kept their distance for a while as the artillery fire from the main battlefield hammered on. When it abruptly stopped, the sudden stillness after two hours of deafening thunder was remarked by many.

That silence meant that Pickett's Charge was about to be launched, and it was Stuart's signal. He then had twenty to thirty minutes to get one mile south over East Cavalry Field, another mile southwest down Bonaughton Road, then almost two miles northwest up the Baltimore Pike to the rear of Culp's Hill. He could cover that ground in twenty minutes, but it would be close, and he had no time to stop and fight.

Once behind Culp's Hill, Stuart would have dropped off troops, probably the 1,000 mounted infantrymen in Jenkins's brigade, to attack the 3,000 Union soldiers atop Culp's Hill from the rear while Ewell's 10,000 attacked them from the front. His 5,000 remaining horsemen would then have moved across the Fishhook to hit the Copse of Trees from the rear while Pickett's Charge hit it from the front.

Thus divided in half, the Army of the Potomac would have been defeated in detail. The northern half would have had its right wing rolled up by Ewell and Jenkins, while the Union line from the Copse of Trees north was rolled up by Pickett and Stuart. Meanwhile, the blue soldiers deployed in the hook of the Fishhook would have been attacked from the front by the three brigades of Anderson's division and the two brigades each from the divisions of William D. Pender, Rodes, and Early that were arrayed before them. The Union artillerymen, who carried no personal sidearms behind their own infantry lines, would have been killed or driven from their guns by Confederate horsemen, who would have taken them over, turned them around, and fired canister into the rear of Union infantrymen anticipating only Confederate attack from their front. Thus attacked front and rear and with nowhere to retreat, that half of the Union force would have quickly surrendered.

Longstreet says in his memoirs that, had Pickett's Charge been successful, his divisions under Hood and McLaws were ready to "spring to the charge." This would have been nothing more than a pinning attack to freeze that half of the Union army while the other half was overwhelmed. Although neither Hood nor McLaws made that attack, the two brigades of Anderson's division under Cadmus M. Wilcox and David Lang posted with the Confederate artillery received orders from General Anderson, who was with Lee (which means the order came from Lee himself), to attack to their front "in support" of Pickett's Charge while it was fighting at the Copse of Trees. They were specifically ordered, and this is important, to attack "in support" of Pickett's charge, not "as part" of it.

They made that attack, a half mile south of the Copse of Trees, but stopped short of the Union line and exchanged fire with blue soldiers until it was clear that Pickett's Charge had been repelled, at which point they pulled back to their original positions with the Confederate artillery. This attack well south of the Copse of Trees has since been explained by saying Wilcox and Lang got lost in the smoke. But these were tried veterans used to attacking through the smoke that obscures battlefields. They weren't lost; they were simply making a pinning attack to hold the Union troops in place, in support of Pickett's Charge, not as part of it. But it was to be of no avail.

So where was Stuart? Back on East Cavalry Field, as will be explained.

Cavalry on both sides was usually deployed in square formations of two hundred horsemen, twenty wide and ten deep (since horses are longer than they are wide), known as squadrons. For most efficiently controlled movement in any direction, cavalry would be arrayed in a "column of squadrons," with squadrons lined up one behind the other like the cars in a railroad train. But for an attack intended to sweep all before it over a wide battlefield, one would turn that formation ninety degrees and have the squadrons aligned side by side next to each other in what was known as a "line of squadrons."

When the cannonade from the main battlefield ended, the brigades of Hampton, Fitzhugh Lee, and Chambliss came out of the woods and started south in a column of squadrons, a movement formation. Had Stuart wanted to sweep the heavily outnumbered Union cavalry from the field, he could have easily done that with a line of squadrons similar to that used by Custer earlier with the 7th Michigan. Such a formation is difficult to control, however, and it would take valuable time to realign into a column.

Since time was short, Stuart instead decided he could buffalo his way past Union forces in a column of squadrons, using sheer numbers and his enormous reputation to intimidate blue commanders. But he did not foresee a young general who might lead a suicidal attack on him and stop him with a far smaller force. He failed to anticipate Custer, and that was to be his undoing.

The first Union troops confronting Stuart's column were the 600 men of the 1st New Jersey and 3rd Pennsylvania. As the gray horsemen approached, those Union soldiers pulled back on either side and allowed them to pass. The men of the 5th, the part of the 6th not on flank security duty, and the 7th Michigan Cavalry were in the southwestern portion of East Cavalry Field at this time, most of them dismounted and somewhat disorganized in the wake of their earlier fighting.

Custer was with the 7th, and when he saw the large Confederate column heading south, he leaped on his horse and raced across the field to the front of his only reserve, the as-yet-uncommitted 400 men of the 1st Michigan Cavalry. When he got to their front, he took off his hat so they could see his yellow hair, raised his sword, and shouted, "Come on, you wolverines!" Then he turned and, at their head, began trotting north.

The Confederate column was led by Wade Hampton, a big man on a big horse. As the blue force approached, he no doubt thought this was only a feint, that in the face of a rebel force more than ten times their size, they would cut off to the side and take cover, as the 1st New Jersey and 3rd Pennsylvania had just done. But when they got within a few hundred yards of each other, Custer again raised his sword and shouted, "Come on, you wolverines!" then spurred into a hard gallop. As his men raced behind him they spread out into a front three times their normal squadron size, some sixty horses wide.

When they slammed into the Confederate column, the force of impact stopped its leading squadron dead. The sections of the 1st Michigan that overlapped the rebels on either side raced down their flanks, firing their revolvers into the gray ranks. Meanwhile, the 5th, 6th, and 7th Michigan had remounted and proceeded to slam into the western flank of Stuart's force, while much of the 1st New Jersey and 3rd Pennsylvania charged into its eastern flank.

This completely stopped the forward momentum of the column of squadrons, which ground to a halt like the cars of a railroad train. Instead of Stuart getting his men past that last force of 400 men of the 1st Michigan Cavalry and onto Bonaughton Road, they had rather been caught up in a fight that had changed dramatically. Now there were about 2,000 Union horsemen fighting more than 4,000 rebels, and the column collapsed into swirling individual pistol and saber fights. Some twenty minutes or so later, the cannonade opened up again from the main battlefield, only this time it was Union artillery alone pounding Pickett's men. Stuart realized he had missed that narrow window of opportunity, and after more sword banging, he pulled his men back up on Cress Ridge, with no pursuit from Custer and his much smaller force.

Most historians since that time have dismissed the fight on East Cavalry Field as a meaningless event in which the two sides simply fought for the joy of fighting. But that is an inaccurate assessment, as was made clear by Lee that evening. Lee had sent General Imboden and his cavalry brigade away from the battlefield on special duties, some to guard Lee's wagon train while others went out into the Pennsylvania countryside to round up livestock. Imboden returned the evening of 3 July, long after the fighting had ended. When he finally saw Lee late that night, his first comment to his commander was that this must have been a hard day for him. Lee agreed that it had been. Then, according to Imboden's official report, he made the following statement:

> *I never saw troops behave more magnificently than Pickett's division of Virginians did today in that grand charge upon the enemy. And if they had been supported as they were to have been—but, for some reason not yet fully explained to me, were not—we would have held the position and the day would have been ours. Too bad! Too bad! OH! TOO BAD!*[13]

Now what did he mean by "if they had been supported as they were to have been"? Two of the brigades in Pickett's Charge may not have made it all the way across the field before turning back, but he clearly didn't mean that, and he also did not mean support by artillery, which had hammered Union lines for two hours. I believe the only reasonable explanation is the arrival of Stuart's men behind Culp's Hill and behind the Copse of Trees. And that, as we now know, was precluded as a function of the spectacular personal courage shown by George Armstrong Custer on East Cavalry Field. There, he stopped Stuart's column and in so doing probably saved the Union.

# TWELVE

## *The Wilderness*

After the battle of Gettysburg in early July 1863, Lee and his army retreated into the Shenandoah Valley. Meade followed him on their march to the south, but cautiously. By 24 July, the Army of Northern Virginia had passed through the Blue Ridge mountain range and back into central Virginia, with the Army of the Potomac moving slowly in its wake. Lee finally set up around Culpeper, between the Rapidan and the Rappahannock rivers, and both armies rested and reorganized.

Since Union forces had triumphed at Gettysburg, thus blunting Lee's thrust north, the Army of Northern Virginia was home but on the defensive once again. On 4 July Vicksburg had fallen, which meant that the Confederate states of Texas, Louisiana, and Arkansas were separated from the rest of their new nation by a wide Mississippi patrolled by Union gunboats. In Tennessee, Rosecrans was pushing Bragg's smaller army south toward Chattanooga and the northern borders of Alabama and Georgia. And finally, the blockade was beginning to tighten and a Union expeditionary force was hammering the coastal defenses of Charleston, South Carolina.

In light of this sudden set of crises, the decision made in Richmond was to send Longstreet's corps to reinforce Bragg in the hope of staving off a Union drive across Georgia. But Longstreet first sent two of his brigades to Charleston to try to hold off what increasingly looked like the inevitable expansion of Union bridgeheads along the islands and coastline of the Atlantic seaboard.[1]

When Lee left the Shenandoah Valley, Imboden stayed there with a small force of about 3,000 men, a mixture of cavalry, mounted infantry, and a small infantry brigade. Soon enough, Lee ordered that infantry to join him east of the Blue Ridge, leaving Imboden with no more than 1,500 mounted men.

Ramseur had retreated as part of Rodes's division, all the way to Orange County Courthouse, south of the Rapidan River, where he stayed with his men for six weeks of rest and recovery undisturbed by Yankees. Even this brief spate of peace, however, maintained its military character as the men went through a certain amount of drilling and the occasional review. But Ramseur was most excited about his marriage to Nellie, which was set for 23 September.

He was restless to get home and marry his one true love, which is understandable. But when Longstreet left, he was faced with constant skirmishing that seemed to promise a major battle. And ever the loyal soldier, Ramseur was simply unwilling to abandon the Army of Northern Virginia, even for such a joyous interlude. So he stayed with his men.

Stuart had long wanted to see Rosser promoted to brigadier general and given command of a brigade, but there were no such posts open. Stuart, however, had a long-standing quarrel going on with one of his brigade commanders, William E. "Grumble" Jones. When he and Jones exchanged angry words in September 1862, Stuart had him arrested and tried by court-martial for insubordination. Found guilty, Jones was transferred to southwestern Virginia, which opened a brigade command position.[2] Rosser was soon promoted to brigadier general, and according to Special Orders No. 256 of 15 October 1863, he was given "command of the brigade formerly commanded by Brig. Gen. W. E. Jones."[3]

On 12 October, Lee started what he intended to be a flanking movement against Meade's army encamped to his northeast. But alerted by an early attack, Meade's entire army began to retreat. Stuart's cavalry was already out front, and, after an inconclusive clash with Union horsemen, they continued their pursuit. Leaving Rosser with one field gun near Fleetwood Hill at Brandy Station, Stuart's men rode hard in the wake of the fleeing blue horsemen. Rosser's role was to ward off any possible Union move against Culpeper, where Lee's supply depot was located.

In early afternoon, a large force of Union infantry, cavalry, and artillery appeared from the north, advancing as if they intended to strike in a rearguard action. Rosser was out front as usual, and early on he was wounded in the fray, though not seriously. As he was going to the rear to have his wound treated, he saw that his men on one side appeared to be about to turn and run. Ignoring his wound, he raced back to the front of the men he had seen waver and rallied them, continuing the fight as they slowly gave ground. Before long, the other cavalry brigade arrived with five guns. After arraying these in a line, Rosser's men passed through them and they opened on the Yankees, thus bloodily ending their offensive movement.[4]

For the next few days, there were only inconclusive engagements. On the 18th, Stuart was moving to join several other brigades of cavalry operating under the command of Fitz Lee. But that night, his pickets were attacked by a force that seemed large enough that it might be the entire Army of the Potomac cavalry command. He fell back beyond Broad Run, a deep stream over which there was only one bridge, with no ford in either direction for several miles. From that position, Stuart thought he could repel the Yankees until Fitz Lee joined him.

In the morning of 19 October, the Union cavalrymen

approached the stream and opened fire, but they failed to take
the bridge. Though Stuart still thought he could hold them at
bay, he got a message from Fitz Lee saying that he was near and
could hear the fighting. If Stuart would fall back and lead the
Yankees on, he said, then he, Fitz, could come up and take them
in the flank. His signal would be a single cannon shot, at which
Stuart would turn and the two gray units would trap the blue
between them.

Stuart thought it a brilliant plan, and he began to fall back,
while re-forming his retreating horsemen a few miles away so
that, when the moment came, they might swoop in and kill,
capture, or scatter the startled Yankees. The blue column pursuing Stuart was made up of two brigades, the second of which
was Custer's. The lead brigade got to within a few hundred
yards of Stuart's waiting troops when the signal gun was heard.
Out of the trees raced a cloud of screaming gray horsemen, and
the Yankees, stunned, turned their horses and dug in their spurs.

All Union organization collapsed as they ran, and Stuart's
force, half of which was Rosser's brigade, pursued them as if
they were on a fox hunt. Custer's men in the rear were not so
panicked as those in the lead brigade, and they retired across
the bridge in good order. But they could not get their artillery pieces across, and they also abandoned Custer's headquarters
wagon. The men in the other brigade, however, were still in
flight, scattering into small groups and running for their lives.

After about five miles, the stronger Union horses began to
prevail, and the great bulk of them eventually got away. On a
day they would long remember as "the Buckland Races" the
Confederates captured about 250 prisoners, a dozen ambulances,
Custer's guns, and the official papers and personal effects found in
his headquarters wagon. There can be little doubt that Rosser relished reading Custer's letters and examining his personal affairs.[5]

The next few weeks were relatively calm, broken only by a
few bold attacks from Union soldiers crossing the Rappahannock,

then retiring. But Meade continued his retreat and the Carolina brigade was soon settled in positions behind the Rappahannock. Rodes thought there would be little more action on their front, so he released Ramseur on leave and that eager groom-to-be was soon on a train heading south. He got to North Carolina safely and married Nellie on 28 October, then they went on a honeymoon in the mountains of western North Carolina. This welcome respite lasted almost a full month, a quiet time that could only have been pure ecstasy for both of them.

Ramseur got back to his unit in late November, and for several days Confederate soldiers did a lot of marching and digging, preparing strong positions on the south side of Mine Run while awaiting attack by Meade. Lee had about 30,000 men there, and Meade was moving on them with more than 60,000. But after three days of preparing to defend against a major assault, nothing ever came. Finally, at first light of 2 December, Lee advanced in an attempt to turn Meade's left wing, only to find the Union positions empty. Once again, the men in blue had withdrawn to the north.

After that, Ramseur's brigade withdrew to winter quarters south of the Rapidan River. And although the raging war had quieted, shortages of food bedeviled Ramseur's division, just as it did most of Lee's men that winter. That was a problem that was never really resolved, and despite the peace and quiet of their daily lives, the incompetence of army quartermasters meant only that the many men in gray suffered more than was necessary. But Ramseur, ever aware of the loss of morale that came when men stayed in the same place for an extended period with no action, drilled his men hard, sometimes twice a day. And he was meticulous about the cleanliness of their camp.[6]

When it became clear that there was little likelihood of another Union advance, Ramseur sent for Nellie, and he shared a rented room with her only a few miles from camp. There was very little large-scale fighting in Virginia that winter and early spring, and Dod went to work every morning and came home in late afternoon to long-anticipated nuptial delight. It really didn't matter that they only had this small room, for they were at last together as husband and wife, and they made the most of it. This was a second honeymoon, and it lasted until the first week in April, when Nellie finally left, pregnant and happy.[7]

Back in the Union army, Custer had finally been able to marry Libbie Bacon. He swore to her that he had first been smitten when they met on Thanksgiving Day 1862, and from that day through early April 1863 he had been able to spend a considerable period of time in and around Monroe, during which his focus was on her. Their romance had clearly blossomed, and as her affection grew, he told her how much he wanted and intended to marry her, but as an indefinite sort of plan with which her words to him neither agreed nor disagreed.

Libbie's father had strongly opposed her involvement with Custer, and when he left Monroe, on 8 April, her father forbade her to correspond with him. But he and Libbie had arranged to write to each other through an intermediary. In September 1863, after his summer triumph at Gettysburg, Custer again took leave and went back to his adopted home in Michigan. But this time he returned as a brigadier general rather than a lowly captain and was a much-storied war hero. The people of Monroe, of course, all suddenly recalled that they had been his best friends and they treated him as their own celebrity, a local boy who had become Galahad.

He saw Libbie as often as he could, though such occasions were formal and in the company of others. But they were able to sit and talk together, and on 28 September, as they stood close together at a garden party, he proposed marriage to her and she accepted. This was kept secret, as Libbie feared the reaction of her father. But on 5 October Custer returned to the army, and soon he wrote a letter to Libbie's father, the judge, asking his permission for their wedding. This was serious, and after discussing the matter with his daughter, Judge Bacon wrote back to Custer and gave them his blessing.

In late January 1864, after securing furlough, Custer returned to Monroe, where he and Libbie were wed on 9 February. Their honeymoon voyage was on a train from Cleveland to Rochester, New York, with a stop at West Point. Then they were on to New York City, and finally to Washington, where orders to return to the front awaited Custer. But no major fighting had erupted, and, as a general, he was able to take his wife with him. Over the next few months they spent a lot of time together, including several trips back to Michigan on leave. Finally, in April 1864, Libbie moved to quarters in Washington and Custer returned to the field, but this time he would find himself in the Army of the Shenandoah under General Philip H. Sheridan.[8]

By the spring of 1864, Lincoln had finally found the man who could fight and defeat the Confederates: Ulysses S. Grant. Promoted to lieutenant general on 1 March and given command of all Union armies, Grant began implementing his plan to win the war. He knew that, in order to defeat the Confederacy, he would have to strike at the heart of the Confederacy and destroy not only its armies, but also its support. He set about his task, therefore, by focusing his efforts in three main theaters of operation.

The first would be in Virginia, where the Army of the Potomac would press Lee's Army of Northern Virginia relentlessly. The second would be that developed by Sherman's descent from Chattanooga to take the major Southern hub of Atlanta. And the third, no less important than the other two, would be in the Shenandoah Valley, that bountiful granary in northern Virginia upon which Lee depended heavily for livestock as well as produce.

Unlike Halleck before him, Grant chose to command all Union armies from the field, and he made his headquarters with the Army of the Potomac. Meade was still technically the commander of that army, and Grant left most of the command and administrative decisions to him. His very presence in the field, however, meant that he had the final say on such things as whether or not to launch an attack, how to deploy troops, and so on. The two men operated smoothly enough together, but with the clear understanding that Grant was the senior commander and so made all the important military decisions, tactical as well as strategic.

One of Grant's first orders was to General Ben Butler at Fort Monroe on the end of the Virginia Peninsula. He was told to move his army of 33,000 by water up the James River and land near Petersburg, from where he could wreck Confederate railroads feeding Richmond. If he was able to carry that off, then Grant knew Lee would be forced to send forces to the region to protect Richmond and thus dramatically weaken the defensive line in front of Grant and Meade.

Butler had been a Democratic congressman from Massachusetts, a classic political general with, as he had already shown, virtually no military skills. Grant made sure he was accompanied on this mission by two generals as his subordinates who were trained military professionals. He hoped that they would be able to guide Butler so as to avoid the bungling that might otherwise be expected. Unfortunately, Butler was too bullheaded to listen to them and he ran the operation himself.

On 5 May Butler's naval transports landed his 33,000 men at Bermuda Hundred. This was an irregular peninsula at the confluence of the James and the Appomattox rivers, and when they landed there, Butler's men were less than ten miles northeast of Petersburg. Unfortunately, the peninsula lay between the rivers, and to get to Petersburg, he had to pass through a narrow neck only three miles wide. Beauregard quickly threw together an army of less than 20,000 men, among whom were a lot of teenagers and old men. Butler tried to break out for a week or so and then finally realized he could not pierce the strong line of defensive positions Beauregard had hastily hacked out. And as Grant later recorded the moment in his memoirs,

*He said that the general occupied a place between the James and Appo-*
*mattox rivers which was of great strength, and where with an inferior*
*force he could hold it for an indefinite length of time against a superior;*
*but that he could do nothing offensively. I then asked him why Butler*
*could not move out from his lines and push across the Richmond and*
*Petersburg Railroad to the rear and on the south side of Richmond. He*
*replied that it was impracticable, because the enemy had substantially*
*the same line across the neck of land that General Butler had. He then*
*took out his pencil and drew a sketch of the locality, remarking that the*
*position was like a bottle and that Butler's line of intrenchments across*
*the neck represented the cork; that the enemy had built an equally*
*strong line immediately in front of him across the neck; and it was*
*therefore as if Butler was in a bottle. He was perfectly safe against an*
*attack; but, as Barnard expressed it, the enemy had corked the bottle*
*and with a small force could hold the cork in its place.*[9]

Butler was trapped on a peninsula, and Beauregard had set the
cork in place that kept him tightly bottled up until many weeks
later after Grant's troops had arrived and besieged Petersburg. This
unfortunate experience gave rise to Butler's nickname, "Bottled-
Up Ben," which was to haunt him until long after the war.

When Grant joined the Army of the Potomac, he could tell
that Lee was in too strong a position behind the Rapidan for
him to be able to succeed with a frontal assault. He might try to
turn Lee's left flank, but if he did, that would open to attack his
rear and lines of communication with Washington. It seemed
best, therefore, to try to turn Lee's right flank. That, however,
would require him to go through the same Wilderness that had
been Hooker's undoing a year earlier. But that was the gamble
he would have to take.

On 3 May, Grant crossed the Rapidan at several fords on
Lee's right, and Lee was in motion to stop him the next day.
While Grant had hoped to move quickly through the Wilder-
ness and meet Lee south of it, his columns halted in its middle on

4 May to let their enormous trains close up on them. Lee hoped
to catch Grant in the Wilderness, where the Union's vast superiority in soldiers (about 120,000 to 65,000) and artillery support
would have little to no effect. And that's just what happened.

But Lee was unable to mass his entire army to strike the
Union flank, for on 4 May, Stuart and his cavalry, who might
have told him precisely where the enemy columns were located,
was ten or fifteen miles off to the east near Fredericksburg.
Longstreet and his corps, on 4 May, were as much as forty miles
off to the southwest near Gordonsville, and it would take two
days of hard marching for them to come up. Consequently, Lee
was unable, that day, to deliver the stunning blow he sought. But
in the early morning of 5 May, soldiers from Ewell's II Corps
stumbled into some troops from Gouverneur K. Warren's V
Corps on the Orange–Fredericksburg Turnpike in early morning. So was begun the bloody battle of the Wilderness.[10]

By midafternoon, the two corps present from the Army of
Northern Virginia arrayed themselves facing east, with Ewell
straddling the turnpike to the north and A. P. Hill on the Orange
Plank Road to the south, leaving an open gap about a mile wide
between them. Lee told them not to bring on a general engagement until Longstreet arrived, so they prepared defensive positions and stayed in place.

Now under Grant's orders, however, the Army of the
Potomac was on the offensive, and Warren attacked Ewell, while
Hancock's II Corps attacked Hill. In each case, the Union forces
outnumbered their Confederate opponents by two to one. But
numbers made little difference in that terrain, where the thick
trees and underbrush made any movement difficult and even
vision for any distance was harshly limited.

That day was filled with heavy fighting. Both sides moved
brigades and divisions around on the battlefield, with Yankees
hoping to break through while the rebels sought only survival.
As daylight faded, the repeatedly stymied federal troops had

gained little ground. But Grant, ever confident, ordered them to renew the attack at dawn on 6 May. Lee's men had been fought out and were thoroughly exhausted, so they did not look forward to fighting again on the morrow.

That evening, Lee sent a message to Longstreet to make a night march so as to arrive early the next day. He instantly obeyed and his men started moving at 1:00 a.m. on the 6th, arriving three miles behind Hill on the Orange Plank Road around dawn. But that was about the time Union troops swept forward all along the line and attacked. Hancock was especially aggressive, pushing the divisions of Wilcox and Heth back so harshly that many of their men turned and fled in disorder.

It was around this time that Longstreet arrived, his men trotting forward on the Orange Plank Road in perfect order. Their appearance in formation slowed the disorganized flight of soldiers from the divisions of Wilcox and Heth, men who just had been dealt a severe blow that shattered their structure and drove them back. As Longstreet's corps passed through these stunned gray soldiers, some of his officers stopped and began restoring order to the milling masses.

Once clear of this confusion, Longstreet sent Joseph B. Kershaw's division off to the southeast, where they slammed into Hancock's men. But he didn't push them far before they pushed back. After both sides at this southern end of the line spent most of the morning washing back and forth in attacks and counterattacks, the fighting gradually stopped. But Lee and Longstreet had already planned a Chancellorsville-like turning of the Union's southern flank for the afternoon.[11]

Another danger to the Confederates in late morning was the arrival of Burnside's IX Corps, which Grant sent into the gap in the gray line. Ewell's right flank was occupied by Rodes, with unoccupied ground about a mile wide between him and Hill's left flank. As Burnside's men started to advance into that open space, Rodes immediately recognized the danger. His only reserve was Ramseur's brigade, and Ramseur's official report tells what happened:

> *The distance from General Rodes to Lieut. Gen. A. P. Hill's left being about a mile, General Rodes ordered me to form on Brigadier-General Daniel's right and to push back Burnside's advance. Moving at a double-quick, I arrived just in time to check a large flanking party of the enemy, and by strengthening and extending my skirmish line half a mile to the right of my line I turned the enemy's line, and by a dashing charge with my skirmishers, under the gallant Major Osborne, of the Fourth North Carolina Regiment, drove not only the enemy's skirmishers, but his line of battle, back fully half a mile, capturing some prisoners and the knapsacks and shelter-tents of an entire regiment. This advance on our right enabled our right to connect with Lieutenant-General Hill's left.*[12]

There was a lot of fighting that day on several different fronts. Still, Ramseur's story is compelling, and it seems to conform to what we know of the battle from many other sources, including not only official reports submitted on both sides but also from letters home written by individual soldiers. So it is not at all unreasonable to believe that Ramseur's prompt movement forward on 6 May to fill in that gap may well have been the single act that saved the day for the Army of Northern Virginia. His swift, aggressive movement delivered a blow on Burnside's advance that stopped it cold and that also enabled unification of the front line between those two Confederate corps.

But the boldest stroke by the outnumbered rebels was still to come that afternoon. One of Longstreet's brigadiers had told him of an old railroad cut that went deep beyond Hancock's left and could be used for a flank attack on him. An engineer was sent to investigate, and after he reported back that the cut was as it had been reported, Longstreet sent four brigades into it while launching an all-out frontal assault with the rest of his troops. Hancock's men were busy trying to fend off Longstreet's attack from their front when the flanking brigades burst out of the woods well into their rear. Their rebel yell resounding through the trees terrified the Union soldiers, hit yet again from the rear with no warning. Startled Union regiments began to collapse and run.

Unhappily for Lee, the thick brush further obscured by gun smoke and dust caused some Confederates to fire upon their own men. Longstreet was wounded in the shoulder, and when he went down, it was a crushing blow. Despite the similarities of this event to Jackson's fatal wounding by nervous Southern sentries a year earlier, Longstreet would recover. However, his wound was grievous enough that he would be *hors de combat* for five full months.[13] Lee tried to keep Longstreet's attack going, but the thick brush slowed and disorganized the men in gray, so he finally called it off well before he had driven into the rear of Grant's army and routed it.

As General Porter later told us, that evening there was great consternation in the Union camps when one of his subordinate generals approached Grant and spoke to him both rapidly and excitedly:

> "'General Grant, this is a crisis that cannot be looked upon too seriously. I know Lee's methods well by past experience. He will throw his whole army between us and the Rapidan, and cut us off completely from our communications.'
>
> "The General rose to his feet, took the cigar out of his mouth, turned to the officer and replied, with a degree of animation he seldom manifested:
>
> "'Oh, I am heartily tired of hearing what Lee is going to do. Some of you always seem to think he is suddenly going to turn a double somersault, and land in our rear and on both of our flanks at the same time. Go back to your command, and try to think what we are going to do ourselves, instead of what Lee is going to do.'"[14]

In other words, unlike past commanders of the Army of the Potomac, the prospect of an attack by Lee did not terrify Grant. His mission was to attack and defeat Lee's army, and, despite the expressed fears of some of his officers, that was what he intended to do.

On 7 May, neither side attacked the other as both armies lay in their defensive positions licking their wounds. Both armies had paid a heavy price in blood, with Lee having lost between 7,000 and 11,000 men, while Grant was missing between 15,000 and 18,000 from his ranks. But despite this disproportion in numbers, it was Lee who could least afford the loss: while reinforcements were plentiful in the North, young white men who were not already under arms in the South were in desperately short supply.[15]

Grant realized he was fighting at a disadvantage in the Wilderness, so as soon as dark came on 7 May he pulled his men out of their defenses and moved them a few miles east. But from there, he did not turn them north to seek supposed safety, as so many other Union commanders before him had done after having had their noses bloodied by Lee. Instead, he turned south and told his corps commanders to make all speed for the important crossroads at Spotsylvania Courthouse.

But Lee also knew of Spotsylvania's importance, and an army as large as Grant's couldn't just pick up and move without preparation. During the day on the 7th, Stuart's cavalry had picked up many indications that Grant would be heading south. Consequently, that night Lee ordered Longstreet's corps, now commanded by General Anderson, to pull out of line and prepare to move to Spotsylvania.

# THIRTEEN

## *Battle of Spotsylvania*

At 3:00 a.m. on 8 May 1864, the Army of Northern Virginia
began its long march. Lee's cavalry scouts were out, and they
soon reported that the Union army was also headed south. Lee
knew Grant's goal was Richmond, and in order to get there,
his personal familiarity with the Virginia countryside told him
that Grant had to be headed for Spotsylvania. Lee sent Fitz Lee's
cavalry brigade to get in front of Grant on the Brock Road and
delay him as much as possible. Then he told Anderson, commanding Longstreet's corps, to drive his men hard and try to get
in front of Grant farther to the south and from there to further
slow his advance. Hoping to buy some time, he sent his other
two corps, under Ewell and Early—who had replaced a seriously
ill A. P. Hill—straight to Spotsylvania.

In the spring of 1864, there had been a complete reorganization of the cavalry serving in the Army of the Potomac.
Pleasonton was replaced as cavalry commander by General Phil
Sheridan, a known fighter whom Grant had brought with him
from the West. General Kilpatrick, who had commanded the
3rd Cavalry Division, was sent to join Sherman's army. He was

replaced at the head of that division by General James H. Wilson, an engineer with no cavalry experience but also a friend of Grant's from service with him in the West.

The 1st Cavalry Division's commander, General Buford, had died of typhoid in December 1863, and until April 1864, Merritt had been in temporary command. Then General Alfred T. A. Torbert, a former infantry division commander, arrived and took over, returning Merritt to brigade command. Because he outranked Wilson, Custer and his brigade had been transferred to the 1st Division, so that he and Merritt became brigade commanders in the same division.

During the Wilderness campaign, the 1st Cavalry Division covered the left wing of the Army of the Potomac and guarded its wagon trains. On 6 May Torbert left for a month of medical treatment in Washington, during which time Merritt again took command of the division. That same day, 6 May, Custer's brigade got into a sharp fight with rebel horsemen near Chancellorsville, but was then called back in to protect the wagon trains.

During Lee's night movement on 7–8 May, Fitz Lee did get out in front of Grant's army, led by Warren's infantry column and Merritt's cavalry, and he was able to fight a very skillful delaying action. That same night, the tables were turned farther south, where Wilson's 3rd Cavalry Division was able to drive Rosser's brigade out of Spotsylvania.

On 8 May both armies were around Spotsylvania, and Grant told Sheridan to take his 10,000 horsemen and pass around Lee's left, looking for an all-out fight with J. E. B. Stuart. After that he was to tear up railroad track and cut Confederate communications as much as he could before rejoining the Army of the Potomac.

Sheridan moved at a very deliberate pace, and Stuart, who only had about 4,500 cavalrymen available, could only peck at his flanks. Then he decided to make a stand at Yellow Tavern, ten miles north of Richmond. But the numbers overwhelmed him there, and a man from Custer's brigade shot Stuart in the stomach; he died from the wound the next day in Richmond.

Although that city's defenses were manned by only a skeleton crew, Sheridan decided not to test them, and he returned with his cavalry to the Army of the Potomac by a circuitous route. Grant's immediate assessment of the raid was that it had been a great success. In fact, however, other than killing Stuart, it did very little damage to the Confederates or their cavalry.

By 9 May, Lee's army had set up a strong defensive line some four miles long that would be strong against attacks from the north or east. It was in the rough shape of an inverted V, with Anderson's I Corps occupying the north-facing left leg. Early's III Corps defended the east-facing leg, while Ewell's II Corps was massed at the tip of the V inside a bulging and almost circular defensive position a half mile across, which, because of its shape, was known as "the Mule Shoe."[1]

On 10 May probing attacks against Anderson were followed by an all-out assault by three Union corps under Hancock. But the robust Confederate defensive line, with its carefully planned cross fires, could not be broken. At around 6:00 p.m., a new formation, a column of regiments made up of four lines of three regiments each, punched through the Mule Shoe in some depth. But it was an unsupported attack, and within a few hours it was rejected.

On the 11th little happened. Lee, having anticipated Grant's move south, had pulled all his artillery out of the Mule Shoe. He was readying these guns for movement in parallel with Grant's, but at first light on 12 May, Hancock's II Corps burst through the Mule Shoe. Not met by the artillery fire they had expected, they drove deep over successive trench lines, joined in their attack by Horatio G. Wright's VI Corps and Burnside's IX Corps. For the Confederates, things looked grim.

Then John B. Gordon's division launched a counterattack that stopped the men in blue. But there weren't enough counterattackers and they needed help. Rodes's division occupied the lower left section of the Mule Shoe, and they quickly turned to join Gordon. Ramseur extended his regiments in a line that, facing north, reached far across the Mule Shoe. He shouted orders to them to move forward slowly, to stay in formation, and not to fire their weapons before they closed with the enemy. Then he passed the word that when he shouted "Charge!" they were to move forward at a run and not stop until all the Yankees had been driven all the way back out of the Confederate defenses.

They began to move forward and, despite the explosions and rifle fire from their front, which took several of them down, things were going well. Then, when Ramseur was about to shout the order to charge, his horse was killed and he took a bullet through the arm. Fortunately, another officer who saw him go down gave the order to charge, and his men burst into a run, rifles and bayonets at the ready as they screamed the rebel yell. Somehow Ramseur managed to get up, and, with his arm hanging limply at his side, he rushed forward to join his men in the fight. Despite the pain from his wound, he was caught up in the crucial nature of the battle and refused to leave the field all day.[2]

More Confederate regiments and brigades came up and were thrown into the melee while Lee's engineers scrambled desperately to build another line of trenches. Gordon held the center of the Confederate salient, and James H. Lane had come up on his right. Supported by two brigades from Wilcox's division, they held off furious Union assaults. Ramseur, on the left, was in a very difficult position as more Union troops kept arriving and firing in his front. Rodes threw in Junius Daniel's brigade, but Lee could see that was not enough. It was clear to him that the blue numbers would soon reverse the tide and begin flowing south on the west side of the salient, overrunning Ramseur and Daniel.

Lee turned his horse, Traveller, to the rear and rode off in search of William Mahone's division, which he expected to be coming up on the right rear. When he got near the courthouse, he came upon Nathaniel H. Harris's Mississippi brigade resting along the side of the road. He very quickly ordered Harris forward and rode at the front of the brigade with him to speed the march. As they came within range of Union artillery, shells began to burst around them, and Traveller began to rear excitedly. Lee tried to calm him, but as he went up on his back legs once again, a Union artillery solid shot passed below his belly, missing Lee's foot by inches. If Traveller had not reared, Lee certainly would have been killed, the narrowest escape he had had since the Mexican-American War.

Men from Harris's brigade were alarmed, and many got in front of Lee, urging him to go back. But Lee's battle ire was up, and he refused to turn away. Even so, the men were so insistent that he finally relented, telling them that he would only go back if they promised to drive "those people from our works." They did, and he turned away. But as they got to Rodes, a messenger from Ramseur arrived, saying they could hold out only minutes longer unless help arrived.[3]

Finally, long after dark, the trenches at the base of the salient were ready and the engaged units, all physically exhausted, were told to fall back. They were not pursued by the equally drained federals and so were able to find positions along the new defensive line and get a few hours of rest.

On 13 May both armies were fatigued beyond much usefulness, and no major engagement occurred. Sheridan's cavalry was still off on its raid, so Grant was at a disadvantage for any maneuver warfare in the open. He decided to pull Gouverneur K. Warren's V and Horatio Wright's VI Corps from his right flank after dark and move them all the way around his formation so that they might envelop and turn Lee's right flank in the morning.

But heavy fog and rain that night delayed their movements and the attacks had to be called off. From 14 to 17 May both sides tried to improve their positions. The V and VI Corps were moved back to their former positions, hoping to surprise the Confederates in one last effort to overwhelm their defenses. But when they attacked, the rebels were ready for them, and the men in blue were badly bloodied. After that, even Grant was ready to end the operation. On 20 May he began moving his forces south yet again.

There are several recorded versions of Union losses at Spotsylvania, but it seems fair to say that they were between 17,000 and 18,000. Confederate casualties are more of a mystery, but since they were on the defensive in fortified positions, they were probably fewer than 10,000. But again, the losses had a far greater effect on Lee than on Grant.[4]

At around this time, Ewell fell gravely ill and left the front, so Early was moved up to command his corps. And as the new division commander to replace him, Lee selected Ramseur, who had once again shown his military skill and raw personal courage only a few days earlier. His first operation in that role was on 30 May, when he sent his division forward across an open field to attack an unknown Union force in a wood line. They had gotten halfway there when hidden Union artillery opened up on them, punishing them badly.

Generals in battle are under considerable pressure to make important decisions quickly, decisions on which the lives of soldiers often depend. Errors in judgment are always to be expected, and Ramseur's miscalculation in this case did not lessen Lee's faith in him at all. This became evident to all when, on 1 June, the Confederate secretary of war signed orders promoting Ramseur to the rank of major general.

From 20 May until 3 June there was intermittent fighting as both armies sidled south while still facing each other. At dawn on 3 June, Grant hurled the II, VI, and XVIII Corps against Lee's strong line at Cold Harbor, suffering 7,000 casualties in less than an hour, compared to Lee's 1,500. After the war, Grant would admit that his frontal attack there into the teeth of Lee's defenses was a great mistake that he long regretted.

For the next ten days both armies stayed in their trenches and shot at each other but did little damage. On 7 June, Grant released Sheridan again, this time to try to meet General Hunter's army at Charlottesville. Hunter was expected to defeat or drive off the small Confederate forces in the Shenandoah, then come east out of the valley and connect with Sheridan.

Learning of Sheridan's departure, Lee sent Hampton with two cavalry divisions after him. Then, on 12 June, he sent Early's shrunken corps to Charlottesville, ordering him to find and destroy Hunter's force. After that, he was to move northeast down the Shenandoah Valley and, if possible, cross into Maryland and threaten Washington from the north.

Grant had suffered 55,000 casualties during this campaign, compared to Lee's 30,000. Until this moment, Grant had been rather unimaginative and relied on numbers and brute force. But now he would perform a true feat of military wizardry. Richmond lay only ten miles southwest of Cold Harbor, although the strong defenses that protected it seemed quite impenetrable for the time being. However, almost all the railroads serving Richmond ran through Petersburg, some twenty miles to Grant's southwest. It was on the far side of the James River, but its defenses were not nearly as intimidating as those around Richmond.

So Grant decided to cross the James and seize Petersburg, which would leave only one rail line connecting Richmond with supplies from the South. From there, he could cut that line as well and besiege an isolated and truly cut off Richmond. Lee would then be forced either to submit to the loss of his army at Richmond or to abandon the Confederate capital and maneuver to the west in a last-gasp effort to keep the war alive.

On 12 June, Grant began his move, sending Smith's XVIII Corps by water down the York, then back up the James to

Bermuda Hundred, where Butler's army was still bottled up and inactive. Smith arrived on the 14th, with orders to cross the Appomattox on the 15th and attack Petersburg. Grant's other corps also pulled out of their defenses and moved south on dry land. They were screened by Wilson's cavalry, which moved west aggressively and engaged any Confederate force they found.

Hancock's II Corps was ferried over the James on the 14th while Union army engineers began building a pontoon bridge nearby. They had it finished before midnight, a most impressive structure nearly a half mile long and reinforced to resist the river's strong tidal current. On the 15th, most of the rest of Grant's army crossed the James on that bridge.

At dawn on 13 June, Lee learned that Grant was gone from his front. However, he thought Grant was again just trying to turn his right flank, and so he moved his defenses south a few miles and dug in again. Warren's V Corps set up that day before these new Confederate positions, and Union cavalry kept Lee from investigating anything farther to the east, where most of Grant's army was in the process of moving south to the James.

By 16 June, Grant had pulled off a true military masterstroke that completely outwitted Lee. Now his entire army was south of the James, while most of Lee's force was still north of it. This was a very high-risk and complicated move, but Grant had pulled it off with impressive aplomb.

Meanwhile, after landing at Bermuda Hundred, Smith followed his orders and crossed the Appomattox with his corps and moved against Petersburg. It was defended by strong artillery positions obstructed by ditches and tangles of fallen trees, and Smith made a thorough reconnaissance before attacking. At about 7:00 p.m. he launched his assault, using his own artillery to blast the Confederate positions while his infantry washed over them in waves.

Two of these strong positions, lightly manned, fell right away, and suddenly there was a breach in Petersburg's defenses a mile wide. But Smith waited for Hancock to come up before advancing, and before that happened, Lee was able to get two of his divisions down to Petersburg and fill the gap. Beauregard also pulled most of his men out of the Bermuda Hundred line and used them to bulk up the city's defenses. When Hancock finally reached Smith that evening, he learned to his great chagrin that he was too late and the breach had been closed.

On the 16th Grant and Meade arrived with the IX Corps, and they launched an attack at dawn. Even though it took several more positions, it was bloodily repulsed by Beauregard's counterattack. Butler was finally able to move through what had become only light defenses before him, but when he heard of this, Lee sent Pickett's division down to confront him. In a panicked response, Butler pulled his men back onto Bermuda Hundred. The other Union troops then stopped to reassess the situation, and Lee's army began arriving en masse. Grant would remain in his trenches outside Petersburg without taking it until the following spring, and fighting there slackened dramatically.

Hunger, not surprisingly, became one of the major problems Lee's men inside the city faced. Whether because of incompetent quartermasters or a simple question of supplies coming in to Petersburg by rail from farther south, the men in gray began to suffer from serious malnutrition. The open question was how to procure more food, and one proposed answer from General Hampton was to take food from the Union army. Not dry boxes of hardtack, but rather, beef on the hoof.

Hampton had replaced Stuart in command of Lee's cavalry. One of his scouts had recently come back from a long reconnaissance run with word of an enormous herd of cattle that had been shipped from the Midwest to feed the Army of the Potomac. At the time the cattle were being pastured on farmland on the southern side of the James, only some thirty miles south of Confederate lines at Petersburg.

To confirm this, Hampton sent Rosser with part of his brigade through federal lines with a mission: to bring back copies of recent Yankee newspapers. There was no effective censorship of the press during the war, and information on Union army units, locations, and planned operations was commonplace in newspapers. And sure enough, they found several stories about the cattle and their location, including the number of men in the units guarding them.

Once Rosser had confirmed the scout's story, Hampton made his plans. On 14 September, with Lee's blessing, he led a party of some 2,700 cavalrymen, carrying enough food for five days, through the lines. This party included Rosser's brigade and a lightly equipped engineer company that would build or repair bridges as needed. They moved west and south on a long swing guided by a rail line, then stopped out in the country and spent the night undetected by the Union army. The next day, the 15th, they rode all day, but this time moving back to the east, by then well south and west of the Army of the Potomac. In the afternoon they stopped at the site of what had been, before its destruction by Union soldiers, Cook's Bridge over the Blackwater River. Part of the reason Hampton chose this crossing was because it would not have been expected by Grant's men.

While the men ate, the engineers rebuilt the bridge, which was ready by nightfall. After passing over it, the raiding party moved on into the early hours of morning, with Rosser in the lead. He had been assigned the duty of taking a Union outpost at Sycamore Church, then moving another two miles and capturing the cattle herd, while other brigades moved into flanking positions. They finally stopped and rested until just before the first light of 16 September.

When they approached the outpost, they saw it was a strong one, with some 400 men from the District of Columbia Volunteers on duty. They were all armed with the new Henry sixteen-shot-magazine repeating rifles, and the gate into their little fortress, surrounded by the pointed wooden stakes of a sturdy abatis barrier, was closed. A Union picket detected them and spread the alarm, and suddenly the walls were manned. But Rosser sent his men forward anyway into what turned out to be a brief but rather fierce firefight.

Some of his unhorsed men were able to pull the gate open, and hundreds of gray horsemen poured through it. The men in blue fought gamely, suffering as well as inflicting quite a few casualties. But the superior numbers of the raiders soon had their effect.

Rosser massed his men on the road again and led them forward for a mile or so. They now faced several hundred Union cavalrymen, alerted by the gunfire, mounted and arrayed in a line facing him. Behind them was the target herd, just visible under the lightening gray sky.

Rosser sent a trooper forward with a white handkerchief on the tip of his raised saber to demand their surrender. The response he got from the commanding officer was "Go to Hell!" followed by a volley into Rosser's ranks. The men in gray quickly overwhelmed them, though some of the Yankee horsemen tried to stampede the cattle. However, Rosser's ranks were filled with farmers familiar with livestock, and they soon got them back under control.

Hampton reassembled his men and they all carried out their assigned duties. The enormous herd was moved to the west by farmers drawn from the ranks, while Rosser's brigade, supplemented by the brigade of General James Dearing and the horse artillery batteries commanded by Colonel R. P. Chew, was assigned to hold the intersection of the Jerusalem Plank Road with the main road to the rear of the Army of the Potomac. The cavalry brigade commanded by W. H. F. "Rooney" Lee was assigned as the final rear guard to stay in motion a few miles behind the cattle herd.

Hampton got the cattle across the Blackwater River and was moving toward the Jerusalem Plank Road when scouts told him a large Union cavalry force was in hot pursuit. But this had been expected.

Grant's headquarters had learned of the heist and sent the cavalry divisions commanded by General August Kautz and General David McMurtie Gregg, supplemented by a hard-marching infantry brigade, to recover the herd. Kautz was the first to move, racing down a road to its intersection with the Jerusalem Plank Road, which he suspected the cattle herd would have to pass. Just after the sun had set he came upon Rosser's trailing unit, White's battalion, straddling the road. Rosser had much earlier nicknamed this battalion "the Comanches" because of the fierce recklessness they showed in their mounted charges.

After firing a few volleys at the dark figures coming up, the Comanches moved back a certain distance, then stopped and repeated the fire. That was enough for Kautz, and he turned around and retreated. He reported on the 17th that, after skirmishing with what he first believed to be Hampton's rear guard, he then reconsidered and thought it might have been Gregg's men, so he withdrew two miles.

However, he must have soon reassessed, for it wasn't long before he was back. And although his men advanced cautiously, their rifle fire was pressing to White's men. Greatly outnumbered, White withdrew beyond Union sight. But from right where they had disappeared, Rosser came storming out of the dusk with his whole brigade. Fiercely screaming their rebel yell, they slammed into Kautz's men and sent them flying.

Hampton had told Rosser to make a stand at Ebenezer Church, and immediately after having dispersed his blue pursuers, he quickly built breastworks there with fence rails. His 1,000 men then concealed themselves, awaiting the inevitable blue attack. The herd was by then only three miles behind him, just crossing the Jerusalem Plank Road and so vulnerable.

Beyond sight of the raiding party, Union numbers began to build as reinforcements arrived. Soon enough, Kautz's men could

be seen moving toward the gray defenses, but this time with
Gregg's division as well as his own and the brigade of infantry.
Now some 6,000 blue soldiers, with flanking parties out on foot
and on horseback, moved cautiously back into the open, artillery
pieces firing shot and shell in their support.

While Kautz had already shown considerable caution in his
first attack, Gregg had also shown similar hesitation, both at
Brandy Station and on East Cavalry Field at Gettysburg. But
this was clearly just an unwillingness to risk his men in a stand-
up fight, a demeanor not unlike that earlier displayed by Union
general George McClellan. There must have been enormous
pressure from above to recapture the cattle before dark, however, so back the men in blue came in serried but shaky ranks.
This time, they moved at an even slower pace with only irregular rifle shots fired in Rosser's direction.

Sensing their reluctance, Rosser hurled half his brigade in
a mounted attack against their center. At this critical moment,
Union leadership was lacking, and Rosser's charge hit their line
like a herd of galloping buffalo. The blue line collapsed as most
Union soldiers simply dropped their weapons, then turned and
ran away in great disorder.

Recovery took them a long time, but Kautz and Gregg knew
that no excuses for failure would be accepted at the top. Finally
reassembled, the federals came on yet a third time, their artillery
again pounding at the gray defensive positions. In the interim,
the brigades of both Dearing and W. H. F. Lee had joined Rosser,
so that nearly 3,000 Confederate soldiers lay behind their breastworks. And Colonel Chew's cannon were ready to enter the fray
for the first time.

The Union assault, when it finally came, was stopped cold
in its tracks by deadly Confederate fire, and Chew's guns soon
silenced those of his adversary. As full dark settled on them,
the thrice-rejected Yankees pulled back in the night and broke

contact. The three Southern brigades then moved in the other direction and eventually caught up with the herd.

Somewhat later, they stopped for a few hours' rest, then reentered Confederate lines at Petersburg the next morning. When Hampton finally reached Lee, he reported that his raiding party had moved more than one hundred miles in a long, circuitous route to get well behind Union lines. They had found the cattle as expected and, after a brief flurry, had captured and disarmed their guards, then began their movement back. He had returned with 2,468 fat cattle, several hundred horses and Henry repeating rifles, ten wagons full of Union stores, and 304 prisoners. His loss was ten men killed, forty-seven wounded, and four missing.

Confederate soldiers occupying the lines at Petersburg were able to replace rancid bacon with fresh beefsteak for a long time to come that fall and winter. But orders soon came down, and on 27 September, Rosser and his Laurel Brigade left for the Shenandoah Valley, where they would try to recover Confederate fortunes and stop Yankee depredations of that crucially important "Granary of the Confederacy."[5]

# FOURTEEN

## *The Shenandoah Valley*

During the fall and winter of 1863–64, there was not much military action in the Shenandoah Valley. The farmers there were largely Quakers or members of other religious denominations opposed to war, which meant they were not called to serve under arms. Consequently, they were able to produce a bountiful supply of produce and livestock. As the rest of Virginia's agricultural land was increasingly ravaged and rendered barren, Lee's Army of Northern Virginia became quite dependent on this supply. In the spring of 1864, it was the presence in the Shenandoah Valley of Lee's cornucopia that Grant wanted to end.

Franz Sigel, a German immigrant with little military background, was a prominent figure among other German immigrants. For this reason, Lincoln made him a general officer in the Union army early in the war, though his performance in the field as such was mediocre at best. His big attraction to the president was his ability to recruit and motivate German immigrant enlistees, the only important skill he brought with him.

After having been outwitted, defeated, and humiliated by Stonewall Jackson in the Shenandoah Valley in May and June

1862, Sigel was given command of the XI Corps of the Army of the Potomac for the rest of 1862 and first part of 1863. This corps was largely made up of German immigrants, which meant that Sigel was an important figurehead for them. It was never an independent command of any importance while he held the post, and before the battle of Gettysburg, he was replaced by General Oliver O. Howard.

Sigel didn't hold independent command again until 8 March 1864, when Lincoln, for purely political reasons, had Secretary of War Edwin Stanton name him commander of the Army of West Virginia. And Grant had a mission for the Army of West Virginia, an important mission, though he had been given no choice in its commander.

Even so, he ordered Sigel to assemble some 10,000 men (out of the 24,000 then assigned to his department) and lead them into the Shenandoah Valley. His orders were to cut the Confederate rail lines at Staunton, and then to move on to Lynchburg, Virginia, where he was to destroy the key Confederate rail center he would find there.[1]

This was an important assignment for the overall conduct of the war. But, as it turned out, it was badly handled, primarily as a function of Sigel's poor leadership.

As part of his responsibilities as commander of the Army of West Virginia, Sigel was responsible for protecting some three hundred miles of the Baltimore and Ohio Railroad line. In addition, he was also required to provide some 7,000 men to General George Crook for a somewhat parallel operation that was supposed to move southwest from Martinsburg, West Virginia, and meet Sigel's force in Staunton.

When he started to move south in early May 1864, therefore, Sigel only took about 6,500 Union soldiers—5,500 infantry and 1,000 cavalry—and twenty-eight guns with him. He had learned that the only Confederate military presence then in the valley that might attempt to stop him was about 1,500

Confederate cavalrymen or mounted infantrymen under General Imboden, along with one battery of six guns.[2]

With excellent intelligence from the supportive local populace, Imboden had learned of Sigel's proposed venture and the size of his force by late April. In the face of such a large Union force moving against him, Imboden called for help. His first call was to Lee in Richmond, but he also sent a call to Major General John C. Breckinridge, Confederate commander of southwestern Virginia, whose command included the Shenandoah Valley. Similarly, the commandant of the Virginia Military Institute, General Francis H. Smith, had been told to have his cadets ready to march at a moment's notice.

The three hundred or so teenage VMI cadets then enrolled had been trained in marching, military tactics, and the use of personal weapons from the first day they had arrived at the institute. Modeled on West Point, VMI attracted a student body drawn largely from the sons of the wealthy upper classes, particularly the Virginia planter aristocracy of the time. Solid military training was then thought by Virginians to be a key element of male maturation, and that was VMI's premier attraction.

Given their daily exposure to military realities, VMI cadets had been used to train recruits in Richmond at an earlier point in the war, a job they did very well. Now they might even be called forward with the prospect of actually fighting. But Imboden, Breckinridge, and others insisted their potential use would only be as a last, desperate measure, and only as a last reserve. Lee, meanwhile, was caught up in the battles in and around Spotsylvania, and he told Imboden that he could spare no troops for him, but to rely on General Breckinridge.

Having learned of Sigel's intentions in some detail, Imboden had quickly moved north with his 1,500 horsemen, reaching Woodstock on 5 May. He was then only about twelve miles from Strasburg, where Sigel had stopped with his army of 6,500. Knowing that Sigel would soon learn of his arrival, Imboden

hoped that this aggressive move on his part would at least delay
Sigel for a few days, thus giving time for Breckinridge to send
him reinforcements.

Generally aware of the size of Imboden's force, Sigel was confident he would blow right through it and easily reach Staunton.
Once there, he looked forward to his first significant performance as a commander, the destruction of key Confederate rail
and other logistical facilities. But he was also overly cautious,
and before he began his slow movement south, he sent 500 cavalry out to cover his right flank.

Imboden quickly learned of this movement from the Confederate signal station on top of Massanutten Mountain. Aware
of Sigel's reputation for caution, he realized that flank security
was being sent out primarily to be sure there were no other large
Confederate forces on his northern flank. With this insight and
his own intimate knowledge of the territory from having grown
up in the valley, he thought he could set a trap that would easily defeat or capture this force. If he were able to pull that off,
he thought he might lead Sigel to believe there was a large rebel
host north of the Alleghenies that marked the northern edge
of the Shenandoah and so delay his movement south by at least
several days.

The raids were quickly set up using the 18th and 23rd Virginia cavalry regiments, which would leave Imboden with only
a small mounted infantry regiment to face Sigel's army. On 9
May these units slipped through a mountain gap and sprung
from the woods into the northern Union flanking force, crushing it and driving the terrified survivors north all the way into
Maryland.

Their pursuit ended on 11 May, but that was the day Sigel
moved his force south from Winchester to Cedar Creek, setting
up his headquarters in the mansion of the Belle Grove plantation. Concerned by the defeat of his cavalry force sent out to
cover the northern flank, Sigel also sent a large mounted force

into the Luray Valley, which was parallel to but separated from the Shenandoah Valley by the Massanutten Mountain mass.

The Union move through the Luray Valley was unopposed, but carefully observed by locals sympathetic to the Confederate cause. As this blue force attempted to cross back into the Shenandoah through the narrow gap near New Market, it got quite strung out, a most unfortunate blunder. Imboden pounced on it with the same 18th and 23rd Virginia cavalry regiments, smashing it and scattering the survivors back into the mountain wilds. Imboden claimed to have captured 464 men, while Sigel conceded the loss of 125 and two hundred horses.[3] But these initial battles did cause Sigel to delay, giving the Confederates the time they badly needed to assemble their force in the Yankees' path.

Breckinridge, a man in his early forties from Kentucky, had been vice president under Buchanan from March 1857 through March 1861, and he was one of the defeated Democratic candidates for president in the 1860 election. Breckinridge had studied at Princeton, saw his first fighting as a major of Kentucky Volunteers in the Mexican-American War, and was wounded as a Confederate general at the battle of Shiloh. He was a very smart and widely experienced man who understood the importance of force and timing in war. After receiving Imboden's message, he immediately reached out for the small Confederate forces he had at his disposal. He knew that as many of them as possible must be brought into the Shenandoah Valley, and quickly, to protect it from devastation by Union forces.

The result was that on 14 May Breckinridge and 2,500 troops from southwestern Virginia reached Lacey's Springs, about ten miles south of Imboden's camp near New Market. On that afternoon, Sigel's Union cavalry moving south pressed Imboden's horsemen over Rude's Hill, then through the crossroads town of New Market itself. Still waiting for Breckinridge and his men, Imboden set up dismounted cavalry acting as infantry on the south side of town, their thin line running over the wooded top of Shirley's Hill on the west to Smith Creek on the east.

The blue horsemen had been joined by infantry, and in the last light of day the combined force made a few faint lunges at the gray line, but then drew back. They set up in town that night, and Sigel arrived, confident they would brush away this small Confederate force in the morning. But at about 1:00 a.m. Breckinridge got his force back on the road, and they were joined about 1:30 by the 257 VMI cadets who had gotten out of the torrential rain then falling by resting in a church.

Around dawn, Breckinridge was able to move his infantrymen into the defensive line Imboden had already established, then set his artillery up on Mount Shirley. Soon enough, he was exchanging barrages with the Yankee artillery. After a few hours of this fire, it became apparent to Breckinridge that Sigel was not going to make any offensive movement, so he decided he would attack. He moved his forces forward, with the VMI cadets being held in the center rear as a reserve.

Imboden and his cavalry covered the right flank up to the fast-flowing and unfordable Smith Creek, where they were concealed by a clump of woods. When he rode forward to see what was before him on the north side of town, he discovered he was on the left flank of the entire Union cavalry force. He quickly turned his force around, moved south to a bridge over Smith Creek, then crossed with cavalry and an artillery battery. He was soon set up perhaps a thousand yards to the left rear of the Union cavalry and rapidly began throwing artillery fire into them.

As explosions erupted, horses and riders went down, and there was massive confusion among the blue cavalrymen. Unaware that the woods before them were now occupied by only a thin skirmish line, they turned and rode to the rear to get out of that galling gunfire. But when they did, they opened up the left flank of the Union infantry defenses, which now became the target of Imboden's gunners.[4]

At about the time Breckinridge got his men into position south of town, Sigel arrived on the north side. He quickly appraised the situation and passed orders for his men to fall back to a better defensive position about a half mile to the north. Once there, the Union force only had to cover a front of about a mile between the Shenandoah River and Smith Creek. But his reluctance to seek battle was one of Sigel's major military flaws, and he would pay a price for that here as Southern blood was up and they kept coming hard.

The VMI Corps of Cadets had been moving forward behind a regular Confederate infantry unit. But as that unit suffered casualties, it veered off to the left, thus opening the middle of the front line. The VMI cadets plunged into that opening, moving swiftly across the Bushong farmland, then dividing to get around the Bushong house.

As they were marching north from Lexington, they had occasionally been somewhat patronized by the older soldiers who filled the ranks of Breckinridge's small army. As these fresh-faced cadets moved forward, marching in step in stiff, serried rows, these hardened men gently mocked their youth and inexperience. These comments must have seemed quite appropriate to the soldiers as they jested, for these were boys, not men, with no beards on their callow faces. They had no real experience to match that of Breckinridge's men as soldiers in the field: fighting, killing, and risking their own lives against the Yankees.

But this day, in their tailored uniforms and carefully rehearsed marching formations, they brought a certain spirit, an élan, to the gray ranks that had never been seen before. They were still a bit naive, yes, for they did not yet know the sting of wounds and death they would soon learn. But they were also eager and committed, their youthful idealism pushing them forward as they gripped their rifle butts with sweaty hands, suppressing their strangling fears as they tried to focus on things they had practiced and knew well, like staying in step and in line with their brother cadets marching on either side of them. Their thoughts, however, mattered less than their actions. This day, before the other soldiers on both sides, they would stand in the furnace door and withstand the flaming blasts of war. This day, they would show the world that they were men.

On the north side of the Bushong house was an orchard, and the cadets moved through it to its northern edge, marked by a rail fence. Now they were only two or three hundred yards from the Union artillery batteries that were firing at the whole rebel line, pouring canister into their gray ranks with deadly accuracy.

The cadets stopped at the fence, then began, for the first time, to fire their weapons at the enemy. But the deadly artillery fire continued, and they knew it could only be stopped if they took those guns. After a brief pause, they climbed over the fence almost as one and went streaming and screaming north into the fire-and-death-belching mouths of the Yankee cannon.

As the gray line approached, it became increasingly clear they weren't going to stop. Now suddenly at risk themselves, the Union gunners began to limber up their guns, hitch up their horses, and pull hard down the turnpike to the north. They didn't all make it, though, and the VMI cadets captured at least one Union cannon. And the rest of the Confederate assault all along the line was relentless, hot on the heels of the retreating Yankees. Their wave surged forward, cresting on fallen blue soldiers and hastily abandoned weapons.

In this fight, 257 VMI cadets were engaged as well as six officers who led them. From among that number, two of the officers were wounded, while ten cadets were killed and forty-seven wounded. This became the first and is still the only time that the students of an American college have been called forward and fought in combat. It was an extraordinary and inspirational demonstration of personal courage by very young men. This performance by the VMI Corps of Cadets was stunning in its effect, and it is an exploit of which VMI graduates around the world will long remain fiercely proud.[5]

But as the blue line was collapsing and its soldiers began throwing down their cumbersome rifles and running to the rear, one fresh artillery battery of six guns came forward. It was Battery B, 5th United States Artillery, commanded by Captain Henry Algernon DuPont. Before the fighting started, he and his battery of three-inch guns had been left in the rear and forgotten. But when the blue line began to collapse at around 2:30 or 3:00 in the afternoon, General Jeremiah C. Sullivan's order to come forward finally reached him.

He did so at a gallop, but soon men and officers were flying past him toward the rear, though he never saw General Sullivan, his division commander. Instead, a number of young staff officers paused as he reached them, all giving him conflicting advice or directions and then digging in their spurs and racing farther to the rear.

And that command vacuum endured, for during the battle he did not receive a single order from any military superior. As things turned out, however, that did not matter at all. Having served in the North during the first three years of the war, he had not yet been under enemy fire. But when he was given a field artillery command in the Shenandoah Valley, it was apparent that they would soon become engaged with Confederate forces. DuPont therefore trained his battery very well, and when his fire was needed on the field of battle, he knew exactly what to do.

Given the panicked rout that seemed to be taking place all around him, he decided it might be worthwhile to risk the loss of a few guns in order to cover and protect the retreat of Sigel's entire command. Although he and his battery were in the open along the turnpike, thick smoke covered them and concealed their movements from Confederate commanders. DuPont rode forward beyond the last retreating wave of blue soldiers with one platoon, or two guns, under Lieutenant Charles Holman, and placed them on the west side of the turnpike, from which they immediately opened fire. Their orders were to hold until he returned to them, but under no circumstances to retreat without his personal order.

Then he rode back to the north some five to six hundred yards, where he emplaced another platoon of two guns under First Sergeant Samuel Southworth, but this time on the east side of the turnpike. Finally, he pointed to a small rise another five to six hundred yards to their rear and ordered Lieutenant Benjamin Nash to go into position there, from which he would cover the other two platoons as they pulled back. He told Southworth to open fire as soon as Lieutenant Holman's platoon had passed them, then dug in his spurs and raced back down the turnpike to the south.

This maneuver, known as "retiring by echelon of platoons," was one that DuPont had practiced many times, although he had not yet been called upon to use it in actual combat. Now, however, was his moment, and this specific maneuver was desperately needed to save Sigel's entire force. He could only trust in his men and their training, but he remained confident that they would perform as they had trained and so would succeed.

When he got to Holman's position, they were putting out fast and accurate fire, clearly staggering the gray line of soldiers moving toward them. Within a very short time, however, they could see no other soldiers in blue anywhere around them, and DuPont decided it was time for them to pull back. He told Holman to limber up, then race up the turnpike and to set up in the best position he could find along the turnpike five or six hundred yards beyond that of Lieutenant Nash.

Once Holman and his guns were on their way, DuPont joined Southworth, and they repeated the routine. They again waited until all blue soldiers had gotten past them, and, alone again, DuPont ordered them to cycle to the rear. Next he joined Nash and his guns, which were being fired heavily in their turn while waiting for the last blue soldiers to get well past them. Once these had gotten out of sight, DuPont gave the order to move to the rear and set up again at the appropriate distance beyond Holman's new position.

Though being implemented by DuPont's battery for the first time under fire, the maneuver worked extremely well. And their success was dramatic, for within a half mile or so, the gray pursuit slackened, then stopped. Edward Turner, a history professor at the University of Michigan, later wrote, "The pursuit . . . was retarded by the 34th Massachusetts . . . and also [by] DuPont's battery. This battery did excellent service, firing into the enemy and withdrawing slowly by platoon."[6]

Perhaps more noteworthy praise is that extended to him by a soldier on the Confederate side in that battle. Benjamin A. Colonna fought there as cadet captain of Company D of the VMI Corps of Cadets, and he recorded his memory of DuPont's battery fire as follows:

> The enemy was now, say 2:45 p.m., retreating everywhere in great disorder, and our pursuit continued until about 3:00 p.m., when we found ourselves in front of DuPont's Battery B, 5th Regular Artillery. The audacity of this battery caused us to think that it had a strong infantry support and we paused to form line before advancing further. This caused a delay of fifteen or twenty minutes and allowed the Thirty-fourth Mass., the Twelfth W. Va., and the Fifty-fourth Pa., and perhaps some other troops, time enough to slip through to freedom.[7]

Sigel was quite shaken by this defeat, and when the two armies had broken contact thanks to DuPont, he kept his men going north. But after they had crossed the bridge over the Shenandoah River, Sigel and his men never looked back. The bridge was still in place when the last retreating Union army element arrived there, DuPont's artillery battery. Without orders, DuPont did the only sensible thing: crossing the bridge and then destroying it, thus sealing them off from their Confederate pursuers.

Sigel and his men marched through the night and into the next day, reaching Strasburg the evening of 16 May. For Sigel, as he no doubt realized, that stunning defeat by a smaller Confederate force marked the last combat command his superiors would allow him. On 17 May General Halleck wrote the following to General Grant:

*I have sent the substance of your dispatch to General Sigel. Instead of advancing on Staunton, he is already in full retreat on Strasburg. If you expect anything from him you will be mistaken. He will do nothing but run. He never did anything else.*[8]

General David Hunter had graduated from West Point in 1822 and was therefore one of the oldest general officers to serve on either side in the Civil War. He had resigned his commission in 1836, as a captain, but then had been reappointed a major in 1842, filling the role of a paymaster from that time until Lincoln's election.[9]

Unlike most career army officers, Hunter was quite outspoken in his political opinions and was a strong, even vehement opponent of slavery. After Lincoln's election, Hunter was one of those who accompanied him to Washington before his inauguration in 1861, and he soon became fast friends with the new secretary of war, Edwin Stanton. It is not surprising, then, that he was appointed a colonel of cavalry and, after having been wounded at Bull Run, that he found himself promoted to brigadier general, then to major general.

Hunter had a mixed record in the early years of the war, with perhaps his most famous moment coming on 9 May 1862. Acting on his authority as commander of the Department of the South, he declared, "Slavery and martial law in a free country are altogether incompatible. The persons in these three

States—Georgia, Florida, and South Carolina—heretofore held as slaves, are therefore declared forever free." At the time, Lincoln was greatly concerned about the allegiance of those living in the "border states"—the slave states of Missouri, Kentucky, Maryland, and Delaware that had not seceded. Alarmed by Hunter's rash act without clearance from the White House, he quickly issued a proclamation that Hunter's edict was without any authority and that neither he nor any other military commander had the authority to emancipate slaves.[10]

Despite this abuse of authority, Hunter had made a name for himself, both North and South, and that no doubt saved his job. But he was removed from command of the Department of the South in August 1863, and he filled administrative roles until 21 May 1864. Then he was given the post from which General Sigel had been relieved, the command of the Army of West Virginia.

Hunter went right into action. On 23 May he announced in Special Orders No. 103 that "the whole artillery of this command will report direct to the chief of artillery on the staff of the major general commanding, and hereafter will be completely independent of brigade and division organizations."[11] On the same day, he called Captain DuPont in for an interview.

Captain DuPont's singular actions at New Market had been related to him, so he anticipated meeting just the sort of man he needed. After a brief discussion Hunter found him to be just as he had hoped and perfectly suited for the job. He therefore appointed DuPont chief of artillery of the Army of West Virginia and promulgated General Orders No. 31 to that effect on 24 May.[12]

In this new post DuPont was given command of the four mounted artillery batteries that constituted the artillery brigade of the Army of West Virginia. Although not technically a member of the general's staff, DuPont's position as artillery commander required him to report to department headquarters every day, and he often conferred with Hunter on other official business. He quickly found that Hunter would not interfere or allow others to interfere, whether in battle or elsewhere, with DuPont's command. That, of course, pleased him greatly.

Hunter's task remained that assigned to Sigel before him, so, after receiving reinforcements, he started his movement south into the valley from Strasburg on 26 May. After arriving at Woodstock on the 29th, Hunter received intelligence that General Imboden and his Confederates were setting up a strong defense somewhere north of Staunton, still a dozen miles or more to their south.

One of the Confederate advantages in the valley was that the mountain ranges were riddled with safe refuges from which the 43rd Virginia Cavalry, under the command of Lieutenant Colonel John Singleton Mosby, operated. Tasked with interrupting Yankee lines of communication in any way possible, they were a constant pest to Yankee commanders, and any wagon train had to be carefully guarded lest it be lost to them.

Given this constant threat, Hunter had announced that, after any such attack, he would burn to the ground any town or village nearby, thus destroying the homes of those who had made the attack. He was repeatedly told by men in his command and others that Mosby's men were drawn from the entire Confederacy, not just the Shenandoah Valley, and that any such burning would be futile. But he refused to listen to any such protests and reasserted his threat to burn private homes.

On 30 June, while en route to Mount Crawford, Hunter learned that such an attack had been made at Newtown, where several Yankee wagons and their teams had been spirited away by Mosby's men. Newtown was a small cluster of a dozen houses along the turnpike between him and Winchester, by this time many miles in his rear. Enraged, he immediately ordered one of his regiments of cavalry to go to Newtown the next day and burn to the ground every house, store, and outbuilding found there.[13]

At the time, Newtown was inhabited by women, children, and a few old men. The Union cavalry, under the command of Major Joseph K. Stearns, was met at Newtown by the entire population, who showed letters testifying that they had nursed wounded Union soldiers back to health. They also assured the major that the young men from their town were not serving with Mosby's Raiders, but rather were with regular Confederate army units that were operating far away from the valley.

Stearns was also faced with murmurs of disapproval from his men, who believed it was not part of their duty to burn the homes of helpless women, children, and old men, and some even said they would not obey an order to do so. Finding himself in a difficult situation and also feeling it wrong to so punish noncombatant civilians, Stearns finally decided not to burn the town. He rejoined the Union force at Woodstock and informed Hunter personally of his decision. Though apparently enraged by this, Hunter also must have realized that he may have gone a bit too far with this order to burn Newtown, for he never said another word about it.[14]

When the Union movement south from Winchester was being prepared in late May, General Imboden only had about 1,000 men to stand in the path of Hunter's 8,500. But he was rescued by General William E. "Grumble" Jones, who arrived with another 3,500 men drawn from southwestern Virginia and eastern Tennessee. They set up a strong defensive position just north of the small town of Piedmont, about ten miles north of Staunton.

On 4 June, the Union command once again started to move south, preceded by its cavalry. On 5 June, this mounted blue host smacked into Imboden's horsemen, who stopped them cold. One big problem reported from the lead units was the Confederate artillery fire, which they claimed was hammering them. The one artillery battery moving with the cavalry force sent word back that it was being outgunned, and DuPont raced to the front with two more batteries.

When he arrived, he found that the fire from the Confederate artillery was precisely on target and was devastating the Union guns. Several of the Union artillery horses had been killed, and the return fire of the battery, commanded by a lieutenant of about twenty years old, was confused and inaccurate at best. DuPont quickly told the lieutenant to cut his dead horses out of their harness and take his guns and limbers to the rear. Once he was out of range of the Confederate guns, he told the lieutenant to make his repairs as quickly as possible and then return to the cavalry division. DuPont then set his own two batteries up on either side of the road and opened a counter battery fire that soon found its mark. Within a very short time, the Confederate guns were withdrawn.[15]

The head of the main column arrived just after this had happened, and now DuPont had two more artillery batteries at his disposal. They moved steadily down the road toward Piedmont, infantry deployed on both sides of the road, until they came to a point from which the main Confederate defensive positions could be observed. They were formed in an L shape just north of the town of Piedmont, with one arm anchored on a bend in the river and facing mostly north, the other bending around and facing west along a ridgeline.

The enemy's artillery was firing from three locations, and their impact on the Union force was punishing. Having carefully observed the locations of the Confederate cannon, DuPont massed his twenty-two guns and consecutively put these rebel batteries under concentrated fire. Each in turn was silenced or forced to withdraw, which Hunter noted in his official report: "At 11:30, the fine practice of our artillery had silenced the enemy's batteries."[16]

After the Confederate artillery fire had been eliminated, the first Union infantry attack was launched from the right side of the road. The men slowly swept forward, with DuPont's guns firing over them and finally driving the gray soldiers back over the ridge.

Confederate general Jones now felt the mismatch of numbers, and he launched a furious counterattack to try to stop the wave of blue soldiers. Fighting swayed back and forth as each commander threw in more troops, dismounted cavalry by Hunter and infantry elements pulled out of his right line by Jones. But this drastic move was seen from the Union side as well, and the left end of the blue line swept forward and plunged through the wide gap that had opened in the Confederate line. Now desperate, Jones led another furious counterattack with his last reserves that might have tipped the balance. But at its height, Jones was shot and killed, and Confederate defenses quickly dissolved. More than a thousand Confederate soldiers were trapped against the river and captured, including some sixty officers.[17]

An important part of this victory, of course, was the deadly efficiency of the Union artillery. As Milton Humphreys later said, "the Confederate infantry was much reduced in numbers by the destructive fire of DuPont's guns," adding that "the reader will be struck with the fact that the sad 'day's work,' according to Imboden, did not result from the position, which, though not selected, happened to be an excellent one, but from the unforeseen and almost unparalleled efficiency of DuPont's artillery."[18]

After the battle, DuPont learned that the commander of the Confederate infantry brigade on the left end of their line was a Colonel William H. Browne, and he had been wounded and captured. DuPont immediately went to see him, as Browne had been a member of DuPont's class at West Point. In the spring of 1861, he had resigned before graduation when war broke out in order to serve his home state of Virginia. And now he was a wounded prisoner of war.

When DuPont found him, he had already been treated medically and, DuPont says, did not seem to be very seriously injured. The two talked for some time about the battle, Browne commenting on how the Union forces might have more easily turned the Confederate left flank. DuPont had not seen that part of the fighting and so said nothing. But then they began to talk about the long period of captivity as a wounded prisoner that lay before Browne. DuPont asked him if he had any money, to which Browne responded "not one cent." DuPont then gave him all the money he had on him, which was a ten-dollar bill. The two said their farewells and DuPont rejoined his unit. The next morning, before they began the march to Staunton, DuPont later stated, "I heard, to my great surprise and very great regret, that Browne had died of his wounds during the night."[19]

Hunter reached Staunton on 6 June, then turned left and moved farther southeast on the 10th. But while he and his men rested that day, a more important battle was taking place some fifty miles to their east.

# FIFTEEN

## Cavalry Clashes

Seemingly stalemated after the bloody battle of Cold Harbor, Grant set his eyes on Petersburg. He knew that another army, under General David Hunter, had reached Staunton and would soon turn east and cross the Blue Ridge Mountains. If he could take Petersburg and its railroads and Hunter could take Charlottesville and do the same, that would make Richmond almost untenable, with only the Richmond and Danville railroad line still feeding into Richmond from the southwest.

After leaving Lexington, Hunter moved east out of the valley through the Blue Ridge mountain range and was trying to take Lynchburg, some forty miles southwest of Charlottesville. He had been ordered to wreck that major rail center, then move northeast to Charlottesville and rip up that rail center. Grant intended Hunter to continue his destruction as he moved east, tearing up the Virginia Central Railroad line that fed into Richmond from the north.

According to his master plan, Grant would match the destruction of Hunter by assaulting Petersburg. Once the city was taken, he would wreck the rail net that fed through it and into Richmond, which was only about twenty miles directly north of Petersburg. But in order to take that key rail junction, Grant had to cross from the north to the south side of the James River under the nose of Robert E. Lee's Army of Northern Virginia—a high-risk venture he pulled off splendidly, as we have seen.

Grant then sent Sheridan and two divisions of cavalry on a raid to the west, largely as a distraction for Lee. As he moved, Sheridan was to tear up as much of the Virginia Central Railroad line as possible. Eventually he would reach Charlottesville unless he first reached Hunter's army moving east. Once they met, they would join forces and attack Richmond from the west.

Sheridan left on 7 June, moving up the North Anna River with some 8,000 men in two cavalry divisions under Generals Torbert and Gregg. Two of the brigades in Torbert's division were commanded by two of our men, Generals Merritt and Custer. They were aiming at Trevilian Station, which was just a station on the Virginia Central Railroad, but where Sheridan hoped to begin ripping up the iron tracks, which were a very scarce commodity in the South.

Lee soon learned of this operation, and the next day, 8 June, he sent two cavalry divisions of about 6,000 men to head them off. These were the divisions commanded by Generals Fitz Lee and Wade Hampton, who had a somewhat prickly personal relationship at the time. Since Stuart's death at Yellow Station in May, there had been an intense rivalry between them for overall command of the Army of Northern Virginia cavalry force. And, given his steadily decreasing number of experienced general officers, Robert E. Lee had to be very careful with this situation.

Ultimately, he abided by the technical military lines of authority between two officers of the same grade competing for command, and that was date of rank. Although his nephew Fitz Lee may well have seemed more aggressive and personally reliable to the army commander, the older and more prudent

Hampton had been promoted to major general at an earlier date, which settled the matter. Even so, given the personal tension aroused by their rivalry, Robert E. Lee had carefully avoided circumstances that would make Fitz Lee specifically subordinated to Hampton's command. But this was one moment when it couldn't be avoided, and on this operation Hampton had overall command authority. Of special interest to us is that one of the brigades in Hampton's force, the Laurel Brigade, was commanded by General Rosser.

The Union force moved slowly, hoping to avoid detection, and the Confederate force had a shorter distance to travel, which meant that it got to Trevilian Station on 10 June. Hampton made his camp a few miles west of the station, while Fitzhugh Lee set up at Louisa Courthouse, four or five miles to the east-southeast of Hampton. The Union force, meanwhile, had reached Clayton's Store, about three miles almost directly north of Louisa Courthouse, and its two divisions set up in that region.

It was Hampton's understanding from the intelligence he had received that Sheridan was intending to lead his force to Gordonsville ten miles to their northwest, ripping up the rail line all along the way. To prevent this, he knew he had to defeat it and either kill, capture, or drive away its blue horsemen. That night, he decided on the tactics he would use.

Clayton's Store could be reached from the Virginia Central rail line by two roads. One, the Marquis Road, led directly north from Louisa Courthouse to Clayton's Store. The other, the Fredericksburg Road, ran from Trevilian Station north for a few miles, then swung east and intersected with the Marquis Road just south of Clayton's Store.

Hampton decided the Confederates would strike the first blow, and at dawn his division would head north on the Fredericksburg Road, while that of Fitz Lee moved north on the Marquis Road. The plan called for them to join their forces just before striking the Yankees at Clayton's Store, then they would drive them north a few miles and trap them against the banks of the North Anna River.[1]

That, at least, was the plan. But since Sheridan had a similar plan of early morning attack, things were to work out somewhat differently.

At dawn the next day, Hampton had ordered no bugle calls as he didn't think the Union force knew he was so close. That seemed confirmed when, as his men were saddling up in the predawn gray, they could clearly hear reveille being blown in the Union camps only a few miles to their northeast. Hampton had sent Rosser's brigade to cover a road off to their left and act as his reserve, while keeping the brigades of Pierce M. B. Young (who had been Custer's classmate and friend at West Point until he resigned to fight for the Confederacy) and Matthew C. Butler for the main attack he was about to launch.

Once his men were mounted and in formation, Hampton had Young's brigade lead as his division started up the road from Trevilian Station to Clayton's Store. Fitz Lee would be leading his division north from Louisa Courthouse on the other road at about the same time, and at first light the two branches of the Confederate attack began their move.

But Hampton's force soon made contact with Union horsemen coming down the road toward them. For most of the Yankee soldiers, such a large gray force appearing in their path was an unexpected surprise. Almost all of Butler's brigade had dismounted and was advancing through the thick woods on foot, soon driving the Yankees before them. But it didn't take long for the larger Union numbers to have their effect, and the gray advance ground to a halt, with dismounted cavalrymen from both sides doing their best job as infantrymen firing at each other through the heavy underbrush.[2]

After several hours of heavy fighting, Hampton received word that a Union cavalry force was in his rear. After confirming that, he quickly ordered Butler and Young to break contact, remount, and head south down the road in the direction from which they had come. He also sent word to Rosser to return to Trevilian Station, where a force that appeared to be an entire Yankee brigade was loose in their rear.

As yet unbeknownst to them, this was Custer's brigade.

When Fitz Lee's division was moving up the Marquis Road, the lead regiment ran into what appeared to be a much larger Yankee cavalry force. In a flurry of gunshots, they paused and then pulled back to assess what lay before them. It turned out to be Torbert's 1st Cavalry Division.

Before moving south, Torbert had ordered Merritt's brigade to lead the Union column down the Marquis Road, followed by those of Colonel Thomas C. Devin and Custer. Custer had received the additional order to turn right off of the Marquis Road onto a county road that led through the woods to a point just east of Trevilian Station.[3] When the opening burst of gunfire was exchanged between Merritt's men and those of Fitz Lee, Custer was still north of this contact, concealed by a mass of blue horsemen. When he turned onto the county road, the ongoing firefight was sufficient to distract the attention of the men in gray, and none of them saw Custer's column moving around them through the woods.

It didn't take long for this brigade to come out of the trees along the railroad line, and Trevilian Station was a half mile or so to their right. But Custer instantly realized that he had gotten into the Confederate rear, for arrayed before him was a large baggage train, and without any significant force to defend it. His men swooped in and drove off the few men stationed there as guards, then captured fifty heavily laden wagons and forty ambulances, all with their mule teams in harness, six caissons, and a thousand or so horses. Though Custer did not know it then, these were the horses of Hampton's dismounted cavalrymen, horses that had been led to the rear so they would be safe.[4]

Rosser was off to the Confederate left, and he was recalled to attack Custer's brigade. He moved fast, but as he got near Trevilian Station, he found Union cavalrymen trying to get away with the Confederate horses and supplies they had captured. Rosser soon learned he faced a brigade commanded by Custer, and he slammed into one side of the small Union column from the west, driving it back. Meanwhile, Hampton's returning force nailed Custer's already-stretched force from the north. And from the southeast, completing the virtual circle of enemies around him, came Fitzhugh Lee, who only added to the desperation of the men in blue. And to complete the coup de main, as he approached Trevilian Station Fitzhugh Lee had swept up Custer's own headquarters wagon as well as all of Hampton's baggage train that Custer had earlier captured.[5]

Now attacked from three sides, Custer's men had all dismounted and formed a triangular defensive position, but no part of it was truly protected against gunfire coming in from another side of the line. Things got so tight that, when his color bearer was mortally wounded, Custer tore the flag from its staff and stuffed it inside his own jacket.[6]

Rosser was told by one of his artillerymen that Custer's command only amounted to 1,200 men, and that opportunity was all he could have asked for. After having decided to try to capture them all, he gave the orders to prepare for an all-out mounted charge. But before they got started, Hampton arrived and forbade the attack. Rosser, however, wanted desperately to capture Custer—what a personal triumph that would be!—and he pushed his men hard to keep up the pressure. They fought hard on foot, firing everything they had. But the return fire from Custer's men was just too strong, and they were never able to get the Yankees to surrender.[7]

The fight went on for four or five hours, but despite the disparity in numbers, it was an uneven match from the beginning. All of Custer's men were armed with Colt .44 revolvers as well as breech-loading Sharps or Burnside carbines or magazine-fed

Spencer repeating rifles, and thus were able to put out a much greater volume of fire than their Confederate opponents. Many of the latter also carried revolvers, but virtually none of them had breech-loading rifles or carbines—which meant that their long-barreled, muzzle-loading weapons could only fire two or three rounds per minute, while the Union breechloaders could fire fourteen rounds per minute or more.[8] Because of this firepower difference, then, Custer and his men were able to hang on all afternoon.

Finally, at around 5:00 p.m., Sheridan ordered a brigade from Gregg's division to cut his way in to Custer. Simultaneously, another of Gregg's brigades was sent around Louisa Courthouse, thus hitting Fitz Lee's division in the flank and forcing him to give up his hold. Once the siege had been lifted on that side, Custer had his 7th Michigan Cavalry mount and he led them in a hell-for-leather pursuit of the captured Union baggage trains. He caught up with them and took a few wagons, though not his own headquarters wagon. But soon his small regiment was dwarfed by the host of gray horsemen nearby, so he turned and took his own recaptured vehicles back to Union lines.[9]

Sometime during the attacks he led against Custer's position, a bullet hit Rosser just below the knee of his right leg and broke a bone. Though medicine was quite primitive at the time, a senior officer received more attention and care than a common soldier would have been accorded. Horror stories about medical care during the Civil War are abundant, such as the limited training of physicians and their ignorance of such fundamental things as the sources of infection or the ways in which diseases might spread. They did, however, know other important things, such as the need to clear debris from a wound and to keep it clean. Rosser was fortunate enough to have had his wound so well treated that he did not acquire gangrene or any other serious infection.

Taken immediately to the rear, his wound was treated, and then he was transported by ambulance to the James River. There he boarded a boat that took him back to Richmond, where he endured further medical treatment and a lengthy rest, which he hated. Finally, once he was fully recovered, he resumed command of his brigade near Petersburg on 22 August.[10]

The next morning, 12 June, the Confederate cavalry was gone, and Sheridan's men tore up all the railroad track between Trevilian Station and Louisa Courthouse. Scouts sent out that afternoon found the Confederates in a strong defensive position along the railroad embankment about one mile northwest of Trevilian Station. And so, still not yet ready to give up, Sheridan launched a series of seven attacks in the afternoon against the left flank of the reunited Confederate line, with the last one occurring just at nightfall. All were easily rejected, and eventually, Hampton sent a brigade around Sheridan's position to strike his rear. This surprised the Union force, and after making their last attack at dusk, they withdrew during the night.[11]

Both sides were badly bled. Hampton had brought about 5,000 soldiers into this fight, and he reported a loss from his division of 59 killed, 258 wounded, and 295 missing (killed or captured), for a total loss of 612. Sheridan started with about 8,000 men, and he lost 85 killed, 490 wounded, and less than 150 captured, for a total loss of 725. Fitz Lee's losses from this battle were not reported, but his division was less engaged than was that of Hampton, which means fewer casualties, though of an unknowable number. In any case, even though both sides were badly hurt, that fact was more important to the Confederacy, whose soldiery was drawn from a much smaller population base.[12] But despite the disparity in the size of the two armies, Trevilian Station was clearly a victory for the South, as Sheridan was deterred from moving on to Charlottesville, which he surely would have done had he "won."

Back in the Shenandoah Valley, Hunter's men reached Lexington on 11 June. They were met by sniper fire, some of it coming from the cadet barracks of the Virginia Military Institute, whose cadets had fought at the battle of New Market. DuPont was ordered to return fire, and his guns fired several rounds before receiving the order to cease.[13]

Hunter's force stayed in Lexington for two more days, during which he ordered that all the buildings at VMI be burned to the ground, as well as the private residence in town of the most recent former governor of Virginia, John Letcher. Though before the war he had opposed secession, he also had, more recently, called on all Virginians to resist the invaders. And this, in Hunter's view, justified the destruction by fire of his private home and possessions.

The home of VMI's president, General Francis H. Smith, was spared because of the illness of a family member living there. But all the other buildings at VMI were destroyed by fire. This did not sit well with DuPont, and he and a few other soldiers (including then captain and later president William McKinley) helped carry some of the furniture of one professor's wife, Mrs. Gilham, out of her house before it was put to the torch. One of Mrs. Gilham's brothers, as she pleadingly told Union soldiers, was an officer in the United States regular army. But that made no difference whatever to Hunter, and he had his men burn her house to the ground.

In fact, General Francis H. Smith was not only a West Point graduate from the class of 1833, but his roommate and best friend at West Point was none other than Captain DuPont's father, Henry DuPont. In fact, in 1856 Henry Senior had written to his old roommate Frank, asking if his son could be admitted to VMI as a student.[14] At the time only residents of Virginia could attend VMI, so that was never an option for young Henry, who, after a year at the University of Pennsylvania, ended up a cadet at West Point instead. But it must have been ironic indeed that Captain DuPont found himself witnessing the wanton destruction of a renowned military academy whose superintendent was his father's former roommate and best friend.

The walls of the cadet barracks were stone and so remained standing. The interior was gutted by flame, however, and all other nonstone buildings at the academy, save only the superintendent's home, were reduced to ashes. For Captain DuPont, the cadet barracks were an appropriate subject of Union army destruction. They had, after all, housed and been the base of operations of several hundred uniformed boys who, despite their youth, had fought and killed Union soldiers at New Market.

But the rest of the destruction of what were basically instruments of education and the buildings that housed them he believed to be wanton and wicked. Such destruction by fire was contrary to all conventions of civilized warfare, which, as far as possible, respect the property of institutions of learning. And for Henry Algernon DuPont, only a powerless captain at the time and bound to do the bidding of a stubborn and unthinking general, this affair was far from over.[15]

On 14 June, Hunter and his army set out for Lynchburg, and on the 17th, they engaged Confederate forces some five miles north of that town and forced them back on their entrenchments. Grant had ordered Hunter, upon reaching Lynchburg, to destroy as much of that railhead as possible, then move forty miles northeast to Charlottesville, tearing up the railroad tracks that ran between those two cities as he used them to guide his march. But that night, they heard the loud rumblings of many trains. In the morning, they renewed their advance and were soon heavily engaged.

That day, 18 June, heavy artillery fire came from the still-unknown Confederate force, fire that was frighteningly accurate. The noisy rumbling of arriving trains never slowed all day, and they soon learned from prisoners the meaning of these trains: they were bringing Ramseur's division as well as part of Gordon's, to Lynchburg, with more to follow. These divisions, the Yankee commanders all knew, were major elements of Early's 2nd Corps of Robert E. Lee's Army of Northern Virginia.

They had heard stories from prisoners taken days earlier that Early's entire corps was being brought to defend Lynchburg. These stories, however, had been largely dismissed by Hunter and others at the top as little more than rumors or wishful thinking: Lee was being pressed hard by Grant outside of Richmond, and he simply could not afford to send one of his three corps far away to defend Lynchburg; that much was obvious.

But now the prisoners they captured gave them hard evidence that the rumors were true, and Hunter had to rethink his intentions to take Lynchburg.[16] Having added Crook's infantry division and Averell's cavalry division, his force numbered about 18,000. Unbeknownst to Hunter, however, there would only be about 14,000 men in Early's reassembled force in Lynchburg.[17]

The Union force was low on food and ammunition, but Hunter had planned to resupply himself from the Confederate stocks they would capture in Lynchburg. Unfortunately for the men in blue, he thought Early's corps was much larger than his army, and he was intimidated, if not terrified, by the prospect of facing a larger force. What was he to do? Believing that he now faced an entire corps of Lee's hardened soldiers that far outnumbered his own force, he didn't have to think very long at all. That very night, he turned his men around and raced north, never stopping or even slowing down until he was well into West Virginia.[18]

As Early followed him, he abided by his orders from Robert E. Lee:

*General Early was instructed, if his success justified it, and the enemy retreated down the Valley, to pursue him, and, if opportunity offered, to follow him into Maryland. It was believed that the Valley could then be effectually freed from the presence of the enemy, and it was hoped that by threatening Washington and Baltimore General Grant would be compelled either to weaken himself so much for their protection as to afford us an opportunity to attack him, or that he might be induced to attack us.[19]*

Early did venture into Maryland, where his corps of 14,000 defeated a Union army of 6,000 at the battle of Monocacy on 9 July. Two days later his men approached the northern walls surrounding Washington at a time when they were only thinly manned. However, his entire army was not up then, and he delayed attacking until they arrived, though his riflemen did exchange fire with Union soldiers manning the walls. President Lincoln had always wondered about the Southern soldiers his men faced, and so, out of curiosity, he went to a fort on the northwest wall of the city. According to his personal secretary, John Hay:

> *At three o'clock p.m. the President came in bringing the news that the enemy's advance was at Ft Stevens on the 7th Street road. He was in the Fort when it was first attacked, standing upon the parapet. A soldier roughly ordered him to get down or he would have his head knocked off.*[20]

Lincoln thus became the only man who, as president, came under direct fire from enemy soldiers. And according to legend, the soldier who yelled at him so fiercely was a captain from the 20th Massachusetts Volunteers, a man recovering from his third wound at the time who didn't realize he was yelling at the president: the future Supreme Court justice Captain Oliver Wendell Holmes.

To defend the city, Grant had sent an infantry corps from Petersburg, and they arrived the night of 11–12 July. By the morning of the 12th, the northern defenses of the city were manned by a strong force. Ramseur explained in a letter he wrote to his wife, Nellie:

> *Natural obstacles alone prevented our taking Washington. The heat and the dust was so great that our men could not possibly march further. Time was thus given the enemy to get a sufficient force into his works to prevent our capturing them.*[21]

Early's men turned around that day, and by 14 July they were all safely back in the Shenandoah Valley. Lee had been able to frighten his adversary by sending Early north to threaten Washington, but that would only mean firmer resolve from the Union.

# SIXTEEN

## *Tora, Tora, Tora*

Grant was tired of the Confederacy having access to the Shenandoah Valley for free passage north whenever it wanted. The provisions that land produced for Lee's army hunkered down around
Petersburg also irritated him, and he planned to stop both.

Clearly neither Hunter nor Sigel was up to the task of ward-
ing off Early's army, let alone laying waste to the abundant
agricultural bounty. After this scare from Early's army, Grant
decided to find a general who could prevent another such inva-
sion. There were politics involved, of course, but Grant was
eventually able to appoint the man he really wanted in that post,
a trusted lieutenant he had brought with him from the West
who had most recently commanded his cavalry corps during the
Wilderness campaign.

On 7 August General Philip H. Sheridan took over command of what was then called the Middle Military Division.
But most important, he also took command of the army that
he would lead in the field and use to clear Confederate forces
from the valley, later to be known by the name Army of the
Shenandoah.

In accord with his instructions from Grant, Sheridan was cautious at first, having no knowledge of the terrain or of his enemy. Indeed, he didn't even know much about his own new command. But whatever else he may have been, he was also an aggressive fighter.

Several months earlier, he had crossed swords with General George Meade over his cavalry's ability to catch and defeat General J. E. B. Stuart's much-storied Confederate cavalry. Known widely through the North as "Stuart and His Invincibles," this Confederate force had ridden around the entire Union army on three occasions and had still not been soundly defeated in battle by Union horsemen. When Sheridan proposed leading a cavalry expedition to seek Stuart out and defeat him on the field of battle, Meade, who was technically still the commander of the Army of the Potomac, forbade it. But Grant, who was in the field with the Army of the Potomac and Meade's superior, told Sheridan to go ahead and give it a try.

So it was that on 9 May 1864 Sheridan led all three of his cavalry divisions on an expedition aimed at running Stuart's cavalry force to ground and defeating it. The 1st Cavalry Division was commanded by General Torbert, and it was made up of three brigades, two of which were commanded by Merritt and Custer. The other two divisions were commanded by Generals Averell and Wilson, and Sheridan watched them all very closely.

Sheridan was a harsh disciplinarian, an impatient man with a raging temper, and he tended to make quick assessments of his subordinate commanders. These weren't always fair, but that was the way he operated. If you showed yourself to be, like Sheridan himself, an aggressive fighter who yet retained some prudence in committing your men, then he would not only support you but might even welcome you into his inner circle of protégés. But if he detected in you hesitation or lack of planning or any other leadership flaw, you had little hope of recovery in his eyes.

It was soon understood within his command that if, as a

division or brigade commander under him, you made one error, such as failing to lead from the front in a mounted charge, or even failing to show up with your unit on time for a troop movement, that was all he needed: you had just struck out, even though it was only on one pitch, and you could count on him finding a way to get rid of you.

On this expedition Sheridan paid close attention to the behavior in combat of his subordinate division and brigade commanders. Torbert was not available, so Merritt was made the temporary division commander, and Custer was one of his brigade commanders. The reason Merritt was selected for this command rather than Custer was that, even though they had both been jumped from captain to brigadier general on the same day, 28 June 1863, Merritt was two classes ahead of Custer at West Point and had been commissioned a full year before Custer. Sheridan liked both Merritt and Custer very much, and this technical difference in dates of commission gave him an easy way of choosing between them for temporary command of a division without any personal offense inferred by either.

On that first day, Custer's brigade led the column of horsemen and in late afternoon they came out of the woods to find some 300 Union prisoners being escorted by Confederate guards toward a railroad siding. As the blue cavalry came racing out of the trees, the guards ran into another stretch of woods, though many of them were captured by their former prisoners. And the shrieks from railroad engines signaling them to hurry brought an unexpected shower of Union horsemen crashing down on the massively outnumbered guards. They captured both trains as well as an "immense quantity" of commissary and medical supplies.[1]

The trains were burned, and all the supplies that could not be carried off were destroyed as well. But in his official report, Merritt showed concern over the somewhat impulsive nature of the use of fire:

*A misconception of orders given or some other cause marred the success that might have attended this day's work, as by lighting fires after the capture of the station the enemy were informed of our position and many stores were destroyed which would, as our after experience developed, have been very useful in rationing the men in the command. The success was complete, however, and as it cost nothing in lives or trouble no one felt like taking serious notice of the gaucherie which lost us some of the fruits of a hard day's march.*[2]

The expedition moved on, and on 11 May, it engaged J. E. B. Stuart and his much smaller cavalry force at Yellow Tavern. While the Union force eventually drove the Confederates back, the most important event of the day was, as noted earlier, the mortal wounding of Stuart, who was quickly carried away by ambulance and died the next day in Richmond.

Sheridan's expedition moved on, tearing up Confederate railroad tracks, capturing and destroying crucially important military supplies, and skirmishing with rebel cavalry almost daily. Finally, on 25 May, the expedition ended when it reentered the lines of the Army of the Potomac near Chesterfield Station, having traveled nearly three hundred miles in sixteen days of operation.[3]

During the expedition, Sheridan had observed all his commanders at close range, and his two favorites for the rest of the war would be Custer and Merritt. Now he was ordered to enter the Shenandoah Valley and take on the aggressive General Jubal Early, who had driven Hunter before him. He was very pleased to have two such battle-hardened veterans in command below him, and he would take good care of them.

Sheridan would have three divisions of cavalry with him in the Shenandoah Valley, a force he thought too unwieldy for him to command personally. He therefore made Torbert his chief of cavalry and named Merritt to command the 1st Cavalry Division in Torbert's place. But when Sheridan arrived in the valley,

Merritt's was the only Union cavalry division Sheridan had with him, some 3,500 men strong. His total force included another 22,000 infantry, and he faced about 20,000 men under Early.

On 10 August Merritt moved out and Early steadily withdrew before him. But given the record of Union troops being repeatedly beaten in the Shenandoah Valley, Sheridan had been ordered to exercise caution. By 12 August the Confederates had reached a strong defensive position at Fisher's Hill, and neither Wilson's nor Averell's cavalry division had reached Sheridan. That irritated him, and because of added blunders, both men would eventually be transferred out of the Army of the Shenandoah. He had also heard that Early was expecting major reinforcements of infantry and cavalry from Richmond, and stopping his advance was prudent.

On 16 August Williams C. Wickham's Confederate cavalry brigade splashed across the Shenandoah River and attacked one of Merritt's brigades. But this was only a distraction, for a large body of infantry was moving on the other side of the river and maneuvering to strike Sheridan in the flank. Sheridan pulled back, and Merritt dismounted one regiment of Custer's cavalry brigade on a hill near the ford that the Confederate infantry planned to use. When the rebels began to cross, Custer's dismounted men opened up on them with their repeating carbines and the rest of his brigade charged into the milling Confederates. Those who could got back across the river, but nearly 300 of them were captured in what has been called the battle of Cedarville. Merritt's official report noted, "Great credit is due General Custer for the masterly manner in which he handled his command."[4]

Intelligence reports continued to warn of great increases to Early's strength, although in fact Sheridan's force was about the same size. Even so, Mosby's Raiders continued to attack and steal or destroy supply convoys, which seriously handicapped Sheridan. When word of this reached Washington, Sheridan was ordered to fall back, but on the way to destroy all crops and seize all livestock between Strasburg and Winchester, which his men proceeded to do.

On 28 August, having been reinforced by Averell's cavalry division, Sheridan moved back into the valley, led by Merritt's cavalry. But he was still cautious and attacks by Early's infantry drove them back to old defensive positions. The cavalry continued to skirmish with Confederate horsemen most days, but they did not move forward for nearly three weeks. Finally, on 19 September, Sheridan moved his men forward, following a plan he had devised to trap Early's army at Winchester and destroy it.

But it was a complicated plan, requiring cavalry river crossings before dawn and coordinated assaults. And predictably, although successfully launched, all the good plans somehow went awry. Initially blocked by Confederate infantry in strong positions, Merritt simply waited until early afternoon, when his opponents were withdrawn. Merritt then faced only a light screen of gray horsemen, which he easily crashed through to join up with Averell's cavalry division on the turnpike. Together they moved toward Winchester, their path now blocked by Fitzhugh Lee's thin cavalry brigade.

A saber charge by both divisions sent the men in gray clattering back through Winchester. They took several rebel artillery batteries that had been firing on them, though at the cost of many blue troopers. Finally, their path into Winchester was blocked only by Early's last reserve, which was Breckinridge's infantry division. They were lined up side by side, and Merritt arrayed his own men in a similar formation, a line of blue that was a half mile wide and three horses deep.

At a signal, they charged forward with a shout, and the men in gray, after firing one volley, simply crumpled and were killed, captured, or driven through Winchester. Unfortunately, Wilson's cavalry division had not arrived to stop them on the other side of town, so the larger part of them got away. This was a triumphant day for the Union, and for Custer, but mostly for the division commander, Merritt. His division had carried off a series of six distinct saber attacks that day, the first five by various brigades against artillery positions defended by infantry. And the last was made by the entire division, in which it routed Breckinridge's infantry division and drove Confederate forces out of Winchester. Credited with the capture of 70 officers, 775 enlisted soldiers, and two pieces of artillery, it was a splendid day for the men in blue.[5]

On 22 September Sheridan launched a main frontal attack against Early's defenses at Fisher's Hill. Crook's division turned the Confederate left flank and drove the rebels from their defenses. Averell was supposed to pursue the Confederate cavalry but instead went into camp, leaving Sheridan's infantry to pursue the enemy for fifteen miles during the night. This infuriated Sheridan, and on 23 September he relieved Averell of command, replacing him temporarily with a colonel.[6]

As part of the attack, he had sent Torbert with Wilson's and Merritt's divisions of cavalry down the Luray Valley and so around Massanutten Mountain, with the intention that he would come out south of Fisher's Hill and bar Early's retreat to the south. However, he ran into some resistance from Confederate cavalry, at which he immediately backtracked without even putting up much of a fight. Because of that, Torbert never made it to the south of Fisher's Hill and Early got away clean. One of the cavalry regimental commanders, Colonel James H. Kidd, said, "If Custer or Merritt had been in command it would have been different."[7]

Sheridan was very proud of his cavalrymen, especially Merritt and Custer. But Wilson's lackluster performance on 26 September had again displeased Sheridan and he got him transferred. In his place, Custer was given command of the 3rd Cavalry Division. Men in his Michigan brigade, which was part of the 2nd Cavalry Division and so no longer under Custer's command, were disconsolate. Men in the 3rd Cavalry Division, however, began looking for bits of red cloth to wear around their necks.

In October, Sheridan's men began "the burning," destroying everything in the valley they could find that might be of use to the Confederates. This infuriated Early's men, of course, but in order to stop it they needed more soldiers and more firepower. As it happened, Lee also wanted to reduce pressure on Richmond, and one way to do that would be to start a raging fire of combat in the Shenandoah Valley. Lee therefore sent Early a battalion of artillery, Kershaw's 2,700-man infantry division, and Rosser's cavalry brigade of 600 horsemen.

Rosser and his men arrived in the valley on 5 October. Because Fitzhugh Lee had been seriously wounded at the battle of Winchester, Rosser was given command of his cavalry division, which would include his own Laurel Brigade that he had brought from Richmond. An added benefit to being placed in that command was that Rosser would be promoted to the rank of major general, a reward he had clearly earned.

Rosser's division was made up of three brigades, but because of a shortage of horses and men, his force only numbered about 2,500. Realizing he was outnumbered, Early ordered Rosser not to engage but rather only to harass the federals, who were burning barns and crops while driving off all the livestock they found.

The men in blue were creating a wasteland of the lower Shenandoah Valley, leaving the local residents with little or nothing on which to survive. When one of Sheridan's staff officers was killed by Mosby's Raiders on 3 October, he ordered every house and barn within five miles burned to the ground. But beginning to run short of supplies himself, Sheridan started to withdraw his forces north, down the valley.

Three main roads ran in rough parallel down the valley, known as the Valley Turnpike, the Middle Road, and the Back Road. The Back Road ran closest to and parallel with the

Allegheny ridgeline, and Rosser used that to approach the trailing blue horsemen, who turned out to be Custer's rear guard. On 6 October they first clashed, but the contact was little more than spirited skirmishing. On 7 October Rosser had his men on the move at dawn, but they didn't catch Custer's men until midafternoon, in the midst of a smoking wasteland.

Their attacks were furious, and they drove their opponents back, recapturing several hundred head of sheep and cattle as well as some wagons and teams. But rather than launching any major counterattacks, Custer's men simply continued to withdraw to the north. When Rosser returned this livestock to its rightful owners, he was hailed as the "Savior of the Valley."[8]

By this time, Rosser had followed Custer more than twenty miles, but Early believed Sheridan was leaving the valley and he urged Rosser to push on. Rosser didn't like being so far away from infantry support, but Early's orders left him no choice. Still, he dreaded an all-out attack by Sheridan's 23,000-man army, against which he knew he could not hold out for long.

On 8 October his scouts told Rosser that Sheridan had stopped and was sending a strong cavalry force south on the Back Road. As long as it was only cavalry, Rosser was eager to fight, so he lay in wait, then struck the head of the column in a violent saber charge just north of Toms Brook. The Union cavalry was sent reeling to its rear, and Rosser then withdrew across Toms Brook and set up on the high ridge just south of it known as Spiker's Hill, between the turnpike and the Back Road.

Angered by word that Rosser was being hailed as "Savior of the Valley," Sheridan had had enough. That night, as his commander of cavalry later said in his official report, Sheridan ordered him to "start out at daylight and whip the rebel cavalry or get whipped myself."[9]

Torbert sent those attack orders forward to Merritt and Custer, who were in close contact with each other, their men spread out between the Back Road and the turnpike. Merritt's division numbered about 3,500, while Custer's was 2,500. By this time, all these Union cavalrymen were armed with repeating carbines as well as pistols and sabers, which would greatly add to their firepower.

Early had also sent his other cavalry division forward on the turnpike, which ran down the middle of the valley. Consisting of only about 1,000 horsemen under General Lunsford L. Lomax, they spent the night south of Toms Brook, but stretched across the turnpike itself. Unhappily for them, these men were armed with muzzle-loading rifles and carried no sabers, pistols, or repeating carbines, which would mean a significant handicap for them in fighting Union cavalry. But although they were only three miles apart and effectively next to each other, there was no contact made between these two Confederate forces, which would put them at a distinct disadvantage.

Toms Brook runs at the bottom of steep and heavily wooded slopes, and the crest of high ground on either side alternates between open fields and wooded areas. At dawn Rosser and his staff were in an open area atop the ridge on the southern side, with his cavalry division and his artillery battery arrayed behind him on either flank. Facing them a few hundred yards away on the northern side of Toms Brook, a mass of Union cavalrymen in formation covered the crest, stretching as far in either direction as Rosser could see. The air was electric with tension, but as the sun broke above the horizon, neither side moved.

Then there was a stirring in the federal formation, and a single rider came out in front of the blue ranks. Galloping to the very edge of the precipice, the horseman stopped. There was no mistaking the flamboyant cavalier on that spirited steed: it was Custer, and he and Rosser immediately recognized each other. Turning his horse sideways, Custer grasped his wide-brimmed hat and raised it, then lowered it in front of him and bent forward in a sweeping bow. Rosser raised his own hat and mirrored the bow. An enormous shout that was both a cheer and a challenge erupted from the men on both sides: be on guard, for you now face death at my hands.[10]

No words were spoken by Custer or Rosser, and none were needed. Here were two Black Knights of the Hudson, facing each other and calling for a fair fight with no malice. This formal, gentlemanly salute presaged the best of contests: the two old friends and the finest riders at the academy, drinking companions from Benny Havens and blood brothers for life, now come face-to-face and ready to thrust their cavalry divisions at each other's throats in a mano a mano duel.

A few days earlier, a valley farmer had delivered a note to Rosser from Custer. In it, he reprimanded Rosser for exposing himself too much, since Custer had seen him the day before and had tried to keep his own men from shooting him. He urged Rosser to be more careful so he would live long enough for Custer to give him a good thrashing. Then, after the war, the two of them could get together and laugh about the times they had faced each other.[11]

This face-off at Toms Brook was Trevilian Station all over again, where Rosser and other Confederate commanders had trapped and nearly captured Custer, only to see him rescued at the last moment by Sheridan. But this time, it was more personal. It was Rosser and Custer, each leading his own division of some 2,500 mounted men, sabers drawn and ready. Both men exuded confidence, ready to clash and confident of victory over the other. Their eyes silently declared their personal challenge to each other: may the best man win.

Both generals withdrew from the crests and rejoined their troops. Torbert had ordered Merritt to attack Lomax in a holding action, while the main attack would be against Rosser by overwhelming force. Accordingly, Merritt sent one brigade forward against Lomax, who was in a strong position a quarter mile past Toms Brook, behind Jordon Run. That done, he sent his other two brigades, about 2,000 men, to assist Custer, and they came up on his left flank. This allowed Custer to sidle his forces to his right, with both his wings reaching beyond both ends of Rosser's defensive lines.

Rosser's men were dismounted and waiting in defensive positions behind stone walls and other obstacles, with a mounted reserve in their rear. Both sides had six artillery pieces, and these immediately opened a duel across Toms Brook. Custer dismounted one brigade and sent them down the slope and up the far side in a frontal attack while keeping the rest of his force as mounted reserve. He sent one regiment up the Back Road on his far right flank in an effort to get into Rosser's rear, but they were stopped by part of one brigade that Rosser had posted there.[12]

After several hours of fighting, Custer sent two more regiments to his right flank as reinforcements for his attackers on the Back Road, and Merritt's two brigades under Kidd and Devin on Custer's left made steady ground. Eventually Rosser was down to defending Spiker's Hill from a horseshoe-shaped position, but the superior Union numbers and firepower began to have their effect and it was soon clear he had to withdraw or be overrun. But when he sent word to pull back, a sudden shout was heard on his left from his men being chased from the Back Road by blue horsemen: "We're flanked! We're flanked!" The panic spread as the rest of his dismounted men raced for their horses, and what had started as an orderly retreat soon became a rout.[13]

Lomax's men were already retreating on the Valley Pike, and Rosser's men soon joined them. They ran toward the county seat of Woodstock in their deep rear, and far beyond, moving just as fast as their horses or their legs would carry them. Pursued by Custer, this battle and pursuit are also remembered as the "Woodstock Races," which went on for anywhere from twelve to twenty miles, depending on who you want to believe. But Custer captured all of Rosser's artillery, some 300 prisoners, and all his supply wagons, leaving him in a state of pure delight.

The Confederates fell far south into the upper valley before they were able to recover any semblance of order. When they finally got far beyond Union gunfire, they gradually began to recover their organization, nursing their wounded and husbanding their supplies as best they could. They had been outnumbered and outgunned, there was no doubt about that. Still, it was a humiliating and depressing defeat that Early had to report to Robert E. Lee in Petersburg.

That night, having dug through Rosser's personal things in his captured supply wagon, Custer strutted around Union campfires dressed in the finely tailored uniform of his much taller and heavier friend/enemy. He even wrote a note to Rosser, which he left with a local farmer, informing him that the uniform looked good on him, but next time, to please have it shortened a bit. He later learned that Rosser had received the note, which pleased him greatly.[14] The crushing blow he had delivered at Toms Brook certainly made up for the beating he had taken from Rosser at Trevilian Station.

This victory seemed to confirm once and for all that Union cavalry had complete control over the Shenandoah Valley. There was no Confederate aggression anywhere in the valley, and Sheridan believed that what was left of Early's army had been sent to reinforce Lee at Petersburg. Because of that, he prepared to send the VI Corps back to Grant outside of Petersburg. Fortunately for the Union, Grant told Sheridan to keep the VI Corps in the valley, for Early was a sly fox, and he wasn't quite done just yet.

---

In addition to having lost a battle as well as his artillery and personal effects, Rosser was particularly stung because he had been whipped by Custer. Hungry for revenge, he spent many hours trying to find a way for him to get back at his old friend. Then his scouts learned that Custer was camping in the valley near Old Forge, several miles from Sheridan's main army. Because many of his soldiers were intimately familiar with the lay of the land, he learned that Custer's camp could be easily approached without discovery by moving along back roads at the foot of North Mountain.

On 17 October, just eight days after Toms Brook, Rosser made his move. With General Early's approval, he selected 500 men from his cavalry and mounted an equal number of infantrymen from Grimes's brigade behind them. They set out after dark, their goal that night to capture Custer. There was no moon, and, without detection, the column of two men on each horse approached what they believed to be Custer's location. After dividing his force in half and arraying it so that he might strike the camp from two directions, Rosser gave the signal and both elements rushed the camp.

But despite the fact that their intelligence was only hours old, and to their great distress, Rosser's men found that Custer was gone, and they only captured a strong picket force. They returned to their own camp somewhat disheartened, though they did bring many prisoners back with them. But this attack showed the Union army that the Confederate cavalry's spirit had not been crushed, and it put some of them—not all—on a higher state of alert.[15]

The 18th of October 1864 was a crisp, bright autumn day in Virginia's Shenandoah Valley, the mountainsides lit by yellow beeches, the morning's chill fading as the sun rose. That afternoon, Captain Jed Hotchkiss stood atop the northern peak of Massanutten Mountain and swept his binoculars from side to side, slowly and methodically drinking in the array of Union forces below him.

To his north and northwest, white tents and artillery batteries dotted the woods and fields, the farmland swarming with countless men and horses. The Yankee camp was sprawled across the plain that lay below him, occupying the great central swath of the valley floor north of the confluence of Cedar Creek and the North Fork of the Shenandoah River.

These were Sheridan's men, a force of 30,000 to 40,000 that had been pounding Early's Confederate force of 15,000 to 20,000 for many weeks now. As he pored over the scene, Hotchkiss repeatedly put the binoculars down to work on a map he was sketching, showing positions of infantry, cavalry, and artillery and making other notes on the terrain for Early. Beside him, Confederate general John B. Gordon also used binoculars to survey the scene, as did a few others in their party.

Hotchkiss was a skilled mapmaker, once on the staff of General Stonewall Jackson but now working for General Jubal Early, while Gordon commanded one of Early's infantry divisions. From a Confederate signal station high atop the northern end of Massanutten Mountain, they were exploring Yankee positions through their field glasses, looking for unit locations and weaknesses that they could exploit. At the same time, a similar party under General Pegram had been sent across the Shenandoah Valley to look for flaws in the Union's right flank.[16]

Sheridan had badly punished Early's heavily outnumbered force on several occasions since August and driven it in some disorder upriver to the southern end of the valley, the "Upper Valley." And now, in October, though still outnumbered by two to one or more, Early found himself in a dilemma: the "Lower Valley" had been denuded of food for his men and fodder for his horses. But if he and his men stayed safe and secure in the "Upper Valley," he could not from there perform the duties Lee had assigned him. And those were, first, to deny Yankee use of the Baltimore and Ohio Railroad and the Chesapeake and Ohio Canal; and second, and perhaps more important, to continue to pose a threat to Baltimore and Washington. If convincing enough, that would cause Lincoln to divert significant forces from Grant's Army of the Potomac, an army then pressing

Lee's Army of Northern Virginia back against the defenses of Richmond.

The decision had not been hard, and an ever-aggressive Early was looking for a way to launch a surprise dawn attack. His right flank rested on Massanutten Mountain, and because it seemed such a steep and impenetrable obstacle, he planned to launch an attack around his left wing, against the Union army's right flank. But final plans awaited the return of his two scouting parties and their confirmation of favorable prospects for such a move. He was to be somewhat surprised by what he learned from them.

That night, Hotchkiss showed him the detailed map he had drawn of what lay before him. First of all, the blue forces were arrayed behind Cedar Creek on the west, and the North Fork of the Shenandoah River it poured into on the east. This water-course ran on a roughly east–west line while dipping to the south so that, seen from above, it formed a giant U, within which the Union army was encamped. This river ran very close to the bottom of steep-sided Massanutten Mountain, a piece of terrain so forbidding that Sheridan's army used it as the base against which its left flank rested. They clearly believed there was no possibility of Confederate forces getting past the mountainside that ran so close to the south side of the river, and so the left flank was lightly guarded.

But Hotchkiss had found that there was a narrow trail along the northern base of the mountain that could be used, single file, by Early's men. It was Gordon's idea, Hotchkiss told Early, to have several divisions move down this trail at night and so get around the Union left flank. Once they got past the mountain, as he showed Early on the map, they could cross the river at two fords, then burst into the flank and rear of the still-sleeping blue soldiers at dawn.

Next morning, Gordon confirmed Hotchkiss's intelligence and the possibility of his idea to use the narrow path to get around the Union left flank. Pegram reported that the Union right flank was heavily defended by infantry behind the high, steep banks of Cedar Creek and supported by what appeared to be all of the Union cavalry. That combination would make a successful Confederate attack there almost impossible.

Having heard these two scouting reports, Early suspected that the Union forces did not expect any Confederate attack against their far superior numbers. Because of their overconfidence, he was sure that they were only prepared defensively for an attack launched against the middle of their line or their right flank. And their largely undefended east flank offered just the opportunity Early had hoped to find.

Having spent weeks on end running from the Yankees, the 3,000 men in Dod Ramseur's division were eager for revenge. But Dod was probably more excited by a personal matter than he had ever been in his life. The night before, on the 16th, a signal officer had brought a message that arrived for him by semaphore from Richmond. It read simply, "The crisis is over and all is well." By prearrangement, he knew what this meant: that his darling wife, Nellie, had been delivered of a healthy child and was also well herself. That very day, the 17th, he wrote a letter to his wife: "Tell Sis Mary, for pity's sake, if not for love's sake, write me a long letter about my little Wife and baby."

At the time, women were generally considered indisposed while recovering after childbirth, so he relied on his sister to write him a newsy letter. Before the childbirth, he would not have believed it possible to love her more than he did. But now, a new father sailing high on a wave of emotion, he loved her "more devotedly, more tenderly" than ever before. He thanked God for having brought her safely through the delivery, grateful for the mercy He had shown "both of us." He ended the letter with a heartfelt plea: "Oh me! I want to see you *so bad*. God bless my Darling and may he soon reunite us in happiness & peace a joyful family."[17]

At a time when women very commonly died in childbirth,

this message of her good health was very important and invigo-
rating news. And a healthy child as well—why, all was right with
the world! Still, there was no word as to the sex of the child, so
Dod could not crow too loudly just yet. Even so, he sent for one
of his brigade commanders, Brigadier General Bryan Grimes.

Though not a West Point graduate, and somewhat older than
Ramseur, Grimes was, like him, a North Carolinian. He graduated from the University of North Carolina in 1848 and spent
the next dozen years running the one-hundred-slave plantation
in North Carolina given to him by his father. It was lonely at the
top during the Civil War, and Grimes was one of the few men
with whom Dodson was genuinely comfortable.

His big news for Grimes, of course, was the birth of his child.
After the two men shared Dod's joy, Grimes left, only to learn
that he, too, was a new father. He returned to Ramseur's headquarters tent and shared this joyous news with his friend. This
time, they sat at the foot of an old oak tree and talked in a more
leisurely fashion of their wives, their children, and their futures.

Dod was overjoyed not only by the birth of his child but
also by the good health of his wife, Nellie. As an exception to
his normally serious, even grim demeanor, Dod wore a white
flower in his lapel. Yes, the war was still there, but this joyous celebration of life almost required some outward sign of
Dod's true joy. And through the bloody combat that lay ahead,
the white flower was there to remind all that Dod was truly
rejoicing the great events that had just taken place back home in
North Carolina.[18]

Early sent Gordon and Hotchkiss out immediately to investigate the practicability of his forces using the trail at the base of
the mountain. Within a few hours, they reported back that it was
usable by infantry, but not by artillery. But their reconnaissance
had also found two fords across the North Fork of the Shenandoah they could use, and Early sent out engineer teams to mark
and improve the trail. When couriers came back reporting that

they were able to provide a serviceable pathway, Early sent for his division commanders, and at a meeting around three o'clock in the afternoon, he gave them their orders for the attack.

That night, soon after full dark, Gordon would lead three divisions, his own as well as those of Pegram and Ramseur, on that narrow path at the base of the mountain. They would be nearly 9,000 men, and moving single file meant it would take them many hours to cover no more than a few miles. That prompted them to start at around eight o'clock that night, and commanders all the way down made sure their men secured or left behind anything loose that might clank or rattle. But with this early start, Early and Gordon both thought they should be able to get in position behind the Union left by about three or four in the morning. They would then wait silently in place until 5:00 a.m., the moment of mass attack.

The next units to move into position would be the divisions of Kershaw and Gabriel Wharton, who would lead their men, another 5,000 rifles, directly north to the banks of Cedar Creek in the center of the Union line.

Kershaw's division was arrayed perhaps one mile west of the ford that Gordon's divisions would use to cross the North Fork of the Shenandoah. They were only a few hundred yards south of Bowman's Mill Ford, which they would use to get beyond Cedar Creek.

After dark, Wharton's division was placed on the Valley Turnpike a few miles west of the bridge, with the artillery guns and their caissons waiting behind them. Early was reluctant to move these weapons closer before the attack was launched lest the creaking of their wheels be heard in the Yankee camps. But once the attack had been launched by Gordon's force a few miles to the east and Kershaw's a mile south of the bridge, Wharton was to approach the bridge and get his force across it as soon as the VIII Corps defenses had been driven back by Kershaw's and/ or Gordon's men.

Rosser, meanwhile, would lead his division of cavalry, less William H. F. Payne's small brigade of fewer than 500, against the far right of the Union line, which also lay behind Cedar Creek. He would need much less time to move into position, but when the other attacks erupted, he was to charge across the creek with his 1,500 horsemen and smash into whatever Union forces he found there.

Reconnaissance as well as the Gordon-Hotchkiss party had led Early to believe that two divisions of blue cavalry would be there, but Rosser was to be prepared for anything. His mission was not to defeat his enemy counterparts, particularly because he would, no doubt, be heavily outnumbered. Rather, he was to make a pinning attack that would freeze the blue cavalry in place while gray infantry swept through the Union camps and killed, captured, or routed their occupants.

Lomax and his 3,000 cavalrymen, meanwhile, would be sent east ten miles toward Front Royal on a roundabout route and were expected to arrive next morning on the flank and rear of the Union's northernmost VI Corps. Unfortunately, this significant Confederate mounted force—more than half the cavalry Early had at his disposal—must have gotten lost, for they never appeared on the field of battle next day.[19] This would be a major loss to Early, but it was simply unpredictable at this planning stage.

After a careful synchronization of watches, the generals returned to their units and set the wheels in motion.

Union commanders, of course, were still prisoners of the idea that no Confederate force could make their way over or around that rough terrain on the far side of the Shenandoah, where Massanutten Mountain seemed such an impregnable barrier. That confidence meant that only pickets along the river and a small force of cavalry covered the left end of their line, while they had built strong positions behind and covering Cedar Creek in their center and right.

Their confidence at the time would have seemed, to an out-
sider, more than reasonable. After all, Sheridan and his men had
driven the Confederate army in the Shenandoah down the valley before them over the past few weeks, and no significant resistance had encumbered their movements.

Sheridan and his generals, therefore, were sure that Early's
small force (later determined to have been roughly 14,000 infantrymen, supported by 5,000 cavalrymen and 1,000 artillerymen
manning forty-odd guns) would not attack their much larger
Union force (22,000 infantrymen, 7,500 cavalry, and 1,800
artillerymen manning eighty-five to ninety guns) in their camp
behind Cedar Creek.[20]

The Yankees felt they were in a strong defensive position,
and the looming mass of Massanutten only further bolstered
their confidence. The men in blue slept soundly that night. But
while they slept, a daring Confederate stroke was taking shape.

# SEVENTEEN

## *Cloudburst*

Moving all night on little more than a pig track between the river and the steep mountain, much of it in single file, three Confederate divisions made the very passage Union generals thought an impossibility. Led by their scouts, who had explored the region in daylight, and helped by a nearly full moon, the men in this long gray serpent slithered slowly and silently toward their target.

They crossed the Shenandoah at two fords, and Gordon's division was preceded by Payne's cavalry brigade of 400 that had been detached from Rosser's division. These gray horsemen quickly cleared the small Union cavalry units posted as sentinels beyond the ford, but even this did not warn of the impending attack. Such scattering of pickets and sentinels by enemy cavalry detachments was not uncommon, and the blue horsemen simply fled without seeing the large infantry force that followed. When they reported the incident to their night watch commanders in the rear, they were no doubt met by the same indifference with which, over the past few months, similar reports of cavalry scuffles along their line of sentries had been met. But this time, it was at their peril.

The gray infantrymen soon reached a dirt road running north, and they followed it until they had passed a certain white house Gordon had noted from the mountaintop the previous day. There they halted, then simply faced to their left, moved forward a few hundred yards, and lay down. The glow of Union campfires among the shadows of white tents before them were so close that they could almost feel their warmth.

By 3:00 a.m. nearly 9,000 rebel soldiers had begun to quietly assemble along a line at their final launching positions. Within shouting distance of the Yankee camps, the men lay still and spoke only in rare hushed whispers as their comrades joined them, the line of riflemen slowly growing longer and thicker. Once in position, they rested quietly, many of them even sleeping soundly for a few hours while they awaited the signal to attack.

All were in place by 4:00 a.m. when a thick ground fog rolled across the valley floor, a murky mist that would even better conceal the scope and scale of the looming Confederate surprise. Thousands of men in butternut gray lay quietly in position as the fog rolled over them, some of them having been in position for several hours. Then, just as first light filtered faintly through the gray fog covering the valley floor, the synchronized watches of the generals all reached 5:00.

The first attack was made by Kershaw's men, a mile or more to the left of Ramseur's line and waiting south of Bowman's Mill Ford. Early had accompanied Kershaw, and at 4:30, he sent a specially prepared detachment across the ford to clear the sentinels posted on the other side. Aided by the fog and darkness, they captured nearly every one. Then Kershaw's division crossed Cedar Creek at Bowman's Mill Ford and formed a line facing north and very close to the tents of the 1st Division of the VIII

Corps. At 5:00 a.m. they burst into the Yankee camps from the dark, firing and screaming and soon killing or capturing the men from that division who didn't get away.

Off to their left, Wharton's division lay in wait to rush across the bridge over Cedar Creek, though it would have to wait for the success of Kershaw's attack. Hotchkiss had warned them that the bridge was strongly covered by men of Crook's VIII Corps as well as by sixteen cannon. Arrayed in three positions and covering the bridge and the area north of Cedar Creek in that region, those cannon would speak death to any who moved too soon.

On two ridges north of Cedar Creek and facing south were the guns of the VIII Corps artillery brigade, commanded by Captain Henry Algernon DuPont. These were the guns of three Union batteries—one regular army battery (six three-inch rifled guns), one Pennsylvania Volunteer battery (six ten-inch Parrott guns), and one Ohio Volunteer battery (four ten-pound Napoleons).

At around 4:45 a.m. gunfire from Rosser's probe on the Union right flank a few miles away awakened DuPont. At first he thought it was men chopping wood. But as he sat up, he listened intently and knew it was gunfire from somewhere off near the end of their right flank. Everyone knew that if the rebels were to attack anywhere, this would be their target. But such an attack might also be followed by Confederate infantry charging across Cedar Creek and coming at them directly from the south. It was against such a threat that his sixteen cannon had been placed atop those ridges, and he was suddenly wide awake.

As DuPont dressed he called for his horse and ordered the bugler to sound "Reveille." He at first considered having "Boots and Saddles" sounded, which would have meant that horses were to be harnessed and batteries made ready for immediate action. But then he reflected that they had been called to arms as a drill at 2:00 a.m. for the previous three or four nights, all of which proved to be false alarms. He thought that it might unnecessarily alarm the infantry sleeping in tents all around them, so he decided to let it go.[1]

His cannon were emplaced in three positions on the crest of two ridges running east and west, facing south and covering the bridge as well as ground on either side of it. The ridges were about four hundred yards apart, and the caissons, the horses that pulled them, the forge, and other equipment of the batteries were conveniently kept in the ravine between them. Twelve of his guns were on the southern ridge and four on the northern, which was slightly higher. If they were hit from their left flank, it would be virtually impossible to turn the guns, which meant they would be unable to repel enemy troops coming from that direction. But according to higher-ups, the steep mountainside so close to the water made such an attack simply impossible.

Then gunfire and the rebel yell burst on him like a fire-breathing dragon from somewhere in DuPont's left rear. Somewhere close—too close, and he was as shocked as the suddenly awakened men who were still in bed. He shouted orders for every man to go to his battle post as his orderly brought his horse. His voice could barely be heard over the din, but the screams and gunfire so close by spurred all of his men to their battle positions.

Then his orderly arrived with his horse, and he leaped on and dug in his spurs. He had not thought to specify a color, and his mount was a pale gray mare. This initially disturbed him, for it seemed a color too bright on a night when enemy troops would be looking for targets. But that was no more than a faint thought that drifted through his mind and disappeared as he raced to the position of the regular army battery atop the southernmost ridge.

The storm of gunfire came from the attack by Kershaw's men off to his left, while more gunfire still, from the divisions of Ramseur, Gordon, and Pegram miles away, filled in the background. On command and uncomfortably close in DuPont's left rear, Kershaw's 3,000 men had leaped to their feet and were now storming through the VIII Corps camps, howling and firing at anything that moved. Their surprise was complete, and the Yankees who came out of their tents and didn't get away were shot down or bayoneted.[2]

But hundreds of yards from the initial burst of flame, not all Union soldiers immediately ran. Here and there, some stalwart leader would gather a dozen, fifty, two hundred men around him and try to stem the tide, an act of great and selfless courage. A regiment prepared for a dawn reconnaissance was placed in their trenches. But as they faced south, they were in precisely the wrong place and were easily rolled up by the advancing rebels hitting them from their left side. Given the numbers, these very brave few were quickly surrounded and overwhelmed.

DuPont raced for his guns as the storm rolled closer. He shouted down into the ravine and ordered his first sergeant to harness and hitch as rapidly as possible. Then he raced up to the regular army battery, six three-inch rifled guns. When he got there, he could see that the Pennsylvania battery, six ten-inch Parrott guns that were a quarter mile down the ridge from him, was being overwhelmed by gray forms, and the crew members who had gotten to them were being bayoneted or dropped by clubbed muskets.

DuPont jumped off his horse at the regular battery and was informed by Lieutenant Henry F. Brewerton, the battery commander, that all six guns were loaded with canister. But because of the fog, he could see no enemy to his front and was reluctant to fire. The sounds of troops moving in the dark, intermittent gunfire, and creaking wheels came from their left front, and though they didn't know it at the time, this noise was no doubt Wharton's men and Early's artillery approaching the bridge.

DuPont told Brewerton to hold his ground and fire blindly to the front until he could see enemy soldiers coming at him through the fog. When they got that close, he was to abandon the limbers and run the guns down into the ravine by hand. DuPont, meanwhile, would get other limbers to the bottom of the hill to receive the guns (a limber was a two-wheeled horse-drawn carriage that was used to move an artillery piece).

Leaping onto his horse again, DuPont galloped to the bottom of the ravine to find the drivers and gun crews of the regular battery working feverishly to get the horses harnessed and hitched. He told the first sergeant to detach the limbers from the caissons and take them to the bottom of the hill, where they would be ready for the guns. Next, he raced over to the Pennsylvania battery's camp on the east and yelled at them to clear out, else they would be captured. Then he galloped to the Ohio battery on the northern ridge, four ten-pound Napoleon guns.

These guns specifically targeted the bridge, and DuPont told their commander, Captain Frank C. Gibbs, to open fire with two of his guns on the lead element of Wharton's Confederate division, which could then be seen in the dim light approaching the bridge. As these two guns began to fire at targets beyond the bridge, DuPont told Gibbs to send the other two guns a few hundred yards to their left rear, to a higher point on the same ridge, and open fire from there. At the same time, he was to order his battery wagon, caissons, and any other equipment the crews could snatch up to the rear.

The two guns ordered to the other end of the ridge soon left while the other two kept up their fire and kept the rebels off the bridge. As Early himself later acknowledged, their fire was effective enough that Wharton's men were stopped until they could bring their own artillery forward and fire on this galling Union battery until it (the Ohio battery) was withdrawn.[3]

Within minutes, the crews of the two guns ordered to higher ground were back, saying that when they got there the spot was being overrun by Confederate soldiers. DuPont then ordered the Ohio battery to withdraw to the north up the turnpike, and

this was quickly done. Even so, men in gray entered their position just as the last piece was being pulled out.

Lieutenant Brewerton with the regular battery, meanwhile,
kept up his fire until the enemy was within twenty-five yards of
his position. After a last blast of canister, he had the guns pulled
from their limbers and followed DuPont's orders to run them
downhill by hand, where other limbers awaited them. Unfortunately one of his guns got hopelessly tangled in the bushes, so
they spiked it before they left it behind. The other five got away,
but one man was killed as they fled, and Lieutenant Brewerton,
the last man out, was captured.

Now DuPont and the gun crews found themselves at the
bottom of a ravine with high ridges on either side, both occupied by screaming, shooting rebel soldiers. Clearly they were in
great peril, filling a space not unlike that between two spread
fingers of a hand placed palmdown on a desktop. But the rebels on both ridges did not realize there were Yankees in the
ravine between them, and, helped by the darkness and the fog,
the Union men raced to the west. Somehow they got to the
turnpike ahead of the two Confederate swarms running atop
the ridges along with them, and they managed to turn north.
The roadway was now crowded with soldiers in blue, and they
simply joined the flight.[4]

DuPont had been able to extricate five of the six guns from
his regular battery as well as all four guns of the Ohio battery.
But as they fled north, he was surprised to see troops from the
XIX Corps entering their entrenchments, which all faced south.
That was precisely the wrong direction, and unless they left the
entrenchments and faced to the east, they would all be rolled up
and captured.

Even the 2nd Brigade, 2nd Division, XIX Corps, already
awake and prepared to make a reconnaissance in force to the
south, was caught in that dilemma. In the dark and confusion,
they entered the rifle pits to find they were facing south. But,

that being simply the wrong direction, the attacking rebels hit them broadside on their left. The later report by their commander, Colonel Edward L. Molineux, confirmed as much:

> At about 5.40 a.m. I heard the sound of heavy musketry in the direction of the position of the Eighth Corps, and apprehending an attack immediately ordered my command into the rifle-pits, throwing out a few sharpshooters to give me early intimation should an attack be made on my front, only to soon be overrun.[5]

So DuPont had seven of his guns captured by Kershaw's men, who came in shooting and screaming from their left rear, though one of them had been rendered inoperable until it could be drilled out again. Even so, the fact that he got away with nine was quite a feat.

When he heard the attack on the Union left erupt, Rosser led two of the three brigades in his cavalry division, some 1,600 men, in a probe against the Union right flank. His third brigade, under Colonel Payne, was tasked with driving off the mounted pickets along the Shenandoah River in front of Gordon's men. Once that was done, he was to make a dash to Sheridan's headquarters in the Belle Grove mansion, where they hoped to surprise and capture him.

But this was to be a vain effort, for, unbeknownst to Early and his planners, Sheridan had been away for several days in Washington and at the moment of the dawn attack he was still gone. In his absence, command had passed to General Wright, who was a solid and reliable man. But he was nowhere near the bold and aggressive leader from the front that Sheridan had shown himself to be.

In concert with the other attacks, and with no more than 1,200 men, Rosser's force had driven in the Union pickets along Cedar Creek, a sudden blow accompanied by fire over their heads from their own horse-drawn artillery. He followed this with a dash across the creek, dismounting one of his brigades and using them in the attack as infantrymen.[6]

But they would be no match for the well-armed, though hurriedly dressed, Yankee cavalrymen they would face, many of them also on foot and firing their repeating carbines at the attackers from the cover of a wood line. Rosser's men were easily stopped, but they kept up a pestering fire on their Union counterparts. Although they were unable to drive off the blue horsemen, Rosser's force was a loud and dangerous distraction that only further confused that end of the Union line.

Early knew from Hotchkiss that this part of the Union line was defended by what looked like two large cavalry divisions. That was accurate, as it turned out, and Rosser faced some 7,500 men in the 1st Cavalry Division under Merritt, supported by the 3rd Cavalry Division under Custer, whose camp was still farther upstream.

Rosser had pleaded with Early the night before to be allowed to accompany Wharton's or Kershaw's division in the attack, moving north on their flank and killing or capturing the crowds of blue soldiers they could expect to be chasing across open fields. But Early would have none of that, for he wanted Rosser to keep the much larger Union cavalry force occupied and off the infantry field of battle at all costs. That was the purpose of his attack, which Early ordered over his subordinate's objections. Although he sulked at this rejection of his proposal, Rosser's bold thrust across Cedar Creek seemed, at first, to be doing the job quite well.

Merritt's division had been moved to the Union right flank, with Custer's on the same side of camp but even farther out. Both were four miles or more from the point of attack, and their first notice was faint, though heavy, gunfire. But no orders arrived, and the attack was a true surprise throughout the army. Confusion and consternation raced through the awakening ranks of Union soldiers, even here among the as–yet–untouched cavalrymen. Still, as a sort of background noise, the increasingly loud crash of gunfire and the deep boom of cannon echoed from the left of the Union line, presumably the site of the main fighting. But coming from some three or four miles away, there was no sense among the Yankee cavalry commanders as yet of a Confederate breakthrough.

Colonel J. H. Kidd had replaced Custer in command of the Michigan brigade when he was promoted to major general only days earlier. That night, the much-harried 7th Michigan Cavalry Regiment that Custer had led in a charge at Gettysburg manned the picket line along Cedar Creek and was part of Kidd's brigade in the 1st Cavalry Division under Merritt. A courier soon arrived from Merritt telling Custer to rush to the support of the pickets. As soon as his men were armed and mounted, he brought the rest of his new command up and confronted the rebel horsemen who had driven his pickets back.

He was soon joined by the division's reserve brigade under Colonel Charles R. Lowell, and together they had some 2,000 men armed with sabers, repeating carbines or rifles, and revolvers, all mounted on strong, grain-fed horses. They faced a smaller number of Southerners, who also carried sabers, but most primarily armed with single-shot, muzzle-loading carbines and a scattering of pistols. Their starving mounts were bony and weak, and it really wasn't much of a contest as Custer's men rather easily drove Rosser's men back across Cedar Creek.

But by now it was becoming clear that the attack on this flank was no more than a distraction from the main Confederate infantry attacks to their south and east, and the gray horsemen broke contact. So what were Kidd and Lowell to do? Having received no orders from their division commander, General Merritt, other than to support the pickets, they were confused. Then a courier arrived on a lathered horse with orders from

General Torbert to leave three of Custer's regiments to stave off Rosser and bring the rest of their men to the left side of the Union line, which was collapsing.[7]

Meanwhile, the blue response to the mass infantry attack on its left flank was nothing less than sheer panic. Shouts of terror blew through Union tents like wind, driving half-dressed and unarmed Yankee soldiers before it. And close behind, a wave of blazing rifle barrels and steel bayonets emerged from the dark with no warning, a wave so wide and deep that it carried all in its way as it crashed through the Union camp. After a few hundred yards, some scratch forces in blue were hurriedly assembled. But they, too, quickly collapsed before the butternut tide.

Black powder smoke came with the loud gunfire, and as it wafted through the Yankee tents before them, that sharp odor of gunsmoke nipped at the nostrils of thousands as they were jolted awake. But resistance was futile, and as men sprang from their cots they pulled on clothes and shoes and maybe grabbed for their weapons, then joined the terrified rush of soldiers in blue streaming away from the crash and thunder.

First the 4,000-man VIII Corps was overwhelmed and virtually dissolved, followed within less than an hour by the collapse of the 9,000-man XIX Corps. The claws of terror gripped them hard as they fled the noise and confusion, all capped by the terrifying rebel yell. But as they moved west and north some valiant officers made lines from the soldiers of various blue regiments and brigades, all repeatedly trying to slow the tide and set up some kind of organized resistance. Some of these lasted seconds, some minutes. But, as relentless as time, the flame-belching wall of gray kept blowing great gaps in the lines of blue defenders before gobbling them up.

Now supported by fire from the 5,000 men in Kershaw's and Wharton's divisions coming up on its left from the south, this joint Confederate attack met only spotty resistance. Within an hour or so of the opening blasts, sunlight began to split through the fog. By 7:00 a.m. the blue sky had widened and the soldiers on both sides could actually see their enemies. But the men in blue trudging north, desperate first for survival and then for some sort of safety, seldom even slowed down.

As Ramseur's men lunged forward, they, too, captured a few Union artillery pieces, which they promptly turned around and fired at their fleeing foes. And the gray mass rolled on, pursuing the men in blue like hounds after a wounded deer.

By eight o'clock, Ramseur's men could see Belle Grove mansion a mile or so in front of them. Union men from the VIII and XIX Corps seemed to be reestablishing order in that area, and Union cannon were seen pointing their way from the crest of a small hill. Officers seemed to be trying to deploy hundreds, maybe a thousand Union riflemen in defensive positions around the top of that hill.

A mile or more to the northeast, Ramseur's men cleared the streets and buildings of Middletown. Early rode up and dismounted to talk to Ramseur and Kershaw. The men in gray were truly ebullient at this point, having participated in a genuine rout of a much larger Yankee force. Before speaking with Early and Kershaw, Ramseur took a minute to speak to Major Henry Kyd Douglas, a Virginian about his age who was an old friend and was serving as one of Early's aides: "Douglas, I want to win this battle, for I must see my wife and baby."[8]

But a Union position on a hill only hundreds of yards to the west of that town, a hill crowned by a cemetery, became the thorn that slowed and then stopped this end of the Confederate line. It was held by an unknown Union force, but it put out a storm of fire, and Early suspected it might be the entire Union VI Corps of some 9,000 men.

The Union force defending that hill was only one division, fewer than 3,000 men. But it was able to repel repeated, though somewhat disjointed, attacks made by single brigades from four divisions. The entire progress of the line stopped as Early concentrated his fury on this stubborn position. This was a single hot spot, a strong Union position that stopped the entire rebel wave while Early dealt with it.

But Early would lead no charges here, and he finally massed most of his artillery south of Middletown, from where they opened fire. A half hour of repeated pounding on the cemetery-masked position finally drove the Union soldiers back as part of the continuing blue retreat to the north.

Early was elated by this, shouting, "The sun of Middletown! The sun of Middletown!" This was the name by which he wanted his triumph remembered.

Like most important fighting generals on both sides, Early was a West Point graduate. While there, he had studied Napoleon, a man who was generally recognized as the greatest battle captain of all times. After the battle of Austerlitz in December 1805, in which he destroyed both the Russian and Austrian armies, Napoleon was known to have loudly proclaimed this victory as the *soleil d'Austerlitz*, or the sun of Austerlitz. Now Early was trying to establish the name of this, his own great victory, as an evocation of Napoleon's.[9]

But he was a bit premature, and commonly recited American folklore of the time should have warned him: never count your winnin's at the table 'til the dealin's done. And the dealin' wasn't quite done.

The Confederate force of five divisions on a line perhaps three miles wide renewed its drive north of Middletown. But before they had gone more than a half mile, word came to the division commanders from Early to stop and reassemble.[10] When they did, of course, the forces they were pursuing did not slow down at first. As Ramseur and the other division commanders reassembled and dressed their ranks, they fired a few artillery rounds at the men they had defeated, but then occupied themselves with distributing more ammunition to their men.

Now that they had stopped, Ramseur saw through his field glasses that the Yankees had also seemed to stop and were perhaps trying to reassemble about a mile north of the new Confederate line. Gordon was furious at this break in their momentum, and he raced back to Early's position to protest the halt. He insisted that they keep up their pursuit and drive forward to dislodge the Union VI Corps, a unit of several divisions he felt were still largely untouched by the Confederate triumph.

Early tried to calm Gordon down, insisting that now, in midmorning, the battle had already been won and the Yankees would disappear once it began to get dark. Gordon would have none of that, insisting that the VI Corps would not move unless it was attacked. But Early wouldn't hear of it, and he stuck to his order to stop the attack and realign their forces in a defensive posture. That ended it, but Gordon was still unhappy as he rode back to his men, and he would fiercely promote his argument long after the war had ended and Early was dead in his grave.[11]

Early, however, felt he was right and that his men needed to rest and regroup. After all, the surprise had been total and the rout complete, a Confederate martial success in the Shenandoah Valley of the sort they had only dreamed of until this moment. Their dawn attack had been a smashing victory over a force under Sheridan twice their size, an army whose men were driven terrified from the field. And in their shock and panic, they had abandoned without a thought not only many of their cannon but also their bountiful supplies of tents, food, armament, clothing, wagons, and horseflesh. No, Early thought, those men had been whipped, and there wouldn't be any fight left in them for a long time to come. Now it was time to let his men rest and recover from a long night's march and hard day's fight.

More than a thousand Union soldiers had been captured, many of them having not even gotten out of their tents. Among them was the surgeon assigned to the VIII Corps artillery, John Knight. A man in his early sixties, Knight should never have been there at all, but his fervent and patriotic pleas to the artillery commander, Captain Henry Algernon DuPont, had been compelling enough that he was allowed to stay forward with the men manning the guns of the artillery batteries. But now that he was captured, only a hard time of hard marches lay before him.

These prisoners were among the first trophies Ramseur and other commanders had sent south on the Valley Turnpike, followed by wagons loaded with captured goods of all sorts, ranging from weapons and ammunition to plentiful food, food his men desperately needed. Fortunately for him, Knight's skills were immediately recognized, and instead of joining the crowd of other Yankee prisoners moving south, he was allowed to join the Confederate medical personnel and worked in their aid stations, treating freshly wounded men as they were brought in.

As the men in blue continued their retreat to the north, most of the Union soldiers captured were immediately herded south. That was relatively easy, as the unwounded prisoners could walk under their own power. But it took a while before groups of soldiers from the supply train following up the attack could organize and load the captured goods and supplies onto the captured wagons. Pulled by captured horses and mules, they were sent back "up" the Valley Turnpike to the south.

As it turned out, some—the exact number or proportion will never be known—of the Southern soldiers who stormed through the Yankee camps were fatally seduced by the full pantries left behind. Early would later use their absence as a major excuse for having stopped his forces in their advance at about 9:30 or 10:00 that morning.

Confederate forces were then about a half mile north of Middletown, arrayed on a rough line running about three miles east to west, when their assault against Yankees retreating to their north suddenly stopped. But when the gray line stopped, it didn't take long before the blue soldiers they were chasing, now mingling in some disorder a half mile or so to the north, noticed this and stopped running themselves. And it was this halt in the pursuit that would later be used, by Gordon and others, to attack Early for having let the spectacular victory won that morning slip through his fingers.

In Early's defense, it is certainly true that, having had little to put in their mouths for many months beyond rancid pork, board-hard biscuit, and tobacco, some men in gray had simply stopped there to eat. As the morning lengthened into afternoon, still others were able to leave their ranks after they stopped and slip back to the Union tents. And it was very difficult indeed to pull these half-starved men away from the ample stocks of fresh meat, bread, and coffee—real coffee!—the Yankees had left behind. It would have seemed that only heartless men could force these half-starved men back to their units, men who had spent the previous night moving into position for the attack and were now utterly famished.

But unit cohesion at this point was all-important. It was a fact that, in their movement, certain divisions had gotten intermingled with others. This was particularly true for the men in Gordon's division, which had started the attack on the far right of the Confederate line. But by the time they had passed Middletown, their division had moved all the way to the left end of that same line. And while there undeniably was a certain amount of plundering by some of those soldiers that added to the confusion, it would seem from the evidence—as loudly promoted by Gordon after the war—that such plundering did not have any major effect on the fighting capabilities of any of the Confederate divisions that day.

This is unambiguously apparent because, from the time the Confederate line stopped at around 10:00 that morning until fighting began in earnest again at around 4:00 p.m., there had clearly been enough time for stragglers to have been gathered up and returned to their units. And despite his protestations to the contrary in his reports and later, Early soon realized that he should have continued the attack rather than stopping it. He acknowledged as much to Hotchkiss when he was sent back to Richmond days later to carry maps and messages to General Lee. In Hotchkiss's own words:

"General Early told me not to tell General Lee that we ought to have advanced in the morning at Middletown, for, said he, we ought to have done so."[12]

Subordinate officers from the Confederate divisions had already sent teams back to the Yankee camps to round up stragglers in the Union camps and return them to ranks. This was important, for although the Yankees had been sent flying, an orderly pursuit might still be required to assure the victory, and they could not afford to lose masses of riflemen who were busy plundering the camps.

Other commanders in the rear were charged with gathering up abandoned spoils, a logistical task now taking place far to the rear. Confederate commanders must have been annoyed by any thinning of their ranks brought on by this almost-desperate slaking of thirst and hunger. But they were all exhausted and famished, and those creature comforts would be tended to later. For now, the Yankees were on the run, and it was up to the men in gray to keep them running.

In the past, Ramseur and other division commanders had had deserters shot, and while this might have been justified now, only their prompt return to ranks was demanded. Indeed, given the splendid victory they had just won, any of the division commanders would have been very reluctant indeed to have their own men shot or even punished for failing to return to ranks this day. Up all night without food or drink, after which they had won a great victory, it was hard to be angry at them now for doing no more than feeding their ravishing hunger, clothing their half-naked bodies, or trying to shoe their bare feet.

Ramseur had stopped his division a half mile or so north of Middletown, and many miles north of these Union army encampments. Earlier, he and the other division commanders had met individually with General Early, who, the day before, had adopted this high-risk, high-reward attack proposed by Gordon. It had been a thunderbolt success, but then Early had stopped their pursuit of the fleeing foe. Having predicted to his division commanders that the whipped Yankees would withdraw that night, Early thought he had done enough.

With his division west of the Valley Turnpike and in the middle of that Confederate line, Ramseur turned his attention to important logistical measures required for his men, such as acquiring more ammunition and seeing to its distribution. To his left were the divisions of Kershaw and Gordon, to his right those of Pegram and Wharton. To anyone looking to their left from Ramseur's location, it might have seemed that Kershaw's men, and particularly Gordon's, were rather strung out across the valley floor and didn't seem to have pinned the left end of their line to any strongpoint. Rosser's cavalry division was supposed to cover that left flank, and gray horsemen could be seen through the dust at the far left end of the line. But Lomax and his force of 3,000 horse, supposed to cover the Confederate right, were nowhere to be seen. Payne and his small brigade of 300 men were all there was at that end of the line, but they could easily be overwhelmed if attacked by the thousands of blue horsemen known to be out there somewhere. Perhaps Early was right and the whipped forces in blue would disappear with the dark. Still, it must have made Ramseur and the other commanders uncomfortable when they saw through their field glasses that the Yankees a mile or so to the north seemed to have stopped running.

But Dod hoped Early would be proven right, and now was a time for rest for his men and a sense of deep satisfaction. If the Yankees did disappear into the night, he knew that this great victory would mean he could go home for a week, home to hug and hold Nellie and their new baby.

Only twenty-seven years old, he was a newly promoted major general commanding a division that had just won a great victory over Sheridan's men. And he had learned that he was a father as well—his inner elation, both with family and now with this truly stunning professional accomplishment, was unbounded.

With the battle over, Dod could turn his thoughts to home. At a time when women commonly died in childbirth, he felt such a great sense of relief that Nellie had lived and was even in good health. And they had a new baby—why, words could not express his feelings! The white flower was still in his lapel, a sign of his joy that ignored the heat of battle. And this surprise dawn attack that had driven one of the best generals in the Union army and three of his infantry corps from the field—why, this was truly a triumph to savor!

But it really wasn't quite over just yet. . . .

# EIGHTEEN

## *Counterattack*

While it is true that Early had a splendid victory within his grasp after he had driven Union forces beyond Middletown, he made one great error—a blunder, really—that ultimately cost him that victory. And that blunder was his failure to vigorously follow up his successful surprise dawn attack, to pursue that beaten blue army and make sure that, as a legitimate fighting force, it had been completely shattered and destroyed. Only then should he have rested his men and allowed them access to the Union goods and supplies, the food and clothing they had captured that were the immediate trophies of their victory.

This concept of sealing a victory with a strong pursuit of the vanquished foe has long been recognized in military teachings and traditions. As Early's words remind us, in U.S. Army circles from the early nineteenth century until the present time, Napoleon has long been seen as the single "Great Captain" of European history. His battlefield performance, therefore, remains to this day the centerpiece of most formal military studies, both in Europe and in the United States. And because all of the great generals on both sides in the Civil War had been educated at

West Point, Napoleon's battlefield performance was the lodestar by which they guided their own steps and against which they measured the actions of others.

There have been countless victories in military history, most usually followed by a pursuit of some sort. But the most relevant to Civil War leaders, of course, came from the Napoleonic Wars. And the model was Napoleon's pursuit of the beaten Prussian army after the October 1806 joint battles of Jena and Auerstädt.

In those contemporaneous battles, Napoleon and Marshal Davout led an army of 130,000 against a Prussian force of 200,000. Before the battles, Napoleon divided his force in half, intending to overwhelm one portion of the Prussian army while Davout kept the other, larger element busy.

In fact, on the same day both generals defeated the enemy they faced and drove them from the field. In this initial defeat of two enormous armies, Napoleon inflicted 35,000 casualties at a loss of 15,000 and captured several hundred cannon. But Napoleon knew that, if he let them go, the Prussian survivors would retreat, recover, and once again pose a military threat to him. He therefore mounted a pursuit that remains the gold standard: over thirty-three days, he killed or wounded yet another 25,000 Prussian soldiers, took 140,000 prisoner, and captured a thousand cannon, all at a negligible cost to his own Grande Armée.[1]

Napoleon, then, was the model best known to Civil War generals, and his actions offered examples from which they could and did learn, some better than others. In the summer of 1862, let us recall, Confederate General Thomas J. "Stonewall" Jackson marched his men more than six hundred miles up and down the Shenandoah Valley. Their speed earned them the sobriquet of "Jackson's foot cavalry" and he was able to use maneuver, surprise, and pursuit to win five significant victories, leading a force never larger than 17,000 gray soldiers against a combined Union force of 60,000 men in blue.

It would seem, then, from this evidence he provided early in the war, that Jackson had learned his Napoleon very well indeed, a reputation that endures. But such military expertise was rare. So, early in the war, Jackson was intent on tutoring then captain (later brigadier general) John Imboden, an aggressive young officer who served under him in the valley but who had had no military experience whatever before the war. In one of his private instructional sessions, Jackson told him:

> there are two things never to be lost sight of by a military commander: always mystify, mislead, and surprise the enemy if possible; and when you strike and overcome him, never let up in the pursuit so long as your men have strength to follow; for an army routed, if hotly pursued, becomes panic-stricken, and can then be destroyed by half their number.[2]

Two of the great military theoreticians of all time were Carl von Clausewitz and Antoine-Henri Jomini. Both men were participants in the Napoleonic Wars, and both later wrote books about their ideas on the fundamental elements of fighting a war. Jomini's work is entitled *The Art of War*, published in 1838, while that of Clausewitz is entitled *On War*, published in 1832.

Different ways and means of either attacking or defending are among the major issues discussed in both books. As a follow-up to a successful attack, of course, the immediate need for an energetic pursuit by the victorious commander is almost a given. Jomini says:

> A pursuit should generally be as boldly and actively executed as possible, especially when it is subsequent to a battle won, because the demoralized army may be wholly dispersed if vigorously followed up.[3]

The guidance one finds in the work of Clausewitz goes into somewhat more detail, and his words seem especially pertinent to our Cedar Creek situation. In book 4, chapter 12, "Strategic Means of Exploiting Victory," he says:

> *Pursuit of a beaten enemy begins the moment he concedes the fight and abandons his position. . . . At this juncture, victory, while assured, is still usually limited and modest in its dimensions. Little positive advantage would be gained in the normal course of events unless victory were consummated by pursuit on the first day. . . . A prolonged struggle on the battlefield calls for exertions that complete the exhaustion. Moreover, the winning side is in almost as much disorder and confusion as the losers, and will therefore have to pause so that order can be restored, stragglers collected, and ammunition distributed. For the victor, these conditions create the critical phase. . . . At this point, too, a general's freedom of action bears a heavy handicap—the whole weight of human needs and weaknesses. Each of the thousands under his command needs food and rest, and longs for nothing so much as a few hours free of danger and fatigue. There are very few men— and they are the exceptions—who are able to think and feel beyond the present moment. Only these few, having accomplished the task at hand, are left with enough mental energy to think of making further gains—gains which, at such a time may seem trifling embellishments of victory, indeed, an extravagance. The voice of the other thousands, however, is what is heard in the general's council; it is conducted up a channel of senior officers who urge these human needs on the general's sympathy. The general's own energies have been sapped by mental and physical exertion, and so it happens that for purely human reasons less is achieved than was possible. What does get accomplished is due to the supreme commander's ambition, energy, and quite possibly his callousness. Only thus can we explain the timorous way in which so many generals exploit a victory that has given them the upper hand.*[4]

That section from Clausewitz seems to break the quality of victorious generals neatly into two classes: the hard-driving strict disciplinarians who push their men on in pursuit of a beaten foe, and those sensitive to human frailty who are willing to stop and let their men rest and recover, even if that means letting the enemy units get away untouched. If we look at the Confederate generals on the field the morning of 19 October, it seems clear that both Jomini and Clausewitz, or any other competent military theorist, would have praised Gordon's will to pursue the retreating Yankees while they were still in flight. Similarly, they would have condemned Early's willingness to let his men stop and rest, content that the beaten men in blue would simply disappear that night.

In the United States, a military commander's success, from the lowest platoon level all the way up to the command of armies, has always been measured by his performance of his two primary duties. The first and most obvious duty is the performance of his assigned mission, whether that be taking a hill or securing a crossroads or bringing ammunition to the front. But the second and equally important duty, which is often interactive or even competitive with performance of mission, is protecting the welfare of his troops. When food is short, a good company commander eats last, and before settling in for the night, a good platoon leader physically walks around and checks the fields of fire and other details important to the defensive positions occupied by his men.

How a leader balances these two duties, of course, always depends on specific circumstances, and there are clearly occasions when the leader will see that one or the other dominates. Added to that sometimes difficult judgment is the fact that the higher you go up a chain of command, the more distant commanders become from the circumstances faced by their men. This is not unimportant, for in order to win battles or wars, commanders must make hard decisions that often result in the loss of life or limb for some of their men. And as Napoleon famously said, "the general who cannot look dry-eyed upon a battlefield will cause many men to die needlessly."

This is an important leadership point, and it might be an easier shorthand for us here to simply refer to victorious generals as "hard" (pursuit) or "soft" (rest and recover). Under that definition, and in the battle as we have seen it so far, Gordon can be seen to have been a "hard" general, while Early was "soft." For an army commander, then, sympathy for the lot of the soldier can be a very dangerous thing indeed. So if Lincoln wanted to win the war, he clearly had to find some "hard" generals to lead these by-now battle-hardened men in the Army of the Potomac.

Given the development of the Civil War until that time in what was known as the Eastern Theater of Operations, which meant primarily northern Virginia, Early's assumption would have probably been safe and correct at any earlier moment. That's because every Union commander in the Eastern Theater before the arrival of Grant and Sheridan had either retreated as fast and as far as he could after having been defeated, or after victory failed to pursue his beaten enemy.

Had the routed Union army at Cedar Creek been commanded by any of the Union commanders who had operated in the Shenandoah Valley before Sheridan—meaning primarily Sigel or Hunter, both of whom were men of limited battlefield ability—they clearly would have continued their retreat, certainly back to Winchester or farther. And the same would have been true for any of the commanders of the Army of the Potomac to date:

- After McDowell lost the first battle of Bull Run, his men were routed and ran all the way back to Washington.

- After each of the six battles on the peninsula during the "Seven Days"—all of which were Union victories or draws—McClellan kept retreating all the way back to the protection of Union gunboats on the James River.

- After the severe beating he took in the second battle of Bull Run, Pope retreated with his army all the way back to the outskirts of Washington.

- At the battle of Antietam, despite the fact that McClellan had captured Lee's detailed plans and outnumbered him two to one, he refused to commit his reserves and so the battle ended in a draw, with Lee retreating back into Virginia the next night with no Union pursuit.

- After Burnside's repeated bloody attacks against Lee's outnumbered men in strong defenses were all stopped cold in the battle of Fredericksburg, he retreated back across the Rappahannock River.

- After Hooker's Army of the Potomac was badly whipped at the battle of Chancellorsville, he also retreated back across the Rappahannock.

- And even after the battle of Gettysburg, where Meade did nothing more than hunker down in his defenses and endure Lee's repeated attacks over three days, he failed to mount any serious pursuit of Lee as he retreated back into Virginia.

But now Lincoln had finally found his general in Grant, and when he came east, he brought Sherman and Sheridan with him. All three, unlike their predecessors at the top in the east, were "hard" generals.

Sherman was sent from Chattanooga to take Atlanta while Grant came to Virginia and hurled the Army of the Potomac into Lee. But this time, if he lost an individual battle, as, say, in the Wilderness, Grant did not run north for protection. Rather, he pulled back and then turned his forces to their left and attacked again. Turning left meant Grant was leading the Army of the

Potomac south toward Richmond, rather than turning right toward Washington and safety, as all his predecessors had done.

Now Grant had sent Sheridan to wipe out Confederate resistance in the Shenandoah Valley. In Washington for several days for a top-level conference before the battle of Cedar Creek, he was on his way back and had reached Winchester the night before it erupted. And this was not Frémont or Hunter returning to his beaten troops. This time, Grant had sent a hard general to put an end to rebel resistance once and for all. But now, after Early's booming success that morning at Cedar Creek, Sheridan's task of cleaning out the valley was suddenly at risk.

———

When the Confederates stopped their pursuit at around 9:30 or 10:00 that morning, General Wright, who was the acting Union commander in Sheridan's absence, tried to reestablish some order among his men. Wright had been badly wounded in the chin earlier that morning, and as he raced from place to place on his lathered horse, shouting orders, his blood-and-gore-soaked beard gave him the appearance of something between an enraged Moses coming down from the mountain and an avenging angel. But he knew his duty, and he was almost desperate as he sought to stem the flow of blue soldiers to the north by taking the few units that retained cohesion and forming an east–west line on which to post them.

His most important discovery in this expanding Union crisis was the 2nd Division of the VI Corps in a hastily formed defensive position about a mile north of Middletown on the Valley Turnpike. Wright used that as his base, giving orders for the men of the XIX Corps, several units of which had retained some structure in their retreat, to form on their right, or west, side. The survivors of VIII Corps were too widely spread out and disorganized for him to hope that they might make up part of his front, so he told his subordinates to have them sent to the rear of VI Corps, where they would form a part of his reserve. He also ordered all of his cavalry to form on the east side of the line, outside of the VI Corps, where he felt the greatest threat.[5]

Although the rebels had stopped driving them back and the fighting appeared to be over for the day, there was still tremendous confusion among Union ranks. Some soldiers obeyed orders and formed up as best they could, while others just kept on moving north. And despite the enduring confusion, the attacking gunfire from Confederate forces had ended, and order was slowly returned to Union ranks under General Wright's command.

---

As VIII Corps and XIX Corps were collapsing early that morning, the cannon fire could be heard as far away as Winchester, some twenty miles to the north. General Sheridan was awakened by an unsettled colonel, though no one yet knew what the cannon fire meant. And as he awakened, the colonel proposed two immediate explanations: it could just be exploration by fire being made by that XIX Corps brigade scheduled to make a deep reconnaissance down the valley that morning; or it could be a larger battle.

The one possibility that immediately brought Sheridan fully awake was the thought that perhaps that message they had gotten off the Confederate semaphore the other day predicting Longstreet's arrival and a major attack on Sheridan was real after all. There were a lot of other possible explanations as well, but few of them were good.

As the cannonade continued, Sheridan dressed, ate, and gathered his staff and 300-man mounted escort. Then he warned them that only the well mounted would be able to keep up with him, for as they all knew, the horse he would ride was simply magnificent.

A big black stallion seventeen hands high from the Black

Hawk stock of Michigan, Rienzi had been presented to him by the officers of the 2nd Michigan Cavalry when he was their colonel. The presentation took place in the spring of 1862 in Rienzi, Mississippi, where the 2nd was then stationed, and after which he was named. He was a handsome horse who always held his head high and was not the slightest bit disturbed by gunfire, and Sheridan rode him in every major engagement after that for the rest of the Civil War. Rienzi walked so fast that other horses had to trot just to keep up, and he was such a remarkable mount that he was recognized at a distance by Union soldiers, who knew he carried Sheridan, a man they loved and always heartily cheered.

That morning he mounted Rienzi—a name he would change to Winchester after this battle—and dug in his spurs. This was to be a ride widely celebrated in the North and retold time and again in a poem. "Sheridan's Ride," written by Thomas Read within days after the battle, was to become an American patriotic standard. It was to be recited not only at Republican political gatherings before the November elections of 1864, but also by uncounted American schoolchildren over the next century and more.

Sheridan and his party didn't get far south of town before they ran into crowds of wagons and soldiers, some wounded but most of them not, moving north and choking the roadway. Retreating soldiers told him that all was lost at Cedar Creek, but he rode on, now riding cross-country but parallel to the turnpike clogged by fleeing wagons and soldiers. And as he rode and various retreating soldiers recognized him, they loudly cheered him and often turned around and began moving back toward the battlefield in Sheridan's wake.[6]

In Sheridan's own words:

> *My first halt was made just north of New Town, where I met a chaplain digging his heels into the sides of his jaded horse and making for the rear with all possible speed. I drew up for an instant, and inquired*

*of him how matters were going at the front. He replied "Everything is lost; but all will be right when you get there."*[7]

After perhaps an hour's ride, Sheridan came upon the 1st and 3rd Divisions of the VI Corps, roughly assembled on the western side of the turnpike. He learned from officers among them that the men of the XIX Corps had stopped their retreat and begun to coalesce again a mile or so to their east and south. Sheridan resumed his ride, staying parallel to the turnpike but now moving on its western side. He passed large masses of blue soldiers off to his west, realizing that these must be the men of the XIX Corps, perhaps of the VIII Corps as well. And though they were still some distance away, his large black horse out in front of the party was recognized, and their distant cheers for Sheridan and his return were wind in his sails as he rode on.

After what must have been a few miles, he saw a large group of blue soldiers ahead near the turnpike. It was late morning, sometime around 10:30 or 11:00, when he finally reached what turned out to be Getty's 2nd Division of the VI Corps and a few regiments each of Merritt's and Custer's cavalry. These were the last organized Union units of any size arrayed before the enemy's front. They were poised to fill the role of rear guard by attempting to block any further Confederate advance, though by this time the men in gray seemed to have stopped their attack.

Clearly Sheridan was grateful to these men for standing firm when the rest of the army dissolved around them. And he remembered that, for after the battle he told Halleck that he wanted Merritt and Custer promoted to the rank of major general, and without the normal delays caused by red tape. In accordance with his wishes, the promotions were officially announced before the end of the month.[8]

As he approached, one man rode out to meet him: General Torbert, the commander of the cavalry corps. "My God!" he exclaimed, "I am glad you've come!" And once again, as

Sheridan approached the men in blue, he was met by their exultant cheers. He then rode along the rear of that VI Corps division, and among their rear ranks he saw officers and men from the collapsed VIII Corps, seemingly all of them joining in the shouts of praise and thanks for his return. One of these he recognized was Colonel Rutherford B. Hayes, who at the time commanded the 2nd Division of that corps and was destined later to be elected president of the United States.[9]

Sheridan assessed the size of this force and spoke with General Getty, the division commander, then rode off a few hundred yards to that division's west. After passing through a gully, he dismounted on a small hill, which he informed his staff would be his headquarters. Then he began sending couriers out to find commanders and bring them to him, while others carried orders for various other infantry, cavalry, and artillery commanders, though many of them and major parts of their units would be difficult to find.

Within a few hours, the 1st and 3rd Divisions of the VI Corps responded to Sheridan's courier-borne orders and began to reappear from the north, now seeking to reestablish their VI Corps as a single unit. Sheridan rode up to each division in turn and spoke with their commanders amid loud cheers from their men. Then he pointed out where they should be placed on either side of the 2nd Division.

When the three divisions had formed a solid front line, Sheridan rode down it at a slow canter, his hat raised in a salute to them. Many throats were shouted hoarse in jubilation at their leader's seemingly miraculous return. And now these proud men in blue who had been surprised in the night and disgracefully driven like sheep, now they were once again empowered psychologically by the sudden appearance before them of their valiant war chief.

This was the man who, over the past weeks and months, had led them in repeated battlefield triumphs over the same Confederate army, the very men in gray who had surprised them before dawn. With him again at their front, they quickly recovered their sense of self-worth, their pride in their manhood and in being important constituent parts of this Union army. And they all knew from the very moment of his arrival that, today, as he led them forward, they would whip those men in gray once again! They had done it before and they would do it again. Now was the moment for vengeance!

It took a number of hours, but after he had sent his staff racing around with his orders, Sheridan was gradually able to reassemble most of the XIX Corps and place them in line next to the VI Corps. He also secured each flank with a division of cavalry, as Wright had been attempting to do before Sheridan's arrival. Now he had a line longer than that of the Confederates he faced, a line of perhaps 17,000 infantrymen flanked by 3,500 men from Merritt's cavalry division on his left flank and 3,000 more under Custer on his right. And this front line was supported by thousands more infantrymen from the VIII Corps, men whose organization had dissolved but brought up the rear as a sort of reserve force. At around 4:00 p.m. they started their movement to the south.[10]

---

In the center of the Confederate line, ammunition supplies were being distributed when a courier rode up in a boil of dust. Leaping from his lathered horse, he ran over to where General Ramseur and his staff stood talking of administrative matters. The courier handed a scribbled sheet to a captain, who scanned it, then passed it to his commander.

It was a warning from the Confederate lookout station high atop Massanutten Mountain, a post that offered, as Gordon and Hotchkiss had learned, an open view of the valley many miles to their north. As the general read it, his face tightened. Then he raised his binoculars to his eyes, scanning the valley floor to their northwest.

The message was a bit unsettling. It said that large Yankee forces were assembling a mile or two off to their northwest, and seemed to be moving south in a wide line, though Dod could only see sections of it in the distance. But it was clearly moving their way. Off to the right, he could also see a large mass of blue cavalry, and they seemed to be moving south on the eastern side of the blue force.

Were they really coming back for more? Ramseur was a bit unsettled, and a sour taste grew in his throat as his stomach churned. This was not what Early had predicted, of course, though Ramseur had dreaded it. At around 10:30 that morning, when they stopped north of Middletown, he had been restless and had agreed strongly with Gordon that, after realignment and refurbishment of arms, equipment, and ammunition, they should have continued their attack. They should have hit the barely touched VI Corps as they reeled and the remnants of VIII Corps and XIX Corps streamed past them in panic, seeking only personal safety.

Had they struck while the iron was still hot, he was sure the men of VI Corps would also have collapsed and run for their lives. Instead they had simply waited for the Yankees to disappear while they rested in the open, both wings suspended in air. Early had been confident the Yankees, once smashed, would continue to flee, even the little-engaged VI Corps. As it turned out, of course, he had been wrong. Dead wrong.

Around noon, Gordon and Kershaw had sent a line of skirmishers to probe the Union positions to their north, still a mile or so away. These quickly brought on a storm of rifle fire from a line of woods to their north, a fire that told them that at least some of the formerly retreating Yankees had formed solid defensive positions.

But Early dismissed that news, confident they had hit nothing more than a rearguard force placed there to delay Confederate pursuit. No, he told Gordon again, they are still in headlong flight, and by nightfall, even that rearguard element will have disappeared as well.

Gordon was stunned. If Early was not going to pursue the Yankees beyond this point, fine; as commander he had the right to make that decision. But he couldn't just leave his troops strung out in the open with both flanks open and little or no apparent cavalry support. Gordon asked Early why he did not just reassemble his troops, send all their booty south in captured wagons, and simply follow them down the turnpike, going to a better defensive position from which they could have both wings covered. Thus arrayed, and even though outnumbered, they could have made any Union attack on them very bloody indeed.[11]

But after several more hours of observation through field glasses, it was clear that the Yankees were no longer fleeing north. Instead, they seemed to have re-formed and, if the accuracy of the men atop Massanutten could be trusted, were moving back toward them in what appeared to be an attack mode.

Now the devil had turned on them, and there would be hell to pay.

Ramseur quickly sent messages to regimental commanders, telling them to dress their ranks and be prepared for an attack from the north. While he was satisfied that his own division was in a strong enough defensive position, he also looked down the gray line through his binoculars in both directions.

To the right, Lomax and his 3,000 horsemen were supposed to be covering that flank, but they had never even appeared that morning, and no one, even Early, seemed to know where they were. In Lomax's absence, the only Confederate cavalry covering their right flank was the small 300-man brigade of Payne's cavalry that had preceded Gordon in his attack.

A few hours later even Early began to feel some concern over the potential of a Union attack, for there had just been several fierce and repeated Union cavalry attacks on his right flank. Because of his own major cavalry absence there, Early had ordered Pegram's and Wharton's divisions to form a solid defensive position with infantry and artillery to ward off any further cavalry attacks. And these Union cavalry attacks had not been supported by infantry or artillery, so perhaps they did not pose any real threat. But the limited and mixed evidence of Yankee intentions could be read either way. All he could do was wait and hope that he had guessed right. But as his mind worked over what he saw before him and heard from couriers, his confidence faded.

Yes, the infantry might hold them off for a while, but even so, it was clear that a large force of Union cavalry—and Early thought they had around 7,000 or 8,000 horsemen at their disposal—could easily ride around either flank not defended by their own cavalry and hit them in the rear, an attack to which they were most vulnerable.

Since around noon, that same enormous body of blue horsemen could still be seen through the dust a mile away to the northeast, and as they stayed there, they worried Early more and more. He knew that if thousands of Union cavalrymen descended on that wing, they would swallow up Payne's tiny force, and whatever the infantry and artillery defenses over there might be, they could easily ride around them and hit the Confederates in their most vulnerable rear.

Off to his left, however, things appeared to be even worse. There was no such in-depth defensive troop arrangement, and he could see no physical feature—no hill, no stream, nothing whatever—against which Gordon might have tied that end of his line. But he had learned from Gordon that Rosser's small division of cavalry, perhaps 1,200 to 1,500 men, was supposed to be covering that flank, though he saw only flashes of gray horsemen a mile or so down the line, and even these sightings were rare. Was Rosser really out there?

While he recognized Rosser's skill as a cavalry commander, what would he do if that end of the line was attacked by a much larger host of blue cavalry? Still, he could see no Union cavalry over there through his binoculars, so perhaps they were safe. For now. He stayed a bit anxious, however, as he received information from both flanks that it appeared one division of cavalry threatened his right while perhaps two more threatened his left. But as yet they had no infantry or artillery support, so perhaps things weren't as threatening as some of his subordinate commanders seemed to think, even though both wings of the Confederate line were uncovered and hanging out there "in air." He consoled himself with the same fiction he had proclaimed earlier, that the Union infantry troops were still retreating, too badly beaten to be reorganized and returned to the field of battle.

Having uncovered wings was a great flaw in the deployment of troops in combat, but it was a flaw that had been forced on Early by the conditions they found as his men drove the Yankees to the north. But after hours of standing in place with no visible movement or other activity whatever on either side, Gordon and Ramseur and the other division commanders must have wondered why Early hadn't done anything about this flawed defensive position.

Without orders or even permission to move forward, they simply stood in place from around 10:30 that morning until nearly 4:00 in the afternoon. And as they waited, both ends of their line—particularly the left—were simply hanging out there entirely uncovered and dangerously vulnerable. This was a major error in their present array, one that the Yankees, should they return and attack, were sure to see and exploit.

Now Ramseur started to be concerned. He had first hoped Early might be right, that the Yankees had been whipped and were through fighting for the day. But this message from the signal station atop Massanutten Mountain seemed to indicate just the opposite, for apparently the Yankees were coming back. To fight. Again.

And he simply could not ignore the evidence he saw through his field glasses. True, the Yankees had been totally surprised and badly whipped early that morning. But apparently, having been allowed to withdraw without fierce Confederate pursuit, they had reassembled a mile or more to the north of Ramseur's position. And now, still vastly outnumbering the gray soldiers on the field, they were coming back to fight. Only this time they were not disarrayed by surprise, and they would be the attackers, while the outnumbered men in gray would have to try to stand their ground.

When Wright moved Custer's division to the left wing, he had left three regiments behind to make Rosser think he still faced a division or more. The ruse was successful, and exchange of gunfire from a distance was the only combat between those horsemen. Then when Sheridan arrived and sent Custer back to the right wing, he told him to "take charge of affairs on the right." This was a pretty broad charge, and Custer, of course, took full advantage of it.[12]

As Sheridan started his long line of soldiers moving, it was impressive. And as this line grew nearer, Gordon realized that the Union infantry and cavalry would reach beyond the end of his line. He also had a growing gap between his division and that of Kershaw on his right—he had sent couriers to Early asking for troops to plug the gap, but had gotten no response.

Finally, he raced back to Early's position and urged him to send men forward. But Early had no troops to send, and he told Gordon to simply stretch his line even thinner, even if that meant creating gaps between brigades or even regiments. He did send some artillery forward, but that final gesture disgusted Gordon. And as he rode back to his men, he realized that even the guns would arrive too late to stave off the blue horde then descending on his lines.

————

As Sheridan's reconstituted army began its frontal assault on the Confederate line, it was initially stopped by a wave of gunfire.

Ramseur, ever aware of the importance of his image as commander, had a horse shot from under him, but he quickly
mounted another. And despite the physical and psychological
weight of their attack, those troops attacking his division were
quickly driven back.

Off to his left, however, Ramseur could see that blue elements were clawing at Gordon and Kershaw. Farther down the
line, he knew that Gordon had detached an entire brigade that
lay in wait. When the Union forces hit that end of the line, they
were suddenly hit from their right side by a hail of bullets and a
roar of rebel yells. Startled, stunned, and stung, those who could
lurched hurriedly back the way they had come, seeking only
safety from this galling fire.

Beyond and somewhat in front of that fight, Ramseur saw
horsemen in a cloud of dust, the gray lit by tiny sparks that were
muzzle blasts as the two sides hammered at each other. Distance
obscured the fighting, but he knew Rosser had arrived there to
cover that end of their line and he hoped that fierce gray warrior
would drive off his attackers.

In fact, Rosser had eventually figured out that he was opposed
by only three regiments, and had driven them north, chasing
them until he got to the left end of the Confederate infantry
line. From about 10:30 on, this line was about three miles long,
and he stopped his men at its western end and held them in a
defensive posture. Now, around 4:00, the Yankee infantry attack
on their entire front was accompanied by cavalry hitting Rosser
on their left flank, and probably Payne's small force on their
right as well. Rosser might be able to hold his own, but he feared
for poor Payne and his 300 horsemen. And the enormous number of blue horsemen who were known to be on the field made
him cringe.

Ramseur saw Yankees were coming forward again to attack
Kershaw on his left as well as his own men. And they did hit
his line, though once again his men drove them back. Gunfire

was being exchanged all the way up and down the line, but the rebels seemed to be holding their own. Then the greater numbers finally began to weigh in, and even Rosser's men began to waver.

At the far left end of the Confederate line, Custer poured his men through the gap between Rosser's cavalry brigade and the rest of the infantry line. And Custer's men never even slowed down, racing down the back of the gray line and firing into the riflemen from the rear with their pistols or repeating carbines. And now those men, hit from the front by blue riflemen and the rear by blue horsemen, also began to waver.

Ramseur knew that panic was fatal, and that seemed to have been loosed at the left end of their line by Custer's breakthrough. Some of Gordon's men down there were the first to break, and at first they only drifted away as lone soldiers or in small groups, even as the Union infantry in front of him returned to the attack. His own men rejected the Yankees once again, but the numbers were just too great, and he ordered his men to move back about two hundred yards and take position behind a stone wall near a clump of woods.[13]

They all seemed to make it to the stone wall safely, from which they were in a better position. But then he saw that even larger numbers of men were fleeing from Gordon's division far off to his left, and now some were slipping back from Kershaw's line on his immediate left as well. He rode down to that end of his line, yelling at the top of his lungs to his men to hold their ground, when his second horse was hit and went down. He got up off the ground, not shaken but angry as he watched not only larger groups of Kershaw's men join the flight but also some of his own men.

Ramseur still had at least 300 or 400 men in front of him, good soldiers all, who were firing from behind that stone wall and driving yet another Yankee attack back. They were under fire now from Yankee artillery moving south on the turnpike

and almost even with them, and he sent word to the artillery
battery off to his right, a battery that Early had sent to him, to
direct its fire over there. Although he was surprised as well as
angry to see his own men turn and run, he was also very proud
of those who stayed.

As a third horse was brought to him, Ramseur knew his men
would stay there and fight maybe until dark, which, by then,
couldn't be more than an hour away. But if they couldn't make
it till then, he hoped their fight would be long enough to give
those who were retreating—no, running away—the time to get
to a safe area in the rear, an area where they might re-form and
be led back into the fight. For he would *never* give in! Now he
was also fighting for Nellie and their new baby, and he would
*never* give in! *Never!*

He had put his foot in the stirrup and begun to swing up into
the saddle when he was hit and knocked to the ground by a bullet or a piece of artillery shrapnel that smashed through his ribs
and ripped deep into his chest.[14] A lieutenant and several startled
soldiers nearby picked him up and slumped his body over the
saddle. Then they held Ramseur in place as one of them took
the reins and began leading the horse to the rear.

As soon as some of his men in line learned that their division commander was down, they turned and fled for the rear
themselves. When they did, the line broke, and the remnants
of Ramseur's gray force resisting the Yankee advance simply
melted away.

Once Ramseur's men broke, the few remaining men in the
Confederate line buckled, and soon enough, all the gray soldiers at Cedar Creek who had not been killed or captured
were in headlong retreat. It soon became abundantly clear that,
because of many factors that must have included the arrival
of General Sheridan on the field, the rout of the Union army
by the Confederates early that morning had been completely
reversed.

When the Union forces drew up before their advance that afternoon, the two batteries remaining from DuPont's artillery brigade were assigned to the left, or eastern, end of the line, stationed on or immediately next to the turnpike itself. Only cavalry was beyond them, protecting their left flank as they opened fire.

With all the caissons that carried his ammunition having been destroyed or captured, Captain DuPont had to do a certain amount of juggling. He found a limited amount of abandoned ammunition and moved it into the limber chests of some of his guns, all the while keeping up his fire on the Confederates. He sent the other limbers to the rear to be filled and returned to the firing line. And his fire seems to have been quite effective: he reports having put his guns into position a short distance north of Middletown, from where

> *I was able to get an enfilading fire upon a battery of the enemy and a portion of his infantry line which were making a determined resistance at a clump of woods on the west side of the turnpike. Some very effective firing was done with solid shot from Gibbs's 12-pounder guns and with percussion shells from the rifled pieces of Light Battery B, Fifth United States Artillery. The enemy soon gave way in great confusion.[15]*

It can never be known for certain, of course, but the enemy positions DuPont describes firing upon and driving off correspond closely to Ramseur's infantry position flanked by a Confederate artillery battery. There is, therefore, the distinct possibility that Ramseur may have been hit by shrapnel from a round fired by one of DuPont's guns, which, if true, would be a sad communion between old friends.

When DuPont was rejoined by his three other guns with

their limber chests full, he moved them down the turnpike as rapidly as possible, first at a trot and then at a gallop as the gray forces fled south before them. When he reached the high ground near Cedar Creek on the west side of the turnpike, he had his men set up and they opened fire on the disorganized masses before them, some of the fugitives being no more than six hundred yards away but fleeing fast. The first few rounds burst in the midst of the crowded troops, causing them to avoid the turnpike and scatter into the adjoining fields, but continuing south.

Demoralization had clearly taken over in the gray ranks, and the area to their front was littered with vehicles that had then been abandoned, often overturned or smashed by collisions—caissons, cannon, ambulances, and wagons of every sort. The Union cavalry was moving into range in front of DuPont, and he gave the order to cease fire as soon as those horsemen were in danger of being hit.[16]

———

Custer brought his entire force around to the Union right flank in preparation for Sheridan's attack, and he had detailed one brigade to ward off Rosser's cavalry division. Then Yankee bugles sounded the charge. As the Union force galloped closer, the Confederate cavalrymen at first fired one ragged volley from their saddles, gave ground, then turned and raced back across Cedar Creek. Their own artillery on the south side of that creek covered the crossing and deterred their pursuers, and a stalemate resulted, with both forces standing their ground a half mile or so apart from each other with the creek between them. While this was not the smashing success some of them had hoped for when they began the charge, still, unbeknownst to most of the blue riders, they had accomplished the task Custer had given to their commanders to protect the Union flank from Rosser's horsemen.

When the main Union infantry first hit them head-on, the Confederate defenses held. As the fire from blue soldiers began to swell, however, some gray troops tried to make an orderly withdrawal, their officers apparently hoping to find better defensive positions. Then as the fire from the blue ranks pounded at them, this orderly withdrawal turned into a confused scramble. On the Union right, the defenses of the main Confederate line began to crack, then to crumple as squads of soldiers turned and moved toward the rear. Panic was in the air, and the men moving in this pullback soon took up a hurried trot. Soon enough, almost every gray position dissolved, and the rout was on.

The Union cavalrymen chasing their foe rode hard, soon outdistancing the infantry line they were supposed to support. But the soldiers in gray, quickly realizing that this wave of blue horsemen might cut them off from the bridge across Cedar Creek, began to run, many of them tossing their rifles and knapsacks aside to speed them in their flight. It was getting dark now, but there appeared to be a strong Confederate line forming south of the bridge. In addition to their rifles, these men also had two cannon, with which they hoped to cover the bridge for their fleeing fellows in arms.

But Custer was able to cross with two regiments at a ford about a half mile northwest of the bridge, unseen in the gloaming by the Confederates who were forming that makeshift line south of Cedar Creek. His men dug in their spurs, and they soon came swooping down out of the gray, one regiment hitting them in the front, the other in their left flank. The Confederates were able to get the few guns they had left limbered up and pulled off, and the line fired perhaps one volley at the horsemen. Then they, too, turned and ran, many abandoning their weapons in their haste. This appears to have been the last organized resistance offered by the Confederates at the battle of Cedar Creek.[17]

Several more regiments from Custer's division continued the chase down the turnpike, which was increasingly blocked by abandoned ambulances, caissons, forges, and other wagons. A few miles farther south, a key bridge at Spangler's Mill that had

been damaged earlier was broken down by racing Union cavalrymen, and many vehicles were stuck there until still more
Union cavalry caught up with and captured them.[18] Among
these wagons was the ambulance carrying General Ramseur,
who was still alive but grievously wounded.

There have been many stories told about how Ramseur
was captured, one being that Custer himself, riding among the
ambulances, recognized Ramseur's voice, while another says
that Union horsemen asked the driver who was in his ambulance and received the response, "The general told me not to
say." Both stories are romantic, but a more realistic account is
provided by a man who claimed to be not only an eyewitness
but also a central figure in the event; his description, being much
less colorful, is therefore more probably accurate.

John Knight, surgeon of the VIII Corps artillery, as was
recounted earlier, was captured in his tent when the first wave of
Confederates swept through the VIII Corps camp. Recognized as
a physician, he was put to work treating the wounded in Confederate aid stations. When the retreat was under way, he was walking among the ambulances carrying wounded men south and
was close to the one carrying Ramseur. When the column was
stopped because of the fallen bridge and Union cavalrymen came
racing by, it was clear that their capture was only a matter of time.

Major Hutchinson of Ramseur's staff was also walking next
to his ambulance when he noticed that the surgeon, Knight, was
a Union officer. He turned to him and said, "We surrender to
you, sir!" Knight accepted the surrender of the general, two staff
officers, and two orderlies and ordered the ambulance to turn
around and return to Cedar Creek. As they approached Union
lines south of the bridge, he announced that he was escorting his
prisoners to VIII Corps headquarters at Belle Grove plantation.

When they arrived there, Ramseur was carefully carried up
the steep steps and into the house, where he was laid out in a
large bedroom. By this time, he was only occasionally conscious,

having bled profusely and been administered heavy doses of laudanum, an opium-based painkiller of the time. As word got out, many friends from the old, pre–Civil War army stopped by to visit him. Sheridan visited, as did his old friends as cadets at West Point and drinking buddies from Benny Havens, Merritt and Custer.

Perhaps the last old friend from the academy to arrive was DuPont. Having just arrived at Belle Grove famished and looking for a place to lay his head, he had been told that Ramseur had been captured, mortally wounded, and was inside the main house. This news "so acutely shocked and distressed me that I forgot my own necessities and hastened upstairs to see him."[19]

They had been close friends for all four years they were together at the academy. During DuPont's last year at West Point, he had lived across the hall from Ramseur, and the two had developed a particularly tight and warm personal friendship. And now, although DuPont had graduated at the very top of the class of May 1861, he was still only a captain. Custer, who had graduated at the very bottom of the class of June 1861, and Merritt, who had graduated in the middle of Ramseur's class of 1860, were major generals. But that was irrelevant here and military rank was ignored by all, for they were drawn together again as West Point brothers to comfort one of their number on his deathbed.

DuPont came into the room as quietly as he could, then sat on the bed rail. He reached out and gently took Ramseur's hand in his. When he did, Dod opened his eyes and looked at him, then spoke the last words that can reliably be attributed to him:

"Oh, DuPont, you don't know how I suffer!"[20]

After that, Ramseur closed his eyes, but from what DuPont has told us, he did not again lapse into unconsciousness for a long time.

In that place and at that time, only three or four years out of the academy, they all came together, in their minds and hearts, as bonded brothers once again. Though the outward signs of their uniforms said something else, they silently and reverently returned to that close personal friendship that had been born in their teenage years and had slowly and tightly been annealed over four years at West Point.

And now, in their presence, one of the brothers was dying. Not even politics or the Civil War, in which they fought so fiercely with or against each other, could threaten that bond.

Once again, they were simply brothers and best friends.

Brothers and best friends for life.

DuPont himself relates what followed that night:

*Ramseur and I had been on terms of most friendly intimacy during the four years we served together at West Point, and although his own surgeon and adjutant-general were present, he turned to me in his suffering and never relinquished his grasp of my hand until the anesthetic given to relieve his agony had rendered him unconscious, which condition until the end came.*[21]

More laudanum was administered, and Dod finally faded into unconsciousness, his hand turning limp in DuPont's. After that, the old friends gradually left.

The next morning around 10:00 a.m., without ever having regained consciousness, Major General Stephen Dodson Ramseur quietly slipped away.

# NINETEEN

## *Valley Conquest and Rosser's Raids*

At Cedar Creek, Early's command had been badly beaten, and they lost many men and much materiel as they fled south. The Union cavalry pursuit ended the night of 19 October, but Early's men kept moving far to the south. However, over the next few months he took his small army or sent parts of it back down the valley, mostly just to harass Sheridan. On 11 and 12 November, Rosser's cavalry skirmished inconclusively with Union troopers, but these engagements were really trivial to Sheridan.

On the night of the 12th, Early withdrew to Fisher's Hill, and on the 14th to New Market. From there Kershaw's division was returned to Lee at Petersburg, and General George B. Cosby's cavalry to Breckinridge in southwest Virginia. The valley had been burned over and picked clean by Sheridan's men, and a hard winter lay ahead, not only for the veteran Confederate soldiers still operating there, but also for the civilian farmers and their families who lived there.

Since he was now commander of a division of cavalry, Rosser was promoted to major general on 4 November. But obtaining sufficient food for his men and forage for his horses was a constant and gnawing problem. Finally, when his quartermaster told him on 20 November that he could feed the horses for only another week, Rosser knew he had to do something.

His scouts told him that the South Branch Valley of the Potomac across the Allegheny Mountains in the new state of West Virginia had not been ravaged by Sheridan's men, and there were plentiful supplies of food and fodder in that region. He asked permission of Early to go there and gather sustenance for his men and horses, and his formal authorization for such a venture was quickly given. But from among the 3,000 men present for duty in the cavalry division he was then commanding in Fitzhugh Lee's absence, he found fewer than 600 men who were mounted well enough to make what he knew would be an arduous march.

They left their camp near New Market on 26 November and headed north. They passed through the Alleghenies at Brock's Gap and spent the night at Matthias, some twenty miles from their starting point. Early next morning, 27 November, they pushed on and reached the town of Moorefield in West Virginia at around 1:00 p.m.

The goal selected by Rosser for this raid was the U.S. Army's New Creek Depot on the Baltimore and Ohio Railroad line, some sixty miles north of New Market as the crow flies. But the limited roads through the rough, mountainous terrain they would have to cross would make the trip perhaps twice that distance. The depot consisted primarily of large warehouses filled with food, forage, and ammunition. And because of the importance of these supplies, two Union forts protected them, forts that had repelled two earlier Confederate cavalry raids sent to capture them. Rosser, however, was not to be easily deterred.

The largest and most important of these defensive installations was Fort Kelley. Set on the south side of the upper waters of the Potomac River, the fort was surrounded by solid earthworks that were defended by some 1,200 men and a half dozen cannon.

Local residents in the area sided mostly with the Union cause, so cautious avoidance of civilians by the Confederate invaders was crucial. Rosser knew, therefore, that a surprise attack would be the only way he might hope to succeed.

He had hoped to get help from a local partisan ranger command, which was 150 men from E Company of the 18th Virginia Cavalry, commanded by Lieutenant Jesse C. McNeill. But when McNeill's rangers showed up at a river crossing specified by Rosser in his orders, they were engaged from high ground by a Union detachment. Not content to remain on the defensive, McNeill broke contact, then led his men on a flanking move. When they exploded from the forest on the surprised Yankees, the outnumbered and terrified men in blue ran for all they were worth. And although McNeill captured fifty prisoners and one artillery piece, some of the Union soldiers got away safely.

When McNeill told Rosser of this, neither of them knew if the retreating Yankees had gone to Fort Kelley. But even if they had not, Rosser felt sure the men there would have learned of this action and so would be on the alert for a Confederate attack.

On 26 November, a reconnaissance party under Major P. J. Potts had left Fort Kelley to search the Alleghenies through which Rosser's men had passed. On the 27th, Potts and his men spotted this rebel force without being seen themselves, and they got away on a mountain path. They spent the next day wandering through the mountains while trying to avoid this large Confederate party, and they wouldn't return to Fort Kelley until the 29th, when their intended alert to the garrison was far too late.[1]

Because of the partisan ranger action on the 27th, Rosser knew he had to attack as soon as possible. That meant a night march, and on the morning of the 28th the raiders were within a few miles of the fort. But before he struck, the general in gray had another card up his sleeve.

Early that morning, one of the Confederate scouts learned

from a friendly local that the reconnaissance party under Major Potts that had left on the 26th was expected back at any time. And as outnumbered as he was and had always expected to be, this was Rosser's moment for high-risk trickery.

After having sent a party downstream a half mile to cut the telegraph line, Rosser launched his attack around noon. But this was not to be a typical saber-waving, pistol-firing, rebel-yelling gray cavalry attack. Instead, the leading twenty horsemen in Rosser's column were clad in captured Union blue uniform coats and they simply walked their horses slowly down the middle of the road. Thinking this was the Major Potts party returning from their patrol, sentries and pickets stationed along the road to the fort merely smiled and greeted them pleasantly as they passed, only to be captured by the gray troopers who rode behind. Too late to send a message back and too frightened for their lives to fire their weapons, the captured Union sentries gave no warning of the oncoming Confederate column.

Wearing the uniform of the enemy in order to impersonate one in combat is a clear violation of the laws of war long agreed to by western civilized nations, at the time most recently specified in the Lieber Code of 1863. The person captured and found guilty of such an act is usually treated as a spy and punished by death. However, during the Civil War, both sides almost routinely had some of their own soldiers who volunteered to do so put on captured enemy uniforms and then go across the lines in an effort to gather intelligence. But this was a very high-risk venture, as capture and identification as an enemy soldier often meant summary execution on the spot.

In this case, there was always the chance that, if the Confederate column had been driven back and any of the twenty soldiers wearing blue Union uniform coats had been captured, they might well have been shot and killed for what was referred to as their "perfidy." But these are the sorts of risks that were taken in the Civil War and, when practicable, are also taken by both sides in all wars. This time, Rosser got away with the deception he had ordered, and it worked.

When they rode through the main gate unopposed, the rebel raiders found their Union counterparts relaxed and eating lunch. Rosser's men first took control of the cannon, and as soon as the blue soldiers realized what was happening, most surrendered without any resistance. A certain number of Union soldiers were able to get away and cross the river, and some of them hurled long-range rifle fire back at the Confederates. But these few parting shots were in vain, for the Confederates were by then in charge of both forts, and there were no Union troops anywhere nearby who might hope to turn the tables on them.[2]

The man responsible for the defense of New Creek Depot and Fort Kelley was Brevet Major General Benjamin F. Kelley, who worked out of Cumberland, Maryland. But the commanding officer in place at New Creek was Colonel George R. Latham of the 5th West Virginia Cavalry, and he was able to get away with some of his men who crossed the river. He was, however, to hear much more from within the Union army of his inability to turn away this raid.

It was not long before the last hiding Union soldiers had been found and captured, and complete Confederate control of both forts at the depot had been fully secured. Rosser then sent Major E.H. McDonald and the 11th Virginia Cavalry, a 300-man force, to take the small town of Piedmont. Only five miles away, it was the site of an important railroad repair center, and McDonald was told to destroy as much of it as he could. But on their way there, Captain John Fisher and thirty-five men of a Union unit, A Company of the 6th West Virginia Infantry, blocked their passage through a narrow draw.

A fierce firefight erupted, and although the Yankees were initially in a strong defensive position, they were soon turned by the horsemen and driven across the river. Even so, they continued to fire on the rebels while they wrecked the rail facilities at

Piedmont. But their efforts were in vain, for McDonald's men caused considerable damage to the railroad repair facilities, then put the associated buildings to the torch. After they had burned everything they didn't wreck, McDonald and his men did not return to Rosser at New Creek, but rather just made their own way back across the Alleghenies to the Shenandoah Valley.

To Rosser's great delight, he found that they had captured far more at New Creek than they could possibly transport back to the Shenandoah Valley. Their spoils included tons of flour, meat, molasses, sugar, coffee, and forage for animals as well as enormous supplies of clothing, weapons, ammunition, and military equipment of all sorts. They would also start back to Virginia with about 700 prisoners, 160 cavalry horses, 40 mules, eight pieces of artillery, and hundreds of wagons, many of them filled with other army supplies.

As soon as he was able to organize what would be a heavily overloaded caravan, Rosser led it back into the Allegheny Mountains. In order to make sure he truly got away with his booty, he drove his men well into that night. Their sleepy lack of vigilance, however, coupled with the rough mountainous country they were moving through in the dark, allowed about half of the Union prisoners to escape.

While he was busy at New Creek, Rosser had sent foragers out into the surrounding countryside. They had returned with more than four hundred head of cattle as well as some sheep and horses, and their number was simply added to this highland victory parade. With his caravan of wagons overloaded with food, forage, and numerous military supplies, he was joyfully received on 2 December when he arrived back in the valley.

An embarrassed General Sheridan, of course, was furious, and he made sure Colonel Latham was tried by court-martial within weeks. Charged with neglect of duty, disobedience of orders, and conduct to the prejudice of good order and military discipline, Latham was found guilty. Under these shameful circumstances, he was sentenced to discharge from the U.S. Army, a sentence that President Lincoln, normally lenient and forgiving, upheld. But this was not to be the end of the story.

In addition to having been the acting commander at Fort Kelley, Latham had also just been elected to Congress from the Second District of West Virginia. After his dishonorable discharge, he was seated in Congress on 4 March. And on 9 March the War Department revoked his dismissal and had him honorably discharged. And it is not at all clear that this was just political, because the incidence of Confederate raids across lines into Union safe havens was being seen in a new light.

On 21 February these same McNeill's rangers slipped into Cumberland, Maryland and, in the middle of 8,000 Union soldiers, were able to kidnap and get away with Major General George Crook, commander of the Army of West Virginia, as well as Brevet Major General Benjamin F. Kelley. From Cumberland, Kelley had been Latham's boss at New Creek, and Crook had long disparaged and dismissed officers below him who had been surprised or captured by fast-moving Confederate rangers or other raiders. Now, having been caught himself, he had to acknowledge that these "irregulars" were not the ragged incompetents he had earlier thought them to be. And clearing Latham's record may have been part of Crook's self-imposed penance for having made a false assessment and then used it as the basis on which he had punished certain subordinates.[3]

The December weather in the Shenandoah Valley that year was particularly harsh, such that military maneuvers or operations of any sort seemed all but impossible. Even so, Grant wanted Sheridan to cross the Blue Ridge Mountains and wreck the Confederate rail center at Gordonsville. And so it was that Sheridan planned one last operation for the middle of December 1864.

The main thrust from Sheridan would come from Torbert, who would lead some 8,000 men in two cavalry divisions,

Merritt's 1st and William Powell's 2nd, through Chester Gap
in the Blue Ridge Mountains. Their goal would be to break
up the Virginia Central Railroad near Charlottesville and Gordonsville. At the same time, Custer would lead the 3,000 men
of his 3rd Cavalry Division up the Shenandoah Valley, this primarily as a distraction intended to hold Confederate forces in
the valley.

On 19 December, the blue columns left Winchester, stepping out into freezing, snow-covered, and unwelcoming enemy
country. Custer moved straight up the valley, while Torbert's
men got through the mountains. But men and horses in both
columns suffered greatly from the cold. Though the men carried
food for themselves and grain for the horses, their movement
through snow and ice and slush was slow and difficult. And since
there was no shelter for the men, at night they built fires if they
could find dry wood, and then simply lay down and slept on the
ice- and snow-covered ground.

Early still had signal stations atop various mountains, and he
had been monitoring these Union army movements through signals and by telegraph. He was told of the two columns, a small
one in the valley and a larger one going through the mountains.
On 20 December he sent Rosser racing down the valley with
around 750 men to strike the smaller column. The larger column looked like it was heading for Harrisonburg, so he sent
Wharton's division of under 2,000 men there, giving them the
added burden of having to leave through a hailstorm.[4]

Custer reached Lacey Spring, some nine miles north of Harrisonburg, on the evening of 20 December. Rosser's force also
got to Harrisonburg that night, and he went forward to make a
reconnaissance with a local man who guided him to the federal
encampment. A cold rain was falling, turning the roads into
muddy mires, and the rain soaked both men and horses, then
froze solid. Soldiers and horses on each side suffered from this,
but they suffered equally. Rosser's men moved through the bitter

weather, and as they approached, Custer's men were totally unsuspecting.

Moving forward quietly on foot in the dark, Rosser was pleased to see that they didn't have to avoid pickets or sentries because none had been posted, a colossal error for a Union commander at that time and place. They got to within a hundred yards or so, and, judging from the number of campfires, it was clear that they were outnumbered four or five to one. Their only hope was in a night attack with no warning that might overrun part of Custer's command. But upon reflection, Rosser realized that the number of Union soldiers was just too large to expect that their first strike would result in a total rout. Still, in love and war, you just never know. . . .

Rosser returned to where his men were waiting in a long column of fours. From there, he simply led them forward until their column encompassed one end of the Union camp. Then, with no bugles or other signals, he had them face left and move forward into the camp, shooting into the tents or at the half-clothed Union soldiers who came bursting out of them. Within a few minutes some Yankees began to return fire. But most were so shocked by the gray wave that swept over them that they just grabbed what they could and ran.

The rest of the division was awakened by the gunfire, and most who were not yet under fire themselves secured their horses, then saddled and mounted them as quickly as they could. When Custer realized one side of his camp was being overrun, he didn't know how large a Confederate force he faced. He quickly saw that in a confused firefight in the dark night his men might shoot more of their own number than rebel soldiers, so by shouted and repeated orders he was able to extract most of his force and move them to the north, down the Valley Pike. But some of his men were unable to even find, let alone saddle their mounts, and Rosser captured many prisoners as well as horses and equipment. Now it was Rosser's turn to gloat.[5]

After Rosser and Wharton had left, Early sent Lomax with his cavalry to Gordonsville, in case the other Union column had been headed there. Once he got confirmation of Custer's rout by Rosser, Wharton's division was brought back and part of it was sent by rail to Charlottesville. Thomas Munford's cavalry brigade was also sent there.

After he had deployed these units, Early went to Charlottesville himself. When he got there on 23 December he learned that the larger column, two Union cavalry divisions under Torbert, had been held in check by Lomax near Gordonsville. A brigade of Confederate infantry soon arrived in Gordonsville from Richmond, and when they saw them approaching in formation, the blue horsemen quickly retired back through the mountains. Early himself then returned to Staunton, where he made his winter headquarters, with Wharton's infantry division and Rosser's cavalry encamped nearby.[6]

But hunger once again returned as an increasingly serious problem among Early's troops. Indeed, without food or forage, Rosser had to release many companies on leave. Theoretically, they were going home to recruit new soldiers, but actually they were being sent to their homes that they might be able to adequately feed both themselves and their horses and simply survive the winter. This was a genuine crisis, and Rosser was looking for any way possible to resolve it. And as he listened to his scouts and thought about his situation, he came up with a rather novel approach.

He had learned that at Beverly, another small town in West Virginia, there was another major Union supply depot. This gold mine of supplies, defended by a garrison of about a thousand Union troops, lay on the other side of the Allegheny range, though it was some seventy miles west of his winter camp near New Market. The raid he had led on New Creek Depot, of course, had required him to march a similar distance across the mountains to his north. But this time he could expect the bad mountain roads to be obstructed by ice and snow, which not only added to the difficulty of such an operation but also promised even more misery for his soldiers.

Rosser's fundamental principles of leadership would not allow him to ask his men to do something that he would not do himself. But with the bitter winter that had descended on them, this proposed operation looked like it would be far more difficult and dangerous than the November raid on New Creek, so he spread the word of his proposed raid within his division and asked for volunteers.

There were many men who wanted to go with him, but because he could only come up with three hundred horses he thought fit for the venture, he would only allow that number of volunteers to accompany him. To get to Beverly, they would have to pass through land ravaged by war with little or no sustenance for man or beast. The few roads they might use to get through the mountains were steep, rocky, and all but impassable with the deep snow that had been falling on them for weeks. The few people who lived there were just as tough as the land on which they lived, and most of them were bitter opponents of the Confederate cause. And if Rosser were to try this with any hope of success, it soon became apparent from information he was able to gather that they should make the attack from the north, where fewer Union pickets, patrols, or outposts covered the roads.

On 7 January, the 300 men set out for Beverly. They went through the Buffalo Gap and moved down the Staunton and Parkersburg Turnpike. Several of the raiders were natives of the county in which Beverly was located, and they rode at the front as guides. They started up the mountains, the road covered with unbroken and often deep snow. Even so, they got to the crest of the Alleghenies around sunset.

During the night, a heavy rain turned mountain streams into torrents, and the next day they had difficulty fording many of these. The most intimidating watercourse of all, however, was the wild Jackson River. Screwing up their courage, they plunged into the white water, and after one man and his horse were swept away and lost, the rest of them emerged whole on the far side.

Later that day, a courier from Early with orders recalling Rosser and his men from a mission considered far too dangerous arrived at the Jackson. But unable to cross the increasingly wild water, he returned to the Shenandoah Valley. Only by so narrow a margin were the raiders able to avoid orders that would have recalled them and ended the venture that grew riskier with every mile they put behind them.[7]

The men were moving on narrow mountain trails, and on 10 January the heavy rain they had endured for two days turned to snow. Their march became a brutal ordeal, but Rosser kept them going all night, arriving outside Beverly at around 4:00 a.m. on 11 January. They rested for several hours, and then, just as the first gray streaks began to light the sky, led their horses on foot and approached a large field of tents.

After they had overpowered the first sentries who challenged them, a few Union soldiers recognized them as Confederates and opened fire. But the Yankee officers were all comfortably quartered in heated buildings in town, and none of them slept with their enlisted men in the tent city. Consequently, with no effective leadership, the blue soldiers began surrendering by the hundreds.

Word of the raid soon reached the officers, and many of them attempted to get back to their men. But Rosser had a line of mounted men ready at the edge of town, and the confused officers who came running down the street were dispersed or captured by the raiders before they got anywhere near the tents.[8]

Rosser quickly assembled his captured soldiers and other booty and got them back on the road to the Shenandoah Valley. He reported 572 enlisted men and 8 officers captured, 6 killed, and 32 wounded, while having lost only 1 man killed and 1 seriously wounded from his own force. He also captured and brought back with him one hundred horses, six hundred rifles, and, most important, ten thousand rations.[9]

Their march was slow, and because of the harsh weather, both prisoners and their captors suffered from the cold. However, the men in gray all rode horses, and so the march was easier for them than for the men in blue. And the psychological boost these 300 raiders must have felt as they guarded twice their number while moving them slowly toward their Confederate prisoner of war camp destination must have made up for a lot of cold hands and feet.

Meanwhile, Grant was pressing Sheridan to destroy the Confederates in the valley once and for all, then come through the Blue Ridge Mountains and wreck the railroad lines as well as the river and canal transportation facilities at Lynchburg. From there, he was to move south and meet Sherman's army coming north through the Carolinas. Their joint actions, he reasoned, would basically destroy the ground on which the rebellion stood and the war would be brought to an end.[10]

On 27 February Sheridan set out with 10,000 cavalrymen and artillery support to accomplish that mission. But Early, then at Staunton, had allowed many of his men to go home for the winter, and he had little force available to resist.

At Mount Crawford, Rosser and about 500 cavalry tried to slow Sheridan's advance so that Early might gather more troops. The fords over the North River were largely impassable because of melting snow and heavy rain, which delayed the men in blue for twenty-four hours. But once Union horsemen had gotten across upstream, they flanked Rosser and sent his men into headlong retreat.[11]

And Sheridan's pursuit was relentless. He finally caught up with Early on 2 March near Waynesboro. Arrayed for battle with about 1,000 infantry supported by Rosser's command of no more than 100 horsemen and a few artillery pieces, Early's men made a brave stand. But it was a hopeless situation for the last Confederate force that still resisted the Union army in the Shenandoah Valley, and Custer flanked them with three regiments while hitting them squarely from the front.

The whole gray line collapsed almost immediately, and then individual soldiers ran for all they were worth, leaving behind for capture by Sheridan's men everything of any military significance, including Early's baggage wagon. The rebels scattered to the winds, and Sheridan's men had no resistance left to fight or organized retreat to pursue. They had finally conquered the Shenandoah Valley and now it was time for them to pass through the Blue Ridge Mountains and help end the war.

# TWENTY

## *Appomattox Campaign*

After the small army under Jubal Early was destroyed as a fighting force at Waynesboro on 2 March, some 1,300 rebel soldiers were captured by Sheridan's force. Custer suspected that both Early and Rosser were hiding in town and so had the buildings there carefully searched. But Early had slipped away with a handful of other horsemen and within a few days got over the Blue Ridge Mountains on back trails. He eventually reached Petersburg and reported to Lee, but there was nothing left of his army. And with his dreadful loss at Cedar Creek widely known throughout the South, his days of Confederate command were over.

Rosser stayed in the valley and within a few days was able to assemble about 300 of his horsemen who had been on leave. They followed the 1,300 prisoners, now guarded by 1,200 Union soldiers, as they moved north up the Valley Turnpike toward Winchester. Rosser was even able to send unarmed men in at night to mingle with the prisoners and encourage them to revolt when he struck.

But these plans were to come to naught. When Rosser did

hit the Union expedition on 4 and 6 March, his attacks were quite feeble and easily repelled. And the Confederate prisoners simply ignored these brief flurries of gunfire and just kept trudging north as they were bidden by their captors. Realizing that he could not rescue these prisoners, Rosser turned around and headed south into the "Upper Valley" once again.[1]

Sheridan's cavalry force poured through the Blue Ridge Mountains by way of Rockfish Gap and into Charlottesville. That town's mayor, carrying a white flag, met him a mile outside of town. After a day of rest there, Sheridan broke his force into two columns.

The first was Custer's 3rd Cavalry Division, which was directed to follow the Virginia Central Railroad, tearing up track and destroying associated facilities as they came to them. The second was Devin's 1st Cavalry Division, ordered to similarly destroy military facilities along the James River or any associated canal systems. Sheridan rode with Custer, and Merritt, as the overall commander of both cavalry divisions, rode with Devin. Both columns were moving toward White House on the Pamunkey River, where Grant had supplies awaiting them.[2]

Spring rain, coupled with creeks and streams overflowing with snowmelt, slowed their progress considerably. After a week, the columns reunited, but movement continued to be slow, the only external constants being rain and mud. And the only internal constant in this expedition's mission performance was its steady and unrelenting destruction of the last shreds of life still adhering to the already-desiccating Confederate corpse.

Having captured some 2,000 rebels along the way and destroyed all supplies and militarily useful facilities they came across, the column led by Devin with which Merritt rode finally reached White House on 18 March. Many of their mounts had broken down during the last few weeks, and more than a week was spent resting the troops and reshoeing those horses considered still serviceable. Even so, nearly 900 men had to be left behind without horses when, on 27 March, Merritt led both cavalry divisions south to join Grant's force outside Petersburg.[3]

After failing to free the Confederate prisoners captured at the battle of Waynesboro, Rosser led his small cavalry force to the east of the Blue Ridge Mountains and for many days hovered on Custer's flank, but never really had enough force to attack him in any meaningful way. Finally, on 16 March, he joined Longstreet's corps, and they decided to cross the Pamunkey River together in front of Sheridan's cavalry and force them into a fight. But before a satisfactory pontoon bridge could be built on that river, General R. E. Lee called them both to join him in the defenses around Petersburg. By this time Rosser had been able to recover many of the men from his cavalry division whom he had sent home during the winter, and when they got to Petersburg, their number approached 1,100.

The wide arc of the Confederate defensive line east of Petersburg was nearly thirty-five miles long and so at some points thinly manned. But the most important part of the line was its right wing, which protected Lee's last remaining supply line into Petersburg, the Southside Railroad. The key Confederate defensive position there was at the crossroads of Five Forks, from which White Oak Road crossed the Southside Railroad and led into Lee's rear. If that position were taken by Union forces, Lee would no longer be able to remain in Petersburg or Richmond.

Grant, of course, was well aware of the importance of Five Forks, and he decided to extend Union lines to the west with two of his infantry corps and Sheridan's cavalry, from where he could attack or outflank Five Forks. On 29 March he sent Sheridan's cavalry to his extreme left flank, with orders to Warren's V Corps to follow. Sheridan now had the 1st and 3rd Cavalry Divisions under Merritt, plus another cavalry division, the 2nd Cavalry Division of the Army of the Potomac under General George Crook, for a total of 9,000 crack cavalrymen. But the rains had turned the roads into quagmires, and although the fields appeared to be solid, the first horse who stepped into one soon foundered in a sea of seemingly bottomless mud. This was a major handicap, and Custer's entire division was assigned to corduroy some of the roads used by Sheridan's army, often using abandoned Confederate muskets for the task.

On 30 March Sheridan sent Merritt forward to test the Confederate defenses, and his men skirmished with rebel pickets all day long. In every case, when pressed, they withdrew into solid fortifications reinforced with timber around Five Forks. Clearly they had no intention of withdrawing from that key position. But this was just what Sheridan was looking for: a good fight.

On 31 March Merritt led his 1st Cavalry Division under Devin and one brigade from Crook's division against the Five Forks fortifications. Once they had driven in the pickets, the fall of the main position was surprisingly quick. But that was because Pickett and the 14,000 veterans he controlled had come out of their positions and moved around Merritt's left flank, between him and Crook's division. And then Confederate cavalry joined Pickett's men in attacking Crook's division.

Merritt rapidly pulled his men back, but Crook was still separated from him by gray soldiers. Sheridan was behind Crook, and his men threw up strong log defenses while calling both Merritt's and Custer's divisions to join him and try to stop the gray wave. Custer arrived in late afternoon, in time for his dismounted cavalrymen and their repeating rifles or carbines to help beat back Pickett's infantry attack. Merritt got there just before dark, and by first light on 1 April, Sheridan was ready to go again. Yes, they were outnumbered by the men in Pickett's division. But that force was unsupported and dangerously overextended.

In fact, Pickett was also anxious about being out so far in front of his own lines, and during the night he had pulled back to Five Forks. At dawn on 1 April he held a strong position in the defensive fortifications, his infantry flanked by cavalry under Fitzhugh Lee and Colonel Thomas Munford. Rosser's division was held in reserve, guarding the wagons about two miles in the rear of Five Forks.

On his way to that position the previous day, 31 March, Rosser had crossed a river in which the shad were running. Food was short for the officers as well, and so he borrowed a seine from a local farmer and waded into the river with some of his staff. Soon enough, fresh fish were cooking over an open fire, and for the first time he could remember, his staff ate all they wanted and still had a lot of good food left over. Among Confederate forces in 1865, such a situation was almost too good to be true. But this was not an opportunity to ignore, and Rosser saved a few big shad for an impromptu feast with his brother generals. That evening, once he had gotten his men set in place, he invited Generals Pickett and Fitz Lee to join him the next day, 1 April, for what promised to be a festive lunch.

The fish were cooked over an open fire, and as they ate, there seems little doubt that, in Southern tradition, the three men also drank some kind of alcohol as well. This was one of the few chances they had ever had to truly relax among friends. In the face of the overwhelming blue war machine that pounded on them every day, the laughter, ribaldry, and song they shared then must have gone a long way toward stabilizing their shaken psyches. It is no surprise, then, that the impromptu party went on for several hours, well into the afternoon.

Tragically for them, of course, was the fact that their feast coincided exactly with Sheridan's all-out effort to take Five Forks. It remains unclear how much difference their presence at the front lines that day might have made, or even if there was any hope at all left for the life of their self-proclaimed new nation. But whatever the longer odds may have been, the absence of Pickett and Fitz Lee from their respective commands clearly hurt the Confederate cause.

That morning, Merritt had been ready to attack Five Forks at first light, but Warren's V Corps was still not in position, so the movement forward was delayed. Finally, at around 4:00 p.m., Warren's men charged over the barricades on the Union right, followed by an assault by Merritt's dismounted troopers on the left. There was little heart left in the Confederate defenders and, after little resistance, they turned and ran, pursued by the Yankees for as much as six miles before dark.[4]

Rosser and Pickett and Lee were quite relaxed, ignorant of the ongoing battle because the noise of gunfire at Five Forks was totally absorbed by a dense pine forest that lay between them. As the afternoon wore on, several couriers arrived with news of Union breakthroughs. Finally, two men from Rosser's division arrived on lathered horse, reporting that Union troops had broken through on all the roads the Confederates were guarding and were closing in on White Oak Road. This silenced the generals, but after listening for a few seconds, they heard no noise of battle at all. Convinced these incidents must be minor, they went back to the shad and the laughter, never realizing that noise from Five Forks would have been buffered by the thick forest that lay between them.

Finally, at around 4:00 p.m., Pickett asked for a courier he could send to his men at Five Forks. As he always did, Rosser provided two couriers, one to ride ahead but always within sight of the other. That meant that if the first courier were captured or shot, the same message carried by the trailing courier had a much greater probability of getting through.

This time, the advance rider had not gone a half mile when he was captured by blue soldiers who came swarming out of the woods, and the second courier came racing back with the news that there was a large body of Union soldiers well behind Five Forks. Pickett and Fitz Lee tried desperately to get back to their now-fleeing units, while Rosser stayed where he was, and his men did successfully impede some of the Union pursuit. Unhappily for the Confederacy, no one sent word to Robert E. Lee of the massive defeat, news he didn't learn until the next morning.

Lee knew right away that, with his southern flank turned, he could no longer keep his army in Petersburg or Richmond. On the night of 2 April, therefore, they began their slow move to the west. Lee hoped to join Joseph Johnston's army in North Carolina, and to get there, he needed to reach the Danville Railroad line many miles to the west. Rosser moved at the rear of the column, his cavalry protecting Lee's meager wagon train.

In the flurry of orders he had to give when he left Richmond, Lee had made sure food for his troops was sent forward to Amelia Courthouse. But only disappointment awaited his weary column when they got there, for bungled commissary orders meant there was nothing there for them to eat. Lee knew he could go no farther, so he stopped his column and sent wagons out into the country to collect what food they could.

The results were disappointing, and it cost Lee a full day. When his men picked up their gear and moved west the next day, few of them could have expected their agony to go on much longer. On 6 April Merritt's cavalry cut between Longstreet's corps and that of Ewell. Repeated cavalry attacks slashed through their formations and burned all their wagons, resulting in the surrender of about 10,000 men—a third of Lee's remaining troops—and 6 Confederate general officers. On that same day, Grant sent a detachment of about 1,200 infantry and cavalry to destroy a key bridge that carried the Southside Railroad line over the Appomattox River, the High Bridge. But Lee responded by sending Rosser and about 1,500 veterans from his own and Fitz Lee's division to stop them. And stop them they did, capturing some 780 men and driving the rest off. This was to be Rosser's last fight in the Civil War.[5]

On 7 April Merritt pressed his two cavalry divisions, driving them hard toward Appomattox Courthouse. Sheridan's intent was to keep Lee from reaching Lynchburg, where he hoped to feed and supply his men. Custer's 3rd Cavalry Division was in the lead, galloping hard, although it wasn't until late afternoon on the 8th that they reached Appomattox Station. There, four trains laden with supplies awaited Lee. Sheridan soon arrived on the scene and, destroying one train and moving the other three beyond Lee's reach, sent the following word back to Grant:

"If General Gibbon and the Fifth Corps [Union infantry] can get up tonight we will perhaps finish the job in the morning. I do not think Lee intends to surrender until compelled to do so."[6]

That night, Lee called his two corps commanders, Longstreet and Gordon, and his cavalry commander, Fitzhugh Lee, to his tent. After discussing their bleak prospects, he ordered the cavalry, at first light on 9 April and with the full support of Gordon's infantry, to attack the Union forces blocking their path. If they were only cavalry, he continued, then his men should drive them off and continue their march. If, however, there was also a sizable body of Union infantry in front of them, he should so inform Lee. If that were to be the case, Lee informed them, then appropriate steps would be taken for the surrender of the Army of Northern Virginia to Grant's Army of the Potomac.

During the night, Union infantry did join Sheridan's force at Appomattox Station in large numbers. By dawn it was clear on both sides that Lee's last desperate escape hatch had been closed and the game was over. Couriers were soon bearing messages between Grant and Lee, and his formal surrender occurred that day in the McLean farmhouse.

After the surrender document had been signed by Lee, the commanders on both sides returned to their troops. Sheridan then purchased from McLean the small table on which it was signed and gave it to Custer, along with a letter to his wife, which read:

*My Dear Madam,*

*I respectfully present to you the small writing table on which the conditions for the surrender of the Army of Northern Virginia were written by Lt. General Grant—and permit me to say, Madam, that there is scarcely an individual in our service who has contributed more to bring about this desirable result than your gallant husband.*

*P. H. Sheridan, Major General, Commanding*

Rosser, however, saw the surrender coming and managed to get away with his cavalry division before that happened. And because he was not physically present with the Army of Northern Virginia when Lee surrendered it to Grant, he felt he was technically not bound by it. He led his men to Lynchburg that night, then disbanded them while he rode to Danville with his staff, seeking orders from President Jefferson Davis. But Davis was gone when he got there, though he did receive orders from Confederate secretary of war General Breckinridge to collect as many Confederate soldiers who had not been paroled in Virginia as possible, and then to obey the orders of the governor of Virginia if President Davis still could not be reached.

He later said he had gathered about 500 men and was preparing to lead them across the Mississippi to continue the fight—a daunting task, to say the least. Riding to Hanover Courthouse to bid farewell to his wife and children, however, he was no sooner inside the house than it was surrounded by Union cavalrymen and he was captured. After being released on parole, he went back to his men at Swope's Depot and distributed parole papers to all of them, thus releasing them from Confederate service and allowing them to return to their homes. And so, for Tom Rosser, George Custer, Wes Merritt, Henry DuPont, and all the other earnest patriots on both sides, the Civil War finally came to a close.

# TWENTY-ONE

## *Old Soldiers*

After the Civil War, the immense armies on both sides were demobilized, and most soldiers on both sides returned to civilian life. The entire Confederate army, of course, simply went out of existence, though after a certain period some Confederate veterans did join the U.S. Army as enlisted soldiers. In May 1865 there were just over a million volunteers still wearing the Union army uniform, but a year later there were only about 11,000 volunteers still on active duty.

After the end of the Civil War, most of the volunteers were mustered out as soon as possible. Merritt, Custer, and DuPont, however, were all regular army officers and they stayed in uniform, intending to make a career of their service. Some volunteers were kept on active duty, much to their distaste, because of a French army in Mexico.

In 1864 the French were interested in exploiting Mexico's rich mines and Napoleon III placed his puppet Maximilian of the Hapsburg family on the throne of Mexico, supported by a French army landed in that country. The U.S. government objected that this was a violation of the Monroe Doctrine, but because of the Civil War it could take no military action.

After the war, and as a sign of American concern, Sheridan was sent to Texas with some 50,000 volunteers. Merritt and Custer went with him, retaining their rank of major general of volunteers and each commanding 4,000 cavalrymen. Now faced with a U.S. force prepared to back up its government's demands, the French announced in August 1865 that they would withdraw their army from Mexico, and the volunteer units in Texas began mustering out and sending their men home. On 28 December 1865, many generals of volunteers were mustered out of the service, including Merritt and Custer.

Both automatically reverted to their regular army rank of captain, and each was given an extended leave of absence. Merritt, still a bachelor, went for a long vacation trip to Europe, while Custer took Libbie back to her home in Monroe, Michigan. He then traveled on his own to Washington and New York City, exploring any other professional opportunities that might have been open to him. But he found nothing else that attracted him as much as the army did, and he and Libbie decided to make a career of the service. For Merritt, there was really never any such question, for he was committed to the army come what may.

By November 1867, with virtually no volunteers left in service, the regular army numbered about 54,000. The American people have never been happy with a large standing force in peacetime, so this force was further reduced by Congress to 45,000 in 1869, and again to 27,000 in 1876. That number remained constant until the Spanish-American War erupted in 1898.

Because of the vastly reduced size of the postwar army, those who wanted to stay in uniform faced dramatic reductions in rank. But Grant was commanding general, and his favorite subordinates, Sherman and Sheridan, were able to retain their status as general officers. Merritt and Custer, in turn, were protected by Sheridan and each of them managed to attain the rank of lieutenant colonel.

Regiments were normally commanded by colonels, which is the rank both had sought, but politics precluded that. Still, in those days colonels commanding regiments assigned to the western frontier were often absent for extended periods. That often left the actual hard duty of field command to the affected regiment's deputy commanders, its lieutenant colonels.

From early in the nineteenth century, the federal government had been attempting to control Indian tribes in the West. Most tribes on the Great Plains were nomadic, following enormous buffalo herds and moving their villages of buffalo-skin tepees and large herds of horses regularly. It was clear, however, that neither buffalo herds nor the nomadic lifestyle of tribes of buffalo hunters could coexist easily with white families living on and farming the fertile land of the Great Plains.

In an attempt to eliminate violence between white settlers and these tribes, large sections of the West were set aside by the government in Washington as Indian reservations. After payment of some sort, many chiefs agreed that their tribes would live on these designated lands where they would be left to themselves without white interference. They also were given the promise that if needed, they would be housed, clothed, and fed by the white man on those reservations.

In more recent times, the plight of Native Americans, a more appropriate title than "Indians," has begun to be recognized. By what right, for instance, did the white man interfere with the age-old ways of life that Native Americans had inherited? That moral question was never really asked as white men and their families moved west, pushing Native Americans aside to farm the land. Justified as "manifest destiny," that assessment is more an observation than an explanation, for the flood of white men moving west was basically unstoppable. And as we look at the behavior of American soldiers, white settlers, and Native

Americans in the late nineteenth century, we must carefully avoid judging them under twenty-first-century standards.

The postwar army had two major duties: occupying the former Confederate states, which went on until 1877, and protecting settlers moving west from attack by hostile Indians. Merritt and Custer, of course, wanted to be where the action was, which meant on the western frontier. Both were lucky enough to obtain assignments there.

Merritt served with the 9th Cavalry, one of the famous "Buffalo Soldiers" regiments made up of black enlisted men and white officers. They were assigned to western Texas, where he fought against Comanches and Apaches. Custer was to serve with the 7th Cavalry in the northern Great Plains, where he fought against Sioux, Cheyenne, and Arapaho.

By the end of the Civil War, the transcontinental railroad line had been completed, and the Homestead Act of 1862 had been passed into law. It provided for the transfer of 160 acres of "unoccupied" public land to each homesteader on payment of a nominal fee after five years of residence. In addition, European immigrants were flooding our shores—out of the thirty-five million whites living in America in 1870, roughly five million were foreign born. The immediate result was an avalanche of white settlers moving west.[1]

As they moved west, settlers simply assumed that they would be protected from Indian attacks by the U.S. Army. In order to do that, part of the U.S. Army's protective role involved setting up army forts along the major trails leading west. This, however, was an act that truly enraged many of the tribes inhabiting those areas.

Unrest between Indians and the ever-growing number of white settlers mounted, with many killings occurring, both of white men and Indians. A climax of sorts was reached when more than 500 white settlers in Minnesota were killed by the Sioux in 1862. Eventually, 303 Sioux were captured, tried, convicted of murder, and sentenced to death, though Lincoln pardoned all but 38 of these men. Those 38 Sioux warriors, however, were publicly hung in the town square of Mankato, Minnesota.[2]

But massacres occurred on both sides. In 1863–64, with few army troops available, there were repeated attacks in Colorado on white settlers in their cabins or moving on trails. Finally, a white family was brutally murdered near Denver. The state governor called out the state militia, and in November 1864 some 700 members of the Colorado Volunteers descended on a Cheyenne-Arapaho village and killed more than 400 Indians in what is remembered as the Sand Creek Massacre.

In the northern Great Plains, the army's leaders soon realized that their Civil War tactics of forcing set piece battles would not work against the Indian tribes, who kept great herds of horses and so were very mobile and elusive. The army's horses were fed grain, while the Indian mounts relied exclusively on grass or whatever vegetation they could find. When snow covered the ground their horses were badly undernourished and very weak, which limited Indian movement. The tribes, then, tended to set up somewhat permanent winter camps, usually near streams or rivers.

As movement west of settlers ballooned after the end of the war, Indian depredations increased dramatically, as did white attacks on Indians, and innocents on both sides died violent deaths. But the federal government had established reservations for the tribes, and it was when they left these territories that most of the bloodletting occurred. The U.S. Army, then, became the government's agent to punish raiders or force the return of tribes to their reservations.

But the Indians did not want to go back to the reservations, where they were often cheated and starved. On 21 December 1866, 80 infantrymen under Captain William J. Fetterman and Lieutenant G. W. Grummond were sent out from Fort Phil Kearny in present-day Wyoming to rescue woodcutters under attack. They were met and then surrounded by more than 1,000 warriors from the Sioux, Cheyenne, and Arapaho tribes and all 82 soldiers were killed.[3] Lieutenant General William T. Sherman, commander of the Department of the Missouri, was furious. On 28 December 1866, he wrote to General U. S. Grant, commanding general of the U.S. Army, saying:

"We must act with vindictive earnestness against the Sioux, even to their extermination, men, women, and children. Nothing less will reach the root of the case."[4]

This was strong language, but it was not uncommon, for white settlers were terrified by Indians and looked to the army for protection or retribution. As the attacks continued, it was increasingly difficult for the army to protect settlers from their passive, defensive positions in frontier posts. But the army's commanders tried to change that when they adopted an offensive strategy of total war on "hostile" Indians who refused to return to their reservations. Their first effort remained pacification, and they decided to trap the tribes in the winter with converging columns, then kill their ponies and force them to move back to the reservations on foot.

In the fall of 1868, warriors from Chief Black Kettle's tribe of Cheyenne were accused of committing quite a number of atrocious killings of white settlers, and General Sheridan decided to send Custer and his 7th Cavalry to attack his village on the Washita River. His final orders were to "kill or hang all warriors and bring back all women and children."[5]

On 27 November 1868, Custer had surrounded the village and he attacked from three directions at dawn. His men killed 105 warriors and brought back 53 women and children, though there were doubtless other women and children who were killed during the fight. He destroyed fifty-five lodges and all their food supplies, and also slaughtered about seven hundred of their ponies, forcing the surviving people to return to their reservation.[6]

Merritt's 9th Cavalry was commanded by Colonel Edward Hatch, and their enlisted men were former slaves recruited in Louisiana. A small number of them had served in the U.S. Army during the Civil War, and only one could read and write. However, they were put through extensive training, and in March 1867 began moving to Texas. Their duty was to protect travelers from Indian attacks on a western segment of the seven-hundred-mile road between San Antonio and El Paso. They would operate out of Fort Stockton, commanded by Colonel Hatch, and Fort Davis, commanded by Lieutenant Colonel Merritt.

The Indians of concern were Comanche and Kiowa who were few in number but masters of raids. Even so, the most serious fighting for the 9th Cavalry would be with Apaches out of the mountains of southern New Mexico. But there was little bloodshed, and in 1867, only two of his soldiers were wounded in action.[7]

In September 1868 a band of Mescalero Apaches had stolen stock from a wagon train at Fort Stockton. Merritt sent sixty men under his best lieutenant in their pursuit, and they soon caught them, recovering the cattle and two captive Mexican children while killing twenty-five Apaches. It was the biggest success the 9th Cavalry had known since they had arrived in Texas.

Early in 1868 Merritt had hired a local schoolteacher to educate his men in basics. Classes were held every day of the week but Saturday and Sunday, and attendance was mandatory. He also established daily infantry and cavalry drill and made sure his men acquired habits of good hygiene and sanitation. Consequently, morale was high, and over a twelve-month period in 1867–68, the 9th Cavalry had only 48 deserters, while Custer's 7th Cavalry had 456 in the same period. Part of this was because many former slaves saw the army as a legitimate career, while a major portion of Custer's men were looking for a refuge from the law or a free ride partway to the goldfields in California.

In January 1869 Merritt fell and a wagon rolled over his left arm, breaking it badly. There were serious complications, and the arm would trouble him for the rest of his life. On 3 September 1869 he left Fort Davis on medical leave to have it cared for, and he would end up gone from Texas for longer than even he expected.[8]

In early 1871, he went on a lengthy trip to Europe, visiting England, Italy, Austria, and Germany. It is unknown whether he traveled alone, but in May 1871, while still in Germany, he married Miss Caroline Warren of Cincinnati, Ohio. Apparently he had found true happiness with her, for he requested and received an extension of his leave, not returning to the U.S. with his new wife until September 1871. Then it was back to the lower Rio Grande and the 9th Cavalry, where the couple remained for several years. They finally left Texas for good in May 1874 and once again spent eight months touring Europe on leave.

DuPont, who finished the war as a brevet lieutenant colonel, reverted, like all the others, to his regular army rank of captain. But he decided to make a career of the army as well and stayed in uniform. He sequentially commanded an artillery battery, then a battalion, and finally, as part of the occupying army in Virginia, all of Fort Monroe. From 1870 through 1873, he commanded Fort Adams in Newport, Rhode Island, for certain periods while also serving on a board of U.S. Army officers charged with assimilating the tactics of the infantry, artillery, and cavalry.

In July 1874 DuPont married Mary Pauline Foster, then resigned his commission on 1 March 1875 and went on a year-long delayed-honeymoon trip to Europe. When he finally came home to Delaware, he became first the director of the Wilmington and Northern Railroad Company, and in 1878, once he had learned the ropes, its president and general manager. He filled that post for twenty years.

At the end of the war, Rosser had a wife and hungry children, and he had to find a way to feed them. He scrambled around for a few years, working for various mail and banking services, none of which worked out. Eventually he decided to try to find a practical application for his five years of education in engineering at West Point.

Having left a few weeks before graduation, he had no diploma from the U.S. Military Academy. Additionally, his Confederate experience, even as a general officer, caused potential employers in the North to simply shy away from him. Finally, in 1868, he went to St. Paul, Minnesota, and took a job with the Canadian Pacific Railroad Company as a simple axman, helping clear a path through wooded areas and dutifully sending money home every payday.

He was a strong man and a good worker, impressing his employer so much that he was promoted within a month. But looking for more, he joined the Northern Pacific Railroad as an engineer in construction work. He soon rose to be the engineer in charge of surveys and construction as the Northern Pacific pushed a line west through what are today's states of North Dakota and Montana.

Because of his military experience, Rosser was named to head an engineering party that laid a line in September 1871. Despite open hostility from Indian tribes, the U.S. government very strongly supported construction of the railroad line. Rosser's expedition was therefore protected by 500 U.S. Army soldiers, 50 Indian guides, and two Gatling guns under General Joseph N. Whistler, and needed equipment and supplies were carried by one hundred wagons.

After five weeks, the expedition had gone through the badlands of the Little Missouri and reached the Heart River. When Rosser returned to Fargo, he sent for his wife, Betty, and their four children. After setting them up in a converted tent in the new town of Fargo, Rosser continued his engineering expeditions. But the next summer, when he was absent, tragedy struck on 20 August 1872, when their youngest child died of cholera. Named John Pelham Rosser after his West Point roommate and best friend, the baby's death was a major blow to Rosser. Because the closest doctor was more than one hundred miles away, he and Betty decided that she and the children should move to Minneapolis, where there was medical care available.[9]

In the summer of 1873, the Northern Pacific sent a surveying party to explore and mark out the unfinished section of the line from the Missouri River into Montana beyond the Yellowstone River. This was a serious intrusion into country where they could expect to be attacked by any Sioux or Cheyenne warriors they ran into who had ventured off the reservation to hunt. Rosser again was the chief engineer on this expedition, and the U.S. Army sent 1,700 soldiers to act as escorts under the command of Major General David S. Stanley.

After the Civil War, it was a custom that men who had held brevet general's rank but remained in uniform at a lower regular army rank continued to be addressed as "General." Stanley's command included infantry, cavalry, and artillery as well as Indian scouts. And the cavalry regiment under Stanley and accompanying Rosser happened to be the 7th U.S. Cavalry, commanded by none other than Brevet Major General and regular army lieutenant colonel George Armstrong Custer.

As he lay in his tent one day, Custer heard a familiar voice outside: "Orderly, which is General Custer's tent?" He sprang to his feet and said, "I know that voice, though I haven't heard it for years! Come in and welcome!" Custer recorded the reunion that followed in a letter he wrote to Libbie on 26 June 1873:

*It was my old friend General Rosser. Stretched on a buffalo robe, under a fly, in the moonlight, we listened to one another's accounts of the battles in which we had been opposed. It seemed like the time when, as cadets, we lay huddled under one blanket, indulging in dreams of the future. Rosser said the worst whipping he ever had was that of Oct 9th (well do I remember it) when I captured everything he had, including that uniform of his now in Monroe. He said he had*

*been on a hill, watching our advance, and, through his field glasses,*
*recognized me, so sent for his Brigade Commanders and said, "Do*
*you see that long-haired man in the lead? Well that's Custer, and*
*we are going to bust him up. . . . And so we should have only you*
*slipped another column around us, and soon my men were crying*
*'We're flanked. We're flanked,' and then some broke out and ran,*
*and nothing could stop them."*

From the moment Custer first heard Rosser's voice, boyish glee overcame them both, and they were to spend many evenings lying on the same buffalo robe beside the campfire or inside a tent, reminiscing about the overwhelming nature of the lives they had each lived: starting as brother cadets at West Point, followed by major moments fighting each other as warrior kings, and now ending on the high plains as they worked jointly again, as the brothers they had always been, to ease the progress west of white settlers. That made for a very heady brew of brother-enemy-brother, one that I expect, in the annals of American history, has not been far surpassed by any other young men setting off as close companions on the voyage of life.

Rosser and Custer were together for about five weeks, until the last days of July 1873. Many days they would ride together ahead of the engineering party for ten or twelve miles and mark the path the rail line would follow. But they were well aware of their environment, and they were always accompanied by eighty-odd cavalrymen. Their party came under fire several times from hostile Sioux warriors, but they returned to the main camp at the end of every day. It was the sort of brotherhood that defies written description, but they surely relished it.

Then the party reached the Yellowstone River, and a steamboat arrived carrying one of Rosser's assistant engineers. It was his turn to rough it now, and Rosser would return to see his wife and children in Minneapolis. He and Custer bid each other a fond farewell, promising to stay in touch and hoping to work again on a future railroad engineering expedition. But unbeknownst to both, this was to be the last time they would see each other.

Three years later, in June 1876, Custer led his 7th Cavalry north through the Bighorn Mountains, looking for a large village of Sioux and Cheyenne who were off the reservation. Two other large columns of cavalry were moving south toward Custer, with the idea that the three converging columns would trap the Indians. Their intention was to force them back onto the reservation, but it was expected that this might well involve some heavy fighting.

On the morning of 25 June, Custer's scouts found the village lying north of them along the Little Bighorn River. Thinking they had been seen and afraid the Indians would flee, he divided his regiment into three battalions. He sent one battalion, under Captain Frederick Benteen, on a scouting mission and ordered another, under Major Marcus Reno, to approach the village from the south.

He then led the third battalion toward the far northern end of the village, where he and more than 200 of his troopers met an enormous force of warriors. He sent his bugler back with a last desperate order to the others to come forward, but it went unheeded. The soldiers who rode forward with Custer were killed to a man in a battle about which we know almost nothing.

The other two battalions were able to reunite and stave off heavy Indian attacks that day and the next. They were finally rescued when the Indian village disappeared in the night and the other two army columns moved south along the Little Bighorn to find them on a hilltop.

There was a great national outcry, and many refused to believe it, that Custer, the great Civil War hero and Indian fighter, had been killed by Indians. But it was true. And he had many enemies as well as friends, people who loudly charged that he was a selfish glory hunter who cared nothing for his men or the Indians he slaughtered. The Sioux and other Plains Indians were innocents who were trapped and run over by waves of greedy white men, and Custer was their willing instrument. And those charges have reverberated, loud and long, even into the twenty-first century.

Indeed, the white man's treatment of Indian tribes has been shameful. And Custer was a flawed man who performed poorly in caring for his men on several occasions. He had also been rather vain during the Civil War, sometimes seeking credit for conquests or captures made by other units. A newspaper reporter, at his invitation, accompanied his command whenever possible, and there is no doubt that he loved the limelight.

But there is also no doubt that he was an extraordinarily courageous cavalry commander who led charges from the front and seemed to know no fear. Some called his actions rash and too risky, and these charges were often accurate. But his commanders loved the victories he won, and his men simply worshipped him.

And finally, on a wholly different field of battle from those of the Civil War, "Custer's luck" had run out, and he was dead.

Rosser was stunned by the news, and he wrote a long letter to the editor of the St. Paul *Pioneer Press*, part of which reads as follows:

> It was expected that when the expedition was sent out that Custer and the Seventh Cavalry were to do all the fighting, and superbly did a portion of them do it. As a soldier I would sooner today lie in the grave of General Custer and his gallant comrades alone in that distant wilderness, that when the "last trumpet" sounds I could rise to judgment from my post of duty, than to live in the place of the survivors of the siege on the hills.
>
> I knew General Custer well; have known him intimately from boyhood; and being on opposite sides during the late war we often met and measured strength on the fields of Virginia, and I can truly say

*now that I never met a more enterprising, gallant, or dangerous enemy*
*during those four years of terrible war, or a more genial, wholesouled,*
*chivalrous gentleman and friend in peace than Major General George*
*A. Custer.*[10]

When Merritt returned to duty in January 1875, he served as a staff officer in Chicago until 1 July 1876, when he was promoted to colonel and given command of the 5th Cavalry Regiment. He spent the rest of that summer and fall chasing the Sioux and Cheyenne who had killed Custer that June, only to have them find refuge in Canada or back on their reservations. In November 1876 Merritt took the 5th Cavalry to Fort D. A. Russell in Wyoming.

In January 1879, he was appointed one of three members of a Court of Inquiry that met in Chicago to examine the conduct of Major Marcus Reno, who had been Custer's second-in-command at the Battle of the Little Big Horn. After spending a month hearing testimony from twenty-three witnesses, the Court said that, under the circumstances, Reno was justified in not moving forward to support Custer and then retreating into a defensive position. This was far from a glowing endorsement of his conduct, but Custer was dead and he couldn't be brought back to life by beating on survivors.

Wesley and Caroline would live at Fort Russell, Wyoming until 1880, when the regiment was moved north ninety miles to Fort Laramie and two more years slowly passed. Finally, on 1 September 1882, he took over as superintendent at the United States Military Academy at West Point, New York. And even with the broad array of experiences he had lived in uniform, the five years during which he filled that post came as close to true personal bliss as anything he ever knew.[11]

In 1886 Rosser bought a two-hundred-acre farm near Charlottesville with a very large Victorian house called Rugby Hall. Two more children had been born to him and Betty in the West, and they happily moved to this, their final home in the state where both had been born. He would occasionally engage in some of the back-and-forth arguments in letters to the editor of various newspapers, finding fault with some former generals on both sides in the Civil War while applauding others. But mostly he was finally home to rest and live out his days in peace.

When war with Spain came in 1898, Rosser wanted to show his allegiance to the United States of America and so applied for a commission in the U.S. Army. President McKinley, in a political act both positive and palliative, responded by commissioning him a brigadier general of volunteers on 10 June 1898. But his health was not the best, and so Rosser spent his time in the uniform of the U.S. Army in Georgia, where he trained conscripts who were preparing to fight in Cuba. And ironically enough, the men he trained were members of infantry regiments from Minnesota, Ohio, and Pennsylvania, Yankees to a man!

Rosser spent that summer drilling these men, but, given the short duration of the war, they never went overseas and he retired in November 1898. But he had finally been able to serve in the blue uniform he had aspired to wear while a West Point cadet, and he retired after service as a general officer in both the Confederate States Army and the United States Army, a rare honor and privilege.

Rosser was one of the few former Confederate generals, such as Longstreet and Mosby, who adopted the Republican Party as the best hope for the nation. He supported President McKinley and Teddy Roosevelt, whom he particularly admired for his military service in Cuba. He expressed his rationale as follows:

*No one can deny that the North has prospered under Republicanism, nor is there any denying the fact that the South has not prospered under Democracy. Nature has blessed the South with a soil and climate superior to that of the North. Then, shall we be expected to admit that, under like conditions, the South is not equal to the North*

*in a fair field of business competition? My experience, which has been*
*extensive, will not allow me to admit it, but on the contrary, I deny*
*it. . . .*

   *I regard the Republican party as the only national party in the*
*field. It is enterprising, aggressive, and patriotic; it has on hand and*
*unfinished a great work of clearing off the debris left in the fields by*
*Spain after the war was over, which both Democrats and Republicans*
*put us into.*[12]

In 1901 Rosser ran for governor of Virginia but was unable to
win the Republican nomination. In any case, a Democrat won the
governorship, but that made his run for office no less disappointing to him. In 1905 President Theodore Roosevelt appointed him
postmaster of Charlottesville, a post he filled for the next five
years. On 29 March 1910 he lost his last fight to pneumonia, and
his great heart beat its last. As a soldier he had won many victories, and he acknowledged only one defeat. That was when he
was beaten by Custer at Toms Brook. But he had fought a good
battle, and the man who defeated him was a true brother.[13]

He had lived a full life, a general officer in both the Confederate States Army and the United States Army. His life was a
worthy symbol of the disunion and reunion of our states.

On 16 April 1887 Merritt was appointed brigadier general
in the U.S. Army. This was a mighty culmination to his career,
and it was all he had ever hoped to attain. With his new rank
he was entitled to departmental command, and he and Caroline
left in early July to assume command of the Department of the
Missouri in Fort Leavenworth, Kansas. There was little Indian
strife by then, and his one major accomplishment was his troops'
management of the Oklahoma Land Rush on 22 April 1889. In
1887 he wrote a section of *Battles and Leaders of the Civil War*,
entitled "Sheridan in the Shenandoah Valley," and in 1890 two
articles for *Harper's Magazine*. In one of them, "Three Indian
Campaigns," he used his own experiences to describe fighting

against various Indian tribes, and he was, to say the least, not sympathetic with their plight.

In July 1891 he moved to St. Paul, Minnesota, where he took over command of the Department of Dakota. By then, the Indian Wars really were over, and economic hard times swept the country. With no war to fight, the main engagement of his troops was protecting railroad facilities from strikers and unemployed workers. This went on for several years. While a railroad bridge was burned and soldiers had to disperse some rioters, Merritt's men were also involved in other minor violence associated with these labor disputes.

But Merritt's attention was focused on Caroline, who was very sick. He took her to New York for treatment and then to the softer climate of Fort Monroe, Virginia, for rest. Unhappily, she died of "chronic diffuse nephritis" on 12 June 1893 at the young age of forty-four. Though they never had children, they had spent twenty-two happy years together, and Merritt buried her in the West Point cemetery.

With Caroline gone, he filled his days with work as best he could. But he still shone brightly in uniform, and on 25 April 1895, at the age of fifty-eight, he was promoted to major general, the highest rank then obtainable in the United States Army. He moved to Chicago, where he took over command of the Department of the Missouri, which meant everywhere west of the Mississippi save only the Pacific region.

Living in Chicago was to be most enjoyable for him. His work there was primarily administrative and, supported as he was by many staff officers, not terribly taxing. He traveled extensively through the West and spent the months of January and February 1897 inspecting army posts in Texas, then continued into New Mexico and Arizona in a private railroad car provided by the Chicago and Eastern Illinois Railroad Company. That trip was markedly different from his early days in Texas with the 9th Cavalry Regiment after the end of the Civil War.

Merritt grew closer to his family members from southern Illinois, some of whom had ended up in the Chicago area. His service also brought him into close contact with Chicago's business and civic leaders. One of his closest friends was Norman Williams, a wealthy lawyer and businessman, and he often stayed at the Williams's suburban mansion. He became particularly close to their daughter Laura, a bright and attractive woman in her midtwenties.

In April 1897 he was appointed commander of the Department of the East, working out of Governors Island in New York Harbor. Things were quiet enough for him until 24 April 1898, when Spain declared war on the United States. The next day the United States declared war on Spain, and immediate plans were made to attack Spanish forces in Cuba and Puerto Rico. Then on 1 May, Admiral George Dewey defeated the Spanish fleet in Manila Harbor and sent word that if a U.S. Army force were sent, it could easily take Manila.

The commanding general of the U.S. Army in Washington was Nelson Miles. It was decided that he would command the Caribbean operation while Merritt, the second-ranking general in the U.S. Army, would command an expedition to the Philippines. During the month of June, 11,000 soldiers sailed to Manila in three detachments. But once arrived, there were political complications.

There were some 12,000 Spanish troops inside the walls of Manila, besieged by an equal number of armed rebels under command of the European-educated leader of the recently proclaimed Philippine Republic, Emilio Aguinaldo. They had been fighting the Spanish for several years and had finally gotten the upper hand and controlled all of the island of Luzon except the capital city. They were not strong enough to take the city, but Aguinaldo thought the Americans had come to help them win their independence and would help them take Manila. But

American political leaders had imperialist aims and sought to control the Philippines, not free them.

The Spanish commander, General Fermin Jaudenes, was in somewhat of a box. He did not have the strength to defeat the rebels, but he was reluctant to surrender as he feared his men and their families would be subjected to bloody retribution for the harsh rule that Spain had inflicted on the Philippines. He therefore opened secret negotiations with Merritt through the Belgian consul. He had to put up some resistance, so he agreed to put up a show of opposition at the outer walls, but then pull his troops back and surrender the city to the Americans.

Merritt did not share this agreement with his subordinates, and on 13 August, the U.S. troops opened fire on the southern walls of Manila. The defenders were quickly routed, and after about an hour of fighting, the Spanish showed the white flag and surrendered. American forces then occupied Spanish barracks and basically took over control of the city from them. Merritt was appointed a delegate to the peace conference that would open in Paris on 1 October, and he sailed for Europe on 30 August.

He arrived in Paris on 3 October, and Laura Williams met him in London, where they were married on 24 October. He was sixty-two but fit and trim, and she was twenty-seven, gay and gorgeous. After their honeymoon in Europe, they came back to New York in mid-December. As the commander on Governors Island, he was a celebrity in New York, and for the next two years, he and Laura were caught up in that city's social whirl.

After he retired in June 1900 they spent three months in Europe, then they moved to their last home, in Washington, D.C. Again, he was a prominent figure much sought as a guest or lecturer. But after the age of seventy, he began to fade. Finally, on 3 December 1910, at the age of seventy-four, he died of arteriosclerosis. As one last grace, Laura made sure that his wish to be buried at West Point with his first wife, Caroline, was fulfilled.[14]

---

On Saturday, 7 February 1914, a hearing of the U.S. Senate Committee on Claims was held to hear testimony on Senate Bill 544, a bill introduced by Senator Henry Algernon DuPont of Delaware in 1913 "for the Relief of the Virginia Military Institute of Lexington, Va." The bill proposed that:

> *the Secretary of the Treasury be, and is hereby authorized and directed to pay to the Virginia Military Institute of Lexington, Virginia, out of money in the Treasury not otherwise appropriated, the sum of $214,723.62, in full payment of all claims of said Institute for the damage and destruction of its library, scientific apparatus, and the quarters of its professors in June, eighteen hundred and sixty four by the military authority of the United States.[16]*

As recounted earlier, back on 11 June 1864 General David Hunter's army had taken the Virginia Military Institute. Colonel J. M. Schoonmaker was commander of the cavalry brigade that was the first Union force to reach the VMI grounds. Colonel Schoonmaker sent the following deposition, which was introduced as evidence:

> *I was Colonel of the 14th Pennsylvania Cavalry, in command of the First Brigade of Averell's Cavalry Division, and led the advance of General Hunter's army when he moved south from Staunton on June 11, 1864, on what is known as Hunter's raid on Lynchburg. On arriving at the outskirts of Lexington there was some firing from skirmishers, which halted us until General Hunter came to the front and ordered the shelling of the Virginia Military Institute, but with no response following same, and my recollection is that I was the first one to enter the Institute building, finding the cadets' school books*

*open on their desks and diagrams partly finished on blackboards, and no trace of the building having been occupied by Confederate forces, placed it and the Washington College [today's Washington and Lee University, which closely adjoins VMI] buildings under guard. Some time after General Hunter advanced his main army into Lexington and sent for me, taking me severely to task for not having burned the Institute, which he did the following day, and it was my understanding at the time that General Hunter also intended burning the Washington College buildings. I have no hesitation in stating that I considered at the time the burning of the Institute for military reasons unnecessary and unwarranted.*

In his testimony before the Senate Committee on Claims, Senator DuPont said that he could personally accept the destruction of the cadet barracks since they were apparently the source of rifle fire upon his troops. But the destruction of the other institute buildings, which included the library filled with books, other academic buildings with various scientific equipment used for academic instruction, and even the homes of professors, was "a wholly unnecessary destruction of private property and not justified by the rules of war." He remembered in particular the then future president William McKinley, who at the time was a staff officer, expressing the same views and even helping him to literally carry furniture out of some of the homes in which a number of older women lived alone.

DuPont explained to the committee that VMI was a military school only so far as the instruction and discipline of the students were concerned. Its purpose, he went on, was to educate teachers for the Commonwealth of Virginia, and a number of boys were given a free education there in return for their later teaching for a certain term of years within the state.

At the time, DuPont said, there were no organized athletics, and military training was part of the curriculum at many schools throughout the land. It was felt that military exercises would not only improve the physical condition of the boys but would also keep them out of trouble. That was the idea of all these schools, DuPont went on; it was not for the purpose of educating the pupils to fight, he said, adding that no one even thought of such a thing when he was a child before the Civil War.

A key witness was the chief of staff of the U.S. Army, General Leonard Wood. Born in 1860, he had heard only later in life about General Hunter's 1864 destruction of VMI, though he knew none of the details. Senator Key Pittman of Nevada asked if the Confederates, had they captured West Point during the Civil War, would have been justified in destroying the buildings of that military institute. Wood said that they would not be so justified. But the question really turned on whether a given institute contributed to the enemy's prosecution of the war. If that would involve the destruction of all colleges where the military art was taught, said Wood, then that would mean the destruction of all agricultural and mechanical colleges then in existence, and that would clearly not be justified.

When he made this specification, Wood was referring to those colleges that maintained regiments of trained men as actual or potential commissioned officers. Under the Land Grant Act of 1862, military instruction was required at every land-grant college or university, including a minimum of three hours of drill each week. General Wood said that despite its name and the fact that it produced a great many officers each year, the Virginia Military Institute was not a military institution. Rather, it was a school of broad general culture and engineering.

General Wood said that the formation of VMI as an organization was not dissimilar to Norwich University in Vermont, which sent seven hundred of its graduates into the Civil War. It was a distinct military organization, and yet it was in every essential a college or educational institution training men for civil life.

Senator Pittman asked General Wood if he was willing to

give it as his opinion that the destruction of VMI by General Hunter was unnecessary and not in accordance with the general usages of civilized nations in war. General Wood responded that it was both unnecessary and not in such accordance, and that he would regard it very much as he would regard the destruction of Norwich University if the Confederates had gotten up into that part of the country.

The bill was passed by the Senate, and in early 1914, as often happens, a conference between the Senate and the House of Representatives lowered the amount that would be appropriated. It was sent to the White House and as Private Act No. 264, 63rd Congress, it was signed by President Woodrow Wilson. It states:

"Your claim for amount appropriated by Congress as compensation for damages and destruction of library, scientific apparatus and the quarters of professors in June 1864 by the military authority of the United States has been allowed as shown in the following statement, and settlement certificate No. 107860 has this day been forwarded to the Secretary of the Treasury for payment."

The award was in the amount of one hundred thousand dollars.

That meant that VMI did not get every penny Senator DuPont thought the federal government owed it because of the army's wanton destruction of its property in 1864. That was partly because DuPont's bill claimed more than eighty thousand dollars in interest, which was not granted. But the institute did get one hundred thousand dollars. And in 1914 that was a very large sum.

In 1864 DuPont had been forced to watch his commanding general wrongfully burn VMI to the ground. But in 1914, and only because of DuPont's own efforts as a senator, the former artillery captain was able to see justice finally done: VMI was bountifully repaid by the federal government for the misdeeds of

Tom Carhart

an angry old general during the Civil War. It was another fitting closure to the division of our nation by the Civil War, a healing of old wounds that still reverberates well into the twenty-first century.

DuPont left the Senate on 4 March 1917, his public life over. He retired to his estate at Winterthur, Delaware, where he managed an experimental farm looking into more productive ways of growing food for the American people. On 31 December 1926, he quietly died in his sleep.

The last two stanzas of the West Point song "Alma Mater" are important here:

> *And when our day is done,*
> *Our course in life has run,*
> *May it be said "Well Done,"*
> *Be thou at peace.*
> *Long may that line of Gray*
> *Increase from day to day*
> *Live, serve, and die, we pray*
> *West Point, for thee.*

The six men we have looked at here grew to be brothers as West Point cadets. Then, when our country divided, they fought with and against each other as soldiers. And when our country reunited, the survivors loved each other once again, but this time as older and wiser brothers.

In many ways, their lives mirror that of our young nation.

These words, then, are a fitting epitaph for each of the six: Well Done.

Be thou at peace.

# NOTES

## INTRODUCTION

1. Alan Aimone, "U.S. Military Academy Civil War Resources and Statistics" (West Point, NY: U.S. Military Academy Archives, 2008), drawn from *Decennial Register of Graduates and Former Cadets* (West Point, NY: U.S. Military Academy, 1999), 2–5.

## CHAPTER ONE

1. William A. Shelton, *The Young Jefferson Davis* (Manchester, NH: Ayer, 1981) 41–43; Clement Eaton, *Jefferson Davis* (New York: Macmillan, 1977), 14.
2. Russell F. Weigley, *A Great Civil War* (Bloomington: Indiana University Press, 2000), 150–54.
3. Ibid, 227.
4. Robert K. Krick, "The Confederate Experience at Spotsylvania's Bloody Angle," in *The Spotsylvania Campaign*, ed. Gary W. Gallagher (Chapel Hill: University of North Carolina Press, 1998), 96.
5. Gary W. Gallagher, *Stephen Dodson Ramseur* (Chapel Hill: University of North Carolina Press, 1985), 26; Frederick L. Ray, "George Custer and Stephen Ramseur," *America's Civil War* (July 2003).

6. *Salem (IL) Advocate*, 24 March and 6 October 1858, 6 December 1860.

7. Don E. Alberts, *General Wesley Merritt* (Columbus, OH: General's Books, 2001), 13–18.

8. David Schenck, unpublished manuscript, *Sketches of Maj. Gen. Stephen Dodson Ramseur*, Wilson Library, University of North Carolina, 12.

9. Millard K. Bushong and Dean M. Bushong, *Fightin' Tom Rosser, C.S.A.* (Shippensburg, PA: Beidel Printing House, 1983), 1–3.

10. Philip Mercer, *The Gallant Pelham* (Wilmington, NC: Broadfoot, 1995), 14–18.

11. Jeffry D. Wert, *Custer* (New York: Simon & Schuster, 1996), 17–25.

12. Virtually all the various verses written and sung over the years are collected in the USMA Archives, West Point, NY, although the creativity of individual cadets or West Point graduates is not to be discounted here, and there are no doubt verses sung at different times that are not to be found in the academy's formal records.

## CHAPTER TWO

1. This concept was perhaps best articulated by Senator Henry Hammond of South Carolina in a famous speech he delivered to the U.S. Senate on 4 March 1858, in which he described blacks as the "mudsills of society," the natural lower class who perform the drudgery and menial duties necessary to support a society of higher-class whites. He contrasted that with the North's "hireling class" of manual laborers and "'operatives,' as you call them, are essentially slaves." This is captured in an article on page 1 of the *New York Times* of April 26, 1875.

2. James D. Richardson, comp., A Compilation of the Messages and Papers of the Presidents, 1789–1902, vol. II pp. 640–56.

3. Theodore Crackel, *Mr. Jefferson's Army* (New York University Press, 1989).

## CHAPTER THREE

1. Morris Schaff, *The Spirit of Old West Point* (New York: Houghton, Mifflin & Co., 1907), 17.

2. Stephen E. Ambrose, *Duty, Honor, Country* (Baltimore, MD: Johns Hopkins University Press, 1999), 147–51; James L. Morrison, *The Best School* (Kent, OH: Kent State University Press, 1986), 74–76.

3. Tully McCrea, *Dear Belle* (Middletown, CT: Wesleyan University Press, 1965), 18–20.

4. Ambrose, *Duty, Honor, Country*, 154–55.

5. Ibid., 155.

6. Jay Monaghan, *Custer* (University of Nebraska Press, 1959) 26-7.

7. Ambrose, Op.Cit., 137.

8. Ibid., 138.

9. One of Napoleon's central tactics in battle was known as *manoeuvre sur les derrieres*, or "maneuver on the enemy's flanks and rear," which he used with great success in more than 90 percent of his battles. This, however, requires dividing your force in the face of the enemy, a high-risk venture few generals have attempted on a real battle-field. But Lee used this approach with great success at Cerro Gordo and the Pedregal, two major battles of the Mexican-American War, and at the Civil War battles of Second Manassas and Chancellors-ville. There is also strong and compelling circumstantial evidence that he attempted the same sort of maneuver at Gettysburg as briefly described in chapter 12.

10. As a member of the West Point class of 1966, I actually lived in those same barracks for four years.

11. Letter from H. A. DuPont to his mother, 14 July 1856, DuPont family collection found in Winterthur Library in Winterthur, DE.

12. Letter from H. A. DuPont to his mother, 1 November 1856.

13. Ambrose, *Duty, Honor, Country*, 131.

14. Letter from H. A. DuPont to his aunt, 8 May 1857.

15. Letter from H. A. DuPont to his mother, 3 October 1858.

16. Mary Elizabeth Sergent, "Classmates Divided," *American Heritage Magazine*, February 1958.

17. William Hassler, *Colonel John Pelham* (Chapel Hill: University of North Carolina Press, 1960), 5.

18. Mercer, *The Gallant Pelham*, 24.

19. Gallagher, *Stephen Dodson Ramseur*, 14.

20. Hassler, *Colonel John Pelham*, 4.

21. Letter from M. G. Adelbert Ames to Fred R. Martin, 21 February 1901, as quoted in Mercer, *The Gallant Pelham*, 18.

22. Ambrose, *Duty, Honor, Country*, 152–53.

23. Schaff, *The Spirit of Old West Point*, 26–27.

24. Watts would resign his commission after graduation and was wounded four times in the Civil War, reaching the rank of major in the Confederate army.

25. Schaff, *The Spirit of Old West Point*, 66–67.

## CHAPTER FOUR

1. *Dred Scott v. Sandford*, 60 U.S. 393 (1856).
2. John M. Carroll, ed., *Custer in the Civil War* (San Rafael, CA: Presidio Press, 1977), 80.
3. Schaff, *The Spirit of Old West Point,* 137-40.
4. Alberts, *General Wesley Merritt*, 20.
5. Gallagher, *Stephen Dodson Ramseur*, 21.
6. Sellano L. Simmons, "Count Them Too: African Americans from Delaware and the United States Civil War Navy, 1861–1865," *Journal of Negro History* 85, no. 3 (Summer 2000):183–90.
7. George W. Turner, who was killed at Harpers Ferry on 17 October 1859, graduated from West Point in 1831, while Henry DuPont's father graduated in 1833.
8. Letter from H. A. DuPont to his father, 29 October 1859.
9. Gallagher, *Stephen Dodson Ramseur*, 27.
10. Schaff, *The Spirit of Old West Point*, 154.
11. Alberts, *General Wesley Merritt*, 26–28.
12. Gallagher, *Stephen Dodson Ramseur*, 28–29.
13. Ambrose, *Duty, Honor, Country*, 169.
14. Letter from Sam Houston to Thomas L. Rosser, 17 November 1860: USMA Archives, West Point, NY.
15. Mercer, *The Gallant Pelham*, 31–32.
16. Bushong and Bushong, *Fightin' Tom Rosser*, 11.
17. Letter from H. A. DuPont to his mother, 5 January 1861.
18. Letter from H. A. DuPont to his mother, 10 April 1861.
19. John M. Carroll, *Custer in the Civil War* (Presidio Press, San Rafael, CA, 1977) 83.
20. Schaff, *The Spirit of Old West Point*, 196.
21. Ibid., 201–2.
22. Ibid., 207–8.
23. Bushong and Bushong, *Fightin' Tom Rosser*, 13.
24. Unfiled Slips and Papers, Confederate Records, U.S. Archives, Washington, D.C.
25. Letter from John Pelham to Marianna Pelham Mott, 26 March 1861, Garrison Family Papers, Sophia Smith Collection, Smith College, Northampton, MA.
26. Masonic Collection, MSS. Division, Alabama Department of Archives and History, Montgomery, AL.

27. Rick Atkinson, *The Long Gray Line* (Boston: Houghton Mifflin, 1989), 104.

28. Carroll, *Custer in the Civil War*, 84.

29. Tully McCrea, quoted in Schaff, *The Spirit of Old West Point*, 220.

30. Bushong and Bushong, *Fightin' Tom Rosser*, 13.

31. James L. Morrison, *The Best School in the World: West Point, the Pre-Civil War Years, 1833-1866* (Kent, Ohio: Kent State University Press, 1986) 134. For a more thorough examination of the West Point honor code and its development, see the splendid new book by Lewis Sorley, *Honor Bright* (Boston: McGraw Hill, 2009).

32. Hassler, *Colonel John Pelham*, 10.

33. Mercer, *The Gallant Pelham*, 36–37; Hassler, *Colonel John Pelham*, 9–10.

34. I list the other "border" slave states at the time as just Missouri, Kentucky, and Maryland, because West Virginia was not yet a state. The delegates of the forty western counties of Virginia whose citizens opposed secession had met in Wheeling and formed their own government loyal to the Union. They then seceded from Virginia, but were not recognized and accepted as a new state by President Lincoln and the U.S. Congress until 20 June 1863.

35. Record Group 153, Records of the Judge Advocate General, National Archives; Carroll, *Custer in the Civil War*, 83–89.

## CHAPTER FIVE

1. Schenck, *Sketches of Major General Stephen Dodson Ramseur*, 32.

2. *Raleigh (NC) Register*, 31 July 1861.

3. Carroll, *Custer in the Civil War*. 90.

4. Ibid., 91–93.

5. William T. Poague, *Gunner with Stonewall* (Jackson, TN: McCowat-Mercer Press, 1957), 9.

6. Stephen W. Sears, ed., *The Civil War Papers of George B. McClellan* (Cambridge, MA: Da Capo Press, 1989) 70.

7. Bushong and Bushong, *Fightin' Tom Rosser*, 16–17.

8. Letter from H. A. DuPont to his mother, 5 August 1861, USMA Archives and Special Collections, West Point, NY.

9. Letter from H. A. DuPont to his aunt Sophie DuPont, 25 August 1861, USMA Archives and Special Collections, West Point, NY.

10. Letter from McClellan to Mary Ellen McClellan, 16 August 1861, in Sears, *Civil War Papers of George B. McClellan*, 85–86.

11. John Esten Cooke, *Wearing of the Gray* (Bloomington: Indiana University Press, 1959), 118–20.

12. Charles G. Milham, *Gallant Pelham* (Washington, DC: Public Affairs Press, 1959), 59.

13. Letter from McClellan to Mary Ellen McClellan, 10 October 1861, in Sears, *Civil War Papers of George B. McClellan*, 106.

14. Jay Monaghan, *Custer* (Lincoln: University of Nebraska Press, 1959), 64–66.

## CHAPTER SIX

1. Official Records of the Union and Confederate Armies (hereafter "OR") Series 1, Vol. 11, Part 3, 526.

2. OR Series 1, Vol. 11, Part 1, 536–43.

3. Ibid., 573.

4. Ibid., 526.

5. Ibid., 153, 198–99, 651, 914.

6. David J. Eicher, *The Longest Night* (New York: Simon & Schuster, 2001), 279.

7. Vincent J. Esposito and John Robert Elting, *A Military History and Atlas of the Napoleonic Wars* (New York: Praeger, 1959), 45.

8. Schenck, *Sketches of Major General Stephen Dodson Ramseur*, 33, 34.

9. OR Vol. 11, Part 1, 574–75.

10. Ibid., 663.

11. Ibid., 663–64.

12. OR Vol. 11, Part 2, 515.

13. Henry B. McClellan, *I Rode with Jeb Stuart* (Bloomington: Indiana University Press, 1958), 75–76. Interestingly, this McClellan was a cousin of the Union commander. Having been born in New Jersey and educated at Williams College in Massachusetts, he moved to Virginia before the Civil War and ended up serving in the Confederate army as Stuart's adjutant general.

14. OR Vol. 11, Part 2, 517.

15. Ibid., 794–95.

16. Bushong and Bushong, *Fightin' Tom Rosser*, 20.

17. OR Vol. 11, Part 2, 795.

18. Emory M. Thomas, *Bold Dragoon* (New York: Harper & Row, 1986), 136–37.

19. OR Vol. 11, Part 2, 521.

20. Ibid., 522.

## CHAPTER SEVEN

1. OR Vol. 12, Part 2, 725–26.
2. Ibid., 726–27.
3. Ibid., 755.
4. Ibid., 753–54.
5. Todd S. Berkoff, "Battle of Brawner's Farm," *America's Civil War* (September 2004).
6. Alan T. Nolan, *The Iron Brigade* (Bloomington: Indiana University Press, 1961), 95; Berkoff, "Battle of Brawner's Farm."
7. Berkoff, "Battle of Brawner's Farm."
8. OR Vol. 12, Part 2, 755.
9. Ibid., 737.
10. Eicher, *The Longest Night*, 327; A. Wilson Greene, *The Second Battle of Manassas* (Fort Washington, PA: Eastern National, 2006), 54.

## CHAPTER EIGHT

1. Heros von Borcke, *Memoirs of the Confederate War* (New York: Peter Smith, 1938), Vol. 1, 192–97.
2. Ibid., 212–13.
3. OR Vol. 19, Part 1, 30.
4. Jennings C. Wise, *The Long Arm of Lee* (Lynchburg, VA: J. P. Bell, 1915), 43–46.
5. James M. McPherson, *Crossroads of Freedom* (New York: Oxford University Press, 2002), 3.
6. James M. McPherson, *Tried by War* (New York: Penguin Press, 2008), 133–34.
7. OR Vol. 19, Part 2, 395.
8. Mercer, *The Gallant Pelham*, 96; Hassler, *Colonel John Pelham*, 97–98; von Borcke, *Memoirs of the Confederate War*, Vol. 1, 250–51.
9. Von Borcke, *Memoirs of the Confederate War*, Vol. 2, 30–32.
10. *Register of Graduates and Former Cadets* (West Point, NY: U.S. Military Academy, 2005), 1568.
11. OR Vol. 19, Part 2, 684, 699.
12. Custer's courtship of Libbie is taken from Marguerite Merington, *The Custer Story* (New York: Devin-Adair, 1950), which is a thorough study of letters between the two placed as much as possible in the context of the time. This section is taken from pages 46–51.

## CHAPTER NINE

1. Von Borcke, *Memoirs of the Confederate War*, 117; Hassler, *Colonel John Pelham*, 146–50.
2. This version of Pelham's bravery at Fredericksburg is from von Borcke, *Memoirs of the Confederate War*, 117–19; Lee's statement is from John Esten Cooke (one of Stuart's staff officers), *Wearing of the Gray*, 122.
3. OR Vol. 21, 547.
4. Ibid., 553.
5. W. W. Blackford, *War Years with Jeb Stuart* (New York: Charles Scribner's Sons, 1945), 90.
6. OR Vol. 25, Part 2, 640, 651.
7. Von Borcke, *Memoirs of the Confederate War*, Vol. 2, 187–88; McClellan, *I Rode with Jeb Stuart*, 210–11. Von Borcke and McClellan were both there when Pelham was killed, but there are many other and differing accounts available. For an interesting analysis, see Robert J. Trout, *Galloping Thunder* (Mechanicsburg, PA: Stackpole, 2002) 649–53
8. Milham, *Gallant Pelham*, 230–33.
9. OR Vol. 25, Part 1, 59.
10. Schaff, *The Spirit of Old West Point*, 133; Cooke, *Wearing of the Gray*, 124.
11. OR Vol. 25, Part 1, 60.
12. Cooke, *Wearing of the Gray*, 118–19.
13. Ibid., 116–29.
14. Bushong and Bushong, *Fightin' Tom Rosser*, 42–43.

## CHAPTER TEN

1. Gallagher, *Stephen Dodson Ramseur*, 48; letter from Ramseur to Ellen Richmond, 25 December 1862, Folder 6, Ramseur Papers, Southern Historical Collection (hereafter "SHC"), Wilson Library, University of North Carolina, Chapel Hill, NC.
2. Many people have speculated on the causes of Jackson's death, but perhaps the most concise treatment can be found in "The Last Illness and Death of General Thomas Jonathan (Stonewall) Jackson" by Beverly C. Smith, M.D., which first appeared in the summer 1975 issue of the *VMI Alumni Review* (Virginia Military Institute Alumni Agencies, Lexington, VA).

3. Letter from Ramseur to Ellen Richmond, 11 February 1863, Folder 7, Ramseur Papers, SHC.

4. Letters from Ramseur to Ellen Richmond, 8, 11, 12, and 17 February 1863, Folder 7, Ramseur Papers, SHC.

5. Most of the details of the battle of Chancellorsville that follow are taken from Vincent J. Esposito, *The West Point Atlas of American Wars, Vol. I* (Praeger, New York, 1959) 84–91.

6. OR Vol. 25, Part 1, 995.

7. Esposito, *West Point Atlas, Vol. I,* 87.

8. OR Vol. 25, Part 1, 996.

9. Douglas Southall Freeman, *Lee's Lieutenants* (New York: Charles Scribner's Sons, 1942) Vol. 2, 594–98.

10. OR Vol. 25, Part 1, 949.

11. Ibid., 947.

12. Ibid., 886.

13. Letter from Ramseur to Schenck, 10 May 1863; letter from Ramseur to Ellen Richmond, 17 May 1863, Folders 1, 6, 7, Ramseur Papers, SHC.

14. OR Vol. 27, Part 2, 305.

15. Douglas Southall Freeman, *R. E. Lee* (New York: Charles Scribner's Sons, 1935), Vol. 3, 58–59.

16. OR Vol. 27, Part 2, 305.

17. The story of these two grand reviews is told in much detail by Emory M. Thomas, *Bold Dragoon* (New York: Harper & Row, 1986) 214–20.

18. OR Vol. 27, Part 1, 33.

19. Thomas, *Bold Dragoon,* 216.

20. Monaghan, *Custer,* 125–27.

21. Fairfax Downey, *Clash of Cavalry* (New York: David McKay, 1959), 136–38.

22. Alberts, *General Wesley Merritt,* 58–59. Though the Confederate commander was probably either Wade Hampton or Fitzhugh Lee, neither reported the incident, so his true identity will remain a mystery.

23. OR Vol. 27, Part 2, 546.

24. Robert F. O'Neill, Jr., *The Cavalry Battles of Aldie, Middleburg, and Upperville* (Lynchburg, VA: H.E. Howard, 1993), 39, 40, 60, 152.

25. Ibid.

## CHAPTER ELEVEN

1. Edwin B. Coddington, *The Gettysburg Campaign* (New York: Charles Scribner's Sons, 1968), 220–21.
2. OR Vol. 27, Part 1, 943, 988, 992, 993; *Battles and Leaders of the Civil War* (hereafter B&L) (Secaucus NJ: Castle, 1887) Vol 3, 393–96; Stephen W. Sears, *Gettysburg* (Boston: Houghton Mifflin, 2003), 462–64.
3. Jeffry D. Wert, *The Sword of Lincoln* (New York: Simon & Schuster, 2005), 301.
4. James Harvey Kidd, *Personal Recollections of a Cavalryman with Custer's Michigan Cavalry Brigade in the Civil War* (Ionia, MI: Sentinel Printing Company, 1908), 129-30.
5. OR Vol. 27, Part 2, 554.
6. Ibid., 587.
7. Esposito, *West Point Atlas, Vol. I*, 97.
8. James M. McPherson, *This Mighty Scourge* (New York: Oxford University Press, 2007), 86.
9. Walter A. McDougall, *Throes of Democracy* (New York: Harper, 2008), 470.
10. OR Vol. 27, Part 2, 320, 447, 448; Sears, *Gettysburg*, 371.
11. John W. Busey and David G. Martin, *Regimental Strengths at Gettysburg* (Baltimore: Gateway Press, 1982), 194.
12. McClellan, *I Rode with Jeb Stuart*, 338.
13. Imboden, John "The Confederate Retreat," in Battles and Leaders, Vol. 3 (New York: The Century Company, 1884), p. 421.

## CHAPTER TWELVE

1. Esposito, *West Point Atlas, Vol. I*, 117.
2. Freeman, *Lee's Lieutenants*, Vol. 3, 213–14.
3. OR Vol. 29, Part 2, 788.
4. Freeman, *Lee's Lieutenants*, Vol. 3, 251–53.
5. Ibid., 260–63.
6. Letters from Ramseur to Ellen Ramseur, 9 and 17 December 1863; 15 and 28 April 1864, Folders 8 and 9, Ramseur Papers, SHC.
7. Letters from Ramseur to Ellen Ramseur, 7, 12, 15, and 17 December 1863; Letter from Ramseur to Schenck, 12 January 1864, Folders 8 and 17, Ramseur Papers, SHC.
8. There are many biographies of Custer, but these details are drawn from Jeffry D. Wert, *Custer* (New York: Simon & Schuster, 1996), 66–69, 112–14, 122–24, 136–44.

9. Ulysses S. Grant, *Personal Memoirs* (New York: Charles L. Webster & Company, 1885–86), 425-26.

10. Esposito, *West Point Atlas, Vol. I*, 118–20.

11. Esposito, *West Point Atlas, Vol. I*, 121–24.

12. OR Vol. 36, Part 1, 1081.

13. James M. McPherson, *Battle Cry of Freedom* (New York: Oxford University Press, 1988), 725–26.

14. Horace Porter, *Campaigning with Grant* (New York: Century, 1897), 69-70.

15. Esposito, *West Point Atlas, Vol. I*, 125.

CHAPTER THIRTEEN

1. Esposito, *West Point Atlas, Vol. I*, 127.

2. OR Vol. 36, Part 1, 1082–83.

3. Freeman, in *R. E. Lee, Vol. 3*, 320, says the story comes from a letter written by Colonel Charles Venable, an eyewitness present at the time; this same "Lee to the rear!" story was also told by John B. Gordon in his *Reminiscences of the Civil War* (New York: Charles Scribner's Sons, 1903), on pages 280–81, when Lee supposedly rode to the front of his division and proposed to lead their attack. It is a wonderful story, and it may have happened twice, although that seems improbable. In any case, Gordon's version is followed by obvious exaggerations, while the details from Venable's version make it seem more credible and so it is repeated here.

4. Esposito, *West Point Atlas, Vol. I*, 131–33.

5. OR Series 1, Vol. 46, Part 1, 944–49; OR Vol. 42, Part 1, 821–43, 946; Bushong and Bushong, *Fightin' Tom Rosser*, 102–10; William N. McDonald, *History of the Laurel Brigade* (Baltimore, MD: Sun Job Printing Office, 1907), 285–98. At an unknown date after the war an account of this raid written by Rosser was printed in the Philadelphia *Times*, and that is also included in this chapter of *History of the Laurel Brigade*.

CHAPTER FOURTEEN

1. B&L Vol. IV, "Sigel in the Shenandoah," 487–88.

2. In a report written long after the end of the war, Sigel claimed that he expected to be opposed by Imboden and 3,000 men, but after any battle such exaggerations of the enemy one opposed and diminution of the number of troops one commanded have long been commonplace in commanders' "after-action reports."

3. B&L Vol. IV, "Sigel in the Shenandoah," 481, 488.
4. B&L Vol. IV, "The Battle of New Market" by John D. Imboden, 483–84.
5. William Couper, ed., *The Corps Forward* (Mariner Publishing, 2005), Foreword (by Keith E. Gibson) and pages 1–7.
6. Edward Raymond Turner, *The New Market Campaign* (Richmond, VA: Whittett and Shepperson, 1912), 93; OR Series 1, Vol. 37, Part 1, 80.
7. Benjamin A. Colonna, "The Battle of New Market," *Journal of the Military Service Institute* (Nov.–Dec. 1912), 346–47.
8. OR Series 1, Vol. 36, Part 2, 840.
9. *Register of Graduates and Former Cadets* (West Point, NY: U.S. Military Academy, 1920).
10. Ira Berlin, Barbara J. Fields, Steven F. Miller, Joseph P. Reidy, and Leslie S. Rowland, eds. *Free at Last* (Edison, NJ: Blue & Gray Press, 1992) pp. 46–48.
11. OR Series 1, Vol. 37, Part 1, 525.
12. Ibid, 531.
13. Ibid, 557.
14. DuPont, *Campaign of 1864 in the Valley of Virginia and the Expedition to Lynchburg* (New York: National Americana Society, 1925) 50–51.
15. Ibid., 56–57.
16. OR Series 1, Vol. 37, Part 1, 95.
17. DuPont, *Campaign of 1864*, 62–63.
18. Milton W. Humphreys, *A History of the Lynchburg Campaign* (Charlottesville: University of Virginia Press, 1924), 45.
19. DuPont, *Campaign of 1864*, 63–64.

## CHAPTER FIFTEEN

1. OR Series 1, Vol. 36, Part 1, 1095.
2. B&L, Vol. IV, Butler, "The Cavalry Fight at Trevilian Station," 237.
3. OR Series 1, Vol. 36, Part 1, 807.
4. Ibid., 823, 824.
5. B&L, Vol. IV, M.C. Butler, "The Cavalry Fight at Trevilian Station," 237–38; B&L, Vol. IV, Theo. F. Rodenbough, "Sheridan's Trevilian Raid," 233–34.
6. Merington, *The Custer Story*, 105.
7. McDonald, *History of the Laurel Brigade*, 253–54.
8. *Arms and Equipment of the Union* (New York: Time-Life Books, 1992), 47, 48, 52, 53, 58, 59; Busey and Martin, *Regimental Strengths at Gettysburg*, 206.

9. OR Vol. 36, Part 1, 803, 804, 1095.

10. S. Roger Keller, ed., *Riding with Rosser* (Shippensburg, PA : Burd Street Press, 1997), 38.

11. B&L, Vol. IV, Theo. F. Rodenbough, "Sheridan's Trevilian Raid", 234; B&L, Vol. IV, M.C. Butler, "The Cavalry Fight at Trevilian Station," 238–39.

12. Ibid.

13. To this day, several of the projectiles from that Union cannon fire are still embedded in the granite walls of the cadet barracks.

14. Letter in possession of the VMI Archives, preserved by VMI archivist Colonel Keith E. Gibson.

15. DuPont, *Campaign of 1864*, 68–69.

16. Ibid., 78–80.

17. B&L, Vol. IV, "Opposing Forces in Lynchburg," 492; Freeman, *Lee's Lieutenants*, Vol. 3, 558; Henry Kyd Douglas, *I Rode With Stonewall* (Chapel Hill: University of North Carlona Press, 1940), 289–90.

18. DuPont, *Campaign of 1864*, 83–85.

19. OR Vol. 37, Part 1, 346.

20. Letters of John Hay and extracts from diary (Washington: printed but not published) 11 July 1864.

21. Freeman, *Lee's Lieutenants*, Vol. 4, 55, 66–67.

## CHAPTER SIXTEEN

1. James Harvey Kidd, *Personal Recollections of a Cavalryman with Custer's Michigan Cavalry Brigade in the Civil War* (Ionia, MI: Sentinel Printing Company, 1908), 293–94.

2. OR Series 1, Vol. 36, Part 1, 812.

3. Ibid., 788–89; Kidd, *Personal Recollections*, 309–17.

4. OR Series 1, Vol. 43, Part 1, 439.

5. Ibid., 445–47.

6. Ibid., 29.

7. Kidd, *Personal Recollections*, 396.

8. Thomas L. Rosser, Scrapbook, Thomas L. Rosser Papers, University of Virginia, No. 1171, Box 2, 107.

9. OR Vol. 43, Part 1, 431.

10. Keller, *Riding with Rosser*, 47.

11. Rosser, Scrapbook, 29.

12. McDonald, *History of the Laurel Brigade*, 305–8.

13. Merington, *The Custer Story*, 249.
14. Ibid., 128.
15. McDonald, *History of the Laurel Brigade*, 308–9.
16. The information for this chapter is interwoven material that comes from Gallagher's *Stephen Dodson Ramseur*, 154–65; Kidd's *Personal Recollections*, 409–24; Keller's *Riding with Rosser*, 49–52; Freeman's *Lee's Lieutenants*, 597–612; Gordon's *Reminiscences of the Civil War*, 327–51; narrations of the battle in *Battles and Leaders of the Civil War, Volume IV* by Wesley Merritt, "Sheridan in the Shenandoah Valley," 500–21, and Jubal Early, "Winchester, Fisher's Hill, and Cedar Creek," 522–530; OR Series 1, Vol. 43, Part 1, 427–46; and sections of Custer's unfinished Civil War memoirs published by John M. Carroll in *Custer in the Civil War* (San Rafael, CA: Presidio Press, 1977).
17. Freeman, *Lee's Lieutenants*, Vol. 3, 599.
18. Gallagher, *Stephen Dodson Ramseur*, 155.
19. OR Series 1, Vol. 43, Part 1, 613.
20. With heavy casualties on both sides, straggling, desertion, and units constantly arriving or leaving, the precise number of soldiers engaged at any given time is an elusive target, with estimates varying widely. The numbers I use here are those that appear in *The Battle of Cedar Creek* by Joseph W. A. Whitehorne and published in 1991 by the U.S. Army Center of Military History.

## CHAPTER SEVENTEEN

1. DuPont, *Campaign of 1864*, 150–54.
2. Ibid., 153–55; Freeman, *Lee's Lieutenants*, Vol. 3, 600–603.
3. Jubal Early, *Autobiographical Sketch and Narrative of the War between the States* (Philadelphia: J.P. Lippincott, 1912), 443.
4. DuPont, *Campaign of 1864*, 161–63.
5. OR Series 1, Vol. 43, Part 1, 333.
6. Keller, *Riding with Rosser*, 50–51; Bushong and Bushong, *Fightin' Tom Rosser*, 133.
7. Kidd, *Personal Recollections*, 410–13; Carroll, *Custer in the Civil War*, 43.
8. Douglas, *I Rode with Stonewall*, 317.
9. David Chandler, *The Campaigns of Napoleon* (New York: MacMillan, 1966), 420–39.
10. Gordon, *Reminiscences of the Civil War*, 340–42; Keller, *Riding with Rosser*, 51; Early, "Winchester, Fisher's Hill, and Cedar Creek"; B&L

Vol. IV, 522–30. Although Early adamantly denies in B&L that he ordered any stop in the assault, Gordon just as strongly insists in his memoirs that he did. But no five divisions attacking on line during the Civil War, even one whose soldiers were as hungry and tired as were those of Early's army here, would have all just stopped their forward movement at the same time in a defensive formation spread across the valley unless that was done pursuant to an order from their commander, General Early, which makes Gordon's argument compelling.

11. Gordon, *Reminiscences of the Civil War*, 352–72.
12. Hotchkiss, *Make Me a Map of the Valley* (Dallas: Southern Methodist University Press, 1973) 241.

## CHAPTER EIGHTEEN

1. Esposito and Elting, *A Military History and Atlas*, 57–68; Dupuy and Dupuy, *Military Encyclopedia* (New York: Harper Collins, 1986) 750–51.
2. B&L, Vol. II, 297.
3. Antoine H. Jomini, *The Art of War* (Philadelphia: J.B. Lippincott, 1862), 221.
4. Clausewitz, *On War*, trans. by Michael Howard and Peter Paret (Princeton: Princeton University Press, 1976), Book 4, Chapter 12.
5. Carroll, *Custer in the Civil War*, 43.
6. B&L, Vol. IV, Wesley Merritt, "Sheridan in the Shenandoah Valley," 500–521.
7. Ibid, 519.
8. Sheridan, *Memoirs* (New York: Charles L. Webster & Company, 1888), Vol. 2, 82.
9. B&L, Vol. IV, Merritt, "Sheridan in the Shenandoah Valley," 518–19.
10. Ibid., 219–20.
11. Gordon, *Reminiscences of the Civil War*, 346–47; Keith S. Bohannon, "The Fatal Halt," in *Shenandoah Campaign of 1864*, Gary Gallagher, ed. (Chapel Hill: University of North Carolina Press, 2009) 56–78.
12. Sheridan, *Memoirs*, Vol. 2, 82–88.
13. Gallagher, *Stephen Dodson Ramseur*, 161.
14. OR Vol. 43, Part 1, 562.
15. DuPont, *Campaign of 1864*, 171.
16. Ibid., 172–73.
17. OR Series 1, Vol. 43, Part 1, 614; Carroll, *Custer in the Civil War*, 43–46.

18. OR Series 1, Vol. 43, Part 1, 613.
19. DuPont, *Campaign of 1864*, 173–74.
20. DuPont, "Address at Dedication of Ramseur Monument," 16 September 1920, West Point Archives.
21. DuPont, *Campaign of 1864*, 174–75.

CHAPTER NINETEEN

1. McDonald, *History of the Laurel Brigade*, 324.
2. Ibid., 327.
3. Francis Haselberger, "General Rosser's Raid on the New Creek Depot," *West Virginia History* 26, No. 2 (January 1965), 89–90.
4. Early, *Memoirs*, 457; Sheridan, *Memoirs*, Vol. 2, 97–104.
5. OR Vol. 43, Part 2, 821; Bushong and Bushong, *Fightin' Tom Rosser*, 155; Sheridan, *Memoirs*, Vol. 2, 102.
6. Early, *Memoirs*, 457–58.
7. Bushong and Bushong, *Fightin' Tom Rosser*, (Shippensbutrg, PA: Beidel Printng House, 1983) 157;
8. McDonald, *History of the Laurel Brigade*, 339–40.
9. OR Vol. 46, Part 1, 451.
10. Ibid., 48.
11. Ibid., 127.

CHAPTER TWENTY

1. OR Series 1, Vol. 46, Part 1, 528–29.
2. Ibid., 486.
3. Ibid., 480.
4. Ibid., 1117–18.
5. Freeman, *Lee's Lieutenants*, Vol. 3, 709.
6. OR Series 1, Vol. 46, Part 1, 1152

CHAPTER TWENTY-ONE

1. Many books have been written about the Indian Wars, and nothing controversial will be claimed in this book as fact. But one of the best books about the conflicts that occurred on the northern Great Plains is *Little Big Horn Remembered* by Herman J. Viola (New York: Random House, 1999), from which much of the material here related is drawn.
2. Kenneth Carley, *The Sioux Uprising of 1862* (St. Paul: Minnesota Historical Society, 1961), 65.

3. Fairfax Downey, *Indian Fighting Army* (New York: Charles Scribner's Sons, 1944), 44–48.
4. George A. Custer, *My Life on the Plains* (Norman: University of Oklahoma Press, 1962), 123.
5. Clayton K. S. Chun, *U.S. Army in the Plains Indian Wars, 1865–91* (London: Osprey, 2004), 17.
6. Downey, *Indian Fighting Army*, 84–92.
7. Alberts, *General Wesley Merritt*, 206.
8. Ibid., 220-234.
9. Bushong and Bushong, *Fightin' Tom Rosser*, 186–89.
10. *St. Paul Pioneer Press and Tribune*, 8 July 1876, reprinted in the *New York Herald* on 11 July 1876.
11. Alberts, *General Wesley Merritt*, 263-270, 282-288.
12. Rosser, Scrapbook, 105.
13. Bushong and Bushong, *Fightin' Tom Rosser*, 200–202.
14. Alberts, *General Wesley Merritt*, 423–449.
15. Hearing before the Committee of Claims, U.S. Senate, Sixty-third Congress, Second Session, on S.544. The great bulk of this chapter, including the testimony of witnesses, is drawn from the official records of that hearing.

# INDEX